Love in a Time of War

Lara Marlowe was born in California and studied French at UCLA and the Sorbonne, then International Relations at Oxford. She started her career in journalism as an associate producer for CBS's '60 Minutes' programme, then covered the Arab world from Beirut for the *Financial Times* and *TIME* magazine. She joined *The Irish Times* as Paris correspondent in 1996 and returned to Paris in 2013 after serving as Washington correspondent during the first Obama administration. Marlowe was made a Chevalier de la Légion d'Honneur in 2006 for her contribution to Franco-Irish relations.

By the same author

The Things I've Seen:
Nine Lives Of A Foreign Correspondent (2010)

Painted With Words (2011)

Love in a Time of War

My Years with Robert Fisk

Lara Marlowe

HEAD
of ZEUS

An Apollo Book

9 7 5 4 6 8

A catalogue record for this book is available from the British Library.

ISBN (HB): 9781801102513
ISBN (E): 9781801102537

Typeset by Palimpsest Book Production Limited, Falkirk, Stirlingshire

Printed and bound in Great Britain by
CPI Group (UK) Ltd, Croydon CR0 4YY

FSC
www.fsc.org
MIX
Paper from
responsible sources
FSC® C171272

Head of Zeus Ltd

First Floor East
5–8 Hardwick Street
London EC1R 4RG

WWW.HEADOFZEUS.COM

In Memoriam
R. W. F.
1946–2020

Contents

Prologue

It will be the past
and we'll live there together.

Not as it was *to live*
but as it is remembered.

It will be the past.
We'll all go back together.

Everyone we ever loved,
and lost, and must remember.

It will be the past
And it will last forever.

Patrick Phillips, "Heaven"

I am sitting at my desk in Paris on a Sunday evening, hoping to catch up on email before the new week starts.

The phone rings, which is unusual in our era of digital communication. It is the *Irish Times* foreign affairs editor Paddy Smyth. Paddy and I rarely talk, though we have been friends and colleagues for a quarter-century.

"What's happened?" I ask Paddy, fearing I have missed a story on my patch, perhaps a terrorist attack or an assassination in France. I am not eager to write an article that evening, or set off on a story the following morning. It is infinitely worse than that.

"We weren't sure if you heard that Robert Fisk died," Paddy begins as gently as he knows how. At first I am incredulous. This must be some kind of bad joke. My former husband is only seventy-four years old and is fit as a fiddle. I recently saw *This Is Not a Movie*, a documentary about him, co-written by his wife. Robert was still tearing around the Middle East, dodging shellfire and denouncing those he called "the bad guys". Just a year before, when I ran into Robert at Dublin airport, he appeared the very picture of good health and contentment.

"We will publish a piece in tomorrow's paper," Paddy continues. Details are scant, he says. I misunderstand him to mean *biographical* details, rather than facts about Robert's death. I begin to spout information, asking Paddy to share it with whomever is writing the article for *The Irish Times*.

The chronology of Robert's life, which I know by heart, pours out in haphazard fashion. I recall Robert's mock chagrin that his birthday fell on 12 July, the day when Orangemen celebrate the Battle of the Boyne. Attuned to the ironies of history, he recounted that his father, William, whom he referred to as "King Billy", was deployed to Ireland "on the wrong side" during the 1916 Rising. Bill Fisk became the borough treasurer of Maidstone, Kent, for which he was awarded the Order of the British Empire. Robert's mother, Peggy, née Rose, was a housewife and amateur painter who was thrilled to be appointed as a magistrate in her middle years.

I blather on to Paddy.

Robert loved revisiting his own life. His paternal grandfather, Edward, was first mate on the celebrated *Cutty Sark*, so we travelled to Greenwich to see the restored clipper ship. Robert was delighted to find Edward Fisk named in a black-and-white photograph of the crew. He took me to Yardley Court, the minor British public school in Tonbridge to which he was sent as a boarder at the age of nine, and which he hated.

Robert's ineptitude at maths made him ineligible for Oxbridge, but he graduated with a first-class honours degree in Classics from the University of Lancaster. His alma mater later gave him the first of his half-dozen honorary doctorates. He recalled his glee as a schoolboy upon discovering "the dirty bits" in the erotic poetry of Catullus. His favourite joke about ageing television correspondents was that they were still waiting for their laundry to come back after they covered the Battle of Thermopylae.

Though he was in some ways a quintessential British public-school boy, Robert was also a pacifist in perpetual revolt against authority. He got himself expelled from cadet training by destroying his rifle. "I love the wily rebel who threw his rifle in the river / And the little boy in you who wanted to drive steam trains," were the first lines of the first poem I wrote to him, in 1987.

Robert had a following in Ireland, a country he came to love with his first serious journalistic assignment, covering the Troubles in Belfast for *The Times*. Though he was lucid about the excesses of the IRA, he saw Northern Catholics as underdogs and victims. He would later compare their status to that of Shia Muslims in Lebanon and Iraq.

Robert's doctoral thesis at Trinity College Dublin became *In Time of War*, the definitive book on Irish neutrality during the Emergency, as World War II is known in Ireland. He bought the cottage opposite Finnegan's Pub and Maeve Binchy's house in Sorrento Road, Dalkey, before I met him. We later built our dream home, imitating the style of the Ottoman mansions that adorn Beirut, overlooking the sea in Dalkey.

When, in 1976, the foreign editor of *The Times* asked Robert if he wanted to go to Beirut to cover the Lebanese Civil War, Robert said he "felt like an Arab king being offered a country by Winston Churchill". The assignment changed the course of his life. For the next forty-five years – fifteen of them with me – Robert interviewed generals and guerrillas, wounded civilians and their tormentors. He knew more about the region's history than many of its inhabitants did. He accurately predicted its future.

When Anwar Sadat signed the Camp David accords with Israel, Robert wondered in print if the Egyptian autocrat had signed his own death warrant. He saw how Israel's 1982 invasion of Lebanon radicalised and Islamicised the region. He warned that the evacuation of Palestinian fighters after the siege of West Beirut left women and children defenceless, a premonition of the Sabra and Chatila massacres which he covered with award-winning eloquence.

When Yasser Arafat concluded his ill-fated Oslo peace accords with Israel in 1993, Robert explained to my naïve bosses at *Time* magazine why it could not work. He knew that Israel would not give East Jerusalem back to the Palestinians or stop seizing Arab land in the West Bank, and that the Palestinians' right of return, as consecrated in UN General Assembly Resolution 194, was an existential and irreconcilable issue for both parties. Under the Oslo accords, he said, Israel would turn the PLO into its policemen. He predicted that the 2003 US and British invasion of Iraq would destroy Iraq and hand it on a platter to the Islamic Republic of Iran.

Robert's message never varied. He regarded war as the total failure of the human spirit. He railed against the double standards that led journalists and politicians to regard violence by Muslims as "terrorism", while Israel, the US and NATO were never labelled "terrorists" for the civilians they slaughtered. He protested endlessly that the Palestinians were not responsible for the Holocaust, but that Arabs needed to admit that the genocide had happened. He denounced those who equated criticism of Israeli actions with anti-Semitism. He said every war contained the seeds of the next one.

Robert's immense physical courage was matched by his moral courage. He braved hate mail and condemnation by media pundits and government officials. Although he was not alone in criticising the tyranny and corruption of Arab despots, Robert was far more daring than most of his colleagues in investigating the criminal ravages of US and Israeli military offensives. He never forgot that the Armenian Holocaust was the first genocide of the twentieth century. He refused to allow the dispossession of the Palestinians to be erased from history.

In the Middle East, too, Robert had a following. Arab universities invited him to lecture. Diplomats and Arab officials were eager to meet him. When Vintage Books republished T. E. Lawrence's *Seven Pillars of Wisdom* in 2008, they asked Robert, perhaps the Englishman most closely associated with the region since Lawrence of Arabia, to write the preface. Lawrence wrote: "The people of England have been led in Mesopotamia into a trap from which it will be hard to escape with dignity and honour." This was, Robert wrote, "exactly what happened to us in Iraq" at the time of the 2003 invasion.

Robert understood Europe and its history equally well. Amid the euphoria over the fall of the Berlin Wall and the disintegration of the Warsaw Pact, he told me, "Watch out. I know what Eastern Europe is like. Ugly, right-wing, neo-fascist nationalists will start coming out of the woodwork." When commentators enthused about the possibilities of the internet and social media, Robert predicted they would be a powerful vehicle for disinformation and indoctrination.

Robert was not only a journalist and historian, he was a master of the English language, *il miglior fabbro*. A Lebanese colleague told me Robert's descriptions were so vivid that reading one of his articles was like watching a video of the event. They were translated often into Arabic and republished in Beirut newspapers. The Arabic version of *Pity the Nation*, his masterpiece about the Lebanese Civil War, was also a bestseller. Though Robert's spoken Arabic was rudimentary, I watched him painstakingly check every line of the Arabic translation before it went to print.

Some of these details were recorded by obituary writers at the beginning of November. To me, they provide only the faintest outline of the man who was the most important influence in my life, the man who gave me Lebanon, Ireland and journalism. No one ever loved me as much as Robert did. No one hurt me as much either. There was never anyone like him.

I have lost him for the second time, I keep thinking as I tune in and out of the telephone conversation with Paddy. He says *The Irish Times* learned of Robert's death from a hospital source, but the newspaper lacks independent confirmation. In shock and confusion, I think there is some doubt about his demise. So I hang up and dial the house we built together in Dalkey. We kept the same telephone number when we moved there from the cottage in 1999. It was my Dublin phone number for twenty years. I never dialled it after Robert remarried in 2009, but I still know the number by heart.

His widow answers the telephone. She is poised, but I can hear the strain in her voice. "He went to Vincent's hospital with a high fever and pneumonia on Friday night," she says. I had spoken to her only once before, in the late 1990s, when she rang our hotel room in Tehran. I am intrigued by her unplaceable accent.

"Was it Covid?" I ask.

"No. They wasted time doing a Covid test, and while that

was happening, he had a massive stroke. He never regained consciousness. He didn't suffer... The church service and burial will take place tomorrow."

"Why didn't you call me? I would have come over for the funeral."

She says she didn't know how to reach me.

"What time is the service? Where is it?"

"In the chapel in Dalkey at 11.30. The hearse will go to Kilternan cemetery around 12.30."

"I will try to come over," I say.

"There are limits on the numbers because of Covid – a maximum of twenty-five," she cautions. "With all the people who confirmed, we are probably twenty-five already. The church said they cannot and will not accommodate more. You can stand outside if you want to, but the weather is cold and windy.

"Robert loved this country. He was very proper about obeying Irish regulations," she continues. "He had many friends but also enemies. I don't want Robert's funeral to be marked as one where rules were broken... You can come to the outdoor part, at the cemetery."

We hang up and I look at the clock. It is already 8.30 p.m., too late to catch a flight to Dublin that evening. I do not know what Covid regulations are in force, or how many flights are operating. I ring my friend Patricia O'Brien, Ireland's ambassador to Paris, who is immensely sympathetic.

"The first flight is not until 10.40 a.m. You cannot make it to Dalkey in time for the church service," Patricia says. "But you could make it to Kilternan cemetery by 12.30."

I buy an Aer Lingus ticket online, and ring Louis Deacon, the friendly Dublin taxi driver who often helps me. He will meet my flight and drive me straight to Kilternan.

Robert was eleven years older than me, but I always thought I would die before he did. My parents and grandparents died young. His father, whom Robert resembled physically, lived to be ninety-three. I assumed he would live that long, if he could continue to elude violent death in the Middle East.

At the end of the day, this man who cheated death a thousand times died of natural causes. Robert used to imitate the *clack-click* sound of the bolt being released on a Kalashnikov pointed at his chest by an angry gunman. Being a war correspondent had taught him how easy it was to die, he said. It took only the slightest misjudgement over crossing a road, or the way one looked at a gunman.

Robert was a force of nature. I used to tell friends that living with him was like being plugged into a 220-volt electrical socket. I find it impossible to believe that I will never see him again, never hear his cheery voice, unless in dreams. I dreamed of him on the Friday night he died. The romantic in me wants to believe he was saying goodbye.

I sit in the back of the taxi, wrapped in an old, long black wool coat and the black beret that Robert said made me look like a Resistance heroine or an IRA gunman. I keep my eye on my watch as we speed down the M50. "How much farther is it, Louis? We must be there by 12.30."

Louis is not accustomed to my being ill-tempered and impatient. He exits the highway one off-ramp too soon, and we wander. I nearly lose my sang-froid. Since 1983, I have kept hundreds, probably thousands, of appointments with Robert. Countless times I travelled with a quickened heartbeat, excited at the prospect of our reunion, not wanting to keep him waiting. We met in airports and hotels, at border checkpoints and at our homes in Beirut, Paris and Dublin. In Kuwait City and in Sarajevo, our bulletproof vests clanked "like turtles", Robert said, when we ran into each other's arms. This is our last rendezvous, my only chance to say goodbye. I must not miss it.

A double rainbow hangs above the pretty wooded valley of Kilternan, the length of the horizon. The wind is icy, but mercifully it isn't raining. An Irish army piper in a kilt is lifting bagpipes from the boot of a car in the otherwise empty parking lot.

"Are you here for the Fisk funeral?" I ask. He nods Yes. "They haven't arrived yet?"

"No," the piper says. "You'll see them coming. They have to enter there, where you did. There is only one entry."

Despite the cold, I feel easier waiting outside, pacing and watching for Robert's arrival. At long last the black nose of the hearse inches into the cemetery drive, followed by a few cars. The piper takes up his place behind the hearse. Three women alight from the first car. I recognise Catherine Sheridan, our dear neighbour from across the road in Dalkey. "Hello, Lara," a woman in a long black velvet cloak with a jewelled broach says to me. We are wearing face masks because of the pandemic. I do not recognise Robert's widow, whom I have seen only in press photographs and film posters.

A mahogany coffin with brass handles can be seen through the display windows of the hearse, covered with a large spray of white lilies and mixed purple flowers. I greet a few old friends, starting with the broadcaster and author Olivia O'Leary, who has been close to Robert since Belfast in the 1970s, and her daughter Emily Tansey. Conor O'Clery, the great *Irish Times* correspondent who was, like Olivia, a colleague from Belfast, and who covered the Soviet invasion of Afghanistan with Robert, is there with his Russian-Armenian wife Zhanna. It is an added cruelty that we cannot hug one another.

Robert's widow and Catherine take the lead, directly behind the hearse, as we walk the few hundred metres to the waiting grave. I fall to the back, beside Conor and Zhanna. "He was the love of your life," Zhanna says softly, out of earshot of the other mourners. It is the most moving thing that anyone says to me after Robert's death, and I nod, stifling a sob.

The widow and Catherine sit on a bench overlooking the grave while a vicar says a few words. I had expected the actual burial to take place in our presence, shovelfuls of earth to be tossed atop the mahogany coffin. Instead, a large panel covered with fake grass is dragged over the dark rectangle into which the casket has been lowered. My journalist's curiosity kicks in. Do they think it too upsetting to fill in the grave in our presence? Are they going to reuse that shiny mahogany coffin? Will Robert be buried in a linen shroud, like a Muslim? It occurs to me later that gravediggers and shovels must be a thing of the past, that the cemetery will use heavy machinery to complete the task.

IN LOVING MEMORY, ROBERT FISK, 30 OCTOBER 2020, says the brass plaque on the astroturf with the floral spray. The double rainbow still hangs on the horizon, as if it had been arranged for the occasion, like the Irish army piper. I can hear Robert quoting *Hamlet*: "And flights of angels sing thee to thy rest!"

An officer who helped organise the brief ceremony approaches me. "I remember you from Tibnin," he says kindly, referring to the Irish UN battalion headquarters in southern Lebanon which Robert and I visited often. "You must feel very sad too. I am sorry for your trouble."

The widow and Catherine stand up and walk a few metres away. I slip onto the bench facing the grave. "I thought we would be buried near my family, but it was not to be," she says, chatting with other mourners. "We'll be here now. Robert always said, 'I want to be wherever you are'."

My mind races back to a time when we planned for our deaths as a precaution, given the violence of the Middle East. Before we moved to Beirut together in 1989, we drew up wills, leaving everything we owned to one another. A friend found it terribly romantic, but we treated our possible demise as something to be laughed at. Robert told me that he wanted this inscription on his tombstone: *Robert Fisk, Foreign Correspondent, Beloved of Lara.*

In those days, Robert wanted to be buried in the cemetery outside St Patrick's Protestant church in Dalkey, "with my feet to the east, to face the good Lord on Judgement Day." He was only half-joking, for although Robert was not religious, he was steeped in the Anglican tradition.

Robert used to remind me that each year we unwittingly pass

the anniversary of our own death. Muslim Arabs believe that God inscribes the date of our death on our foreheads with the tip of his index finger. So 30 October 2020 was the invisible date on Robert's forehead.

"Is there life after death?" Robert frequently asked friends and interviewees. He said it as a joke, but I think he genuinely wondered. If there is an afterlife, he promised he would be the first journalist to file from there. Perhaps he is already interviewing God. I imagine him furiously typing up the interview, as he always typed, with only two fingers. Surely there are no deadlines in heaven? In life, Robert devised elaborate schemes to sneak copy out of Soviet-occupied Kabul and various Arab dictatorships. How would one transmit copy from the great beyond?

I imagine Robert's alert, intelligent face, the way he raises a finger to say, "Now hold on a minute, Mr God...", the way he peers quizzically over his eyeglasses to signal, "You have *got* to be kidding." I feel certain Robert has tough questions for God. He liked to recount the story of Winston Churchill's son Randolph reading the Bible in one sitting, on a bet from Evelyn Waugh during World War II. From time to time, Churchill's voice could be heard through the tent flap exclaiming, "Isn't God a shit!"

Robert admired William Howard Russell, the Irish-born correspondent for the London *Times* who is considered to be the first modern war correspondent. During the Crimean War, Russell angered the British establishment, all the way up to Queen Victoria, by denouncing what he saw as the needless sacrifice of British cavalrymen in the Charge of the Light Brigade.

Russell went on to cover the Sepoy Rebellion against the British East India Company, and the US War of Secession. He met Abraham Lincoln and later witnessed the 1870 Battle of Sedan, embedded on the Prussian side, in the Franco-Prussian war. Napoleon III was captured at Sedan, precipitating the Paris Commune and the advent of France's Third Republic.

No other correspondent, I suspect, could match Robert's record, unless it was the great war reporters of the two World

Wars. Robert seemed to regret having missed those conflicts, whose history he knew in detail. He long kept his father's medals from the Great War in our china cabinet in Paris. A photograph of one of his father's medals appears on the dust jacket of his last book, *The Great War for Civilisation*.

By the time I met Robert, he had already survived the Lebanese Civil War, the Iranian revolution, the Soviet invasion of Afghanistan and the beginning of the Iran-Iraq War. Together we reported the last years of the Lebanese Civil War, the 1990s' war between the military and Islamists in Algeria, the break-up of Yugoslavia and two Iraq wars. He was the only western correspondent to have interviewed Osama bin Laden three times. Those interviews grew out of my chance meeting with Jamal Khashoggi, the slain Saudi journalist, in Algiers in 1991.

Robert liked the phrase "Let's wind the tape back." Usually it was during an argument, to lead one back to the start and renegotiate a misunderstanding. As I sit on the bench in Kilternan cemetery on that cold November day, staring at his grave beneath the arc of a double rainbow, I mentally wind back the tape, through our saga of love, adventure, and heartbreak.

When we rushed to Dubai to cover the downing of Iran Air flight 655 by the *USS Vincennes* in July 1988, I saw for the first time what an extraordinarily lucky and resourceful journalist Robert could be. He was still with *The Times* then. I covered the story freelance for *The Irish Times*.

We spend a sleepless night driving from one Gulf port to another, in the hope of chartering a boat to Bandar Abbas, where the bodies of the victims have been taken. The tiny emirate of Sharjah allows British citizens to leave without exit visas. In the middle of the night, correspondents from the *Guardian, Daily Telegraph* and *Independent* board a boat bound for Bandar Abbas. As a US citizen, I am not allowed to depart.

Robert makes a snap decision on the quayside to stay with me. "I hope you realise how much I love you," he says as the small boat pulls out of the harbour. "I just watched my competitors sail away on a story without me, to be with you." He later tells me it was one of the most difficult decisions he ever took as a journalist.

Robert's romantic sacrifice pays off. The following morning, on the spur of the moment, the Iranian embassy in Dubai organises a press plane to Bandar Abbas. The journalists who chartered the boat are considered illegal aliens and are detained for twenty-four hours, while the rest of us come and go and file our stories. No wonder some of Robert's rivals are jealous to the point of fury.

The Iranians have taken the wreckage of the Airbus, and the remains of the 290 civilians who were killed when the missile blew the airliner apart, to a warehouse cold-storage facility. Intact corpses of men and women are lined up in plastic bags and plywood coffins, sorted by gender. Male reporters are not allowed to look at the women. Arms, legs, heads, and torsos are piled up at one end of the gymnasium-size cold room.

We are then bused to the former Intercontinental Hotel, where the Iranians offer us a lunch of grilled lamb. After what we have just witnessed, the mere sight and smell of meat makes me feel sick. "Come with me," Robert says, leading me to the hotel telex room, in a cubbyhole behind the reception desk. He charms the telex operator and sits down immediately, composing his front-page news story directly onto the keyboard. The line cuts after a few hundred words, but Robert files more from a payphone at the airport, after begging airport staff for Iranian coins and getting London to ring him back.

Robert's tour de force on the Iranian Airbus story isn't over. That night, the Iranians fly us back from Bandar Abbas to Dubai on a civilian airliner, the first to repeat the trajectory of the downed aircraft. While most of us sleep with exhaustion, Robert befriends the pilot and interviews him. The pilot explains that the *Vincennes*' military transponder could not communicate with the civilian airliner. In Dubai, Robert interviews civil aviation sources who confirm what the Iranian pilot has told him.

The days when Abraham Lincoln told William Howard

Russell that *The Times* was "one of the greatest powers in the world" are long over. Robert has been dismayed to watch his newspaper grow more right-wing and sensationalistic under Rupert Murdoch's ownership. His editors want speculation about a kamikaze airliner, not evidence of the US Navy's incompetence. I witness a furious telephone argument in our Dubai hotel room. The incident eventually prompts Robert to leave *The Times* for *The Independent*.

When radio technicians asked Robert to speak on the telephone so they could test sound levels, he invariably quoted Yeats's poem "When You Are Old". Since his death, I joke with friends that I have become what I always knew I would be one day: a nostalgic old lady. Yeats's text, with its portent of lost youth and lost love, feels incredibly poignant.

Memories of Robert flood back, especially the happy and funny moments: our Christmas mornings in Dalkey, drinking champagne as we open presents beneath the tree; the surprise birthday parties I threw for him in Beirut; the way we sang "Lili Marlene" and "A Nightingale Sang in Berkeley Square" with our interpreter Ljiljana Matijašević as we drove through Serb-held parts of Bosnia. Ljiljana had survived the Blitz in London.

In May 1989, during General Michel Aoun's "war of liberation" against Syria, we travel to Jounieh, on the Maronite coast north of Beirut. The doorman of the Aquarium Hotel shows us three jagged cones from Katyusha rockets, half-buried amid singed shrubbery in the hotel's flowerbeds. Two days earlier, the Syrians fired a barrage of so-called "Stalin's organs" from West Beirut. "The hotel gardener was working in the field across the street. He was cut in half by a rocket," the doorman says, pointing to the place where his colleague died.

I am still thinking about the unfortunate gardener when our evening aperitif on the hotel balcony is interrupted by blinding flashes of white light and deafening explosions. Another Katyusha bombardment. I race into the bathroom and cower beneath the sink. Robert follows, to comfort me. "Damn! I forgot my gin and tonic," he exclaims. As the explosions continue, Robert runs back to the balcony to retrieve his drink.

Robert had an uncanny sense of danger, the result of instinct as well as experience. He seemed to have antennae tuned to the proximity of kidnappers, gunmen and high explosives. In the wake of the Iraqi rout from Kuwait in 1991, we ventured into south-eastern Iraq. I still worked for *Time* magazine then, and my editors were urging me to go to Basra. Robert and I head up the highway with a driver, then stop. "I don't like this road," he says. "People go up it, but no one comes back." I grudgingly return to Kuwait City with him. "Where are you?" the chief of correspondents gasps when I call New York. He is extremely relieved that we did not continue to Basra, because all the journalists who went there were taken prisoner by Saddam's forces.

After covering the 1991 war from Saudi Arabia, and the liberation of Kuwait, we travel to southern Turkey and northern Iraq, to witness the exodus of up to a million Kurds who have been driven out by Saddam. It has been a hard trek. At the PTT office on the Habur Bridge between Turkey and Iraq, I am dismayed to learn that my visa to Baghdad has come through. My editors at *Time* want me to go to Amman to collect it, immediately. Baghdad is only 500 kilometres away, as the crow flies. But in the Middle East one is often forced to travel by circuitous routes. It takes two days to retrace my steps and reach Baghdad.

On arrival at the Al Rasheed Hotel, I turn on my shortwave radio to hear: "The British war correspondent Robert Fisk has been arrested by Turkish authorities." Robert saw Turkish soldiers stealing food and blankets from Kurdish refugees at a mountain camp called Yasilova, which he reached after he was mistakenly shunted onto a CIA helicopter. US agents and British Royal Marines are engaged in a tense standoff with the Turks there. Of course, Robert filed a story.

Alan Parker's 1978 film classic *Midnight Express*, about an American student sentenced to life in prison in Turkey, flashes through my mind. I have visions of my lover being mistreated or tortured. I find a colleague from Reuters news agency in the coffee shop of the Al Rasheed. "If your partner was arrested in Turkey, what would you do?" I ask him. "I would go there immediately," he answers.

Robert is released before I can organise the journey. He has told a Turkish court that he was "shocked, shocked to see the Turkish army betray the high ideals of Mustafa Kemal Atatürk, who my father taught me was a titan of the twentieth century". In those pre-Erdogan days, when Atatürk's memory as the founder of the modern Turkish state is still sacred, no formulation could be more awkward for a Turkish court. *Shut this guy up, get him out of here,* they must have thought. Robert relishes telling me about his adventure.

I see Robert arriving at our suite in the Majestic Hotel in Belgrade with an enormous bouquet, purchased under bombardment, to apologise for having accidentally de-programmed the French mobile phone I use to file our stories. I remember him weeping with joy on learning that he has won yet another press award. He had at least eighteen British and international press awards, more than any other foreign correspondent. They filled several shelves in his library in Dalkey.

яэ

Robert was part Tintin boy reporter and part James Bond. As the years passed, a third Robert superseded them: an unrelenting crusader for wronged and oppressed peoples, who catalogued atrocities and injustice with frightening intensity. The job of a journalist was "to be neutral and unbiased on the side of those who suffer", he said.

Robert was fearless, and his fearlessness was contagious. "You are going there to report, not to die!" he insisted whenever I expressed anxiety about heading for a war zone. "Don't be so vain as to think that the bullet (or shell or bomb) should choose *you* among thousands of people!"

These memories rush at me in haphazard fashion as I sit beside Robert's grave. I get up to go, and notice that the rainbow is still there. I glance around at the lingering mourners and begin to recognise friends of Robert whom I have not seen for decades. All wear masks over wrinkled faces. Their complexions are ashen and their hair is white, like a ghastly Halloween disguise. I feel like Proust's narrator at the end of *In Search of Lost Time*, when, reunited with the characters of the novel, he is stunned by their decrepitude. We buried our youth with Robert.

I doubtless look as old and haggard as the others, but in my mind, I am a twenty-six-year-old researcher/associate producer for CBS News. I have a powerful sense of Robert's presence inside the casket beneath the flowers and astroturf panel. But the man I imagine is a youthful thirty-seven-year-old, merely napping before he heads out on yet another exclusive story. I have mastered the art of time travel and turned the dial back thirty-seven years, to a time when we were hungry to learn and love and when it meant so much to be alive. I have gone back to the beginning.

I

The Beirut Hoover and Appliance Company

Had we but World enough, and Time,
This coyness, Lady, were no crime...
The Grave's a fine and private place,
But none, I think, do there embrace.

Andrew Marvell, from
"To His Coy Mistress", 1681

I fell in love with Robert Fisk in the office of the Syrian Information Minister on a cold December morning in 1983.

About two dozen journalists have crowded into the minister's top-floor office in a dusty, crumbling high-rise on the western outskirts of Damascus. Meetings with Arab cabinet ministers usually involve sitting on garish brocade and gold chairs or fake leather sofas while imbibing tiny glasses of scalding, sugary tea, but it is a sign of the tense times that no one offers tea and we remain standing. Hafez al-Assad's Syria is supporting the Druze and Muslim militias who are fighting Israel and Ronald Reagan's America in neighbouring Lebanon. The region is going up in flames.

We want to know something, anything, about Lieutenant Robert O. Goodman, the US airman who has been shot down by Syrian surface-to-air missiles in the hills east of Beirut. Goodman is the Syrians' prisoner, and they will hold him for a month.

Robert stands a few feet away from me, throwing me sideways glances and winking. He seems to have springs in his legs. His wiry, elastic body bounces up and down with irrepressible energy. The Irish would say he is full of divilment.

Robert's scruffy, boyish appearance contrasts with his reputation for erudition. He has tousled light-brown hair, crooked teeth, a ruddy complexion and pleasing blue eyes. His wire-rimmed glasses are smudged. Though he wears a belt, his trousers fall around his hips, so his shirt tails are hanging out. He hitches up his trousers with one hand while pushing the shirt tails down inside the waistband with the other. The shirt tails pull out again within seconds. He also cocks his head at an angle and blinks with one eye. These nervous tics never interrupt a constant flow of words.

Robert travels light. Unlike the rest of us, he carries no

reporter's bag, no tape recorder. Just a small notebook and an old-fashioned pencil which he holds up as if he is about to throw it at a dartboard. A Lebanese press card and a British passport protrude from his shirt pocket. His questions reveal more about the situation than the minister's turgid replies.

Robert sidles up to me the moment the press conference is over. "So, Miss Lara, how are you enjoying Damascus?" he asks. A colleague from CBS introduced us in the coffee shop of the Sheraton Hotel that morning. It was Robert who alerted me to the minister's press conference. "You probably won't learn anything, but if you are trying to work here, it's a good idea to put in an appearance."

I had read Robert's articles in *The Times* almost every day since Israel had invaded Lebanon in June 1982, at my desk in the CBS bureau in Paris. I remember his horrifying accounts of the Sabra and Chatila massacres, and his reports on the bombing of the US marines and French paratroopers in Beirut, just five weeks before I left Paris for Damascus. I am almost surprised to find that the famous, intrepid war correspondent exists in real life, even more surprised when he shows an interest in me.

I was still an undergraduate French major in California when Robert moved from Belfast to Beirut to be *The Times*'s Middle East correspondent in 1976. The Vietnam War had just ended. The Lebanese Civil War, and the presence of Yasser Arafat and the PLO, made Beirut a world news centre, the place to be for aspiring journalists. More than any other correspondent, Robert owned the Lebanon and Middle East story.

I have been in Damascus for eight days. This is my first trip to the region, and I am struggling to prepare a CBS *60 Minutes* programme about Syria's pivotal role in the war between Israel and its neighbours. Our leisurely documentary, which will require weeks to shoot, edit and broadcast, has been overtaken by events.

In 1983, Hafez al-Assad is the Middle East's pyromaniac fireman, igniting fires in Lebanon so that he can demonstrate how badly Syria is needed to put out the flames. He is a cruel and murderous dictator, but consistent, even idealistic, in his way. He sees himself as the ultimate defender of the Palestinian cause, and will never capitulate to Israel and the US. When the Muslim Brotherhood threatened his hold on power, Assad ordered his fundamentalist subjects to be slaughtered in their tens of thousands. Robert was the only western reporter to reach Hama when it was under siege by Assad's troops in February 1982.

Now *60 Minutes* presenter Mike Wallace is ringing me every day from Manhattan, demanding to know why I have not yet landed an interview for him with Assad. Wallace is a millionaire celebrity television journalist whose pugnacious interviewing style is known to most Americans. He cannot comprehend that Assad could not care less about appearing on what was then, as we often boasted, the most watched television programme in the US. As a fallback, I have lined up foreign minister Farouk al-Sharaa, who speaks English well from his days at Syrian Airlines.

To make matters worse, Mike Wallace made a pass at me on our previous shoot, a story about NATO in Germany. "You know what the *droit du seigneur* is, young lady?" he intones menacingly down the phone line from New York. "Well, this time you won't escape."

Every day, I call the information ministry and the office of Gebran Khourieh, Assad's press spokesman. The title is a misnomer, since Khourieh speaks rarely, if ever. (I will finally meet him a decade later, when my editors at *Time* magazine and I at last interview Assad.)

The Syrian government deals with the press the way it deals with diplomats in negotiations. No one says no, but nothing happens; nothing is scheduled. The information ministry is there not to disseminate information but to block it. Assad is the only man in the country who has the right to take decisions.

I make the rounds of the Palestinian groups and interview diplomats. I have brought a portable typewriter to Damascus, to type notes for Wallace and producer Barry Lando, who is Canadian. Barry asks for a simple, historical explanation of the Palestinian claim to statehood. I put the question to Syrian and Palestinian sources and am hit with a barrage of verbiage. I am out of my depth.

Enter Robert Fisk, who knows everyone and everything but wears his learning lightly. "My boss, Barry Lando, is arriving from Paris this afternoon," I tell him as we chat after the press conference. "Can *60 Minutes* invite you to dinner?"

Barry is a friend, and I know he will be impressed that I have lined up an evening with the famous Robert Fisk. We go to Damascus's only French restaurant, La Chaumière. Over pepper steak and Lebanese red wine, Robert gives us a crash course in Middle East history and the war in Lebanon. Not only does he bring clarity to confusion, he is a great raconteur.

The three of us share two bottles of Château Ksara. Then Robert orders Irish coffee. It is so good that we have three each. Then we walk back through the silent streets of Damascus to the Sheraton. "Is this safe?" Barry asks as we set off.

"There is no place safer than an Arab dictatorship," Robert replies. "Nothing happens here unless it is *meant* to happen." He points towards the street where Alois Brunner, the ageing Nazi war criminal, lives quietly, raising rabbits on his roof, under the assumed name Georg Fischer. As we walk past the defence ministry, Robert pantomimes torture in the underground cells.

I meet Barry in the coffee shop the next morning. Neither of us has slept a wink. The penny drops. "It's the Irish coffee!" I blurt out. When I run into Robert in the lobby, he shows no sign of fatigue and proposes dinner again that evening. Of course, I say. I am eager to resume the conversation. But is it all right if Barry joins us?

That evening, I sit opposite Robert in the Sheraton coffee shop, with Barry beside us like a chaperone. We eat mezze and drink more Lebanese wine. By the end of the meal, Robert and I are leaning across the table, staring into each other's eyes.

Barry finally realises he is *de trop*. "Oh," my boss says, suddenly embarrassed. "I guess I'd better be going."

Robert invites me to his room and we become lovers. He leaves for Beirut the next morning. The tone of our encounter has remained casual, light-hearted. Robert has a Finnish girlfriend waiting for him in Beirut. I am going out with an Irish-American television journalist in Paris, and I am in the process of moving to New York to work for CBS there. Robert is the courageous, funny, sexy and intelligent lover I have dreamed of, yet I despair of forming any kind of lasting relationship with him, because he seems to have a girl in every port; because he has told me that his idea of happiness is to curl up alone with a book and a cup of hot cocoa.

A few weeks later, I receive a Christmas card, c/o CBS in New York. It is a copy of a nineteenth-century lithograph by David Roberts, showing the Roman ruins of Baalbek, and is signed The Beirut Hoover and Appliance Company. Robert does not want to provoke any jealous scenes, he explains later.

In the meantime, I meet another Robert in New York, an aspiring young Canadian film producer. For the sake of clarity, my brother Bob later nicknames him Robert the First. And although I had met him first, family and close friends will refer to Robert Fisk as Robert the Second.

At CBS, I am assigned to the morning news, which means getting up at 2.30 a.m. five days a week. Try as I might, I cannot adapt. I find it impossible to sleep during the day or go to bed before eight o'clock in the evening. I live for several months like a zombie. I have almost forgotten that I passed the foreign service exam several years earlier. When the State Department tracks me down to ask again if I would like to be a diplomat, I jump at the opportunity to escape from an inhuman work schedule.

For four years, Robert Fisk and I stay in touch somehow, without email, mobile telephones or social media, across time zones and halfway around the world from each other. He posts a birthday card from Cyprus to my Manhattan address the following

April, around the time I am packing to move to Washington. It is marked Private, and contains one of his favourite quotes from *Antony and Cleopatra*:

> Age cannot wither her, nor custom stale
> Her infinite variety. Other women cloy
> The appetites they feed, but she makes hungry
> Where most she satisfies.

After six months training at the Foreign Service Institute in Virginia, I am appointed vice-consul in Barbados. On the eve of my departure, Robert the First, the Canadian film producer, proposes marriage.

"Are you sure?" I ask him.

"No. But you are leaving and I don't want to lose you," he replies.

I am not sure either, but he is a kind, gentle man and I think I love him. I am twenty-seven years old. Most of my friends are engaged or already married. One should not base a life decision on such shaky premises, but I nonetheless start organising a wedding in Barbados.

One afternoon in the late summer or early autumn of 1984, the telephone rings on my desk in the consular section. It is Robert Fisk. "I was thinking of taking a Caribbean holiday. Could I visit you in Barbados?" he asks. "Why don't you come to my wedding?" I reply. I have pegged Fisk for a ladies' man, and I don't want to be part of his harem. My reply must sound flippant, but my heart is pounding. I desperately want Fisk to show up and prevent me from making this mistake.

The night before my wedding, I tell Robert the First that I cannot go through with it. "You can't do this to me," he says. "My family have flown all the way from Vancouver."

My younger sister Marie tries to comfort me while I weep in bed. "All my friends get cold feet. It's perfectly normal," she says.

At sunset on New Year's Eve 1984, on the patio of my house

on the beach in Barbados, I marry the wrong Robert. It will take three years to undo my error.

Until the last moment, I have fantasies of Robert Fisk arriving on a white horse to spirit me away. Or bursting into the ceremony when Judge Sandra Mason asks if anyone can show just cause why we should not be married, like Dustin Hoffman in *The Graduate*.

Despite the fact that I am now a married woman, the following Christmas Robert Fisk sends me a romantic card of Frederic William Burton's *The Meeting on the Turret Stairs*, from the National Gallery of Ireland. A poster of the painting, which shows the tragic parting of Hellelil and Hildebrand before he is to be executed by her seven brothers on her father's orders, will later hang on the wall of our bedroom in Beirut. "No word from you for months," the card says. "And what about that trip to Ireland? Do write – with love, Robert."

My eighteen-month tour of duty in Barbados ends. I successfully lobby for a post as junior science attaché in Paris. I know nothing about science, but the science counsellor, a prominent American physicist, needs someone with good French. My husband is still in Manhattan, pursuing his career as a film-maker. He promises to move to Paris and we intend to put my diplomat's housing allowance towards the purchase of an apartment, as allowed by State Department regulations. In the meantime, I rent a studio flat with jungle wallpaper in the rue du Faubourg Saint-Honoré, a few blocks from the US embassy.

Robert Fisk asks to visit me in Paris in the summer of 1986. I have not seen him for two and a half years, but I am lucid enough to know that if I see him, I risk being unfaithful to my husband. I agree to a rendezvous, then panic. I send Fisk a telegram. "Too terrified. Don't come to Paris," it says. He telephones me in stitches of laughter. "Lara, Lara, dear Lara," he says. "What a priceless message! Now I really *must* come to Paris!"

I book a hotel room for Robert across the street, with the idea that we will wave platonically at one another from a safe distance.

I am obviously lying to myself, because I buy champagne and foie gras at the embassy commissary. We spend two riotous days together. The interlude leaves me feeling hung-over and guilty.

The other Robert has second thoughts about moving to Paris when his first feature film receives encouraging reviews. "I can't. It's too foreign," he says. I know my marriage is doomed if I stay in Paris, and I am weary of the State Department. So I resign and move back to New York, with the intention of writing a novel.

I work in our dark, ground-floor apartment in Greenwich Village while my film-maker husband edits videos uptown to make a living. Robert Fisk telephones occasionally from Beirut or Dublin, London, Cairo or Dubai. He has a new nickname for me and starts our conversations with the words, "How is the novel going, Jane Austen?" I poke fun at the cards he sends me from Ireland, of thatched cottages and wet cows. The latter become a joke between us. At Christmas 1986, he writes that he is "leaving the island of wet cows and rainy lanes" for Beirut, "the city that haunts me almost as much as my little village in Ireland". It was "smashing" to talk to me on the telephone he says, adding that he intends to see me in the New Year.

French friends ask me to look after their apartment in the rue de Tournon in Paris during their summer holiday in 1987. I accept eagerly. One hot night in August, Robert Fisk holds my hand across the table at the Brasserie Muniche in the rue de Buci. "Do you love me?" he asks. "I suppose I do," I answer shyly. Those words change everything for him.

Robert is covering the Tanker War, in which Iran and Iraq, and Iraq's American and Saudi allies, attack each other's merchant shipping in the Persian Gulf. He has caught a terrible cold, probably from moving between extremely hot outdoor temperatures and ice-cold air-conditioning. He is sweating and running a high fever, but nonetheless makes love like a trooper.

In the morning, still ill, Robert bashes out a 1,000-word profile of Iran's Hashemi Rafsanjani on a French keyboard, pecking away with two fingers. It is the first time I see him write a newspaper story, and I am stunned by the speed and ease with which he turns out flawless copy, without notes or reference material, never correcting or rewriting.

In his rush to catch a flight back to the Gulf, Robert arranges for *The Times*'s copytaker to call my friends' apartment. Before leaving, he gives me a crash course in dictating newspaper copy. "You have to say every punctuation mark: open quote, close quote, comma, full stop," he explains. "Spell out every name, like this: A alpha, B bravo, C charlie, D delta..." The article creates problems for Robert, because Rafsanjani, who would become president of the Islamic Republic two years later, objects to being called a pistachio farmer.

Adultery with Robert Fisk is becoming a habit. Things take a serious turn after our mutual profession of love in the Brasserie Muniche. I am frightened by the prospect of a messy break-up, of hurting my kind and unsuspecting husband.

Before Robert leaves Paris that morning, I make him promise not to contact me again. No letters, no phone calls. I probably don't mean it, and I probably know he will not keep his promise. I am nonetheless astounded by the campaign that follows.

Between 17 August and 26 November 1987, I receive seventeen letters and three of Robert's own poems. I tell him that Robert is a great name for poets: Bridges, Browning, Burns, Frost, Graves, Herrick, Lowell, Service... and Fisk! Two of his missives run to eight handwritten pages. I do not reread them for thirty-three years, until after his death. They can still move me to laughter and tears. *Une lettre est une âme*, Balzac wrote. *A letter is a soul*.

Over the next three months, we meet for secret trysts in Paris, Dublin, Rome and New York. Language is the weapon Robert uses to conquer my heart, as well as the minds of his readers. Were it not for the letters and poems, which Robert calls "a bridge between us", I might have stayed with my husband.

"Darling Lara – May I call you darling?" Robert begins his first missive, written on *Times* letterhead in Dubai, en route for Tehran after our rendezvous in the rue de Tournon. He says he thinks he can address me as darling, on condition we don't call it a letter. He sends a half-dozen photographs of himself in an envelope marked "Here's looking at you". (We both love *Casablanca*.) In two pictures, he stands on the deck of a ship in the Gulf. You can see the sweltering heat, smell the perspiration. In an older picture, taken in Afghanistan, he wears a rolled pakol hat like the grinning mujahidin who surround him. He has a cartridge belt slung across his chest, and holds a rifle in both hands. He says he misses me, begs me not to say it's too late, as I did in our most recent telephone conversation, and asks me to remember Andrew Marvell's "To His Coy Mistress", which he quotes often.

Robert writes again from Tehran, which he describes as "a dark, grim place for a people who wrote such poetry and made flower carpets that could turn the desert into a garden". He refers to the government of the Islamic Republic as "a necrocracy", government by and for the dead. He believes we often think of one another at the exact same moment, which is doubtless true. He chides me for initially receiving him "primly, all Jane Austen on the sofa, smoothing your skirt and saying, 'so tell me your news' like some very distant friend".

Robert sends three cards from Bahrain and Beirut in September, announcing his imminent arrival at the Essex House Hotel in Manhattan, "barring some lunacy by President R [Reagan] or the Ayatollah", to promote *In Time of War*, his 565-page tome on Irish neutrality in World War II. The copy he sends me is inscribed simply "A long way from Damascus?" to avoid giving my husband reason for suspicion.

Robert arrives in Manhattan on 2 October, without having heard from me. He posts me a frantic letter, saying he does not know if his letters have reached me. He regrets his promise not to call. He is waiting for me in room 1108 of the Essex House Hotel, "staring across Central Park like the itinerant lover you describe". He has spent the morning discussing Lebanon and the Middle East at United Nations headquarters, with men he disparagingly describes as "statesmen" in quotation marks. Their talk about international concern for Lebanon seems far removed from the city he has just left. He cites W.H. Auden's 1930s' poem "Embassy", about diplomats deciding the fate of nations on wide lawns.

Robert worries that he may not hear from me, that his sudden arrival in "my" city may be unwanted and frightening to me. He suggests we could meet in a tea house in Chinatown, or some other platonic setting "where our love could not pass any borders". He jokes about a tryst in the centre of Triboro Bridge, the sort of "industrial romanticism" that a Soviet film-maker might have recorded, "two tiny figures dwarfed by iron girders in the centre of a canyon of traffic".

My husband has gone to Los Angeles to pursue a film project. I resist temptation for a day. Then I take the 7th Avenue Express uptown for a prearranged dinner with girlfriends. It's a solid alibi, and I slip away early to join Robert at the Essex House Hotel.

Robert writes to me in the early hours of the following morning. When he woke up two hours after my departure, he says he was filled with happiness. The pillows and sheets still carried my perfume and he felt I was with him, "in all the intimacy and love you gave me tonight". But the second time he wakes, Robert's mood changes and he feels despair at the thought of the pain he will feel over coming days and months. He says he wept with longing and searched for some hint that my determination to shake him out of my life might not be final.

People who make others laugh are rarely a threat, Robert says, so he tries to make me laugh by telling me that he bought a new suit, blazer, slacks, five shirts and three ties from Louis Copeland, a fashionable menswear shop in Dublin, in the hope of impressing me. He had intended to invite me to lunch, on the supposition that dinner might be awkward for a married lady, and he had no intention of turning up like a country bumpkin. All these clothes hung guiltily and unnoticed in the hotel cupboard when I came to his hotel room at midnight.

Now Robert fears that "our garden of earthly delight" will be taken from us, that I will meet him hurriedly that afternoon with a frown, bringing memories of the previous night "like coloured snapshots in which the colour has not quite been accurately copied, the definition blurred". He fears that our meeting in New York may become mere "fading pictures with negatives unrecoverable".

The fact that Robert lives in Beirut feels daring and adventurous, but it also frightens me. Since 1982, dozens of westerners have been kidnapped, including Robert's close friend the Associated Press bureau chief Terry Anderson. The preceding January, the Archbishop of Canterbury's special envoy Terry Waite was kidnapped while trying to negotiate the release of hostages. I live in fear that Robert too will be kidnapped.

A carload of gunmen tried to kidnap him in West Beirut in 1984. He has told me the story in such vivid detail that I can picture the carload of gunmen pulling up alongside him in Bliss Street, gesturing to him to pull over. Robert has just interviewed a newly freed Lebanese hostage and tells himself, "This is it!" He steps on the accelerator and tears through the crowded, narrow streets, smashing parked cars and ripping off mudguards with the kidnappers in hot pursuit. He abandons his car in front of the Commodore Hotel, where the international press corps stay. Lucy Spiegel of CBS buys him a rum and cola. His hands are sweating and trembling so much that he can barely hold the glass.

Despite my concern for his safety, Robert writes to me on the morning of 4 October 1987 that he feels Beirut may be the best place for him. Pessimism is uncharacteristic of him, but in early October he entertains the possibility that our affair may end soon. I am torn and confused, and he knows it could go either way. Robert has spent more than a quarter of his life in Lebanon already. The fear he experiences there, the dirt of the place, the necessity to be ever watchful are familiar to him. "In its venomous way, perhaps Beirut will give comfort to me," he says.

Robert speaks often of Juan Carlos Gumucio, the only other

western journalist remaining in Beirut since the press corps fled to Cyprus. Juan Carlos works for the Spanish newspaper *El País* and strings for *The Times* when Robert travels. He is a tall, heavy-set Bolivian, a charismatic man with curly, jet-black hair, a bushy beard and laughing eyes, and he is Robert's *compañero*. Juan Carlos and his wife, Agneta Ramberg, the correspondent for Swedish radio, are Robert's neighbours in the Sleit building on the seafront Corniche. They have just had a baby daughter, Anna Céleste, named after the wife of Babar in the elephant comics. Agneta has taken the baby to Sweden. (Agneta and Juan Carlos later divorce. He marries the American journalist Marie Colvin, who is killed by shellfire in the Syrian city of Homs in 2012.)

Because JC, as everyone calls him, bears a passing resemblance to a Hezbollah gunman, his presence makes one feel secure. JC looks fierce but is in reality a human teddy bear. With his Latin lover persona, he delights in dispensing advice to Robert. It was JC who pushed Robert to buy the new wardrobe from the Dublin tailor.

When Robert leaves Beirut for Manhattan, JC tells him that nothing could be a greater challenge than the car ride to the airport through the southern suburbs. Westerners are often kidnapped on the airport road, and JC usually accompanies Robert, as a sort of bodyguard. He sits in the front seat of Abed's battered Peugeot; Abed, whom Robert refers to as "faithful driver". Robert is obviously European, so he sits in the back, holding an Arab newspaper in front of his face, pretending to be reading. They drive fast and refuse to stop at militia checkpoints.

To outsmart kidnappers, Robert books flights under an Arab name but uses his real initials. He travels first-class and does not check bags, because on the return trip the kidnappers will have lookouts in the airport, studying passengers as they disembark and wait for luggage. The snitches telephone ahead to gunmen, who ambush new arrivals on the airport road. Robert is always first off the plane and first out of the airport, so the kidnappers don't have time to organise.

There are things worse than running the gauntlet of kidnappers on the airport road. Beirut is full of people who have been physically mutilated, Robert writes, but there are far more people who have been wounded invisibly. Some are of the hollow laughter variety, others tinkle their voices at the right jokes and have developed an extraordinary capacity to carry on long, complicated conversations while thinking at exactly the same time about other, sadder things. On his return to Beirut, he fears he will understand them better.

Then his spirits rally. This is not self-pity, Robert insists. He says he is a tough, pragmatic and decisive man who always sticks to his decisions. He can think of no better, wiser move than travelling to New York to see me. This is love, he insists, not infatuation. He asks me to make allowances for his occasional arrogance, for I am, he says, a beautiful, elegant American married lady and only an arrogant man would dare pursue me. "I believe in fighting for the woman I love; and you would not love me so much if I did not."

Will he remain a forbidden lover, "all the more desirable but of necessity gone because of what 'forbidden' means?" Robert wonders. Or will he become a memory to be recalled only when I hear about kidnapping or fighting in Lebanon?

Robert says he has no right to expect letters or photographs from me, but will continue to write to me "as intimately and honestly as this letter, leaving nothing of myself out". His letters will be a bridge between us that I may cross at any time. Never hesitate, he says. He will always be there on the other side.

I am surprised, stunned, by his ardour. "I come as true as any lover, wanting to have a baby with the woman I adore, positively desiring to be the father of any child that is yours, happy to give up my career for someone far more important," he writes. He says he wants me to be his wife, not just his lover, and that he fully understands the implications of what he is saying.

On his return to Beirut, Robert writes a poem, entitled "For Lara", dated 10 October 1987. It is my favourite, because it encapsulates not only his love for me but the strange power that Beirut exerts over him and many westerners. Despite electricity cuts, mosquitos and the ever-present threat of kidnapping, the city holds him, in part through the beauty of its snow-capped mountains and the Mediterranean. Danger, I suspect, is an integral part of the attraction.

"I was thinking of you when the lights went out," the poem begins. Robert is sitting on the balcony overlooking the sea. It is hot and the mosquitoes come back, "keen to make a killing on the foreigner in me". He imagines me standing beside the rusty railing and lights a candle. It is midnight in Beirut, 4 p.m. in Manhattan. Robert quotes one of my letters, in which I note that he was not desirous of being possessed: "Salad days and green in judgement. You were right about the rest."

While I sleep, Abed will drive him and Juan Carlos south to Tyre, speeding up through the Hezbollah stronghold of Ouzai, "we silly warriors, notebooks locked and loaded, biros ready to fire". The snow is blinding on the heights of Mount Sannine. The mist has settled on the airport road where kidnappers roam. He will go there yet again, on a journey of love, speeding through checkpoints, his flight booked under another name. It will have been worth it all, he concludes, if I come with him, "faithfully as you stood here tonight".

Robert also sends me the first pages of a novel, which centres on a young British diplomat living in Beirut, who reminds me of Lawrence Durrell's British ambassador, Mountolive. Robert's diplomat character is wary of the Shia Muslim gunmen who prowl the seafront Corniche looking for westerners to kidnap. Like Robert, his fictional alter ego positions a mirror on the balcony, to enable him to watch the gunmen's cars unseen.

When Robert next rings me, I tell him I am trying to find a way of visiting him in Dublin. My "itinerant lover" is, he says, enduring every range of joy, hope and despair, what novelists used to describe as "sweet pain". In yet another letter, he lists all possible negative scenarios. My sister Marie, who lived in Arizona at the time, might persuade me to break off our affair. He jokes that the constitution of Arizona possibly contains "some rugged American bye-laws, in small print but all directed against over-confident Englishmen". Or Tala, my closest American friend in Paris, whom Robert stopped to meet on his way back from New York, might "produce a very negative school report on Master Fisk".

Robert also fears that I might send him a short, carefully phrased note "designed to cool the ardour of your distant Heathcliff". It would, he says, "be doomed to fail in its objective".

Finally, there is the thought and hope he cherishes, that I will fly to meet him at Roissy airport, where we will hold each other for long minutes before speaking.

Robert talks increasingly of our future life together, which will include Dublin. On his way to Manhattan, he buys two books for me, Faber editions of Seamus Heaney's *North* and *Field Work*. "My darling," he writes on the first page of *North*. "I bought these books of my favourite Irish poet for you in Dublin with the notion that one day they may sit on *our* bookshelf."

When Robert speaks of his home in Ireland, I imagine a thatched cottage. He describes instead the terraced Georgian house at 108 Sorrento Road, which will be a second home to us for the next twelve years, until we move to the big house. He sends me a proud description of the single-storey house, built in the 1830s, with heavy, foot-thick walls and a "governessy eagle" above the front door, looking towards Finnegan's pub.

Robert had taken an old photograph of the original eagle, in plaster, to a stonemason in County Laois, who carved a similar bird, but in granite. The sculpture proved too heavy to be raised to the pediment. A builder devised a way of sliding the eagle into position on a miniature railway line. A group of schoolboys formed in the street to watch the goings-on. Robert breaks his own rule about imitating accents to recount their reaction to the elevation of the eagle: "Look, they're takin' the feckin eagle to the top of the feckin Englishman's feckin house on a feckin train."

Within weeks, I will visit the cottage, which is a museum to Robert's life in the Middle East. The book-lined study with a Victorian desk boasts Robert's photographs from the Iranian revolution. A carpet from Isfahan hangs opposite the carved wooden linen chest in the hall. Above the kitchen table there's a framed Crayola drawing by an eleven-year-old Palestinian boy, showing the battle of Tel al-Zaatar. The child has mastered the mechanical details of rifles and anti-aircraft artillery. Guerrillas man the weapons.

Robert no longer hesitates to ring me in Manhattan, in the mornings when I am writing and Robert the First is working at a production company uptown. He tells me Juan Carlos waited a whole hour before asking about me when he returned. "It must have been agony for him. I told him little, except that I am as madly in love with you as ever." As one of the last foreigners in West Beirut, he feels ever more conspicuous. "I get stared at and I am beginning to feel like Gulliver in the land of the little people every time I walk into a restaurant."

In late October, we spend eight blissful days together in Europe. After several days in Paris, we head to Roissy airport without tickets. "Pick any destination," Robert tells me as we stare at the departures board. It feels incredibly extravagant and romantic. I choose Rome. On 29 October in the Via Frattina, Robert buys me a black pillbox hat with a black sash knotted to one side. He calls it my adulterous hat. I keep the receipt, for 39,000 lire.

At our leave-taking in Rome airport, the clerk at the check-in desk asks if we are in love. Robert tells me again that he wants to share his life with me. He has a later flight, so I head through Immigration alone, turning back every few seconds in my adulterous hat, clutching a single red rose. I run to the plane and spot Robert waving through a window.

He is travelling from Rome to Dubai, by way of Athens, Bahrain, Doha and Abu Dhabi. We are years before mobile phones, but he manages to track me down in the terminal at Roissy to tell me again how much he loves me and wants to live with me. I am amazed that he has persuaded Air France to call me to the phone, and I doubt it would have worked in any other country. He tells me later than he spent forty-five minutes on the telephone before reaching me. I cannot imagine how much it cost. Robert's *numéro de séduction* is unbeatable.

And it continues. "I could never have imagined such longing for another human being, for all your love and gentleness and intimacy," Robert says. He recalls rose petals strewn on our bed, the way I snuggled up to him on the windy clifftop at Dalkey, our words of love as we sat in the Ulpia restaurant by the forum in Rome. "I feel quite crushed by it all, like someone who has been to the top of a mountain to watch the dawn but is so overwhelmed by it that he can never afterwards bear to describe it," he says.

I have told Robert of my scepticism, that every love I have known has grown routine and mundane with time. He promises that the brightness and excitement of his love for me will not fade. He says he will leave the Middle East because I want to live in Europe, that the idea of sharing our love in a place where I am happy gives him nothing but joy.

"I will never let you down," Robert promises. For the next thirteen years those words will be sacred to me. I am sure he meant them at the time, but I ought to have considered the adage often quoted by French politicians, that promises commit only the one who believes them. Robert begins addressing me as "Beloved Lara", words he will use for the next twenty-two years.

Robert does nothing by half-measures. He tells me he has broken off with Christina and Majida and Scheherazade, because he wants only me. He sends a page of names and contact numbers for sympathetic parties. They include his parents and the foreign editor and Washington correspondent of *The Times*. He lists numbers for his homes in Beirut and Dublin, and the hotels where he stays in Cairo, Bahrain, Dubai and Damascus. When he tells his desk in London about me, the deputy foreign editor asks, "Is this the woman who files your copy?"

Before I have taken a decision, Robert begins plotting my

exfiltration from New York. He says he cannot possibly ask me to live in Beirut while the civil war continues and every westerner is a potential hostage. He has sought his editors' permission to work out of the Paris bureau.

Robert's most impressive exploit is his 24-hour round-trip journey from Beirut to Manhattan. As Jean Cocteau wrote: "*Il n'y a pas d'amour. Il n'y a que des preuves d'amour.*" There is no such thing as love, only evidence of love.

After our European idyll in late October, Robert continues to telephone almost daily. (Again, I dread to think of the phone bills.) On 11 November, I tell him how badly I want to see him, never dreaming that he will, literally, jump on the next plane. He writes a three-page prose poem while crossing the Atlantic. It begins, "'New York?' the woman asked aboard the plane. 'For just one day? She *must* be beautiful.'" When he tells his driver he is flying to New York to see me, Abed asks if I will come to Beirut.

"Darling, you sound so close! Where are you?" I ask when I pick up the telephone that same afternoon. I race to the Essex House, where Robert has just come out of the shower, and greets me with a towel wrapped round his waist. "You said you wanted to see me! I will always come to you when you need me."

We linger in bed, walk in Central Park, have dinner at an Indian restaurant in West 57th Street. Robert writes to me again on the return journey the next morning, saying he was "in heaven yesterday", that he longs for me and will be thinking of me, loving me, even at the times we cannot talk. He says Juan Carlos is giving him cooking lessons, for my benefit, and that next week will be Italian cooking week in the Sleit building. "Aromas of your lover's experimental pastas, pizzas and lasagnes will waft down among the bearded Shiites strolling the Corniche," he says. If I will come to live with him, he promises never to return to Beirut, unless I will come with him to help pack his things for the move to Paris.

I finally give in to Robert Fisk's Byronic voluntarism, and, truth be told, to my own instincts. There is no longer any contest.

Everything else is drab, compared to the hours I spend with Robert. I feel I will miss out on life if I do not go to him.

When my husband returns from Los Angeles, I tell him I am moving back to Paris. I do not have the courage to tell him about Robert. Two days later, I come home from the gym to find Robert the First distraught and smoking cigarettes, which he almost never does. He has intercepted Robert the Second's latest, eight-page letter. "That turkey sent you a lock of his hair," he says angrily. He casts a sort of curse over me, saying, "You left me for him, and you'll leave him for someone else".

"Turkey? If I were him, I would have called me something much worse," Fisk laughs when I tell him.

On 26 November, Thanksgiving Day 1987, nearly four years after I met Robert in Damascus, I board British Airways flight 178 to Heathrow, wearing my adulterous hat. Robert meets me with a bouquet of red roses. The taxi driver who drops us at the Hyde Park Hotel says our kiss should be in the *Guinness Book of World Records*.

A few weeks later, my estranged husband sends me a letter signed "the real Robert". *Chapeau*. That *is* clever, says the writer in Fisk.

When I look back on the lovers we were then, in 1987, I find us touching, endearing, almost comical. Perhaps one must be young to love so totally and with such abandon. The three months it took Robert to steal me from my husband were our private legend, our foundation. Though the relationship would ultimately fail, the intensity of our courtship gave me the strength to brave many perils, to live as Robert did, for the truth, for the story.

II

Beirut Mon Amour

My heartfelt greetings to Beirut
I send kisses to the sea and houses
And to the rock that is like the face of an ancient mariner
From the soul of her people she makes wine
From their sweat she makes bread and jasmine
How did she come to taste of smoke and fire?

To Beirut
She brings glory from the ashes
And from the blood of the child she cradled in her arms
My city has snuffed out her lantern
Enclosed herself in darkness
Alone in the night

You are mine, you are mine
Embrace me, you are mine
You are my flag, my wave-tossed journey, the stone I carry
to tomorrow
The wounds of our people have blossomed
Their mothers' tears too
You Beirut, you are mine
Enfold me

Lyrics by Joseph Harb, as sung by
Lebanese diva Fairouz, "To Beirut"

December 1987

R obert wants me to see Beirut "just once". He knows he will talk a lot about it, and he wants me to be able to picture his former life once we are living in Paris. Ronald Reagan has banned US citizens from travelling to Lebanon because of the danger that they will be kidnapped. I could apply for a waiver, but Robert says that's not a good idea. "If Hezbollah find permission from the US government in your passport, they'll think you're a spy," he warns.

The Lebanese consul in London offers to put my visa on a separate sheet of paper, the way the Israelis do, so there is no trace of where one has travelled. I decline, on Robert's advice. "If you don't have the visa stamp in your passport, Hezbollah will think you came across the border from Israel. They'll claim you're a 'Zionist agent', and 'Zionist agents' get kidnapped or murdered. It's safer to obey Lebanese law than the Americans."

We fly to Larnaca and board *The Empress* for the eleven-hour crossing to Beirut. Once the ship is underway, we check out the bar and casino, where the ambience is like a cocktail party: low lights, cigarette smoke and the clatter of Lebanese Christians talking, laughing and gambling in three languages. The women wear too much make-up and jewellery. The men pull out wads of hundred-dollar bills. They gamble large amounts at roulette and blackjack, but they won't risk their lives by flying into the airport in Muslim West Beirut.

The ferry is run by the Kataeb, the Phalange party and militia. Its symbol, a triangle representing a cedar tree inside a circle, is emblazoned on the cards and poker chips in the casino, on the cutlery, dishes, drinking glasses and paper napkins in the bar. "You might think that after Sabra and Chatila, the Phalange would disband in shame," Robert says. "But there is no shame in Lebanon. The Israelis changed the name to 'Lebanese Forces' back in 1982, because it made them sound legitimate and official."

There's a framed photograph of the militia's new leader, Dr Samir Geagea, hanging over the bar. He is bald and moustachioed and looks like the sort of man who ties virgins to railway tracks in silent movies.

All Lebanese militias have killed civilians, and individual citizens often have no choice but to support the militia that represents their confessional group. Yet Robert never forgets that old Sheikh Pierre Gemayel founded the Phalange party on his return from the 1936 Berlin Olympics, and named it after the nationalist extremists in the Spanish Falange. Robert could show understanding towards virtually every other group in Lebanon, but he never forgave the Phalange and their successors in the Lebanese Forces for their alliance with Israel, and for repeated massacres of Palestinians. Not all Maronites support fascist ideology, far from it. But Robert questioned how Israel could sponsor a movement whose origins were inspired by anti-Semitic European fascism.

Our cabin is cramped and claustrophobic. The sea is rough. I feel nauseated. We go out on deck for fresh air and drink the champagne Robert has bought in duty-free. He says it's the best medicine for seasickness.

The Mount Lebanon range looms ahead of us at dawn, the snow on Mount Sannine tinted pink and orange by the sunrise. From a distance, Beirut is as beautiful a city as I have seen. But as we approach the coastline, the shell holes and gutted buildings come into focus. Robert points to the hotel district of Minet El Hosn, just west of the port. He tells me that during the Hotel War, in 1975/76, the Phalangists and Palestinians had a sort of shooting gallery between the Holiday Inn and the Murr Tower. The hotels changed hands several times. When they fought inside the same hotel, militiamen threw one another off the upper floors. An AP photographer took a famous photograph of a masked Phalangist playing the baby grand piano in the Holiday Inn, with his assault rifle sitting on top of the piano.

Lebanon's civil war is an accumulation of wars within wars: the Hotel War, the Mountain War, the Camps War. On the quayside in Beirut Harbour we run into a UN official whom Robert knows. "Amal has trapped 20,000 Palestinians inside Sabra and Chatila and Burj al-Barajneh," the official says with a worried expression. "We don't have access to them."

Nabih Berri's Shia Muslim Amal militia is determined to prevent the Palestinian guerrillas of Arafat's Fatah movement from regaining a foothold in Lebanon. Hafez al-Assad put Berri up to it, because he doesn't want to give the Israelis a pretext for returning to Beirut. So Muslim Arabs are killing Muslim Arabs to placate their Israeli enemies. It is far from the first time that Lebanon's civil war has become a theatre of the absurd.

Robert tells the UN man we are going to Muslim West Beirut. "Just for one night. I want Lara to see it."

"Be careful," the UN man says. "The French have been buying out hostages. Hezbollah need to replenish their stocks."

Robert uses the telephone in the port office to ring Juan Carlos. The journalists know that phones are listened to by militias and intelligence services, so they've devised a code. The Syrians are "sisters" or "steel-helmeted ones". Israel is "Dixie", as in the song, "way down south in Dixie". Robert wants to know if it is safe for us to walk across the green line, the three-quarter-mile by six-mile stretch of no man's land between Christian east and Muslim West Beirut. "How's the weather, *habibi*?" he asks JC. *Habibi*, meaning buddy or sweetheart, is the first word of Arabic I learn. In Beirut, nearly all one's friends and acquaintances are *habibi*.

"The weather is fine," says JC. He means there is no shelling or skirmishes – at the moment – and he has seen no cars filled with gunmen scouting for *ajanib* (foreigners). It should be safe to cross.

A plain-clothes Phalangist with a shiny black BMW offers us a lift to the Mathaf, the national museum which marks the Christian end of the front line. He looks a lot like the small portrait of Bashir Gemayel, the Phalangist leader who was assassinated in 1982, which hangs from the rear-view mirror. A small icon of Charbel, the militiaman's name saint, sits on the dashboard.

A sparse but steady stream of Lebanese civilians scurry along what was once a wide boulevard through the former diplomatic quarter. The war has gone on so long that trees have grown from the earthen embankments that militias bulldozed into place to protect themselves from artillery and gunfire. We walk brusquely along the southern side of this maze, keeping close to the wall of the hippodrome, then the Résidence des Pins, where General Henri Gouraud proclaimed the État du Grand Liban in 1920. War has forced the French out of their shell-damaged, Moresque palace, but a tattered French tricolour still flies overhead.

Being against the wall makes you feel secure. If you are out in the open, you make a tempting target for the snipers who haunt the villas, whose façades have been worn down to friable lace by the impact of countless bullets and grenades. Remnants of the divided Lebanese army, the Christian 8th Brigade to the east and the Muslim 6th Brigade in the west, man checkpoints where soldiers cast a desultory glance over one's identity papers. I have not yet grown accustomed to dealing with men in camouflage holding assault rifles.

"Don't worry. They're Leb army. They're harmless," Robert says to reassure me.

To divulge one's identity in Lebanon is a perilous act. I am painfully aware that I carry a blue passport with an eagle and the words *E Pluribus Unum* on the cover. The United States of America, imperialist power and Great Satan. If anything happens to me, the Reagan administration will say it's my fault because I violated the travel ban.

Robert tells me how the city divided into east and west, Christian and Muslim on Black Saturday, 6 December 1975. It started when four Christians were found dead in a car near the electricity company in east Beirut. Bashir Gemayel ordered the Phalange to kill forty Muslims. The militiamen set up a checkpoint at the eastern end of the ring road and checked identity cards. Women and children were left in the cars while men were taken beneath the overpass to have their throats slashed. Muslim militias retaliated by doing the same thing in West Beirut. On both sides of the city, people queued to show their papers. They did not realise what was happening until hooded men wielding bloody knives approached them. Hundreds of Muslims and Christians were butchered in one day.

Things have calmed down since the worst days of the war. There are still Christians who work in West Beirut, and a few Muslims work in the east. Some sects, like Armenians and Greek Orthodox, are considered more or less neutral. And there are mixed marriages. Merchants buy things on one side and sell them on the other. But all risk being taken hostage.

We arrive at the western end of the passage, near the shell-battered Barbir Hospital. Robert has warned me that kidnappers often wait here, on the lookout for potential hostages. Robert spots Juan Carlos, standing next to Abed's orange Mercedes. We walk fast to the car and drive away at speed. Changing cars is an additional precaution against hostage-takers. Abed alternates between an old Peugeot and an even older Mercedes. The Mercedes in wartime Lebanon are not luxury cars for the affluent, but vehicles so old they were exported from Europe as junk, refurbished and endlessly repaired, a testimony to the indestructibility of German engineering.

Robert and JC are like excited tour guides who have been too long deprived of an audience. They seem to take pride in their broken, shabby, murderous, divided city, or perhaps in their own courage and endurance in hanging on there. They want to show me everything.

"Look there, quickly!" Robert says as we drive down Hamra Street, the famous shopping district of West Beirut. There's an urgency in his voice. He doesn't want me to miss anything. "That's the Mövenpick restaurant, where the first Israeli occupation soldier was shot. You can still see the bullet holes!"

I catch a glimpse of the dark holes with torn edges in the aluminium cladding on the restaurant's outdoor terrace, and I remember the bullet hole in the angel's breast in the monument to Daniel O'Connell in Dublin. Robert had shown it to me just a few days earlier, a relic of the 1916 Rising. *What did you do on your holiday? I looked at bullet holes.*

I raise my hand to point and ask a question. Robert catches my hand in mid-air, pulls it down to the car seat and squeezes it. "Don't ever point in West Beirut, my love. It looks suspicious. Don't do anything that will draw attention to yourself."

Our itinerary is dotted with landmarks, often places where westerners have been kidnapped. Robert points with his hand resting on his thigh, beneath the car window, under the radar, so to speak. There, on this innocuous-looking street corner. There, in that banal restaurant. We drive down Bliss Street, past the American University of Beirut. Three AUB professors, the Americans Joe Cicippio and Tom Sutherland, and the Irishman Brian Keenan, are being held as hostages. "That means underground cells, being chained to radiators, being tortured," Robert says.

Cicippio's and Sutherland's wives, Elham and Jean, live on the AUB campus, waiting for news of their husbands. Keenan's sisters, Elaine Spence and Brenda Gillham, campaign for his release from their homes in Northern Ireland.

Just beyond AUB, we pass the twenty-storey Gefinor building, surprisingly unscathed for a Beirut high-rise. "That's where Terry Waite was kidnapped last January," Robert says excitedly. "Islamic Jihad told him to meet them in the underground carpark. Before he went, he came to see me and JC. He had letters for the hostages from their families. He wanted us to make sure there was nothing in them that would create suspicion."

Down the hill at the Spaghetteria, the waiter peers through a crack, then unlocks the padlock on the outer wrought iron door with enthusiasm. "*Ah-ha-laan! Ah-ha-laan! Ah-ha-laan!*" he exclaims when he sees Robert and Juan Carlos, stretching out the syllables of the Arab welcome. We enter a large, once elegant room with bullet-shattered mirrors, dusty potted plants and candles in polished brass shell cases. We are the only clients, and we choose a table far enough back from the plate-glass window that we cannot be seen from the Corniche.

Robert and JC love this place, with its view of the Mediterranean and Mount Sannine. Little matter that most of the food on the menu is not available, or that one runs a serious risk of food poisoning. "How's the fish today?" Robert asks the tall, lugubrious waiter, who wears a white jacket. The waiter raises both eyebrows to signal "No, don't take a chance on the fish". We choose pasta dishes, always safest when refrigerators go off and on. Somehow, the restaurant has managed to keep the white wine chilled. After the meal, Robert and JC choose Cuban cigars from the Spaghetteria's humidor.

The waiter lingers. His brother has been kidnapped and he wonders if there is anything we can do. There are now sixteen western hostages held in Lebanon. For every one of them, there are hundreds of Lebanese. Robert listens patiently. He considers this waiter, a Sunni from Sidon, to be a friend. The waiter knows he can expect big tips from Robert, but their friendship is deeper than that.

The waiter returns to the kitchen. "He is a good man," Robert says, lowering his voice. "He adopted several Palestinian orphans. When the Palestinians were leaving in 1982, I saw him in Beirut port, wandering among the lorries that were taking the guerrillas to the ferry for Cyprus. There was this little vignette: a guerrilla kissing a baby, the baby's mother holding her head in her hands, and an older woman holding her hands up to the man's face, beseeching. I turned back to look at our friend. He was weeping."

The conversation reverts again to kidnapping. "They nabbed Terry Anderson just outside here," Robert says. "He'd been playing tennis with Don Mell, the photographer, and he was dropping Mell off at his apartment in the building next door."

Terry, the AP bureau chief who had fought in Vietnam, had been enraged by the brutality of the Israeli invasion. Terry, the best friend who lived on the third floor of the building where Robert and JC still live, with his pregnant Lebanese partner Madeleine Bassil. Terry, the hostage longest in captivity, nearly three years already, is never far from Robert's thoughts.

Two bearded gunmen dragged Terry into a green Mercedes with a curtain in the back. A third pinned Mell to the wall, at gunpoint. Terry's glasses fell to the ground. "He could barely see without his glasses. I tried to send them to him, through Shia contacts. They told me he'd got them. Terry's kidnappers gave him a Bible. We think that's all he has to read. When he comes out, I expect he'll be spouting scripture."

Through the plate glass window, Robert and JC make verbal note of suspicious cars. Sometimes drivers move slowly back and forth. Sometimes they park on the far side of the Corniche, as if lying in wait. The archetypal kidnap car, they tell me, is a BMW or a Mercedes with no number plates, smoked glass and a curtain in the rear window, like the one that took Terry.

"They're like sharks," I say, watching out the window. "Those cars are like sharks." It may be the effect of the white wine, but Robert and JC are delighted. "That's great! Shark-like cars!" JC exclaims, and I beam at having inadvertently found a *bon mot*. The term shark-like cars enters our vocabulary.

When we finally walk out of the restaurant, my friends want to show me the ruins of the American embassy, just around the corner. We go on foot. The building was shaped like an open U, with a central portion and two wings. The centre practically disintegrated when it was blown up by a suicide car bomber on 18 April 1983. "There was a dead diplomat hanging there, by his feet, in his business suit," Robert says, nodding at the steel girders protruding from the pancaked wreckage.

Sixty-three people were blown up or burned alive, including

dozens of Lebanese queuing for US visas. Ten minutes later a man rang the Agence France Presse to say that a hitherto unknown group calling itself Islamic Jihad had carried out the attack "as part of the Iranian revolution's campaign against the imperialist presence".

The outer wings of the building are a windowless shell, but are more or less intact. It is now home to Palestinian refugees. "*Marhaba,*" Robert shouts hello to a woman hanging laundry two or three floors up. "*Marhaba,*" she shouts back, smiling. She tells us she left Tel al-Zaatar after the 1976 massacre. A refugee from a refugee camp.

We pile back into the car. Juan Carlos tells Abed to drive east, towards Wadi Abu Jamil, the route Terry Anderson's kidnappers took on 16 March 1985. Kidnappers are known to use abandoned buildings on the green line as way stations for hostages.

Abed is surprised, but never questions an order. "Keep going, faster, *habibi,*" JC says as we penetrate ever deeper into the netherworld of derelict buildings. Many buildings, though damaged, retain their original shape and colour and bear the insignia of familiar banks and airlines. This was clearly a vibrant city centre. Now it's a ghost town, a lost civilisation overgrown by jungle-like vegetation. Fluorescent, yellow-green slime oozes down walls, sits in fetid pools on torn-up streets. The colour and stench of broken sewage pipes and God knows what putrefaction.

Abed is fifty-two years old and has been a Beirut taxi driver his whole adult life. A stocky, short Sunni from Mousseitbeh with leathery, sun-browned skin, gentle eyes and a moustache, Abed wears a tweed cap and walks with a limp since he was caught in a militia gun battle.

These streets have been off limits, forbidden by the dictates of self-preservation, for eleven years, but Abed remembers them by heart. They are lodged in his subconscious and their configuration pushes its way back into his fingers that are gripping the steering wheel and into his foot on the accelerator. He has driven journalists through countless bombardments, and he shows no sign of fear, though danger and violent death lurk here too. Deep inside the green line, there are no traffic jams, no motorists, no signs of human life. Abed drives like a Formula One racing car driver, careening around shell holes and corners, speeding up on straight stretches.

We head back through Minet El Hosn, the desolate hotel district that Robert showed me from the Cyprus ferry that morning. Was it only that morning? The Holiday Inn, the Phoenicia, Saint George, Alcazar and Palm Beach. "Look! There are Richard Burton and Liz Taylor walking down the front steps of the Saint George!" JC exclaims. But there are only ghosts and a few refugees in the filthy, gutted ruins.

We are giddy, almost winded, by our wild ride. In 1987, few people venture into the downtown no man's land. "Nobody sees this," JC boasts, as if I have been given an immense privilege. He and Robert undertake to teach me the iconography of the city, the posters and plywood cut-outs of civil war leaders which populate Beirut's walls and streets.

A crude, larger-than-life cut-out of a beneficent-looking Hafez al-Assad stands at the eastern end of the Corniche, just before it peters out in the hotels district. We slow and nod to the Syrian soldiers at the checkpoint. This is the last outpost of Muslim West Beirut – or the first, if you are coming, as we are, from the demarcation line. The soldiers with red berets are Republican Guards, the elite. If the Syrians are expecting trouble, they put on steel helmets, another indicator my friends use to gauge the "weather".

Most of the Syrians are young, poor conscripts from the provinces, dazzled by the worldliness of Beirut. They have never seen the sea before and spend hours gazing at the Mediterranean. They have been told that they are superior to the anarchical Lebanese, with their endless civil war. They believe they are here as peacekeepers, dispatched to save their hapless neighbours from themselves, out of "sisterly" feeling. And yet, despite the wanton bloodletting, the Lebanese have something the Syrians envy: modernity; westernisation; above all, freedom.

It is not safe to go out at night, so we stock up on fresh bread rolls, Kerrygold butter and Danish black lumpfish roe, which we kid ourselves is caviar, at Smith's supermarket in Sadat Street. Robert carries bundles of £250 banknotes, exquisitely engraved with the Temple of Jupiter in Baalbek by the international fiduciary printer De La Rue in Basingstoke. It takes dozens of them to pay for our meagre groceries. "When I first came here, a £250 banknote was so valuable that if I had one, I kept it in the safe," Robert says.

Robert introduces me to Patrick Smith, the genial, half-British, half-Armenian-Lebanese owner of the grocery store. Patrick is tall, with dark hair, eyeglasses and a nasal voice. He wears jeans and a checked shirt and would not look out of place in any grocery store in Europe. But Beirut is not Europe, and Patrick has clung heroically to his business. His shop has been bombed four times, because he refused to pay protection money or because he sold alcohol. If you tell him he is one of the people who keeps Beirut alive, he looks embarrassed and says, "This is my home. And, besides, I make a lot of money."

Patrick seems to live at his first-floor desk, from which he can survey the whole store. He hires bright young people who are reliable and loyal. When Robert refers to them as the Smith militia, Patrick laughs.

To placate the Muslim militias, Patrick now sells no alcohol in the grocery store. Wine and videos can be found at an unmarked, windowless shop down the street. An employee inspects customers through a peephole before letting them enter. We buy two bottles of Ksara 1968 Vieux Millésime, one for us, one for Juan Carlos. Every bottle is numbered, but rumour has it there are far more bottles of Ksara '68 than could possibly have been produced in that year. The winegrower commissioned an artist to design a distinctive, gold-edged label with red and purple swirls for his vintage year. The label is so beautiful that we soak the empty bottle to keep it as a souvenir.

We head down the hillside, past the Hobeich police station into our little corner of Ain al-Mreisse. A company of Syrian troops is billeted in the concrete shell of what was to have been a Sheraton Hotel, just a couple of hundred metres down the Corniche from the Sleit building, where Robert and JC live. Photographs of Kamal Jumblatt, the slain Druze leader, ten years dead, cohabit with images of Assad, who ordered his killing. Jumblatt reminds me of Salvador Dali.

The Sleit building is a five-storey, 1950s' apartment block with two flats on every floor. It is terracotta-coloured, with folding green shutters, and it is surrounded by 30-metre-high palm trees. As in much of Lebanon, if you blocked out the surroundings, you might think you were in Nice or Miami.

"*Fi karaba*?" (Is there electricity?) Robert asks his Druze landlord, Mustafa, on our arrival. The presence, or absence, of electricity is a constant preoccupation. "Sorry, Mr Robert," Mustafa replies with a shrug and an apologetic grin.

"*Malesh*. Not to worry," Robert says.

We trudge up the stairs with the overnight bags we've brought from London, stopping to deliver the Ksara '68 to Juan Carlos on the second floor. He gives me a guided tour of their apartment, which Agneta has decorated tastefully in early Ikea. There's a telex room and a long front balcony overlooking the sea. JC shows me the revolver he has stashed behind the bookshelf in the hall. "Self-protection," he explains.

Robert's flat on the fifth floor isn't nearly as luxurious. It faces the side street, so one has a sideways view of the Mediterranean, and line of sight on the Syrian soldiers in the ruins of the Sheraton. From this distance they look like toy soldiers, milling about the lorries they have parked behind the structure for safety, cooking over open fires.

Only ten months have passed since the Syrians returned to West Beirut to put a stop to the Amal-Druze militia war. A fighter fired a rocket into Robert's kitchen. The hole above the stove has been plastered over but not repainted.

The one-bedroom apartment is functional, with cheap pinewood furniture, a few Kurdish kilim rugs and a laminate desk. The sofa is a relic from the Commodore Hotel, where the journalists stayed in 1982. The hotel was later looted by militias, and pieces of its furniture show up all over West Beirut.

Robert shows me his treasures, including a 10-kilo piece of shrapnel that was fired into the Chouf mountains, the Druze heartland, by the battleship *New Jersey* in 1984. "Feel its weight," Robert says, like a Boy Scout. The jagged edges of the shrapnel are razor-sharp, so he wraps it in a towel before picking it up. "Imagine that hitting your body, red-hot, at high velocity," he adds. I don't want to.

We sip Ksara red, apply lashings of butter to the bread rolls and pile on lumpfish caviar. It is cold. We have only a trickle of tap water and there is no electricity. We face the peril of the airport road the next morning.

I have dined in some of the finest restaurants in Paris, but I remember this meal as one of my happiest. From time to time, I still come across a Lebanese 250-pound note or a Ksara '68 label tucked into a book. Our candlelit picnic above the Beirut Corniche washes over me, with all its original intensity.

Abed comes to fetch us early the next morning. Juan Carlos is taking the same Middle East Airlines flight to London. Robert and I will catch a connecting flight to Dublin, to spend Christmas in Dalkey. JC is bound for Stockholm, to be with Agneta and their baby.

The weather is so foul that we figure the kidnappers cannot possibly be working. The palm trees bend low in the wind and rain. Huge waves crash over the hand railings on the Corniche. We pause to take snapshots of ourselves in front of the churned-up sea, to record the bringing of an American to Beirut, in the midst of a full-blown hostage crisis.

Robert and JC point out more landmarks on the way to the airport. Near the sandy, weed-infested roundabout, which my companions call "kidnap corner", are the ruins of the Drakkar building, where fifty-eight French paratroopers were killed by a suicide bomber on 23 October 1983.

From the road it is still possible to see a large dirt pit where the highway turns south-east at Chatila, a mass grave from the September 1982 massacre, when the Phalange murdered about 1,700 Palestinians. The Kuwaiti Embassy, from where Israeli troops watched the killing with binoculars, still stands nearby. We see Amal gunmen searching Palestinian women at the entrance to the shattered Burj al-Barajneh camp.

When we are on the airport road, on the stretch lined with eucalyptus trees near the home of Sheikh Mohammed Hussein Fadlallah, the spiritual leader of Hezbollah, beside the cut-out of Ayatollah Khomeini, Juan Carlos tells Abed to stop at a *manousheh* stand on the central reservation. Cheese *manousheh* is, along with mezze, one of the great pleasures of living in Beirut. You can find both in other Arab countries, even in Europe, but it never tastes the same.

I sense that Juan Carlos has gone too far. Robert had misgivings about our wild ride through the green line. He doesn't utter a word now, but he is furious with JC. He glowers as shark-like cars slow to stare at the crazy *ajanib* waiting at a *manousheh* stand in the heart of Hezbollah land. *Leave the one with black hair and the woman*, they must be thinking. *Go for the guy with blue eyes.*

Twenty-four hours earlier, I gazed at the plywood cut-out of Maronite President Amin Gemayel in East Beirut. Gemayel wore a natty, three-piece white suit and looked like a Paris dandy, or an ice cream salesman.

Now we slow as we pass a large, unfinished Hezbollah mosque just before the airport. It is made of grey cinder blocks and sports a green dome; green, the colour of Islam. In front of the mosque stands a huge cut-out of Imam Musa Sadr, the vanished Iranian-born Lebanese Shia cleric who disappeared in Libya in 1978 and was probably murdered by Gaddafi. With his beard, turban and flowing robes, Musa Sadr looks like an Iranian ayatollah ascending to heaven. Amin Gemayel. Musa Sadr. There could hardly be a starker embodiment of Lebanon's position on the great fault line between east and west, between Christendom and Islam.

Just after the mosque, at the end of the highway on the left, immediately before one enters the relative security of the airport compound, is a twenty-foot crater where the US marine base stood until it was blown up by a suicide bomber in 1983, seconds before the French Drakkar base. Two hundred and forty-one Americans died in that explosion.

Syrian soldiers open the boot of Abed's car and search our luggage. We carry Robert's treasures: a hand-coloured lithograph of Jerusalem by David Roberts, and a pink Qom silk carpet which he purchased from a Lebanese diplomat's wife. A hundred people queue in the cold outside while the Syrians search for weapons or explosives. The previous month, five people died in a bomb blast inside the airport terminal.

We pause to have our photograph taken for a second time with Juan Carlos, at the door of the Middle East Airlines jet. The aircraft is thirty years old, but it has just been refitted and repainted in California and the word *NEW* is painted in huge letters on the fuselage, next to the cedar tree.

I sink into my front-row seat with immense satisfaction. We made it! We passed between the raindrops, dodged the bullet, whatever. I have just spent twenty-four hours in Beirut and *nothing happened to me*. I am still absorbing what I have seen. Lebanon attracts and repels me. I do not know it yet, but this journey of initiation is the dividing line between before and after, between my settled life and my vocation as a Middle East correspondent.

The steward serves champagne on take-off. Through the cabin window, I study the Beirut peninsula jutting into the sea, the sewage pouring into the Mediterranean off Dahieh, the southern suburbs. When we arrived by sea the previous day, Beirut looked beautiful from a distance, then progressively disfigured as we grew closer. That process is reversed now. With each air kilometre the high-rise buildings more resemble Hong Kong or Monaco. Mount Sannine raises its snowy head. From a safe distance, Beirut is beautiful again.

This was supposed to be our farewell to Lebanon. Through the plane window, Robert watches the city, where he has already spent eleven years, grow small beneath us. He cannot possibly believe he will not return, though that is what he has promised. I see a tear roll down his cheek.

Ultimately, I suspect that Beirut was my greatest rival. Robert saw friends kidnapped and killed there, endured bombardments, shooting and all manner of hardship. Yet Beirut held him. By the time he died in 2020, Robert had spent forty-five years in the Lebanese capital, nearly two-thirds of his life.

Robert used to say Lebanon was a beautiful dragonfly that alights on your arm, then injects you with her poison so discreetly that you do not feel the sting. I think of Beirut more as an ageing mistress with sagging flesh, scars and wrinkles. Her lover tells her he is departing, once and for all. Beirut takes a drag on a cigarette and says with her gravelly, whisky-soaked voice: "Go ahead. Try. You'll be back. You cannot leave me, for I am you."

III

The Fisk School of Journalism

We are waves: our repose spells our death,
Our very being rests on restlessness.

Seventeenth-century Persian poet Saeb Tabrizi

26 January 1988

"My camera!" Robert gasps as we open the door and set down our suitcases. "I left my Nikon on the back shelf of the taxi!"

It is too late to run down the stairs. The taxi has surely gone by now. We have just taken possession of our first home together, a quiet, sunny two-bedroom apartment in a ramshackle eighteenth-century building in the rue Monsigny, in Paris's second district. There is no lift, which is not great for journalists who often travel with suitcases. The walls are crooked, the floor is slanted, and I love it.

The Times is financing Robert's move from Beirut to Paris, so he has kept the taxi receipt, which bears an address in north-eastern Paris. "I've got to find my camera. I'm going there," Robert says, leaving me to unpack.

Although he is a print journalist, not a photographer, Robert often takes his own pictures. He says he wants to be the first writing journalist to win an award for photography. In years to come, he often provides photos to illustrate my articles. In 1996, Robert takes a unique photograph of Osama bin Laden, by the light of a paraffin lamp in bin Laden's camp in Afghanistan. He is delighted when he has the film developed in Beirut. "He looks like Fagin!" – the character in Dickens' *Oliver Twist* – Robert says. The image of a smiling bin Laden, with his head slightly tilted, is the endpaper in *The Great War for Civilisation*.

On that winter afternoon in 1988, I grow more anxious as each hour passes without news from Robert. Mobile telephones do not exist. Our landline has not been installed. It is dinner time when the doorbell finally rings. "I got it!" he says, laughing. "Phew! What a story!"

I will see the same look of joyful triumph on Robert's face, hear almost the same words, when he returns from interviewing bin Laden: "I got him! Phew! What a story!"

Robert sets his camera on the bed and takes me downstairs to the Mellifère restaurant for dinner. He orders champagne before recounting his adventure.

"The taxi company is one man with a phone and a desk. He tells me it is *interdit* to give me the name of the driver. I tell him I am really sorry, but of course I will have to report my stolen property to the police. I'm thinking: some of their drivers must be illegal. The man gives me a long, hard stare. He writes 'Monsieur Heng' and an address in Créteil on a piece of paper and shoves it at me. 'Monsieur, zer iz nos-sing in Créteil *pour vous*,'" Robert says, mimicking the Frenchman's accent with an exaggerated Gallic shrug.

Robert emerges from the Métro in an immigrant banlieue. He hasn't a clue where to go amid the tower blocks. African and Arab toughs stare at him. He asks for directions.

Robert rings the doorbell of Mr Heng's apartment. Our driver from that morning opens the door, dressed as men dress in Cambodia, shirtless and wearing a skirt. Mrs Heng hovers in the background with a little boy. Yes, Mr Heng remembers picking us up, but he didn't see the camera. "Can we sit down?" Robert asks him.

Mr Heng says he took a Japanese man bound for Tokyo to Roissy after he dropped us off. "You mean a Japanese man stole a Japanese camera to take it to Japan? Hmmm," Robert says. "Hmmm" is his standard expression of incredulity.

Robert asks to see the car. Mr Heng leads him to the underground car park, which reminds Robert of Terry Waite's kidnapping in the basement of the Gefinor building in Beirut. Robert goes through the motions of inspecting the boot and back seat of the car. They take the lift back up to the apartment.

"Look, you're from Cambodia. I know all about wars and refugees. I work in the Middle East and I have only sympathy for you and your family," Robert says. "You see, I need my camera for my work. It is my *outil de travail*, like your car is for you... Of course, I will have to go to the police, but I just want you to know that I trust you totally. Here is my business card. If the police give you a hard time, just call my newspaper and I will do everything I can to help you."

A long discussion ensues between Mr and Mrs Heng, in Khmer. "I know my camera is nearby. I can practically smell it," Robert says, regaling us both with his feat, knocking back the champagne. "Mrs Heng goes over to the laundry basket and starts pulling dirty clothes out. My camera is in the bottom of the basket!"

Robert thanks Mr Heng profusely for returning his camera, generously forgetting the original denial. Mr and Mrs Heng insist on driving Robert back to the rue Monsigny with their little boy, free of charge. Robert asks Mr Heng if he would like to be *The Times'* driver in Paris. "At least I know he'll never steal anything from me!" he tells me.

Most people would have given up at the taxi office, I say.

"A good journalist never gives up; never takes no for an answer!" Robert says. "Lebanon has taught me how to deal with people. You have to put yourself in their place, think how your message will be received. Be gentle and respectful. Sometimes it needs a hint of a threat too."

Robert leaves little love notes around the apartment, and in the school ledger where we write regular messages to each other. "My darling," begins a typewritten note with four bullet points, from March 1988. Numbers one, two and three are housekeeping matters: the seamstress whose visit I missed while I was out; the carpenter who came to repair a leaking window; Robert's promise to help with the cleaning.

Then ... wham. Item four. Injustice, murder and Northern Ireland interrupt our domestic bliss. While taking his bath, he listened to a BBC call-in programme about the killing of the three IRA members in Gibraltar. "Two-thirds of everyone on the programme thought it was perfectly OK to shoot to kill and supported the idea even if the wrong people get shot. They also attacked (of course) the 'media'. O Lordy, Lordy. It is unfashionable to be a liberal these days; even worse, perhaps, to be a journalist."

Robert signs off, "I do love you SO MUCH." Here the typewriting ends and he scrawls "yer man".

If there is a shadow on our happiness, it is the professional frustration that hangs over us like a minor ailment. I apply for every job opening I hear of in journalism, and in the absence of salaried employment, struggle to establish myself as a freelancer. *The Times* have let Robert settle in Paris because the newspaper does not want to lose its star correspondent. But he and his editors have different ideas of what his new job is about. Robert wants to do in-depth, often historical, investigative reporting. Despite promises to the contrary, his editors keep sending him off as a fireman on breaking news stories. Robert says he wants to be with *me*, that he has put the fireman's life behind him.

The paper's Paris bureau is in the rue Halévy, across the street from the Paris Opera and an easy walk from our apartment. But their Paris correspondent seems to think Robert is after his job, and initially refuses to let Robert work out of the bureau. He says it's about "the archaeology of the office".

Robert's first big story is a series of reports about the World War II record of Austrian President Kurt Waldheim, who was secretary general of the United Nations from 1972 until 1982. The Waldheim affair combines several of Robert's obsessions: the world war, arrogance and authority, lies and impunity in high places.

During his 1986 campaign to become president of Austria, Waldheim was found to have lied about two important matters. He had claimed that his military career ended in 1942, when he was wounded on the Russian front. From 1942 to 1944, he in fact served as a lieutenant in German army intelligence, with brutal units that executed thousands of Yugoslav civilians and partisans, and deported thousands of Greek Jews to Nazi death camps.

Waldheim also claimed that he never belonged to any Nazi-affiliated group. But he had joined the National Socialist German Students' League one month after the 12 March 1938 Anschluss. Eight months later, he joined a cavalry unit of the Sturmabteilung or Brownshirts, who had been the paramilitary wing of the Nazi party.

Waldheim participated actively in the Kozara Offensive, a vast operation against Serb partisans in western Bosnia in the summer of 1942, during which the Germans carried out mass reprisals, killing 100 Serbs for every German fatality. The Nazis' Croatian allies even awarded Waldheim the Silver Medal of the Crown of King Zvonimir "for courage in the battle against rebels in West Bosnia".

As a German intelligence officer during the operation, he was billeted in a village called Kostajnica, 22 kilometres from the concentration camp at Jasenovac, Croatia, where hundreds of thousands of Serbs, Jews, Communists and gypsies died at the hands of the Croats. Kostajnica was a transit point en route to Jasenovac, and 2,000 people were shot dead there during the summer Waldheim spent in the village.

We spend five days in Zagreb, Jasenovac, Kostajnica, Banja Luka and Belgrade, interviewing Serbs and Croatians and combing through archives. Back in London, at the Public Record Office in Kew, we find an expulsion order against Serbs, signed by Waldheim. Robert goes on to Vienna for more interviews on the same story. Although Waldheim is never proven to have personally committed war crimes, the testimony we record and the documents we discover are part of a body of evidence that establishes his complicity in those crimes.

ℬ

My journalistic career has been on hold for four years, since I left CBS News to join the State Department. Robert introduces me to *The Irish Times* foreign editor Paul Gillespie and encourages me to offer a piece to *The Irish Times* about our December 1987 trip to Beirut.

"What a rush – to have a byline again after all these years!" I write in our message book in January. "It must seem silly to you – who see your name in print so often – but I feel as delighted as a schoolgirl. Thank you for taking me to Beirut – not just for the article. Thank you for sharing your life with me!"

I have become an earnest pupil in what I jokingly call the Fisk School of Journalism. Robert finances my travel and often edits my copy before I send it. "You buried the lede!" he says often. "Say what you *mean*!" Or, most wounding, "That's a cliché!" Clichés are the enemy, the stodge that weighs down one's copy. The word terrorist is the worst cliché of all, because it is used so promiscuously by Israelis, Americans and many of our colleagues, who seem to automatically link it to the words "Arab" and "Muslim".

Robert teases me about my "PhD syndrome" or tendency to over-research stories, thus overwhelming myself with information. This aggravates another handicap, a paralysing fear of the blank page that makes it difficult to begin an article. "Pretend you are writing to a friend. Journalism is *fun*," he says. When Robert praises something I've written, I glow with pride.

"For a journalist, nothing can beat that moment when a great story beckons, when history really is being made and when a foreign editor tells you to go for it," Robert will write years later, in *The Great War for Civilisation*. He often quotes Nicholas Tomalin, the British journalist who was killed by a Syrian missile in Israel during the 1973 Yom Kippur War: "The only qualities essential for real success in journalism are ratlike cunning, a plausible manner and a little literary ability." *Especially* ratlike cunning, he adds.

I know how privileged I am to have a world-class foreign correspondent as my lover and private tutor. At the same time, I despair of ever reaching Robert's level. And I fear being over-dependent.

Robert imparts the big lessons: that history matters, that all wars are evil. We must be on the side of civilians, for they are the victims. It is important to listen and treat them with compassion. He explains the practical details of deadlines, booking travel, transmitting stories. Getting your story over is more important than anything else, more important than eating or sleeping or personal hygiene. Some Arab countries have a blank for the question "Religion?" on immigration forms. Robert always fills in "Journalism".

Don't talk to western diplomats, Robert says. The Arabs aren't wrong when they call embassies nests of spies. The bad guys watch embassies and take note of who goes there. And, besides, we don't need the spies and diplomats anyway. It's our job to know more than they do. We make an exception for the Irish, because they are a friendly, neutral people who do not invade other countries.

ઠa

On 5 April 1988, Islamic Jihad hijacked Kuwait Airways flight 422 from Bangkok to Kuwait. The aircraft landed first in Mashhad, Iran, where it reportedly took on more hijackers and explosives. Authorities in Beirut and Damascus refused to let it land. The plane flew to Cyprus and finally to Algiers. Two airline security agents were murdered during the course of the siege.

The hijackers demand the liberation of seventeen Shia Muslims who are imprisoned for their role in the bombings of the US and French embassies in Kuwait; 1983 attacks for which Islamic Jihad claimed responsibility. The crisis has dragged on for more than two weeks, making it the longest hijacking ever. Three members of the Kuwaiti royal family are among the thirty-one passengers. The hijackers threaten to blow up the plane with the passengers on it. Robert can no longer say no to his foreign editor. We fly to Algiers.

Journalists camp on the tarmac at Houari Boumediene Airport, within sight of the beleaguered Boeing 747. Robert would camp out too if he wasn't with me. It is late at night and we take a taxi to the El Djazair Hotel, but it is full. We drive for what seems like an eternity to the Mazafran, a rundown, cockroach-infested resort outside the city. In the early days of our itinerant life together, Robert apologises for the lack of creature comforts. I gradually become more accepting of hardship – "for the story" – but he continues to tease me, saying, "I'm afraid it's not up to your standards of perfection."

The old Fisk luck kicks in. Overnight, the Algerian interior minister reaches an agreement with the hijackers, believed to be Lebanese Hezbollah members. Robert's colleagues have followed the plane from country to country for sixteen days. He arrives fresh to the story, just in time to cover the resolution and denouement of the crisis.

Early on the morning of 20 April, we watch traumatised passengers disembark from the aircraft. "The worst moment was when they took over the plane," the flight supervisor, Abdul Mounin Mahmoud, tells us. "When they look at you and hold a gun to your face. So cold-blooded. Have you ever seen a shark in the water? The eyes, exactly. They have no expression."

Robert and I have unwittingly crossed paths with the Hezbollah extremist and founder of Islamic Jihad, Imad Mughniyeh. Not for the last time.

I file three articles about the Kuwaiti hijacking over the telephone to *The Irish Times* from Algiers. The copytaker has difficulty understanding me, especially the Arabic names. My American accent doesn't help. While I am battling with the poor telephone line, Robert sketches a cartoon entitled "Horror in the *Irish Times* Copytakers' Room – Marlowe is on the Line!" A cat wearing headphones, with bulging eyes and a dubious expression, sits at a teletype machine. The dictated letters – L Lima, A Apple, R Romeo, A Apple, I India etc. – spell out "Lara I love you."

In May, we travel to London to attend a dinner dance award ceremony at the Savoy. Robert has won an International Journalist of the Year Award, again. I wear a lace dress that I purchased in New York, and a silk stole by Lanvin which Robert buys for me in Paris. My usually scruffy lover is handsome in his dinner suit with the red silk bow tie I chose for him. Our eyes meet often through the dinner. We are brimming with pride. The British author Bernard Levin is seated between us. "Who, may I ask, is this odalisque?" Levin whispers to Robert, referring to me.

Juan Carlos alerts us that Syrian troops are about to enter Beirut's southern suburbs to put an end to the war between the rival Shia militias Amal and Hezbollah. Both are allied with Syria, though Hezbollah is closer to Iran. They've been killing each other for weeks.

Five months have passed since I accompanied Robert on what he said was his last trip to Beirut. I must have reservations about returning, because he writes in our message book, "Our love is more important to me than all the stories and Beiruts and jobs in the world. And remember, *if* we go to Beirut, it does *not* mean we are going to leave Paris or change our lives here."

On 28 May, Robert and I witness the theatrical arrival, on foot, of 2,000 Syrian soldiers in the Bir al-Abed quarter of the southern suburbs. In normal times, we would come here only with the greatest caution. Today, we want to believe the Syrians will protect us.

Syria maintains an ambiguous relationship with the hostage-taking enterprise. It gives Iran its only means of access to Lebanon and allows Hezbollah to flourish. Not once has a Syrian soldier opened the boot of a Hezbollah car at a checkpoint. If they did, they might find a western hostage lying there, wrapped in duct tape like a mummy, suffocating in exhaust fumes. Yet it is standard practice for hostages to be freed in Damascus. They routinely thank Syria for facilitating their liberation.

Ayatollah Khomeini refers to Shia Muslims as the *mostazafin*, the oppressed or deprived. The poor Shia of Lebanon, most of them driven out of homes in the south by the Israeli occupation, have congregated in these suburbs, which are called Dahieh in Arabic. The district lacks the heights and sea views of the

Sunni and Druze quarters on the Ras Beirut peninsula, and the leafy gardens, Ottoman mansions and winding streets of neighbourhoods like Ashrafieh, where the Christians live. Despite the war, it is still possible to succumb to the charm of other parts of the capital. In Dahieh, one latches on to any scrap of loveliness: a smile, schoolchildren playing, a caged bird singing on a balcony.

Dahieh is an ugly, sprawling, urban slum of mean streets, box-like apartment buildings and cinder-block shacks. The women wear chadors. Surly, bearded men leave their shirts hanging outside their baggy trousers, Iranian style. (It is haram, sinful, to show the form of the human body.) Walls are covered with posters of clergy and martyrs. As in other parts of the capital, balconies sag with the weight of electrical generators and satellite dishes. Huge tangles of electrical wires loom overhead, many of them pirated power lines.

A short, stocky, sinister-looking man, wearing a black leather jacket despite the summer heat, walks alongside Syrian officers in the front of the march through Bir al-Abed. He is Abdul Hadi Hamadi, a Hezbollah security chief whose two brothers are in prison in Germany on terrorism charges. Hamadi is believed to have masterminded several kidnappings.

The Syrians have been praised by the US State Department for taking control of Dahieh. The question in all our minds is whether Hezbollah will relinquish power over its fiefdom, or will there be violence? The deployment has been painstakingly negotiated in the hope of avoiding clashes. Fewer than a third of the Syrian troops available are sent in. They bring no armour or heavy weapons. Militiamen will no longer be allowed to carry guns in the streets, but the Syrians will not search houses or Hezbollah barracks for arms or hostages.

A group of scowling Hezbollah members stand in front of the home of a well-known cleric. In other circumstances, they would have weapons, and we would flee from them. Now we stare at each other. "So, you are safe now?" one of them taunts Robert and me.

A little farther on, a family watches the deployment from their garden. The father is tall, thin and bearded. He wears spectacles. Robert says the man has an intelligent face. "He probably reads books. Always go for the guys wearing glasses."

Robert shakes hands with the intelligent-looking man and tries to signal something to me, but I have not yet learned the etiquette of Islamic fundamentalism. I don't know that devout Muslims ban all physical contact with women outside their own families. The bespectacled man shrinks back, staring at my proffered hand as if in horror. "It is for your religious purity. It is for our purity," he explains. His veiled wife nods in agreement. They spent several years in Detroit, where he studied engineering, and they want nothing to do with the American way of life.

"We want a pure world, where people don't get AIDS and children don't shoot drugs into their veins," the man says. "The West has not understood us. We don't want hostage-taking. We are civilised people. You are safe here. You are welcome."

Three *Hezbollahi* pull up in a Mercedes, stop and stare at us. We sense that we are not so welcome after all, and continue on our way.

Hostages. Hostages. Hostages. They are the common denominator of every story in Beirut. When the Syrians go into the southern suburbs, our editors ask, "How will this affect the hostages?" Each time we leave a building, we look around for shark-like cars. Every photograph of Terry Anderson released by his kidnappers is tacked to the bulletin board in the AP bureau, whose staff are Robert's friends.

More than anything else, I fear joining the ranks of Beirut's unfortunate hostage wives. Months later, when Robert does not return as scheduled from a trip to Damascus, I feel certain he has been kidnapped in the Bekaa Valley. The telex is down and we do not have an international phone line, so I go to Patrick Smith's grocery story to use his telephone to call Robert's hotel in Damascus. To my immense relief, the hotel operator puts me through to him. "I am so sorry, darling Lara. I knew you would be worried," Robert says. "I got turned around on a technicality at the border. I had no way of reaching you. I'll try again to cross the border tomorrow." I weep tears of relief, in front of Patrick.

Robert and I don't think they will kidnap me, because I am a woman. For once, Islamist sexism seems to work in my favour. Taking a woman hostage might cast doubt on their manhood. A woman has periods, would require female jailers. None of which will later dissuade Sunni fundamentalists from kidnapping women in Iraq and Syria.

For years I sleep with a hammer under my side of the bed, to use as a weapon if gunmen try to take Robert from the apartment. I develop a habit of filing my nails with a long, sharp Solingen nail file when we drive down the airport road through the southern suburbs. If they pull Robert out of the car, I swear to myself I will gouge out their eyes. It is important to prepare oneself mentally. "Most of the hostages went like sheep," Robert says. "You've got to fight. Surprise them. Go crazy. Become a terrorist. I refuse to spend years chained to a radiator."

I often wonder why Robert is not kidnapped. I believe his attitude is part of it. He is extremely careful to remain on good terms with everyone. "Never have rows with people in Lebanon," he tells me. "You're in *their* country." He describes himself as "a humble dog" and studiously avoids the appearance of arrogance or condescension. Perhaps most importantly, his reporting – especially his coverage of the 1982 invasion and the massacre at the contiguous refugee camps of Sabra and Chatila – is widely translated and reproduced in Arab media. The Lebanese believe he is on their side.

The head of the International Red Cross in Beirut tells me that more than 20,000 Lebanese people have been kidnapped in the first thirteen years of the war. Several thousand are believed to be still in captivity. Yet international media report solely on the fate of western hostages. During our May 1988 stay in Beirut, I have my first article published in the *International Herald Tribune*, entitled "Lebanese Are the Forgotten Hostages".

We stay only twelve days in Beirut on this trip. When the "Trib" publishes my piece on Lebanese hostages, Robert cuts "By Lara Marlowe, Special to the *Herald Tribune*, BEIRUT," out of the paper, magnifies it on the photocopy machine until it fills a whole page, and festoons our apartment with my byline. He is slowly breaking down my resistance.

I gradually build contacts with newspaper foreign editors. In addition to *The Irish Times* and *Herald Tribune*, I publish articles in the *Atlanta Journal and Constitution*, *Baltimore Sun*, *Maclean's* magazine, *Miami Herald*, *Newsday*, *Saint Petersburg Times* and *San Francisco Chronicle*. I can usually retransmit the same telex tape to several papers, but it is a painstaking way to eke out a living, and Robert continues to subsidise me.

Although I report stories from France too, Robert and events pull me inexorably towards the Middle East. Over the telephone from Paris, I interview Intissar al-Wazir about the Israelis' assassination of her husband Khalil, known as Abu Jihad, at their home in Tunis. In Paris, I meet and interview Rachel Hallak, the widow of Dr Elie Hallak, the kind, courageous Syrian-born Jewish paediatrician who was kidnapped from his home in West Beirut. Hezbollah used Dr Hallak to care for sick and wounded hostages, until he too died in captivity.

In late June 1988, Robert and I fly to Dublin for our long summer holiday. Each time we come back to Ireland, we spend at least one evening with our next-door neighbours in Dalkey, John and Sabina Costello. Mr Costello is a retired tram driver. He is tall and thin, with a shock of white hair that reminds me of Samuel Beckett. We buy a bottle of Jameson in duty-free to share with him in front of the fire. Mrs Costello drinks tea. As we leave, she sprinkles us with holy water from a tiny font by the front door, to protect us on our journeys.

We take the train to Belfast, to retrieve Robert's bright blue MG Midget, a relic of his years in Northern Ireland, from the garage of Robert's friend and colleague David McKittrick. David will later co-author *Lost Lives*, recording brief biographies of every man, woman and child who died in The Troubles. We spend the night in David and Pat's big, mock-Tudor house. I instantly warm to their hospitality and sardonic humour. David takes me to the Falls Road and Shankill Road, Milltown cemetery and the "peace walls" between Catholic and Protestant neighbourhoods. "This is a working-class war," he explains. Catholics and Protestants live side by side in his own, upper-middle-class Belfast neighbourhood. "Pat and I are what is known as a 'mixed marriage'," he laughs.

Robert is teaching me about Ireland at the same time as he teaches me about journalism and the Middle East. We head off in his sports car for Derry, then Malin Head, the desolate, wind-battered peninsula where Robert tells me I am almost as close to my native United States as it is possible to be in Ireland. We visit Mullaghmore, County Sligo, where Lord Mountbatten was assassinated by the IRA in 1979.

Soon after we return to Dalkey, the USS *Vincennes* shoots down Iran Air flight 655 over the Persian Gulf. We break off our holiday to race to Dubai, where the Iranian embassy organises a press plane to show us the wreckage and remains of the victims in the Iranian port city of Bandar Abbas. As I recounted in the Prologue, the Iranians have gathered the remains of the 290 passengers and crew in a cold-storage facility, arranging them in three categories: gender, intact corpses and body parts. Only 170 corpses have been retrieved. The rest have been destroyed beyond recognition or have been eaten by sharks.

Nothing from my previous life has prepared me for the smell and sight of 170 bodies laid out in rows on the floor of a cold-storage room. Yet more than the gruesomeness of mutilated corpses and piles of body parts, it is the faces of two females, a little girl and a forty-year-old woman, that stay with me. Three-year-old Leila Behbehani was bound for a wedding in Dubai and still wears the turquoise party dress, white socks and black patent leather shoes that her mother dressed her in on 3 July. Her face is frozen in the expression of a child crying. Zahra Khorasanipour is hauntingly beautiful, lying in her coffin with her long, chestnut-coloured hair falling over her shoulders. She looks peaceful, except for the gash under her left eye.

On the day we are shown the bodies, President Reagan is quoted in the Gulf newspapers as saying that the US "has apologised enough" for shooting down the civilian airliner. A subsequent statement says "ultimate responsibility" must lie with the Iranians for refusing to end the Gulf War. It does not mention that the Gulf War was started by Saddam Hussein with American assistance.

US officials and some western media speculate that Iran Air flight 655 was a kamikaze flight, intent on blowing up the *Vincennes*. Robert and I know instinctively that this is rubbish. Admiral William Crowe, the chairman of the US Joint Chiefs of Staff, lies when he tells a press conference that the airliner was flying outside the commercial air corridor. The combat and navigational data on tapes from the *Vincennes*' Aegis system later prove that the Airbus was well within the commercial corridor. Admiral Crowe says the plane was descending as it approached the ship. The tapes prove that the aircraft was climbing.

The Americans claim that they repeatedly warned the Airbus, but the aircraft's pilot, US-trained Captain Mohsen Rezaian, could not possibly have heard the *Vincennes*' queries and warnings because they were issued on an emergency military frequency. With their usual brash arrogance, the Americans assumed that it was up to others to understand them.

Three years later, Captain Will Rogers III, who ordered that two SM-2 anti-aircraft missiles be fired at the airliner, retires honourably. The crew of the USS *Vincennes* are awarded combat-action ribbons *for shooting down a civilian airliner*. Lieutenant Commander Scott Lustig, the ship's tactical commander for air warfare, even receives the US Navy's Commendation Medal for "heroic achievement".

Robert and I return to Beirut at the end of July for my longest stay yet, twenty-four days. Things are relatively quiet, so I write newspaper features on topics to which I will return over and over. Robert knows every detail of the Armenian holocaust, the dispossession of the Palestinians, the deployment of the United Nations Interim Force in Lebanon. He is loyal to these stories. For years to come, we will report them together.

Lebanon's 150,000-strong Armenian community descends from survivors of the twentieth-century's first genocide, who trekked their way across what is now Iraq and Syria from Turkey. Most settled in the neighbourhoods of Bourj Hammoud and Antelias. Although they have political parties and deputies in parliament, the Armenians manage to remain neutral throughout Lebanon's civil war. More than seventy years have passed since the Turks murdered about one million Armenians, but their descendants in Lebanon remain fixated on events in Soviet Armenia and the disputed enclave of Nagorno-Karabakh.

On one of our visits to Bourj Hammoud, we interview an aged couple in a nursing home, both survivors of the Armenian holocaust. He is 125 years old. She is 97. Both are blind. They listen to Radio Yerevan all day, from parallel beds on either side of a narrow, monastic room. An icon of the Virgin hangs above their headboards. He bears a scar on one cheek, from the Battle of Tannenberg in 1914, where he fought on the side of the Czar's army.

I ask the old Armenian if he has had a good life. His response reminds me of Baudelaire's *J'ai plus de souvenirs que si j'avais mille ans*. It is one of the most memorable quotes I have heard in nearly forty years of journalism. "I hate my circumstances now," he says, "but the things I have seen, no one has seen."

ॐ

Abed drives Robert and me south to Camp Shamrock, the headquarters of the Irish Battalion of UNIFIL at Tibnin. The

UN force was intended to observe an Israeli withdrawal from southern Lebanon, but it takes Israel twenty-two years to leave, during which time UNIFIL acts as a sandbag between the Israelis and the guerrillas who are trying to drive them out. Irish officers brief us on the rivalry between the enemy brothers, Amal and Hezbollah. They introduce us to a local Shia religious leader who is close to Amal. He says Hezbollah's power is waning because Iran has been defeated by Iraq in the Persian Gulf War. We wonder if this is wishful thinking, because UNIFIL prefers dealing with Amal. Nabih Berri's Syrian-backed militia is more malleable, less absolutist, less hell-bent on fighting the Israelis.

Because Hezbollah is funded by the Islamic Republic of Iran, it feels like the artificial creation of a foreign power to many Lebanese. The Iranians have nonetheless sunk roots deeply into southern Lebanon. Iranian doctors and nurses have fanned out across the countryside, and Iran rewards with food and cash Lebanese who wear Islamic dress and attend prayers in the mosque.

At Irish outposts, I learn how Israeli occupation troops and their allies in the so-called South Lebanon Army harass Irish troops, firing tank shells around their positions up to three times daily. The Irish struggle to prevent Israel and the SLA from building still more compounds within the Irish Battalion area of operations, which is already dotted with watchtowers and Merkava tanks in hilltop fortresses.

When the Irish catch Shia militiamen setting booby-trapped bombs to ambush the Israelis and the SLA, they defuse the explosives. The Irish stop militiamen carrying weapons on roads, but they do not interfere with what goes on in the wadis. Commandant Donal Bracken tells me the Lebanese "have a certain right to resist... Most of the villages have armouries. It's not our job to search every house. We stop people who are on their way to making an attack, but not people fleeing after they have made one."

Irish soldiers seem to identify with the local Shia, who, like them, are from rural backgrounds and tightly knit families.

Several draw a parallel between the Israeli occupation and the British in Ireland.

The kidnapping, torture and murder in 1980 of two Irish peacekeepers, Thomas Barrett and Derek Smallhorne – and the fact that their killer, SLA man Mahmoud Bazzi, was spirited out to the US via Israel – continues to poison the Irish Battalion's relationship with Israel and the SLA. It will take forty years for Bazzi to be arrested and extradited from Michigan, where he had become an ice cream salesman. In December 2020, a Lebanese court jailed Bazzi for fifteen years.

In the evening, Irish officers invite us for a drink on the terrace above the wadi. We watch the sun sink over the hills of southern Lebanon, which are tinged purple like Ireland when the heather flowers in summer and autumn. It is almost like being on holiday.

The plight of the Palestinians frustrates and angers me more than any other story I cover. It is not new to me. Issam Sartawi, a PLO leader who attempted to reach a peace agreement with Israel in the early 1980s, and who was assassinated by the psychotic Palestinian maverick Abu Nidal, was a friend. When I visited Damascus on a reporting trip in 1983 – the time I first met Robert – I interviewed officials from all the Palestinian groups and visited the Yarmouk refugee camp.

Now Robert takes me to Sabra, Chatila and Burj al-Barajneh in Beirut, and Ein al-Helweh in Sidon. Six years have passed since the Phalange and the SLA – whom Robert learned were flown in from the south in Israeli Hercules transport aircraft – murdered about 1,700 Palestinian civilians at Sabra and Chatila. He is still sickened by it, still angry.

The massacre at Sabra and Chatila, perhaps more than his interviews with Osama bin Laden, is the defining moment of Robert's career. The killing was still going on when he entered the camps with three colleagues on the morning of 18 September 1982. Each time we go there, he relives the horror of that day and those that followed, of the blood and piles of bloated, rotting bodies. He points out the doorway where he saw an old man in pyjamas, slaughtered in front of his house; the wall where men were lined up and executed with a bullet through the cheek; the place where he attempted to climb over an earthen embankment, only to realise that it was a mound of bulldozed corpses. In his nightmares, Robert places a hand or foot on what he mistakes for a stone or a branch, only to find it is part of a human cadaver.

"We lost track of the number of bodies after one hundred," he recounts. "We found empty whiskey bottles, dead women who'd been raped, with their skirts still pulled up and their legs spread apart. The Israelis gave the Phalangists weapons, uniforms and US military rations. They sent them into the camps and remained in contact with them while the massacre happened. They watched with field glasses from the roofs of surrounding buildings. They dropped flares from fighter aircraft overnight so the Phalange could see what they were doing. And Israel lectures us about 'purity of arms' and 'terrorism'."

In the Palestinian camps, waste flows down rivulets gouged in the centre of narrow alleys. Small, single-storey houses, little more than hovels, are constructed of cinder blocks and corrugated steel. Donkeys carry jerrycans of fuel and water, sacks of flour and tins of cooking oil.

The ritual is always the same. We say hello, *marhaba*. The family invites us into their tiny, clean, sitting room where mattresses wait in a pile in the corner to be spread out on the floor for sleeping. These Palestinians may have been born in a refugee camp in Lebanon, but they tell you they are from Haifa, Lydda or Ramla. The camps are often organised according to where their residents lived in Palestine, neighbours and the descendants of neighbours cleaving to their old proximity, to preserve memories and traditions. The refugees long for a life and a country that most never knew. It is homesickness on a monumental scale, a refusal to, as the former US Secretary of State Condoleezza Rice put it brutally in 2005, "get over it".

In almost every home, one finds a Koran and a photograph of

a "martyred" family member. If you ask, the family can usually produce the deeds and keys to their home in British Mandate Palestine. The further you delve, the greater the loss, the more insurmountable the tragedy, recounted with sorrow but without self-pity over little glasses of sugary tea.

Robert blames the British for this disaster, for having made irreconcilable promises to two peoples, Jewish and Arab. The Balfour declaration of 2 November 1917 promised the Jews a homeland in Palestine, but it also promised to protect the Arab population, which the British never did. In May 2021, an eleven-day war claims the lives of 253 people in the Gaza Strip and twelve people in Israel, showing yet again the inevitable, tragic consequences of this duplicity. For the inhabitants of the Middle East, history never ends, as it never ended for Robert.

ℰ∂

18 August 1988

The Lebanese Civil War drags on. President Amin Gemayel's term of office is over, and the Lebanese parliament is supposed to convene at the Villa Mansour, at the Christian end of the green line in East Beirut, to elect a new head of state.

Seventy-eight-year-old Suleiman Franjieh, who as president of Lebanon invited the Syrians to intervene in the civil war in 1976, is the leading candidate to replace Gemayel. Franjieh has been a personal friend of Hafez al-Assad since the late 1950s. Samir Geagea, the pro-Israel Phalange leader, refuses to allow Franjieh to be elected.

Both are Maronite Catholics, but their confrontation is far more than a question of conflicting allegiances to Syria or Israel. The personal hatred between Geagea and Franjieh originates with Geagea's assassination of Franjieh's favourite son and dozens of his family members. When Franjieh announces his candidacy in

1988, shells are fired across the green line, between Muslim West and Christian East Beirut.

Now Geagea has threatened to shell the parliament building if a vote is called. Robert and I wait outside with a crowd of Lebanese journalists. An AP photographer takes a picture of us standing in front of the wrought-iron gate. Robert is laughing at this Lebanese political theatre of the absurd, but my brow is furrowed. I am bracing myself for the first shell explosion. It doesn't come, because Geagea's men succeed in intimidating enough deputies to prevent the formation of a quorum. At least one deputy says he was held at gunpoint. The vacancy of the Lebanese presidency will precipitate extreme violence over the following two years.

ℬ

Back in Paris, a French publisher asks me to research a chapter of Tom Bower's book about the British newspaper owner, former Member of Parliament and fraudster Robert Maxwell. The project keeps me busy for most of the autumn, while I continue hunting for a job in journalism. Based on my clippings from the summer, the *Financial Times* offers me a job as their contract stringer in Beirut. I accept the offer and we plan to move to Beirut the following spring, once Robert finishes his book on Lebanon, *Pity the Nation*.

Robert banged out his previous book, about Ireland during World War II, on an old manual typewriter in his study in Dalkey. He and the novelist Maeve Binchy, who lived across the street, left their curtains open to see who could start work earliest every morning. When Robert completed *In Time of War* and Maeve finished *Light a Penny Candle*, they met in the middle of Sorrento Road to exchange copies of their books.

I convert Robert to floppy disks and the word processor. Day after day, night after night, he sits in front of the computer, often in his dressing gown, working furiously. I prepare meals and try not to disturb him.

At some point I complain of feeling neglected. Robert leaves one of his cartoon love notes for me. A chastised-looking cat face fills the upper left corner of a sheet of paper. "Maximum hours per day by Fisky – 6. not including atrociously early hours up to 8 a.m. or after midnight," says an annotation in brackets. The body of the text promises, "I will NOT be on the computer 24 hours a day, my darling Lara. Don't you know how very much I love you, my sweetheart? From your man."

Two things ease my qualms about moving to Beirut. The *Financial Times* is a fine newspaper and the only potential employer who has offered me a guaranteed income, however modest. Moreover, Robert has decided that we should buy a pied-à-terre in Paris. "If things get very bad again in Beirut," he promises, "it will be your refuge."

While Robert is writing *Pity the Nation*, I hunt for an apartment. We choose a sixth-floor garret with three small rooms, on the courtyard of a nineteenth-century building in the rue du Cherche-Midi. It has four windows, each with a tiny balcony and a view of the towers of Saint-Sulpice.

Robert's parents help us to finance the apartment. In one of those coincidences that life serves up with such irony, I recognise the son and business partner of the estate agent. He was the spokesman for the Secret Army for the Liberation of Armenia when it blew up the Turkish Airlines counter at Orly airport five years earlier, killing eight people. I interviewed him then for CBS.

We sign for the apartment on 23 November 1988. I start Arabic lessons the following morning. That same week, in Paris, we celebrate the first anniversary of my arrival at Heathrow. "I am more than ever now the luckiest man and I want you to know that you are all my world," Robert writes on his card to me.

Pity the Nation will be published in 1990, to critical acclaim. Robert's publisher, André Deutsch, chooses for the cover James Nachtwey's photograph of an ageing Lebanese woman standing against a shrapnel-pocked wall. Robert is delighted by her fierce expression, which speaks of the way Lebanon destroys its invaders. "This woman is not a victim," he says. "This woman wants to kill you."

At close to 700 pages, Robert jokes that *Pity the Nation* is "a doorstopper". Juan Carlos calls it "Pity the Reader", but I am proud. Proud of having proofread every chapter as it was written. Proud of having suggested that he use Konstantin Simonov's haunting poem "Wait for Me" as the epigram and title for the chapter on hostages. Most of all, I am proud to open the front cover and read the dedication printed in bold type: *For Lara.*

IV

The Mad Artillery General

Let me have war, say I: it exceeds peace as far as day does night; it's sprightly, waking, audible, and full of vent. Peace is a very apoplexy, lethargy; mulled, deaf, sleepy, insensible; a getter of more bastard children than war's a destroyer of men.

Shakespeare, *Coriolanus*, Act 4 Scene 5

On 6 March 1989, the Christian army general Michel Aoun orders the closure of all "illegal" ports in Lebanon, by which he means those operated by Muslims. Two days later he launches a sustained artillery bombardment of Muslim West Beirut.

Aoun says he is engaged in a "war of liberation" to rid the country of 35,000 Syrian troops. There are no Syrians in the Christian enclave that Aoun has controlled since the aborted presidential election the previous September, but he is determined to extend his authority over his Muslim compatriots.

The Syrians retaliate, of course, and the capital is engulfed in one of the most vicious and longest artillery battles of the civil war. The vast majority of casualties are civilians, killed or wounded when they venture out to work or to buy food, or as they shelter in their homes.

The Syrians keep a 130-mm Soviet-made artillery piece on the promontory at Manara, at the tip of the Ras Beirut peninsula, a mile or so from our apartment. Beirutis call the field gun Abu Abdo, meaning father of Abdo, a common Syrian nickname for a tough guy. "Abu Abdo he speak with a loud voice, Mr Robert," our landlord Mustafa says. Robert writes about Abu Abdo as if he were a big dog, hunkered down inside the gun emplacement, the tip of his muzzle peeking over the earthen embankment. Abu Abdo barks every night at ships trying to reach the Christian-held ports of Beirut, Dora, Dbayeh, Zouk and Jounieh. Robert's ingenious transformation of an artillery piece into a barking dog is quoted widely by the Lebanese media.

Robert teaches me to distinguish between the loud, hollow thud of outgoing artillery fire – ominous because it is sure to draw a riposte – and the crashing thunderbolt of incoming artillery fire, which makes the floor and walls shake for several seconds.

On the worst nights, there are continuous explosions. It's a good sign when you hear them, Robert says, "because you don't hear the one that kills you". This is not what I bargained for when I agreed to move to Beirut.

Most nights, we sleep on the floor in the bedroom corridor, to put as many walls as possible between us and a potential direct hit on our building. When the shelling intensifies, we drag our mattresses onto the landing. Several times, Syrian soldiers clatter up the stairs in their helmets and army boots, dragging assault rifles as they step over us on their way to the roof. Mustafa persuades their officer to find another observation point.

Because our apartment is on the seafront Corniche, just a few hundred metres from the Syrian position at the unfinished, derelict Sheraton Hotel, we live literally on the front line of the Aoun war. We move from the fifth floor down to Juan Carlos's old apartment on the second, because one is less exposed to shellfire when lower in the building. JC and Agneta have moved to a more luxurious building a few hundred metres away.

When the shelling becomes unbearable, we flee to the Cavalier Hotel or to the AP bureau in Hamra, where surrounding buildings provide an illusion of security. "My lovely darling, what an awful night!" begins the note Robert leaves while I try to sleep during a morning lull. He draws a picture of two figures sleeping on mattresses on the floor. Little hearts hover above them. Shells burst above the hearts, amid the words "WHIZZ," "BANG" and "WOWHOOM". Robert says he will send Abed back to fetch me at lunchtime. "Would you put $200 in your bag so we can stay at the Cavalier tonight?" he adds.

We decide to pay a call on our tormentor. As our taxi climbs the hills above East Beirut, we contemplate the densely populated Ras Beirut peninsula and the Mediterranean spread out below us like an artillery gunner's dream.

The presidential palace at Baabda is the ground zero of Aoun's "war of liberation". He ensconced himself here in September 1988, when parliament was unable to elect a president. The outgoing head of state, Amin Gemayel, appointed Aoun head of a caretaker government, an appointment rejected by Muslim Lebanese and by Syria, who continue to recognise Selim al-Hoss, a former economics professor at the American University of Beirut, as prime minister. Lebanon has two rival governments, Christian and Muslim, and has never been closer to partition.

The grounds of the palace are a moonscape of craters and shredded trees. We hear an explosion down the hill and Robert tells the driver, "faster, *habibi*". We debate whether we are safer driving fast through a bombardment, and conclude in the affirmative, since speed reduces the time of exposure.

The palace looks like the sort of low, modern stone-and-glass villa one might see in Malibu or on the Côte d'Azur, except that all the glass has been blown out. Lebanese leaders were meant to receive foreign dignitaries in the spacious entry, which is now open to the elements. The taxi driver grudgingly agrees to wait, on the promise of substantial payment. General Aoun's daughter Mireille leads us two floors down to the underground parking lot. She opens a door to Aoun's windowless bunker.

Aoun is short and pudgy, dressed in a camouflage uniform with a general's crossed swords on his epaulettes. There are dark circles beneath his eyes. He has built a career on shelling people from the shelter of bunkers. Mireille and Aoun's aides refer to him reverently as "Le Président Aoun", a title based on no objective criterion.

Aoun studied at the French École Militaire and on a US army base in Oklahoma. More than anything else, his war on Syrian forces is a desperate bid for French, US or UN intervention on behalf of the Christians. It worked back in 1983, when the Lebanese army persuaded US warships to shell Muslim forces at Soukh al-Gharb. But Islamic Jihad proceeded to blow up 299 French and US servicemen. Western governments seem to have understood that entanglement in Lebanon holds nothing but grief for them.

Hafez al-Assad wants Lebanon to accept its "Arab identity".

Like many Maronite Catholics, who tell you they are "Phoenicians, not Arabs", Aoun scoffs at the very concept. "It doesn't mean a thing," he tells us. "The thing that means something is what kind of life you are living. You are free or you are a slave. I want Lebanon to be a western nation with human rights." Mireille gazes adoringly at her father's face during this peroration.

Aoun's "western" aspirations do not deter him and his Phalangist allies from accepting money and weapons from Saddam Hussein. In late May, Aoun's "government" announces a hundred-million-dollar trade deal with Iraq. Saddam has just won the Gulf War against Iran and wants to undermine his fellow Ba'athist and arch-enemy, Hafez al-Assad.

Speaking of human rights, we ask Aoun if he thinks it's fair that the top positions in Lebanon are reserved *in aeternum* for Maronites, including the offices of the president, chief of staff of the armed forces and governor of the central bank.

"There is no problem between Lebanese," Aoun insists, flying in the face of fourteen years of inter-Lebanese slaughter. "The problem is foreign intervention. We cannot carry out reforms in the presence of foreign occupation forces." He stares intensely at us with beady eyes. Syrian troops entered Lebanon under an Arab League mandate, at the request of a Lebanese Maronite president, we note. The slain prime minister, Rashid Karami, asked them to return to West Beirut to end the militia war in 1987.

"And I order them to leave!" Aoun shouts.

Is this really the way to do it? we ask. After all, Aoun has never been elected to public office. More than 150 civilians have already been killed and his bombardment is just beginning. The Muslims say: reform the political system first, then worry about a Syrian departure.

Aoun says the Muslims of West Beirut are "collaborators" because they allow the Syrians to live among them. As for Hoss, why, he is no better than Maréchal Pétain, who provided legitimacy for the German occupation of France during World War II. Hoss is a traitor, Hoss is Judas, Aoun says.

At the end of the interview, Aoun takes the lift with us up to ground level. There is no shelling, for the moment. He blinks like a rodent emerging from its burrow. Aoun has not seen sunlight for a long time. We say farewell to him on the steps of the battered palace.

If Hoss is Judas, then Aoun is obviously the Messiah, Robert writes in a scathing article published by *The Times*. When we next attempt to cross into East Beirut, we are stopped at a Lebanese army checkpoint. Robert's name is on a watchlist. Aoun has banned him from his Christian Ruritania.

I invite a Maronite businessman, the manager of a tile and pre-stressed concrete factory whom I interviewed for the *Financial Times*, to lunch during a lull in the shelling. The businessman is a volunteer aide to Aoun in his spare time. "Aoun says he wants Lebanon to be a western country. Western governments respect freedom of the press, even when they don't like what we write," I plead. "How can Aoun ban Robert?"

"Robert was disrespectful to the president," the businessman protests. He sees banishment as modest retribution for this crime of *lèse-majesté*. Each time Robert sneaks into East Beirut with me, I steel myself for the possibility that Aoun may have him arrested and thrown into an underground cell at the defence ministry building at Yarze.

Neither Aoun, his Phalangist allies nor the Syrians show the slighted compunction about the indiscriminate bombardment of civilians. "There's no such thing as a clean war," Fouad Malik, the chief of staff of the Phalangist militia, says, shrugging, when I ask him how he can justify shelling the Muslim inhabitants of West Beirut.

In any war, it is sobering to report mounting casualty figures. The moment you delve into an individual story, the statistics are transformed into names and faces that stay with you for the rest of your life. Robert and I go to see the surviving members of the Sfeir family in the basement ward of the Pasteur Hospital in the Christian town of Jounieh. Their fatal error was to believe in an

Arab League ceasefire, one of a half-dozen that come and go over the six months of Aoun's "war of liberation".

Six hours after the ceasefire is announced on 11 May, brothers Fouad and Joseph, both construction workers, their wives and six children, sit in the living room of Fouad's small house in the town of Ghadir, on a mountainside north of Beirut, to watch the evening television news. "There is no reason for anyone to fire another shell in Lebanon," they hear Lakhdar Brahimi, the deputy secretary general of the Arab League, say on leaving a meeting with Aoun.

"A few seconds after we heard the Arab say it was safe, the missile came through the window," fourteen-year-old Charbel tells us. "I saw a red flash. Then I heard the explosion. After five minutes, I realised I was still alive. I had the baby on my lap when we were watching TV. When they came to rescue us, they found Chadi in Mama's arms. I don't know how he got there."

Baby Chadi lies in his hospital cot with a soother in his mouth to calm him. His face is swollen, discoloured and spotted with scabs where doctors have removed fragments of metal and wood. He screams and cries out for his mother, Nadia. The Syrian Grad missile that severed tendons and two fingers in Chadi's right hand killed Nadia instantly, and left his father brain-damaged.

Fouad's brother Joseph has rows of stitches zigzagging over his shaved head. He is burned and one eye is damaged. "In fourteen years of civil war, no one from our family was ever hurt before," Joseph says. "We were very careful. As soon as we heard any shelling, we went down to the shelter."

The missile that killed Nadia Sfeir and wounded the rest of her family was one of forty fired from a multiple launcher in West Beirut. "Why do the Syrians do this? To children, to people who have done nothing?" Joseph asks pleadingly. "There weren't any soldiers or barracks. There was nothing military near us."

Though western governments are reluctant to come to the aid of Aoun, a string of dignitaries nonetheless call on him at Baabda. They include François Léotard, a prominent French conservative, and John Cardinal O'Connor, the archbishop of New York. O'Connor describes Lebanon as "the beacon of Christianity" in the Middle East. In a sign of gratitude, Aoun confers Lebanese citizenship upon his foreign visitors. Palestinians who have lived in Lebanon for more than forty years have no right to Lebanese nationality. Aoun's authority to issue passports is debatable at best, but he hands them out to foreign supporters like candy.

Beirut airport has been closed since the start of Aoun's war, so we are on the lookout for ways into and out of Lebanon. Cardinal O'Connor holds a press conference at the Maronite patriarchate in Bkerké. Would there by any chance be room on his helicopter for an American and a British reporter? One of the cardinal's aides says that would be no problem.

O'Connor was scheduled to travel to West Beirut to see Sunni, Shia and Druze leaders after his meeting with Aoun. He cancels the trip, saying he is following advice from Patriarch Nasrallah Sfeir; advice that Sfeir's deputy denies the patriarch gave. "It was a cardinal error," Robert writes, with his usual knack for puns, in *The Times*, regarding O'Connor's failure to travel to West Beirut. On 30 May, we make our way, as agreed, to the helicopter pad north of Beirut, but we are told there is no longer room for us on O'Connor's flight to Cyprus. The cardinal archbishop has taken umbrage at Robert's report.

For as long as the Aoun war lasts, there are only two routes into and out of Lebanon, via helicopter or by boat to or from Cyprus, or through Damascus. We visit Damascus in June, to seek a Syrian perspective on Aoun's "war of liberation", and for a respite from the bombardment. The information ministry offers to take us to the Lebanese towns of Tripoli, Zghorta and Baalbek with a handful of Arab journalists. We jump at the opportunity.

৪ঌ

23 June 1989

The Syrians fly us in a Soviet-made Mi-17 transport helicopter to northern Lebanon. "It looks like a flying tuna can! Do you really think it's safe to fly in?" I ask Robert on the tarmac of the Syrian airbase in Damascus. Robert throws a tender, ironic glance at me, laughs and shrugs. "*Mobarif*, I don't know. We live in *Beirut*, Lara." I understand his meaning: you live in the most dangerous city in the world, and you are worried about taking a helicopter?

"Look, Lara, look!" Robert shouts above the din of the helicopter. "It's Krak des Chevaliers!" The massive medieval castle with round towers and crenellated walls covers the top of a mountain at the north-eastern tip of Lebanon, on the Syrian side of the border. First inhabited by Kurdish warriors in the eleventh century, the property of Knights Hospitaller in the twelfth and thirteenth centuries, the Krak is one of the best-preserved Crusader castles in existence. It seems to put Aoun's "war of liberation" in perspective. What, one may wonder, are a few months of bombardment compared to the two-centuries-long Crusades?

The Syrians are taking us to see the former president of Lebanon, Suleiman Franjieh, who features in what Robert calls his "gallery of rogues". The family's name comes from the Arab word "Franj" or "Franks", which was what the Arabs called the Crusaders. Franjieh is living proof that history never ends in Lebanon.

In 1957, Franjieh led a death squad that machine-gunned twenty members of the rival Douaihy clan in a church at Miziara, near Zghorta. Decades later, his daughter told Robert that Franjieh didn't do any shooting at Miziara; he just directed the massacre from behind a pillar in the church. The Douaihy family are also descended from Maronites allied with the Crusaders, the knights of Douai.

To escape retribution from the Douaihys, Franjieh flees across the border into northern Syria, where he becomes friends with a young air force officer called Hafez al-Assad. In 1976, one year into the civil war and at the end of Franjieh's corrupt and inept presidency, the Maronites are almost overrun by Palestinian and Muslim militias. Franjieh asks his old friend Hafez, president of Syria since 1971, to dispatch Syrian troops, thus making Syria the protector of Lebanon's Maronites and ensuring that future presidents will be subservient to Damascus.

Twenty years after the massacre at Miziara, Franjieh's militia, the Marada or giants, oppose the Phalangists' budding alliance with Israel. Bashir Gemayel sends a murder squad, led by Samir Geagea, to Ehden, near Zghorta and part of the Franjieh fiefdom, to the home of Suleiman's son Tony. The Phalangists make Tony and his wife Vera watch while they shoot their three-year-old daughter, Jihane. Then they shoot Vera in front of Tony, and finally Tony. Their son, named Suleiman after his grandfather, escapes because he is away at school. Old Suleiman keeps the coffined bodies in the family chapel and swears he will not bury them until they are avenged.

Of the many vendettas that blight Lebanon, none are as blood-soaked as those pitting Maronite against Maronite. A Lebanese proverb says *al damm bejeeb damm*, blood begets blood. Robert went to see Franjieh when Bashir Gemayel was assassinated in 1982. "He could not control his delight," Robert recalls. "He told me his only regret was that he played no part in Bashir's killing."

Franjieh is seventy-eight years old now, a sprightly, white-haired man with a leathery face and black-framed eyeglasses. He receives us seated at the head of a large, polished banqueting table in the great hall of his palace in Zghorta. He seems to relish being addressed as *raïs* (president) by the Arab journalists.

Syria is the guarantor of Lebanon's independence, Franjieh tells us, ever the apologist for Hafez al-Assad. Somewhat surprisingly, he admits that when he requested Syrian intervention in 1976, "I never thought they would stay so long." (Syrian troops were to remain in Lebanon until 2005, nearly thirty years.)

I want to ask Franjieh about the massacre of his son Tony, Tony's family and their entourage, about how it affected his life

and events in Lebanon. "I do not wish to stir old wounds but..."
I begin awkwardly, in French. For a brief moment, Franjieh,
the Lion of Ehden, a man rumoured to be responsible for the
deaths of 700 people, appears vulnerable. "*Non. Pas de questions
douloureuses*. No painful questions," he says, and changes the
subject.

ያ&

Our day-long Syrian government press trip is an extraordinary
blend of tourism, political and historical initiation, danger and
adventure; in short, a concentrate of life with Robert. We clamber
back into the clapped-out helicopter in Tripoli for another bone-
shattering flight, this time to the airbase at Rayak in the Bekaa
Valley. Our motorcade passes through acre after acre of hashish
and opium poppies before pulling up beside the magnificent
Roman ruins of Baalbek.

It is late afternoon, and our Syrian hosts seem nervous. Our
small group wanders through the temples of Jupiter, Bacchus
and Venus, accompanied by ten plain-clothes Syrian security
men with AK-47 assault rifles raised to firing position and facing
outwards, covering a 360-degree circle.

We know without asking what our Syrian hosts are worried
about. The Sheikh Abdullah barracks, seat of Iranian power in
Lebanon, looms over the city of 150,000 from the high ground to
the north-east. The former Lebanese army base has watchtowers
and high concrete walls topped with concertina barbed wire.
Five hundred Iranian Revolutionary Guards live there with their
families. The red, white and green flag of the Islamic Republic
flies from the barracks' ramparts, alternating with black flags of
mourning for Ayatollah Khomeini, who died three weeks earlier.
Black flags and photographs of Khomeini adorn every utility pole
and lamppost in the city.

In the Roman ruins, we gape at 62-metre-high granite columns
with capitals of carved acanthus leaves, at friezes of grapevines

and laughing fauns. By what twist of fate did this pagan city, with its monuments to the goddess of love and the god of wine, come to be a stronghold of Shia fundamentalists who have banned wine and all public displays of affection?

The Syrians produce an English-speaking guide for us. He is called Hussein and he talks nostalgically of the famed Baalbek festival, when over decades international stars, including Claudio Arrau, Ella Fitzgerald, Cole Porter, Ginger Rogers and Mstislav Rostropovich, performed on the steps of the temple of Jupiter. "You are the first foreigners I have seen in ten years," Hussein says sadly. "It took 100,000 slaves 250 years to build these temples," our guide continues. The Romans' slaves were mostly Greek and Middle Eastern prisoners of war.

The setting sun turns the granite columns red against a royal blue sky filled with diving skylarks. I am still under the spell of this beauty when we depart for the home of a local businessman. There we are introduced to a Shia cleric called Khalil al-Sheikh. Sitting cross-legged on a Persian carpet, he tells us the Muslim vision of the civil war, the same one we have heard from Prime Minister Hoss in West Beirut. The country's problem is the national pact drawn up by the French, al-Sheikh says. "In the United States, even a black man can be a presidential candidate. But if I, as a Muslim, want to stand for president of Lebanon, I cannot do it."

Al-Sheikh, like our Syrian hosts, tries to minimise the Iranian presence. "They do not interfere in internal politics," he says. "They are here in limited numbers. They are too few to be effective."

But the previous month, we read in Arab newspapers about the 10,000 Hezbollah fighters and 2,000 Palestinians from radical groups who paraded with weapons through the streets of Baalbek for five hours, demanding the destruction of Israel. Fifty Iranian Pasdaran (Revolutionary Guards) participated in live firing exercises, watched by their chief of staff, the Iranian chargé d'affaires from Damascus and Khomeini's personal envoy. After

Khomeini's death on 3 June 1989, the same dignitaries attend a ceremony where all swear allegiance to Khomeini's replacement, Ayatollah Khamenei.

We speed out of Baalbek under cover of darkness. Our driver and bodyguards become nervous when our car is separated from the rest of the motorcade. The driver attempts to overtake another car on the busy highway but swerves into a ditch to avoid a collision. Our Syrian guards jump out, AK-47s at the ready. Within seconds, two cars full of *Hezbollahi* stop to look us over, also brandishing assault rifles, circling like wolves around their prey. They outnumber us two to one.

All the tension of the alliance between secular, Ba'athist Syria and extreme fundamentalist Hezbollah seems to come to a head in that moment. For a few seconds, as cars whizz by on the Baalbek road, our fate is suspended. Syrian guards and Hezbollah extremists look one another up and down, gauge the repercussions of a clash. Finally, a surly gunman speaks. "Who are they?" he asks menacingly, nodding towards Robert and me in the backseat. "Foreigners, going to see General Kanaan," one of our guards responds. The *Hezbollahi* edge back into their cars, their guns still trained on us.

"Jaysus," Robert says softly. "I think we almost got kidnapped."

It is late at night, at the end of a long, eventful day. Our motorcade pulls up to a series of low, nondescript buildings in Anjar, inside Lebanon but close to the Syrian border. General Ghazi Kanaan, the head of Syrian intelligence in Lebanon and the most powerful man in the country, greets us. "This is just a courtesy call, not an interview," warns our minder from the ministry of information. "You must not quote the general."

An aide serves tea and offers cigarettes from a tray. General Kanaan wears an open-necked shirt and slacks, not a military uniform. The man who rules Lebanon with a mixture of diplomacy and force, blackmail and terror looks and acts more like a business executive or the member of an exclusive country club.

"General, my best friend is a hostage in Lebanon," Robert says.

Terry Anderson has been held for more than four years now, and Robert never misses an opportunity to seek information about him and to push for his release. "Terry Anderson is a good man; a journalist like me. He has a Lebanese wife and daughter. Can you help him?"

Kanaan listens quietly. "Yes, I have heard about Mr Anderson, and the others," he says. "Syria is against the taking of hostages. We do everything we can to obtain their release. We believe they are held in small groups of two or three. Even if we knew where they are held, we could not free them by force, because they would be killed."

We ask if the death of Ayatollah Khomeini will change Iran's relations with Hezbollah. Kanaan is surprisingly frank. It will be a good thing if Iran becomes less radical, he says, if it loosens its grip on Hezbollah and the hostages are freed. "They are fanatics," he adds, speaking of the Party of God. "We cannot control them."

Over the following decade, Kanaan will oversee every election in Lebanon and consolidate the grip of Hezbollah over the south of the country. In 2005 he will, like so many of the people we know in Lebanon, meet a violent death, found in a Damascus hospital with a gunshot wound to the head. Bashar al-Assad's government says Kanaan took his own life, but mourners at his funeral chant "Why did you kill him?" If the government murdered Kanaan, it is either because he knew too much about the assassination of the Lebanese billionaire and former Prime Minister Rafik Hariri, or because he was plotting against Bashar.

ᢔᢒ

Back in Beirut, our life settles into an erratic routine of semi-normal life and bombardments. In my desk diary for 1989, kidnappings, assassinations and car bombs are noted alongside appointments for coffee, lunch or drinks with friends and contacts.

We sometimes pop into the Captain's Cabin, below street

level in the rue Adonis, for a beer. The barman is deeply hurt when I mention, in a newspaper article, a cockroach scurrying across the bar. Sunnie Mann, the wife of the British hostage Jackie Mann, drinks there. Jackie was kidnapped on 13 May, the day we interviewed the surviving members of the Sfeir family. He had been an RAF Spitfire pilot during World War II and was later chief pilot for Middle East Airlines. He would be held by a Hezbollah faction for more than two years.

Istambouli restaurant, near the AP bureau and the ruined Commodore Hotel, now a billet for Syrian soldiers, is our lunchtime canteen, because of its sheltered basement location and because the mezze is always fresh. We like the sushi at Tokyo, where the owner, an ageing Japanese woman known as Mama, tells me she would like to flee the bombardment but cannot leave Beirut because her Lebanese husband was murdered and "his soul is not at peace".

Sometimes we drive to the Summerland or Coral Beach resorts, on the southern reaches of the Beirut seafront. Lebanese women sun themselves by the pool while artillery shells explode in the distance. A long closure of the green line provokes panic at the resort clubs, not because West Beirut is cut off from the world, which it is, but because the latest-model swimsuits cannot be brought over from the Christian quarters.

We spend many an evening at Backstreet nightclub, just up the hill in Makhoul Street. Habib, an Orthodox Christian bartender with a handlebar moustache, serves drinks and snacks. Backstreet is frequented by Lebanese journalists and delegates from the International Red Cross. The red and black lacquer interior seems to suggest a Chinese bordello. In other circumstances, it would not be our kind of place. But when the shelling starts, Habib turns up the volume on the stereo so loudly that one no longer hears the explosions. It is almost as if they weren't happening.

We shop for a washing machine and refrigerator for Juan Carlos's former apartment; extravagant purchases, since we have to wait for the occasional arrival of "city power" to use them. I decide to throw a party for Robert's forty-third birthday on 12 July. There can be no question of holding a party after dark, when the city is wracked by artillery bombardments. We opt for lunchtime. "How can you even contemplate such a thing at a time like this?" a friend's mother scolds me. Some of the people I invite say it is too dangerous to venture onto the seafront. Others promise to come, but never show up.

We order salads, mezze and a large chocolate cake from Goodies, West Beirut's only remaining delicatessen. I decorate the apartment with balloons. Juan Carlos makes ceviche, Bolivian-style marinated fish. I contain my fury with JC for starting preparations too late, so the fish is still raw. About a dozen colleagues show up, mostly from AP and Reuters, but also our landlord and his family, and JC's new landlords, an ageing American couple. For a few hours, we eat, drink, smoke cigarettes and laugh. We almost forget about the war.

One week later, the shelling begins as usual after dark. It rises slowly but steadily over several hours. Around midnight we pull our mattresses out onto the landing, but the explosions come faster, louder, nearer. The building vibrates as if in an unending earthquake. It feels like Aoun's last mad fling, the end of the war or the end of the world.

"The Sheraton. Aoun is going for the Sheraton," Robert says. We are so accustomed to the clapped-out army trucks parked in the long grass, and the Syrians' laundry hanging in their open-air billet, that we have forgotten that their proximity endangers us. We run down the stairs to find Mustafa, his sister and nieces crouching against the wall in the ground-floor entry. The only light is provided by candles stuck on the marble floor.

We wonder if Aoun's forces are attempting a landing on the seafront. Around two or three in the morning, we hear a horrific explosion, followed by a continuous barrage of secondary explosions. Aoun's gunners have hit the ammunition dump at the Sheraton. I curl into a foetal position, squeeze my hands over my ears and wait for the building to collapse on our heads. Robert wraps his arms around me.

The wrought-iron front door rattles. Mustafa opens it to let in four Syrian soldiers. Two are carrying a wounded comrade. They tell us he is nineteen-year-old private Yahia Saloum, and ask if he can stay with us. Mustafa brews a pot of tea on a camp stove, which the three uninjured soldiers gulp down gratefully. Private Saloum sits slumped on the bottom step of the stairs, staring at the blood seeping from a shrapnel wound in his chest, his face and dazed eyes illuminated by candlelight, like a Biblical figure painted by Georges de La Tour. He does not speak. There is something unreal, dreamlike, about the racket of explosions and the image of our ghostly group.

The other three soldiers leave us to go back on duty, then return around dawn to carry away Private Saloum, with his arms over their shoulders, as they had brought him in a few hours earlier. He is clearly in shock. "You must take him to hospital," Mustafa urges; they promise to do so. We venture to the front door to see off the wounded man. There is a gaping crater in the road in front of our building. When we return to our apartment, we find a thick layer of dirt covering everything. Explosions in the "West Bank", as Mustafa calls the field across the street, churned up tonnes of earth, which entered our home through slats in the shutters.

I know of Robert's scorn for journalists who "ran away to Cyprus" when the kidnapping started. He calls Cyprus "the island of gossip and gin and tonic". I do not recall him ever expressing fear or fatigue, at least not in those days. Robert has no time for "psychobabble" or talk of post-traumatic stress disorder. "Journalists are not the ones who suffer," he always tells me. "We have the passports and money to leave whenever we want to. The Lebanese cannot do that."

At some point, to my shame, my nerves break, if only for an evening. We have probably been drinking. "Why did you bring me here?" I cry. "I can't stand it any more. You said you would live with me in Paris. I want a normal life."

Two days after what I melodramatically refer to as "the night of the apocalypse", we leave for a break in Paris, crossing the green line on foot, then catching a taxi to the ferry in Jounieh. The boat leaves after dark, when it is less visible to Syrian gunners. As we start boarding, the shelling begins. The explosions are loud and not far away. They smash into the hillside above us or raise great plumes of water in the Mediterranean. I am on the gangplank, at the top of the stairs leading below deck. A Christian woman stops in front of me, paralysed by fear. "Mooooove!" I scream, resisting the impulse to push her down the stairs. I know my behaviour is absurd, because we will be no safer below deck. But I cannot help feeling relieved to reach the hold.

In Paris, I study the graceful buildings through the window of the taxi from Roissy airport. The French capital has never looked so immaculate. I search the Haussmannian façades for shell holes and burn marks and am surprised to find none. War and Beirut have become normality, peace an aberration.

We go to see *Lawrence of Arabia* at a cinema on the Champs-Élysées with wrap-around sound. When Arab forces shell a Turkish encampment, I have an almost irresistible urge to dive beneath my seat. "Pity the men under that," Peter O'Toole (Lawrence) says. "They are Turks," Omar Sharif (Sherif Ali) mutters. "Pity them all the same," O'Toole replies. The exchange becomes part of Robert and my repertoire. "Pity the men under that," we say when witnessing future bombardments.

We return to Beirut via Damascus. The worst artillery battle of the Aoun war starts on 10 August and lasts for a week. On 15 August, the Syrian and Iranian foreign ministers summon an assortment of their allies, some respectable, others much less so, to the Nadi Sharq (Orient Club) in Damascus. Two Hezbollah leaders from the Bekaa Valley, Sheikh Sobhi Toufayli, in turban and robes, and Hussein Musawi, a sleek-looking former schoolteacher with a goatee, attend the meeting. US media claim that Musawi is the "mastermind" of hostage-taking.

Ahmed Jibril, the leader of the Popular Front for the Liberation of Palestine – General Command, the radical Palestinian group initially accused in the West of having planned the Lockerbie bombing eight months earlier, is also present. An ageing, left-wing Palestinian, whose white hair and moustache give him the air of an innocent grandfather, Jibril has become a hired gun for Hojatolislam Ali Akbar Mohtashemi, the Iranian founder of Hezbollah.

We watch arrivals and departures from the street outside, in 30-degree heat. Hezbollah bodyguards glare at us, the way they did fifteen months earlier when the Syrians entered Beirut's southern suburbs. In other circumstances, I suspect they would kidnap us. An Arab colleague dubs the gathering "Terror Inc".

The meeting ends after more than six hours with a commitment to "confront General Michel Aoun's Zionist, imperialist conspiracy". The Druze leader Walid Jumblatt, another member of Robert's "gallery of rogues", greets us on his way out and tells us how glad he is that the meeting is over. A tall, thin, bald man with bulging blue eyes, Jumblatt wears an open-neck white shirt and jeans, which give him the look of the American University of Beirut student he once was.

Aoun is shelling the road across the Bekaa Valley and the artillery battles in Beirut have reached full pitch. We ask journalists' "fixers" and political contacts for help in finding transport to the Lebanese capital. They treat our search for a lift as madness. Jumblatt finds it amusing. He will drive us himself that night to his ancestral palace at Mukhtara. He seems pleased at the prospect of our company; or perhaps he considers our presence a form of protection. In the morning, Jumblatt's men will take us down the mountain to Beirut.

We leave from Jumblatt's office in the fashionable Mezzeh district of south-west Damascus around midnight. The entire staff come out, sleepy-eyed, to salute the departure of the feudal lord they call by the Ottoman title Walid Bey.

At the wheel of his Range Rover, a bodyguard with a Kalashnikov seated beside him, Jumblatt broods for as long as we are in Syria, flicking the radio from Arabic stations to the BBC, listening for news of the meeting he has just attended, and the artillery battles we are driving into. At every checkpoint, the smoked-glass window comes down a few inches and the name Walid Jumblatt is whispered among Syrian soldiers. We are waved through at speed. No identity papers, no documents.

Jumblatt seems more at ease once we've crossed the border. He laughs as he tells us how he abandoned the turbaned sheikhs to search for a beer in the kitchen of the Orient Club. He knows how the conclave will be seen in the West. "I'll never get another visa to Britain!" he moans in his strange, high-pitched voice, laughing.

Jumblatt's father, Kamal, was assassinated in the spring of 1977 because he opposed the Syrian intervention that was ordained by Suleiman Franjieh. Walid Bey was twenty-nine years old at the time, a dissolute youth who liked motorcycles and smoking dope, Czech beer and pretty women. He raced down the mountainside from Mukhtara to find Kamal slumped over the blood-soaked newspaper he'd been reading, machine-gunned to death by two men wearing Syrian special forces uniforms. With cold cynicism, even nihilism, Jumblatt became Syria's most reliable ally in Lebanon. His Druze PSP militia is the only one to join the Syrian army in its artillery battles with Aoun.

We climb the slopes of the Mount Lebanon range, the lights of the Bekaa twinkling behind us and Mount Hermon rising beyond the Bekaa to the south. Just over the crest of Mount Barouk, Jumblatt points to a grove of cedar trees in the headlights. These symbols of Lebanon are being killed by an incurable fungus, he says with what sounds like genuine remorse. "The world doesn't understand that Lebanon never existed," Jumblatt muses as he negotiates hairpin turns. "It was an invention of the French, carved out of Syria for the Maronites. For the French, Lebanon still means the Maronite Christian minority. If Aoun wins this war, he will try to seize our Druze mountains. Syria is not a free country and I don't like their *mukhabarat* [intelligence services], but I would prefer union with Syria to domination by Maronites."

It is after 2 a.m. when we arrive at Mukhtara. Jumblatt's mother, May, and his glamorous Syrian-Lithuanian third wife, Nora, have waited up for us. May chain-smokes and has the ragged air of an ageing French woman novelist, like Françoise Sagan or Marguerite Duras. I am intrigued by the way Jumblatt addresses Nora: "*glaçon de mon cœur*", ice cube of my heart. Servants offer hors d'oeuvres, fresh melon and cold drinks, which we consume seated on red velvet sofas beneath a vaulted ceiling.

In the morning, I throw open the shutters of the guest room where Robert and I have slept, to see a Phoenician marble sarcophagus standing as decoration amid pine trees in the courtyard of the sandbagged seventeenth-century palace. General Aoun's artillery can just about reach Mukhtara. We bid farewell to Walid Bey and climb into a dark Mercedes with two Druze militiamen. One of them drives at high speed down the winding mountain roads while the other keeps watch from the front passenger seat. Robert nudges me when we pass the plaque marking the place where Kamal Jumblatt was assassinated.

The Chouf seems to spill onto the coast road, from which we see the familiar jumble of concrete high-rises, unfinished motorways, vacant lots and shantytowns in the distance. Smouldering rubbish and fires set off by the shelling seem to coat everything with a sooty, oily film. We find Ouzai, the southern entrance to the city, transformed. The Shia slum usually teems with hawkers of kitchen utensils, fruit and vegetables and car parts. This morning there is no traffic jam on the coastal highway. The aluminium shutters are pulled down and locked over shop fronts. Beirut is desolate, abandoned. An estimated 90 per cent of the city's inhabitants have fled. The Red Cross fears a typhoid epidemic because refugees from the capital are camping beside the Litani River, 80 kilometres south of Beirut.

The bombardment continues, so we spend three nights at the Cavalier Hotel before returning to our apartment. Artillery shells have hit the power lines, and West Beirut has been without electricity for twelve days. Without electricity, no water can be pumped. For several hours every morning, the few remaining residents emerge to look for food. By afternoon, the city is silent. The only humans one encounters are Syrian soldiers and militiamen. Flies, fleas, stray cats and dogs dispute piles of rotting garbage.

ঞৈ

We go to the Barbir Hospital, at the Muslim end of the green line, to interview Dr Amal Shamma, the brave paediatrician whose family owns the hospital. Robert has known Amal since the Israeli invasion, when she showed him babies killed by Israeli phosphorus shells whose bodies burst into flames each time they were taken out of water.

In jeans and a T-shirt, with short, dark hair, Amal, who trained at Johns Hopkins and Duke universities, looks younger than her forty-five years. One hundred and thirty direct hits on the hospital building by artillery and tank fire have reduced its laboratory, kidney dialysis room, cafeteria and blood banks to piles of rubble. A shell explosion killed an orderly and blackened the walls of the operating theatre. A tank blew a hole the size of a bed through the wall of what was considered to be the safest ward, so staff closed the hospital for all but emergency cases.

Amal's name means hope, but she says she is losing courage for the first time in fourteen years of war. "We've been shelled many times since 1975," she says, "but all of us feel much worse now. We've reached the point where we don't know why we carry on. Beirut has never been empty like this. At night I go up to the roof and look west over the city, and I don't see anything, not even a candle... The only thing I can react to now is people being hurt or killed. I don't feel anything if I see a house destroyed – or even this hospital. In peace, you live. In wartime you just exist. You don't require as much to stay alive. I don't know if I could learn to have fun, to enjoy life again."

Pope John Paul II blames Syria for what he calls the "genocide". He does not acknowledge that a Maronite Catholic general started this round of Lebanon's civil war. France dispatches five warships, including an aircraft carrier and two frigates "to carry out humanitarian actions". General Aoun is exultant. "I expect [the French ships] to be put at my disposal to assure the freedom of movement in territorial waters," he tells the *France Soir* newspaper. The US sends much of its Mediterranean-based Sixth Fleet to the area when a videotape purporting to show the hanging of US Marine Colonel William Higgins is released, and a group calling itself the Revolutionary Justice Organisation threatens to kill two other American hostages if the US does not prevent France from "committing a stupidity".

The "Nationalist Front", whose formation we have just witnessed in Damascus, denounces the Franco-American build-up as "an act of aggression against the people of Lebanon". The French and American navies remain out of sight, beyond the horizon.

Absurd as it seems, in the midst of all this I am determined to adopt a kitten. *La frivolité nous sauve.* The pet shop in Raouche has a Persian kitten with eyes of two different colours, "like David Bowie", the saleswoman tells me. But $200 seems a lot of money, and I really want a striped tabby anyway. A friend and I vainly try to catch one of the feral kittens that populate the campus of the American University.

"You had better go downstairs. Abed has something for you," Robert announces on 3 September. Our faithful driver holds a bundle of striped fur on his lap. He has tied a yellow ribbon around her neck, and I am moved almost to tears when I see her. We have already decided to call her Walter, after Walter Wells, the editor of the *International Herald Tribune*. He refused to defend me earlier in the year, when the US Navy complained about an article I published regarding a simulated Franco-American hostage rescue mission.

We maintain our choice of name, despite the difference of

gender. After all, Catalani's opera *La Wally* is about a female. Naming a beloved pet after an editor who let me down is our way of mocking Wells, but also of transforming a bitter experience into a source of laughter. Walter is scrawny and covered in fleas. She hides behind the washing machine for several days, but once she grows accustomed to her new home, she is fearless. Our brave puss has known artillery bombardments her whole life and shows no fear of loud noises. When the explosions start in the evening and we run for the corridor or the landing, Walter remains on the front balcony, her eyes following red tracer fire as if it were a dangling piece of yarn.

Robert wants the bathroom, bedroom and his office to be a no-go area for Walter. He draws a cartoon entitled Walter's Wall, with a barbed wire fence and a sign saying "Verboten Halt!!!" A sad little cat face peers over the wall at a structure labelled "Lara-and-Bobby Immigration, No Visas available. Have a nice day".

But Walter wails each time she is shut out. Robert gives up on segregation. Our playful kitten becomes an important part of our life, doubtless a surrogate child, though it annoys Robert immensely when friends suggest this. Walter likes to sleep on the warm telex, and on our stack of back issues of *L'Orient-Le Jour*. Robert says she is a journalist too, that she writes the Paws for Thought and Prowling Abroad columns in *Tooth and Claw* magazine. Like T.S. Eliot's Practical Cats, Walter has many names: WTP for Walter The Puss, GFB for Great Furry Beast. When she begins fetching things like a retriever, particularly toy mice made of rabbit fur, Robert invents the term "Cadog".

Like most lovers, we can be silly and childish in private. Walter integrates our pantheon of animal friends, along with Mus, a plush toy camel that I bought for Robert when we began living together, and Malvine (for the Malvinas islands), a penguin which Robert's mother knitted for him during the Falklands War. They are the subject of innumerable cartoons, greeting cards, jokes and poems over more than a decade. It's a side of Robert Fisk, historian and war correspondent, that few people see.

General Aoun continues raving and firing artillery shells. Like a precursor of Donald Trump, he knows how to whip up a mob of angry supporters and dispatch them on intimidation missions. The US embassy in East Beirut becomes the object of Aoun's wrath. Aoun's supporters stage a sit-in outside the embassy and threaten to cut water and electricity supplies to the compound. Aoun has suggested they might take twenty US diplomats hostage. The ambassador and his staff are evacuated by helicopter to Cyprus on 6 September. State Department spokeswoman Margaret Tutwiler says Aoun intended to expose the US to "a good dose of Christian terrorism".

Aoun, who has almost never left his bunker for the past six months, accuses US Ambassador John McCarthy of having "a fixation about his personal security". He says the thousand-strong mob outside the embassy were just "four or five hundred peace-loving, middle-class teenager children". Ten days later he denounces the US diplomatic mission as a "den of spies" and speaks of a US, Syrian and Israeli "conspiracy of several layers like a club sandwich" to carve up Lebanon.

It feels like the bombardments will never end. On the night of 14/15 September, the shelling is continuous from 9.30 p.m. until 6 the following morning. I am no longer afraid, just weary. By late September, nearly a thousand civilians have been killed in Aoun's "war of liberation". No one has answered the general's pleas to save the Christians of Lebanon. It is obvious that Syrian troops will not leave. Lakhdar Brahimi, then deputy secretary general of the Arab League and an accomplished diplomat from Algeria, begins to make headway in negotiations. Aoun keeps Brahimi waiting for six days for a response to his ceasefire proposal. On 22 September, Aoun makes a two-minute televised address accepting the Arab League peace plan. He rescinds the decision five days later, saying he "didn't discuss details when I accepted the ceasefire" and "couldn't refuse" because of international pressure.

But by that time Brahimi has put in place a mechanism for

ending the war. Beirut port and the airport reopen after a 195-day closure. The Lebanese parliament is scheduled to convene in the Saudi resort of Taif – well out of reach of Aoun's big guns – to conclude a peace agreement.

On 27 September, we dine with Brahimi and a small group of Lebanese journalists beside the pool at the Summerland Hotel. Brahimi "has planted a rose bush in Lebanon's garbage dump", our friend Talal Salman, the editor of *As-Safir* newspaper, writes. Brahimi knows Robert's reputation from his years as Algeria's ambassador in London. He invites Robert and me to travel with him to Taif the following day. We drive with Brahimi to Damascus, where a private Saudi jet is waiting. Brahimi suggests that I purchase a headscarf in the airport. On the flight to Taif, we tell him about the Sfeir family, devastated by a Syrian missile just moments after his promise in May. Brahimi shakes his head and says, with a rare show of emotion, "I so hated that bombardment".

At Taif airport, Brahimi disappears like the Lone Ranger, leaving us to fend for ourselves. The receptionists at the InterContinental Hotel do not want to give Robert and me a room together, because we cannot prove that we are married. Robert lies so vehemently that they finally relent. Henceforward, we tell everyone we are married. Lying about it bothers me more than the fact that Robert no longer talks about marriage.

The Saudi foreign minister, Prince Saud al-Faisal, meets with the dozens of journalists who have flocked to Taif to cover the peace conference. Afterwards, the hotel manager tells me that "Prince Faisal noticed there are lots of ladies and asked what provisions have been made for you. He suggested the hotel pool should be open to you."

I am an avid swimmer, but swimming in Taif turns out to be complicated. A male employee admits me to the pool area at a prearranged time, and locks me in, alone, because no one must see me. I have been asked to wear a black abaya covering in the pool. The fabric floats around me like a black water lily. When I try to swim the crawl, my limbs become entangled in the abaya, to the point where I fear I might drown. I abandon the undertaking.

One morning Robert and I see a large, moustachioed man wearing a gold-edged Saudi robe in the midst of a crowd of Lebanese journalists in the hotel lobby. He is Rafik Hariri, the son of a Sunni citrus farmer from Sidon who went to work as an accountant for a construction company in Saudi Arabia, bought the company and became King Fahd's favourite builder. The rags-to-riches billionaire is financing the Taif peace conference.

Hariri invites us to his villa for a chat. He doesn't like our question about human rights abuses in his adopted country. "Believe me," Hariri says, "one hundred years of dictatorship are better than one day of anarchy." We find him arrogant, because he smokes a Havana cigar and is distracted by an old Hollywood movie on the television set across the room while we talk to him. Despite this inauspicious beginning, Hariri will become a loyal friend to us both.

It takes Lebanese parliamentarians three weeks to agree to increase the number of Muslim deputies, so the assembly is half Christian and half Muslim. The accord says the chamber will eventually outlaw the confessional system of government. It never does.

Aoun does not give up. The homes of three Christian deputies who attended the peace conference are bombed. A new Maronite president, René Moawad, is elected on 5 November. Aoun mobilises another mob the following day. About 2,000 protestors invade the residence of the Maronite patriarch, Nasrallah Sfeir, in the middle of the night. They burn furniture and destroy oil paintings, then try to make the ageing patriarch – the leader of *their* religion – kiss the photograph of Aoun which they have pasted over a portrait of Pope John Paul II. They force Sfeir to say he supports Aoun, not Moawad.

Moawad is assassinated on 22 November when a huge bomb is detonated under his motorcade. Twenty-three people are killed with him. The same method was used to murder the Sunni Grand

Mufti Hassan Khaled six months earlier, and will be used again to eliminate Hariri in 2005. No one is ever prosecuted for killing Khaled and Moawad, but, for the Lebanese, the atrocities have Syrian fingerprints all over them.

Robert and I run into the Algerian general Fodil Cherif, who ensured Lakhdar Brahimi's security throughout negotiations in Beirut, studying the scene of René Moawad's assassination. "Who killed him?" we ask. Cherif raises his right index finger and twirls it in a 360-degree circle. "Lebanon killed him," says Cherif.

Parliament convenes for the third time in two months to elect another Maronite, Elias Hrawi, as president. This session is also held outside Beirut, to prevent the mad general from shelling it. Aoun refuses to leave the presidential palace and bans from his enclave newspapers that refer to Hrawi as president. At the end of January 1990, he starts yet another war, which he calls the "war of elimination", against his former ally Samir Geagea, head of the Phalangist "Lebanese Forces" militia. For the first time since I came to Beirut, West Beirut is a haven compared to the Christian quarters of the city.

Bernard Kouchner, French cabinet minister and a co-founder of Médecins Sans Frontières and Médecins du Monde, the famed "French doctors", arrives with considerable fanfare to rescue the Christians from themselves. Robert, Juan Carlos and I go to the French embassy annexe in the Clémenceau neighbourhood of West Beirut, named after the French statesman, to ask Kouchner if we can accompany his convoy to the Christian quarter of Ashrafieh. Snipers have made the museum crossing impassable and the French embassy is using its influence over the Christians to negotiate a short truce. Kouchner tells us to return the following morning.

"Dr Kouchner has room for the *Financial Times* only," his press officer tells us when we return on 7 February. Kouchner's reputation as a womaniser is well established and I smell a rat. The attempt to separate me from my companions is blatant and clumsy. I refuse to go without Robert and Juan Carlos. Kouchner finds room for all three of us.

The convoy stops on the green line, a dangerous place if ever there was one, because Kouchner wants to have his photograph taken with Red Cross ambulance drivers. "*Bernard a le sens des photos*" – Bernard knows a good picture when he sees one – a colleague from the Agence France Presse remarks sarcastically. We speed past the bodies of three men shot by snipers, scattered at the Christian end of the demarcation line. They tried to cross from Aoun's territory to the Phalangist-held neighbourhood of Ashrafieh. Two slump over steering wheels. The third, an elderly man, must have tried to run, or shelter behind his car, because the door of his Mercedes is open and his body lies on the ground beside it.

Outside the Hôtel-Dieu hospital in Ashrafieh, the French ambassador, René Ala, tells me that Aoun is the legitimate ruler of Lebanon and that he is right to take on the Phalange. Ala deplores the reluctance of the French government to support Aoun. Like many of his compatriots, the ambassador seems to have an irrational weakness for stubborn, egomaniacal generals.

Time magazine wants me to spend a night with a Christian family in their basement shelter. Three days after our trip with Kouchner, I attempt to cross again, with Hussein Kurdi, a daredevil driver from the AP. We come up against a barrage of sniper fire and explosions and are forced to turn back. When we finally make it through the following day, the bodies of the snipers' victims are still where I saw them four days earlier, bloated, blackened and rotting. No one dares move them. I hear the *crack-crack* of automatic gunfire as we drive through the intersection at very high speed. It is my first experience of sniper fire, and it is terrifying, more *personal* than being under bombardment. Artillery is somewhat haphazard. A sniper is aiming at *you*. *Time* does not run a single line of the story they requested. The war between Aoun and Geagea drags on until April, claiming the lives of another 800 Lebanese.

In the end, it is Aoun's mentor, Saddam Hussein, who does for him, by invading Kuwait on 2 August 1990. Saddam, a key western ally against Iran, becomes a pariah overnight. Robert and I travel repeatedly to Bahrain, then Dhahran, in Saudi Arabia's eastern province, to cover preparations for the looming Gulf War. Aoun has become a sideshow.

Hafez al-Assad shrewdly signs up for the symbolic Arab multinational force that is deployed in the Saudi desert as part of the coalition against Saddam. Washington gives Assad carte blanche to dispose of Aoun as he sees fit. By chance, Robert and I are home in Beirut on 13 October, when we are woken at 6 a.m. by loud explosions. "That's an aerial bombardment. The Syrians. Aoun," Robert says, sitting up in bed. From the dining room window, we can see smoke rising above Baabda, eleven kilometres away. More than 700 men are killed in fighting between Aoun loyalists and troops under the Lebanese General Émile Lahoud, allied with the Syrian forces.

Ambassador Ala sends a French armoured personnel carrier to rescue Aoun from the presidential palace. Legend has it that Aoun flees in his pyjamas, sending the French back later to fetch his wife and daughters. He spends more than ten months in Ambassador Ala's residence. I want to write a play, entitled *Mon Général*, in which I imagine that Ala's hero-worship of Aoun is transformed into loathing in the *huis clos* of the residence.

Lebanese army bulldozers dismantle the green line that has separated Christians and Muslims since Black Saturday 1975. The Lebanese Civil War is essentially over, but the hostage crisis and bloodshed continue.

On 21 October, the Maronite politician Dany Chamoun, his lovely German-Lebanese wife Ingrid, and their sons Tarek and Julien, aged seven and five, are massacred at their apartment in Baabda, a repeat of the Ehden massacre of Tony Franjieh and his family. The same man – Samir Geagea – is held responsible. Geagea is the only militia leader to stand trial for war crimes. He serves eleven years in prison.

The Chamoun family are buried in Deir al-Qamar, a Maronite village in the Chouf. Despite their religious and political differences, Chamoun was a lifelong friend of Walid Jumblatt. I see Jumblatt at the funeral, a look of agony on his gaunt face.

ЯЭ

The story of Aoun requires a postscript. On 29 August 1991, French special forces whisk him away from the ambassador's residence to a French naval vessel at the port of Dbayeh, north of Beirut. He spends the next fourteen years in France, where he continues to campaign for a Syrian departure from Lebanon.

In 2005, Aoun returns to Beirut. He allies himself with Hezbollah, whose Shia Muslim fundamentalism and implication in "terrorism" he had condemned so vociferously in 1989. Less than twenty years after close to a thousand Lebanese died and more than 4,000 others were wounded in Aoun's bid to drive Syrian forces out of Lebanon, he forges an alliance with Damascus. In October 2016, when he is eighty-three years old, Aoun is elected president of Lebanon. In September 2017, Emmanuel Macron invites Aoun on a state visit to Paris, the first of Macron's presidency.

In late 2019, the Lebanese pound collapses. Tens of thousands of protestors demand social and economic rights and the resignation of the entire political class. The demonstrations are cut short by the Covid pandemic. Lebanon's standard of living falls to that of an African country. By early 2021, the Lebanese pound is trading at 15,000 to the dollar, one-tenth its value from 1997 until 2019.

On 4 August 2020, 2,750 tonnes of ammonium nitrate which was stored for years in an unsafe warehouse in Beirut port explodes, killing at least 190 people, injuring more than 6,500 and leaving 300,000 homeless. The government – but not Aoun – resigns. True to France's history as progenitor of the Lebanese State, Macron travels to Beirut twice after the explosion. He gives the country's squabbling leaders an ultimatum to work together. At the end of September, he accuses them of "collective betrayal".

Aoun's presidential term will expire in October 2022. As I write this, in August 2021, quarrels between Aoun and three different prime ministers-designate have blocked the formation of a new government for more than one year.

V

Desert Shield, Desert Storm: The Virtual War

Whenever you see hundreds of thousands of sane people trying to get out of a place, and a little bunch of madmen struggling to get in, you know the latter are newspaper men.

H. R. Knickerbocker, winner of the Pulitzer Prize in 1931

On 1 August 1990 Robert and I have just arrived in Paris at the beginning of our long summer holiday. Reports from the Middle East say Iraq is massing troops and tanks on its border with Kuwait. Saddam Hussein has for two months accused the tiny emirate of cheating on its OPEC quota and impoverishing Iraq by stealing its oil. The BBC evening news sounds reassuring. Saddam has promised Egyptian President Hosni Mubarak and Saudi King Fahd that he will not attack Kuwait, but Robert is worried. "I have this terrible feeling Saddam is going to invade Kuwait tonight," he says as we fall asleep.

"Iraqi troops have invaded Kuwait" are the first words I hear on the radio when we wake up the next morning. Robert flies immediately back to Beirut. I keep a luncheon date for the following day with editors at the *Financial Times* in London. They have several correspondents in the region already and want me to go to Damascus.

US troops begin flying into the eastern Saudi city of Dhahran on 8 August. King Fahd is conscious of his title as custodian of the holy cities of Mecca and Medina. It doesn't look good to ask infidels to protect them, so Saudi Arabia, the only country named after a family, is not giving press visas.

Robert rings our friend Joe Khai, a manager at Middle East Airlines in Beirut, and asks how he can get to Dhahran without a visa. Joe says that if Robert buys an onward ticket to another Gulf state – Bahrain, for example – he can transit through Dhahran.

While western journalists are besieging Saudi consulates in Europe and the US, Robert has five hours, from the middle of the night until dawn, on the ground at Dhahran airport. He has recently left *The Times* for *The Independent* and is delighted to offer his new employers a first scoop: descriptions of C-5 Galaxy transport aircraft disgorging Cobra helicopter gunships and missiles, and exclusive interviews with the American servicemen and women being deployed to Saudi Arabia. Little matter that Air Force Major Curt Morris's appreciative comments about his hotel in Dhahran and the Arab food he ate the previous evening are banal. No other newspaper has it. Robert turns the shoulder flashes worn by the US 3rd Airlift Squadron, "Safe, Swift, Sure", into commentary. Here they are, Robert writes, "a Christian army landing in Islam's most sensitive bit of real estate, with a message that has more to do with supermarket delivery times than theology". He describes the Egyptian troops filing down the steps of an Egyptair 737 as "religious camouflage" for those Christian armies.

Robert frequently mentions the Arab belief in the *muamara*, or conspiracy. He and his old friend Ed Cody of the *Washington Post* have often said jokingly that there should be a vacant chair for "the plot" in every interview in the Middle East. In the weeks and months that follow Iraq's seizure of Kuwait, a conspiracy theory takes hold in the Arab world. It goes something like this: April Glaspie, the US ambassador to Baghdad, meets Saddam Hussein on 25 July in Baghdad. "We have no opinion on the Arab-Arab conflicts, like your border disagreement with Kuwait," Glaspie tells Saddam, according to one version of a State Department transcript published by the *New York Times* on 23 September 1990. Glaspie's statement is interpreted as US acquiescence to the Iraqi invasion. If one believes that Glaspie encouraged Saddam, it is only a small step to believe that Washington *wanted* Saddam to invade so the US could deploy hundreds of thousands of US troops in the Gulf and seize permanent control of the region's petroleum resources.

I am reunited with Robert in Bahrain on 12 August. It takes us another two weeks to obtain visas to cross the causeway into Saudi Arabia. On Thursday evenings – the beginning of the Muslim weekend – we try to avoid the drunken Saudis who stagger around Bahrain's hotels and restaurants. There is a special building for them on the causeway, so they can dry out on their way back to Saudi Arabia after the weekly binge.

Bahrain is so cowed by Iraq's seizure of Kuwait that we are asked not to use Bahrain datelines on our reports about Kuwaiti exiles and the use of military facilities by US, British and French armed forces.

"Of course, Exocets are unpleasant," British Rear Admiral Peter Abbott tells us when we visit the guided missile cruiser HMS *York* in port in Bahrain. Iraq has purchased 1,000 Exocet anti-ship missiles from France. The Argentinians used a French Exocet to sink the Royal Navy destroyer HMS *Sheffield* during the Falklands War. An Iraqi jet fired an Exocet at the USS *Stark* guided missile frigate during the Tanker War in 1987, killing thirty-seven servicemen. The Reagan administration blamed Iran.

Fear of Iraqi chemical weapons is omnipresent. The sailors on the HMS *York* confirm that they are trained and equipped for a chemical weapons attack. They refuse to put on protective jumpsuits and goggles for the press. "That is not the sort of news we want people to see at home," an officer says.

An anonymous fax entitled "Precautions in Case of Chemical War" lands in offices and chanceries throughout the Gulf. It advises recipients to seal windows, doors and air-conditioning pipes with masking tape. A column in the *Saudi Gazette* suggests that one should "look out of your windows for birds dropping from the trees, cats, dogs and people dropping and choking, cars crashing, and general panic which are signs of a gas attack". A cold-storage room is the safest place to wait out an attack, the *Gazette* says. Or you should "cover your entire head with a wet towel or blanket ... get into the shower and stay there". And if you have the misfortune to find yourself out of doors at the time of an attack, "You cannot do anything except to accept your destiny".

The obsession with chemical warfare lasts throughout "Desert Shield", the five-and-a-half-month build-up to the conflict, and "Desert Storm", the six-week war itself. US bases in Saudi Arabia keep live chickens as a backup to their gas-monitoring machines.

"You imagine walking around, and your buddy is lying on the ground having convulsions, and you have to inject him with atropine," Private First Class Myra Camacho from Brooklyn tells me the following February.

Building on what it regards as successful management of the media during the Grenada and Panama invasions of the 1980s, the US military devises the pool system to control information coming out of the Gulf War. They combine photographers, print, radio and television journalists in small teams which they take on press junkets to military bases. We are under the supervision of Public Affairs Officers (PAOs) who must clear our copy before making it available to all 1,300 accredited journalists in the form of pool reports.

The pre-war build-up feels like the "phoney war" at the beginning of World War II. Amid a huge exodus of Gulf Arabs and the Asians who do most of the work in the region, we witness the arrival of hundreds of thousands of servicemen and women, and countless tonnes of hardware. By late August, more than 4,000 US troops are arriving daily, on requisitioned civilian airliners, as well as on military transport aircraft. American troop strength will peak at 503,000 the following February.

General H. Norman Schwarzkopf – "Stormin' Norman", the commander of US forces in the Middle East – is a cartoon caricature of a US general: a physically imposing veteran of two combat tours in Vietnam, full of sound and fury. At his first press conference in Dhahran on 31 August, Schwarzkopf swears, "There's not going to be any war unless the Iraqis attack." (Two weeks later, General Michael J. Dugan, the US Air Force chief of staff, is sacked for saying that the US plans a major bombing campaign against Iraq, which is exactly what happens.)

If Saddam Hussein "dares come across that border [with Saudi Arabia] and comes down here, I'm completely confident that we're going to kick his butt," Schwarzkopf says. Iraq's invasion of Kuwait was "not only a mugging, but a rape ... an international rape of the first order. We all tsk-tsk when some old lady is raped in New York and twenty-four people know about it and do nothing," Schwarzkopf continues. "It's not a question of oil. There's not a single serviceman out there who thinks that."

Asked what he knows of morale in the Iraqi military, Schwarzkopf lets loose: "Jesus, I hope it's lousy! I hope they're hungry. I hope they're thirsty and I hope they're running out of ammunition... I think they're a bunch of thugs."

Saudi Arabia is dry, so I drink "Saudi champagne" – apple juice and fizzy water – while Robert prefers alcohol-free beer on the grounds that there *must* be the tiniest amount of fermentation to give it that flavour. I am one of the few journalists who actually *likes* MREs (Meals Ready to Eat), especially the chocolate chip cookies and pasta with tuna. US servicemen teach me how to heat MREs on a tank engine, or in a cardboard box lined with aluminium foil and then left under the desert sun.

Our professional lives revolve around the Joint Information Bureau, in the ballroom of the Dhahran International Hotel. Robert calls it the "Temple of Truth", and is scathing about the incestuous relationship between military officers who long to write newspaper stories and journalists who dress up in combat gear so they can pretend to be soldiers.

On our forays into the desert, we encounter scorpions and sand, endless sand, "sugar-thick or fine as ground salt, brown and white and grey, clinging to the hairs in our ears, lodged between our toes, moist and scratchy between our thighs, blasted like a viscous spray into our faces, slithering up between eyelids and eyes," Robert writes, as only he could, in *The Great War for Civilisation*. "When I close my jaws, I can feel the sand crunching between my teeth."

In the autumn of 1990, one of the most hotly debated questions is whether the deployment of hundreds of thousands of western soldiers will change Saudi society. A group of educated Saudi women take advantage of the presence of the western press corps to drive through the capital, Riyadh. They want the right to drive, but they will not obtain it for another twenty-eight years. The women are promptly arrested and turned over to the custody of male guardians.

I must carry written permission from Robert, as my presumed husband, to take a commercial flight from Dhahran to Riyadh. Although I wear a long skirt and a headscarf on the plane, the Saudi seated next to me stares so intensely that I ask the steward to ask him to stop. "I think he has never seen a western woman before," the steward apologises.

The *Financial Times* asks me to talk to a Saudi cleric. I put on a long dress and headscarf and am about to head across the street from our hotel to the local mosque when Robert insists on coming with me. "You won't get in without me," he says.

We wait outside for more than a quarter of an hour, in scorching heat. When we are finally ushered into the sitting room of Sheikh Saad bin-Faez al-Mudarah, the rector of the mosque, we are introduced to a colonel from the Saudi National Guard. He wears a robe and headdress and sits bolt upright, clutching the armrests of his chair in anger. "Perhaps you are wondering why we made you wait outside in the sun?" the US-trained colonel asks in flawless American English. "We were debating whether you should be allowed in. We in this country believe that men and women should be kept separate." Thereupon, the colonel storms out of the room.

"How long are the Americans going to stay in our country?" Sheikh Saad asks, looking at Robert, not me. "I think that if Kuwait grew carrots instead of extracting petroleum, the Americans would not be here," Robert replies. "*Akid.* For sure," Sheikh Saad nods gravely. However obvious, Robert's observation fits in perfectly with the Arab belief in the *muamara* – the plot.

"As a principle, nobody liked American troops coming here," Sheikh Saad volunteers, "but we are forced to accept it as a temporary measure. There are no problems between our governments, but the cultural differences might be an obstruction to friendship."

At the end of the conversation, Sheikh Saad asks if I would like to meet his wife. This time, Robert must stay behind. We go through several doors to the part of the house reserved for women and children. I am introduced to a pretty young woman, surrounded by toys and small children. Between my poor Arabic and her poor English, we manage to exchange a few words. "What do you think of all these Americans arriving in your country?" I ask her. She bends her head, looking up from under her eyebrows towards her husband, as if seeking instructions. "She thinks what I think," the rector of the mosque replies, jabbing his own chest with his index finger.

The invasion of Kuwait coincides with the advent of CNN and the 24/7 news cycle. Though we spend much of "Desert Shield" and all of "Desert Storm" in Saudi Arabia, some of the most remarkable moments are those we watch on our hotel room television.

For the first four months of the Gulf crisis, Saddam holds about 2,000 westerners hostage, including the passengers of British Airways flight 149, who have the misfortune to be transiting Kuwait when Iraqi troops take over the airport on 2 August. On 23 August, Robert and I are still waiting for our Saudi visas in Bahrain when Saddam stages a grotesque, televised meeting with the British hostages. The dictator draws a terrified five-year-old called Stuart Lockwood to him and strokes his hair. "Are you getting your milk, Stuart?" Saddam asks. "Cornflakes too? Iraqi children cannot get cornflakes."

US officials prove equally cynical in their manipulation of television. On 10 October, a fifteen-year-old Kuwaiti girl called Nayirah testifies before the US Congressional Human Rights Caucus, in perfect English. She and her mother were trapped in Kuwait City by the Iraqi invasion, Nayirah says. After her older sister fled to Saudi Arabia with her newborn child, Nayirah continues, she did volunteer work in a Kuwait City hospital. "While I was there, I saw the Iraqi soldiers come into the hospital with guns," Nayirah says, weeping. "They took the babies out of the incubators, took the incubators and left the children to die on the cold floor. It was horrifying."

Nayirah's testimony is seen by tens of millions of Americans that night and is cited by President George H.W. Bush at least ten times in subsequent weeks. The tale of Iraqi barbarity helps to win public support for the war. Journalists later discover that Nayirah is the daughter of the Kuwaiti ambassador to Washington and an al-Sabah, a member of the Kuwaiti royal family. Her testimony has been fabricated by the Hill & Knowlton public relations agency.

Saudi Arabia is crawling with American PR men, like a certain Mr Lynch from Chicago, who whispers into the ear of Prince Lieutenant General Khalid bin Sultan bin Abdulaziz at his press conference in Riyadh on 29 August. Khalid is the son of the defence minister and is nominally the "Allied Joint Forces Commander". With his wide girth squeezed into military fatigues, and obvious hair implants, Khalid is a cartoon caricature to match Stormin' Norman.

In their respective post-war memoirs, Schwarzkopf and Khalid both write of their difficult relationship. The Saudi prince complains that Schwarzkopf's chair is bigger than his, and insists the American general come to *his* office for meetings. He frets over US troops wearing "classified" maps of Saudi Arabia on T-shirts, and he doesn't like media reports of dancing girls in Dhahran and the celebration of a Jewish holiday on Saudi soil. Khalid's most important qualification, Schwarzkopf suggests, is his "authority to write cheques".

I spend a night in the desert with a unit of the 82nd Airborne Division, the first to arrive in Saudi Arabia. Many expected to be parachuted directly into combat with the Iraqis. Now they are longing for a combat jump. "That's the big dream for the 82nd, to jump in somewhere and start fighting," says Sergeant Robert Moreland from Athens, Texas. "A combat jump would definitely be something to get out of this. If the Iraqis start streaming across the Kuwaiti border, we'll drop behind their lines and cut them off."

Sitting on hard-packed earth while bulldozers erect revetments by moonlight, the men reminisce about the history of their division as told by Hollywood movies. "I was in the honour platoon at Lieutenant General James Gavin's funeral at West Point last March," Captain Jim Huggins boasts. Gavin was played by Ryan O'Neal in *A Bridge Too Far*, about the 82nd's assault on a bridge over the Rhine in 1944. Others recall Gary Cooper as the 82nd's Great War hero, Sergeant York, in the film of that name.

The military are growing impatient. "We're not used to living like bedouins in tents," an Air Force liaison officer complains to me. "The thing that gets you down the most is that nothing is happening," says Private Manh Nguyen, a twenty-four-year-old Vietnamese refugee who made his home in Texas after fleeing Saigon as a child. "We're just like Hollywood, sitting here looking pretty." When Nguyen was a kid in Vietnam, he idolised the GIs from whom he begged chocolate. "They looked like giants to me. I never dreamed that one day I'd be an American GI Joe."

The military use acronyms for everything. My favourite, BMO for Black Moving Object, is some trooper's term for the Saudi women one sees floating around the shops and restaurants of Dhahran. The war ushers in a whole new vocabulary. Iraq's Revolutionary Command Council promises the "mother of all battles". We are introduced to the Humvee (for High Mobility Multipurpose Wheeled Vehicle), the squat machine that replaces the venerable Jeep.

A Humvee has just burned at the 82nd's base camp. "We think the ammunition self-ignited in the heat," says a soldier. Daytime temperatures can approach 50 degrees Celsius. Another soldier worries about the phosphorus shells in the back of his Humvee. "The manual says the inside filler of the canister melts at 140 degrees (60 degrees Celsius)," says Sergeant Tony Figuero, an artillery gunner. "If the filter melts, the liquid phosphorus leaks out. If it gets on your hands, they catch fire and you can't put the fire out."

In contrast to the other wars we cover together, Robert and

I often work separately in Saudi Arabia. I envy his ability to transform the few pool trips he does take into beautiful, literary prose. When he shares the turret of a Challenger tank with a British trooper, for example, Robert writes of the way the tank "dipped and yawed over the desert like a great vessel, its gun barrel the prow, the stinging sand from the tracks a substitute sea-spray".

My editors want conventional copy and official sources. Robert has much more fun wandering around the desert as a "unilateral" or unembedded "pool-buster" than I do in the straitjacket of the pools. He shares his maps with ill-equipped, lost units. He befriends soldiers by promising to telephone their wives, girlfriends and mothers in America when he returns to Dhahran. He spends hours on the telephone calling them from our hotel room.

Robert often goes on stories with Isabel Ellsen, a French photographer who is working freelance for *The Independent*, and with other colleagues he refers to as "the froggy journalists". The French, like Robert, are individualists and rulebreakers. Though he often mocks them, our French colleagues enjoy Robert's subversive sense of humour. To avoid being turned around by Saudi military police, they wear ersatz uniforms, usually parts of their chemical warfare suits. A sympathetic British officer gives Robert a helmet, to complete his disguise.

Robert is spending nights in the desert with Isabel, an attractive brunette the same age as me. He assures me they are just good colleagues and tells me that a well-known US television correspondent is pursuing Isabel but that she spurns his advances. When she takes me to see the Mirage fighter jets at the French Air Force base at al-Ahsa, I have a hunch that the tall, handsome French colonel there is her lover. Isabel and I go to the shopping mall in Al-Khobar. All shops must close at Muslim prayer times, so we stand outside talking. When she isn't covering a war, Isabel tells me, she always sleeps in silk pyjamas and silk sheets.

Isabel may be a seductress, but she is also a good photographer.

That winter, she will take the photograph of Iraqi soldiers surrendering to US troops which Robert chooses as the cover for *The Great War for Civilisation*.

"War is about death," Robert constantly insists, as if to prevent me from being swayed by the propaganda. None of the officers or enlisted men we meet ever seems to consider the effect of these hi-tech, shiny weapons on the human beings they are fired at. They think they are fighting an acceptable, clean war, without risk or responsibility, "in which the tide of information stopped abruptly at the moment of impact," Robert writes.

While we wait for the war to start, Margaret Thatcher's resignation provides a different kind of drama. On our television screen in Dhahran, we see the Iron Lady being driven away from Downing Street with tears in her eyes. "Over a poll tax?" Robert asks incredulously. Thatcher's immortal line, "funny old world", joins our repertoire of favourite sayings.

A few days after Thatcher's resignation, I spend a night with the UK's 7th Armoured Brigade, the so-called Desert Rats. Operation Granby, as the British deployment in Saudi Arabia is called, continues apace, but some of the soldiers express uncertainty about the government's determination. "Most people agreed that Mrs Thatcher should have fought on," says Corporal Jake Malcolm, from Leeds. "Will the next guy have Maggie's resolve?"

The imminence – or not – of a ground war is, like Saddam's use of chemical weapons, a major preoccupation. The men of the 7th Armoured are due to move north, towards the Kuwaiti border. Lance Corporal Michael Oliver, from Darlington, is a "trog" or army driver. He tells me that he'll be driving an eight-tonne Bedford truck filled with ammunition, fuel, rations and water to the front line if there's a ground war. Oliver expects to bring casualties and POWs back on return trips.

Half the British Army of the Rhine are being redeployed to Saudi Arabia. Many are nostalgic for Germany, where it was easier to learn the language and meet women. Their living conditions are more rudimentary than the Americans', in particular the showers and toilets. Unlike the Americans, the British are required to provide their own soap, shaving cream and toothpaste.

So many American women are writing to US marines seeking pen pals that the Americans ask members of the 7th Armoured Brigade to reply to unanswered letters. As a result, the Desert Rats tell me, several long-distance Anglo-American romances are blossoming.

ॐ

Robert and I have our own period of intense correspondence in October and November 1990, when the *Financial Times* asks me to cover the Aoun and hostage stories from Beirut and Damascus while Robert waits for the war to start in Saudi Arabia. It is our first long separation since we started living together in 1987. Because it is nearly impossible to get through to Beirut by telephone, we spend many hours "talking" over the telex machine. The reams of telex paper are a compendium of news, professional worries, travel arrangements and our longing for one another.

We had met Adel al-Jubeir, the Saudi official who will later become ambassador to Washington, then foreign minister and a chief apologist for the murder of Jamal Khashoggi, soon after we arrived in Saudi Arabia that August. A graduate of the University of North Texas, Adel is bright, clean-shaven and efficient. He picks favourites among the 1,300 journalists in Dhahran. We have meals with him and seek his help each time we need a visa to re-enter the Kingdom.

After a brief weekend in Beirut in October, during which we cover Aoun's expulsion from the presidential palace, Robert heads back to Saudi Arabia, but finds himself stuck in Bahrain without a visa. Adel al-Jubeir has suddenly become unreachable. I write to Robert from Beirut on the telex machine: "This not an impressive performance by our friend, is it? Do you think it was something you wrote?"

Robert replies that he suspects it was an article about

Prince Fahd and the Kuwaitis, in which he talked about public executions, human rights "and other undesirable things". Fahd must now approve his visa.

I remember Prince Fahd bin Salman bin Abdulaziz, the deputy governor of Saudi Arabia's eastern province and a grandson of the founding king, from my own interview with him the previous month. Like Adel al-Jubeir, Prince Fahd holds a degree from a US university and retains a veneer of Americanness. When I ask permission to smoke, he glances furtively at the door to his outer office, in the hope that no one is paying attention. I offer him a Marlboro Light, which he accepts nervously. "Please do not tell anyone that I smoked a cigarette with you," Prince Fahd says. Smoking cigarettes, especially with a woman, is considered haram, sinful, in Saudi Arabia.

I ask Prince Fahd about Amnesty International's report on the arrest and detention without trial of hundreds of Shia Muslims in the eastern province that he governs. Fahd dismisses the Amnesty report as fantasy. "What do you want us to do?" he asks, his American manners evaporating. This snide remark from the prince, which I later relish quoting in a talk to the Dublin chapter of Amnesty, sums up the attitude of tyrannical governments to human rights organisations: "Do you expect us to go to the prison every morning and say, 'Amnesty called. Here are your croissants and newspapers'?"

Saudi Arabia is my least favourite country, but I am nonetheless eager to join Robert there. And I fear missing the war if I stay away too long. Robert repeatedly books me on flights to the Gulf, only to have the *Financial Times* postpone my return. On 24 October he writes that he will see me in seven days and "sweep you off for a night in a massive king-size bed". He says he longs for a holiday in which we will "spend all time enjoying ourselves, getting up late, drinking bubbly, and absolutely under no circumstances at any stage contemplating ... doing any work at all".

Our relationship is an incongruous mix of journalism and

romance. In one telex, Robert asks whom he should interview at the Saudi national petroleum and natural gas company Aramco, where I have already reported a story for the *Financial Times*. I send brief profiles and contact details for five Saudi and American executives. He thanks me and adds: "As you said, we make a good team, huh? ... I am thinking most about being with you in Paris and Dublin, roaring fire, red wine, love, Lara and happiness."

Our reunion is postponed yet again, until 10 November. Over the telex on 1 November, I tell Robert it will be difficult to comply with the Saudi ban on public displays of affection when I finally reach Dhahran airport. "I was daydreaming about it today and realised how hard it would be not to hug you and kiss you in public when I see you. This has been I think our longest separation."

Robert says he laughed when he read my words, because he was thinking "exactly same (difficulty of restraining natural Bobby love on your arrival at world's scruffiest airport here)... We'll be together soon, holidays shortly afterwards, Paris and Dublin for Christmas. All will be well, believe me."

Paris and Dublin are the shimmering oases where we will settle when the wars are over. We dream of living in a Georgian house with a fanlight over the door in Ireland. We want to write books and adopt a yellow Labrador puppy. Or at least we think we do. I keep a tiny photograph of such a house, cut from a property advertisement, and an image of a friendly yellow Labrador, in my wallet. These fantasies crop up in our correspondence, especially when we are ill, tired or discouraged.

Rereading our telex exchanges three decades later, I realise how tedious it must have been for Robert to guide me through professional crises over my failed attempts to obtain a staff correspondent's job, and a Lebanese bank that threatened a lawsuit over an accurate story I had published. He was impeccably patient and understanding. One evening when I am particularly despondent, he again mentions our Christmas holiday and alludes to The Dream: "I was thinking today more about houses in the west of Ireland. We must also talk about book-writing and things like that as I have a new offer on the Egypt book etc ... I just want to be with you ... It's the most important whatever happens."

Robert's difficult relations with the British military, and bouts of flu or food poisoning, are other recurring themes, though it is unusual for Robert to be ill. On 26 October, he writes about a trying day. He spent the morning in the desert and "felt dreadful but managed to write story before collapsing into bed". He gets up to attend a British dinner, and is stunned by the mediocrity of the general who is the star attraction. "Here I am wanting to meet the top doggies and I happily walked out because I was so bored. Or maybe there's something wrong with me. Or I'm just ill... I'm very miserable and don't have much interest in being here, work or anything else. Age or experience are making me have little time for fools... I am very short-tempered with folk, including nabobs."

On 1 November, Robert mixes news with anticipation of our reunion. We know telex traffic is monitored and so use our own codes. "Helmets" refers to Syrian troops, "toys" to armour. Robert has heard a rumour that the Saudis are planning a trip to the Red Sea port of Yanbu "to watch the arrival of more helmets with heavy toys". The American Secretary of State, James Baker, is to visit the following week, followed by Mrs Thatcher in mid-November, then President Bush, so we will be busy with news stories. "Now Fisker forgets bullshit news and says I cannot waaaiiittt for you to come, though I hope you have lots of energy for first two three nights etc."

The following day, Robert writes that he is "in the doghouse with the Brits" because subeditors changed the name of a regiment "and of course all kinds of hooty-snooty colonels are claiming it's the worst thing they've read since the rise of the Third Reich". The previous year, the US attorney and author Mike Godwin had promulgated the theory that the longer a discussion goes on, the more likely that someone will compare someone or something to Hitler and the Nazis. We haven't yet heard of "Godwin's law", but Robert is allergic to politicians comparing Saddam, and later Slobodan Milošević, to Hitler. "Bush now claims Saddam worse repeat worse than Hitler which going a bit far," he writes. He has decided to stay away from "fucking PR men ... the snooty little shits" who have complained to editors in London. "So it's back to the gay old days of covering Belfast. I should feel at home. End of bobbygrouse."

On 4 November, Robert is staying at the Hyatt Hotel in Jeddah, to cover the arrival of Syrian troops with their Soviet-made T-62 tanks, which he had predicted three days earlier. He has been up since 5.45 in the morning and has filed an article about the 800 soldiers and 100 tanks he watched disembark. He "wondered if I wasn't fated to spend the rest of my life following same bloody tanks and helmets around the Middle East". He watched Prince Khalid bin Sultan, "our friend the prince with the hair implant" make a long speech before speeding off in an enormous stretch limousine. "Oh Lordy, Lordy," he says, his standard expression of disdain.

Robert's surroundings add to his homesickness. The following day he says he feels "empty inside because you are not with me... I wish so much I was there with you (yes, and with the GFB [Great Furry Beast – Walter, our cat]) and I miss our home so much. This hotel is really grotty... The bedroom carpet smells filthy. (I moved rooms and so did the second one). The air conditioning sounds like a bloody generator and there was human hair all over the bathroom floor..."

In our exchange of 6 November, I mention that Canadian radio is trying to reach Robert. "They want to know if there is going to be a Gulf War and if there are going to be hostages released in Lebanon," I write, tongue in cheek. These are, of course, the right questions, but posed as if one could provide a Yes or No answer. Robert replies with the weariness of a Middle East correspondent who has spent his adult life providing nuanced answers to simplistic queries. "Phew. My God, these people think wars are like cricket matches."

§∂

9 January 1991

Mohamed, the immigration officer at Dhahran airport, is unusually friendly when Robert and I arrive from Beirut to cover the impending war. UN Security Council Resolution 678 gives Saddam Hussein until 15 January to withdraw from Kuwait. There remains the tiniest hope of avoiding a conflict, and it hangs on the meeting in Geneva that night between James Baker and his Iraqi counterpart, Tariq Aziz.

Mohamed invites Robert and me to join him and his friends for dinner while we watch the news from Geneva. It is unusual to be invited to a Saudi home, and we accept eagerly.

Mohamed lives in a nondescript, California-style bungalow. We are shown to the back garden, where he and his friends sit on carpets, leaning against camel saddles, under a tent canopy. All wear Gulf Arab clothing, the *dishdasha* robe and *ghutra* headdress. Meat roasts over a charcoal brazier beside the tent. Platters of mezze and fruit are arrayed on a low table. If it weren't for the black-and-white television droning away in the corner, one would think we had entered an orientalist painting.

We discuss the obvious questions. If Saddam Hussein is so bad, why did Saudi Arabia bankroll him through the 1980–88 war with Iran? (The real answer is nearly 2,000 years of enmity between Persians and Arabs, combined with the Saudis' terror of radical Shia Islam and especially Iran's population, who outnumber Saudis by more than three to one.) "Our government lied to us" about Saddam, Mohamed says simply, adding that he remains King Fahd's loyal servant no matter what happens.

James Baker looks like an undertaker as he walks up to the podium of the InterContinental Hotel in Geneva. "Regretfully, ladies and gentlemen," Baker says, and I suck in my breath, "in over six hours I have heard nothing that suggested to me any Iraqi flexibility whatsoever on complying with the UN Security Council resolutions..."

"So there will be war?" Mohamed's brother asks.

"It certainly looks that way," Robert says.

As if on cue, Mohamed brings out a large tray carrying every imaginable brand of whisky. In Saudi Arabia, where all forms of alcohol are banned. Our host reads the surprise on our faces. "Confiscated whisky. From passengers who try to smuggle it in," Mohamed grins. He distributes tall glasses filled with golden liquid to his guests. They drink it greedily, as if it were water.

Should they stay in Dhahran or flee elsewhere in the Gulf? "It will be just as dangerous in Bahrain or the Emirates," one of the men suggests. "I'd rather go to Europe," says another. "You're cowards – all of you cowards. Have you no patriotism?" shouts a third. For a few tense moments, I think we are going to witness a brawl. The man who calls the others cowards staggers away across the garden.

Robert and I return to the Meridien Hotel at 2 a.m. Later that day, suffering from the only hangover I have ever experienced in Saudi Arabia, I undergo a physical fitness test administered by women from the US Navy and receive a steel helmet, a flak jacket and a set of dog tags engraved with my name, date of birth and social security number.

I am to cover the Gulf War for *Time* magazine, and I cannot help noticing that my male colleagues have found reasons to arrive late. Could they be waiting to see if Saddam will fire chemical weapons at Saudi Arabia at the outset of the war? "It is very important that you reserve *Time*'s slot in the Pentagon pool," one tells me. My fellow journalists arrive four days after the war starts.

I am assigned to Pool 6, with the US Navy. On the 10th and 11th January, I attend a class on nuclear, biological and chemical warfare – NBC to the military – and receive training in first aid and response to a chemical attack. Robert heads to Khafji, on Saudi Arabia's border with Kuwait, early on the morning of the 12th.

The Aoun wars in Beirut have nearly cured me of fear, but this is different. For the first time I will not be under fire with Robert. "Seeing you lying asleep just now, I was filled with sadness that I could not return to my place beside you in our bed, even though we'll only be a few days apart," he writes in the note he leaves before departing for Khafji.

Robert returns to Dhahran the following night and is there when the phone rings at 6 a.m. on 14 January, summoning me for pool duty, for a day trip only. While I shower, Robert writes "6.20 a.m. Monday" at the top of a second note. "I shall read your [pool] reports with the same attention that Walter watches her mouse. Don't worry about your Bobby – he will be waiting for you with kisses and a giant hug (and a cuddle) when you return, my lover. You are all my life, always from your Tiger."

There are a half-dozen journalists in Pool 6, including a Rome-based crew from ABC television and Susan Sachs, a correspondent for *New York Newsday*. Our Public Affairs Officer, Marine Corps Major Jim Maclain, an affable but caustic African-American, shepherds us onto a helicopter – "crowd-killers" the military reassuringly call them – for the short ride to Shaikh Isa airbase in Bahrain. The first trip is a trial run.

As part of our initiation on Shaikh Isa, we are given release forms to sign for vaccinations the following day. US officers encourage journalists to swallow the same pills and take the same injections of anthrax and botulinum toxin vaccines which they are administering to soldiers. "Whatever you do, don't take it!" Robert insists that evening. Of the countless pieces of advice he gives me over twenty years, this is one of the most valuable. More than one-third of the half million plus US veterans of the 1991 war will suffer from the chronic fatigue, muscle pain, cognitive problems, insomnia, rashes and diarrhoea known as Gulf War Syndrome. I am forever grateful to Robert for saving me from such a fate.

I am Robert's spy on the airbase. I tell him about the banner I
see inside an aircraft hangar, showing a US superman clutching
a limp, terrified Arab with a hook nose. I do not include it in my
pool reports, on the cowardly assumption that it would in any
case be censored, and that my editors at *Time* magazine would
not print it. Robert writes about it.

My direct supervisor at *Time*, the Cairo bureau chief, is a
former State Department spokesman who is furious when I later
propose a story about torture under Mubarak while filling in for
him during his holiday. One of the half-dozen *Time* reporters in
Saudi Arabia is a former CIA agent, and I have doubts about a
second. I sometimes wonder if *Time* is just an elaborate cover for
US intelligence, the equivalent of *Pravda* and TASS in the Soviet
Union.

The magazine operates an absurd system under which editors
in New York – not reporters in the field – decide which stories
should be scheduled. The journalists send files to New York,
where the articles are written. Researchers in New York send
endless queries about inane details, but the final pieces usually
miss the big picture. A post-Gulf War internal audit concludes
that *Newsweek* performed better than *Time* because it let
reporters choose and write their own stories.

Our second pool trip to Bahrain, on 15 January, is the real
thing. We are told to pack for three days. The war is about to start.
I tell Major Maclain I would like to interview a navy pilot who
will see combat. He introduces me to a friend of his, Major John
"Smoke" Rader. Major Rader tells me he was a misfit, growing
up amid the peace and love, hippie generation who opposed the
Vietnam War. He is a self-described patriot and "square" who
wants to join NASA's space programme after the war.

Rader believes that the war with Iraq is necessary.

"Have you ever been in a war? Do you know what the weapons
you'll be launching do to people?" I ask.

"Saddam is a bully. He broke international law. The Iraqis are
committing atrocities in Kuwait," the navy pilot replies.

"The Israelis don't obey UN Security Council resolutions either," I say. "They keep stealing Arab land and killing Arab civilians. And the US supports them. The double standard is so blatant."

"You're never going to get justice everywhere. But some justice, sometimes, is better than no justice ever," Rader replies.

In my bunk bed in the dormitory on Shaikh Isa airbase that night, I open the envelope that Robert has marked "to be opened at 22.00 hours 15/1/91". He does not mention what we all know – that the outbreak of war is a question of hours. His tender notes are, as ever, an antidote to the brutality of the world, and in stark contrast to his anger towards the perpetrators of war: "My true love – as you read this, I am thinking of you and loving you and AT THIS MOMENT I am sending waves of love to you. Your tiger has never loved you so much. You are all my life…" He adds an inky cat print, from Walter.

We are woken after a few hours of fitful sleep to go onto the tarmac at Shaikh Isa to interview pilots before they screech down the runway en route for Baghdad. It is noisy and dark. We wear headphones to spare our eardrums. The overwhelming impression of fighter bombers taking off in rapid succession is one of American power and brute force combined with space-age technology. My heart sinks because I sense that we, the West, to which I belong, are embarking on a hazardous journey of unforeseeable consequences.

The sirens sound for a Scud missile alert and we rush to a shelter. No one is certain if we should put on our chemical suits, since Saddam is rumoured to have deployed chemical warheads on his Soviet-made missiles. We brace ourselves for an explosion which never happens. I experience a second Scud alert three nights later, when I find myself locked for eighty minutes in the basement of the International Hotel in Dhahran by the US military. Thereafter, I refuse to go to shelters for Scud alerts.

In the course of the six-week war, Iraq fires a total of eighty-eight Scuds, forty-six at Saudi Arabia and forty-two at Israel. On

25 February, a Scud will hit a barracks used by reservists from the Pennsylvania National Guard in Dhahran, killing twenty-eight and wounding ninety-eight others. It is the single greatest loss of life for the US-led coalition during the war.

When the Scud alert is lifted, we go back to the runway to interview returning pilots. All recount the same thing: that Baghdad "looked like the 4th of July", all fireworks and explosions. The images the pilots describe are on every television screen, tinted green by night-vision cameras and narrated by Peter Arnett of CNN.

Only sixteen years have passed since the end of the Vietnam War. It remains a point of reference for journalists and military alike. Arnett covered Vietnam, as did the Italian journalist Oriana Fallaci, whom I meet one day in a hotel lobby in Riyadh. This is the last war in which I encounter Vietnam veterans, whether media or military.

Memories of Vietnam complicate relations with US officers, many of whom still blame "the media" for their having lost that war. Photographs of the My Lai massacre, the "Napalm Girl" running naked with her body on fire, and the summary execution of a Vietcong guerrilla by a South Vietnamese general played an important part in turning US public opinion against the war in Vietnam.

We listen to the BBC World Service on a transistor radio at breakfast in the canteen on Shaikh Isa airbase on the morning the war starts. Seven B-52 bombers have flown "the longest strike mission in the history of aerial warfare", making a return trip from Louisiana to Saudi airspace to fire cruise missiles at Iraq. The US-led coalition has already flown hundreds of sorties and downed an Iraqi MiG fighter.

The Bush administration has appealed to Israel not to retaliate for the Scuds which Iraq launched at Israel. "Israel is being attacked and they're not allowed to defend themselves," my colleague Susan Sachs from *Newsday* mutters angrily over her cornflakes.

"They'd better not retaliate," Major Maclain says, equally angry. "Because the Israelis make trouble all over the Middle East and we're tired of cleaning up their shit." Maclain and Susan glare at each other. The tension between them is palpable.

Before returning to Dhahran, Pool 6 interviews a US colonel who gives each of us a small American flag which he says was carried in an aircraft on a bombing mission over Baghdad on the first night of the war. "You are warriors too," he tells us. I am not a warrior. I find the remark inaccurate, misplaced and in bad taste. If I were Robert, I would say so. But I suppress a feeling of unease and remain silent.

The pool system and the huge imbalance between western and Iraqi forces make it possible for the Americans to create the impression of a clean, video-game war. On 10 February, my pool is flown to an airbase in south-west Saudi Arabia to see Secretary of Defence Dick Cheney and General Colin Powell, then chairman of the joint chiefs of staff, unveil the new F-117 Stealth attack aircraft. The bomber's uneven surfaces are designed to deflect radar detection. It looks like an intergalactic junkyard.

CNN shows countless images, taken by unmanned cameras positioned on bombers, of laser-guided "smart bombs" striking their targets. The majority of reporters and servicemen and women return to the US without visiting Iraq or Kuwait when the war ends. Perhaps understandably, they, like the US public, have the impression nobody died in the 1991 Gulf War.

A 1993 UN report estimates that between 142,500 and 206,000 Iraqi deaths, civilian and military combined, are directly attributable to Desert Storm. The US suffered 148 fatalities, of which nearly a quarter were due to "friendly fire".

Attention focuses on the wizardry of weapons, not their effects. I had visited a Patriot missile battery three weeks after the invasion of Kuwait. These weapons are meant to protect US troops from Saddam's Scuds. They look like railway boxcars, tilted skywards. "You kind of grow attached to them," US army captain Joe DeAntona, who is assigned to an air defence artillery unit, tells me. "You get to think of the missiles like family. We paint names on the top of their carriers. I let the soldiers name them."

On 23 January, Pool 6 flies with the "Raiders" squadron of Marine Air Group 13 in a KC-130 Hercules jet tanker over the Persian Gulf. Ours is one of four tankers ascending in "stairway to the stars" formation. The tanker is "parked" at an airborne filling station at 18,000 to 20,000 feet. Below us, Victor tankers from the RAF refuel British Tornadoes and Jaguars. Above us, US Air Force tankers are refuelling their fighters.

It is hard not to see a certain beauty in the elaborate aerial ballet. The only analogies I can think of come from natural science. F-18 fighter jets speed towards us like hornets, hover, insert their probes into hoses resembling tulips, then suck fuel from the tanker. The KC-130 crew refer to the hoses, drogues and probes as "male" and "female" apparatus.

The refuelling process seems almost poetic, divorced from the bombing campaign it is enabling. (I can hear Robert admonishing me in my head: "Come on, Lara. Don't tell me you've been dazzled by their hi-tech weapons. That's what they want!") There are only the faintest reminders that we are covering a war. "Our fighters are going to work real hard on messing up somebody's day," Lieutenant Colonel Arlen Rens comments. He has no fear of an Iraqi attack. "We've got hundreds of guys whose sole goal in life is to be an ace. You just say the word 'MiG' and they'll be all over them like flies over sugar."

At the end of January, *Time* magazine publishes a two-page spread entitled "Inside the High-Tech Arsenal" which calls weaponry "the star of the war" and "state-of-the-art showpieces". Sea-launched Tomahawk cruise missiles "are the real technological marvels", it adds.

Over 80,000 tonnes of bombs are dropped on Iraq, more than on Germany during World War II. *Time* describes the bombing in such terms as "pinpoint strikes" and "pinpoint accuracy".

Robert analyses the claims made for "smart" weaponry in the

1991 war in *The Great War for Civilisation*. He cites a report by the US state auditor, the General Accounting Office, which declares that the claims made for Stealth fighters, Tomahawk missiles and laser-guided bombs were "overstated, misleading, inconsistent with the best available data or unverifiable". Only 8 per cent of the bomb tonnage dropped on Iraq were guided munitions. The Stealth bomber had a 40 per cent success rate, the same as Patriot missiles fired at Scuds over Israel. Patriots destroyed 70 per cent of Scuds over Saudi Arabia. Robert is enraged by what he calls "rubbish language". Several years later, I see him nearly reduce my sister's father-in-law to tears in a Paris restaurant. The ageing American engineer designs TOW anti-tank missiles, and Robert wants him to know what the missiles do.

I agree with Robert on the fundamentals, though I sometimes wonder if the 1991 war is not justified. "Don't you ever forget that war is about death," he says again.

"So what would *you* do about Saddam invading Kuwait?" I ask.

"Well to start with, I wouldn't have supported Saddam. The Americans and French *created* Saddam. They gave him all the weapons he wanted. The CIA gave him maps so he could invade Iran."

"You didn't answer the question. You always go back to history. What do you do now that it's too late? There has to be a cut-off somewhere. Surely you cannot just let Saddam keep Kuwait?"

"But the bombing campaign isn't liberating Kuwait; it's destroying Iraq!"

"We all agree that war is bad, but don't you think it's necessary sometimes?" I ask. "Didn't Hitler have to be stopped, for example?"

"Not *you*, Lara! Don't tell me you've jumped on the World War II bandwagon? Saddam Hussein is not Hitler. Kuwait is not the Sudetenland or Poland. And John Major is definitely not Winston Churchill! All this rubbish about 'the allies'. Our politicians seem to think they are refighting the Second World War. It's obscene!"

At 4.30 on the morning of 13 February, two US Stealth bombers drop 2,000-pound bombs on the Amariya air raid shelter in Baghdad, killing at least 408 Iraqi civilians. It is the worst American atrocity of the war. In his briefing that evening, General Richard Neal, the US deputy director of operations, states that the bombing was deliberate and "legitimate", since the US believed the shelter was being used as a military bunker.

Robert and I are staying in the Hyatt in Riyadh, where Neal gives his briefing. Robert is enraged. While I pursue stories assigned by *Time* editors the following day, he meets a former US Air Force general who is now a senior targeting officer for the Royal Saudi Air Force, with access to all US photo reconnaissance and satellite imagery. The general is one of hundreds of whistleblowers who contact Robert over the years, because they know he dares to challenge authority.

"There's not a single soul in the American military who believes that this was a command-and-control bunker," the US general tells Robert. Iraqi military often bring their wives and children into bunkers with them. When that happens, the Americans do not hesitate to bomb them, the source says.

In the event, the shelter appears to have been purely civilian. The BBC reporter Jeremy Bowen visits it on 14 February and says there was no evidence of its use as a military shelter. General Neal says military signals came from the bunker. But Charles Heyman of Janes World Armies later reports that the signals in fact came from 270 metres away.

The women and children who sleep in the shelter are incinerated by the heat. Charred human hands are discovered fused to the ceiling. A woman known as Umm Greyda, who lost eight children in the bombing, moves into the destroyed shelter and becomes caretaker of the memorial. Photographs of many of the victims line the walls.

౸ə

On the day Robert files an exclusive story about the Amariya shelter bombing, based on his interview with the distraught American general in Riyadh, he finds time to think of me. We sleep badly at night because of the constant racket of US warplanes taking off and landing. I am exhausted, and I miss our cat Walter, who is being looked after by a cleaning lady in Beirut in our absence. Robert wants to cheer me up.

I return from my interviews around Riyadh to find a trail of love notes leading like stepping stones across the bedroom floor. Each note fills an A4 piece of paper. They say, all in capital letters: "LARA'S LOVER ADORES HER!"; "LARA IS THE BEST"; "LARA IS WONDERFUL; I LOVE LARA".

Unknown to me, Robert has borrowed the tiny photograph of Walter that I keep in my wallet. Our cat faces the camera, balanced elegantly on her two front paws. Her coat is shiny. Tiger stripes undulate down her body like bracelets or the rings of a tree. Walter's ears are pricked up, listening. Her yellow eyes stare and she has an almost human expression. One would swear she is smiling.

Robert has enlarged the picture many times on the hotel's photocopy machine. The next three stepping stones are one-page enlargements saying, "Hi, Valentine Girl; Happy Valentine's Day!" And "Be my Valentine – from your Bobby". The path culminates with a metre-high poster of Walter taped to the hotel room wall. It is perhaps 100 times the size of the original photo. Her ears, face, body and paws are Sellotaped together like a crazy quilt.

I've received many Valentine's Day chocolate boxes and bouquets over the years. But no gift ever gave me such pleasure, or made me laugh as hard, as finding Robert's blown-up portrait of Walter The Puss while US warplanes thundered overhead. It still makes me laugh today, three decades later.

VI

Kuwait, Kurdistan, Iraq: The Real War

This is war then: All is well.
The missiles bomb the cities and the airplanes
   bid the clouds farewell.
It is nothing but a corpse which grows and stretches...
Between time and time,
Between blood and blood.
All is well.

> Fadhil Al-Azzawi, from "Every Morning
> the War Gets Up from Sleep"

On 24 February 1991, General Schwarzkopf sends 100,000 troops into Kuwait and southern Iraq. The land war has finally started.

Iraq has been ravaged by nearly six weeks of bombing. The much-anticipated and equally dreaded ground war will last for only 100 hours. Robert hitches a lift to Khafji, on Saudi Arabia's border with Kuwait, courtesy of Sky News. There are dire predictions of the landmines, snipers and flaming oil-filled trenches that supposedly await us on our path to Kuwait City.

"My darling Lara," Robert writes to me from Khafji on 26 February, the eve of the liberation of Kuwait. He finds a journalist returning to Dhahran to bring his letter to me. "I miss you so much. I have been waiting for you here all day, numb and cold and longing to see you." My own lift to Khafji has fallen through. "I keep hearing your views on things (your voice often gives me a commentary on what I see) … Thank you, darling, for the sleeping bag and the cookies and newspapers …" He tells me about the cats in Khafji, "mighty beasts that purr round me in the night" and expresses anger that his article of the previous day was "pushed on to page 3 to make room for some bloody Riyadh briefing". He had never expected things to move so fast. "We can shortly fly out if they'll just decide to close down the war!"

News of the Iraqi rout begins to reach us. The war is obviously ending. I arrange to leave for Kuwait early the next morning with the Saudi army, to whom the Americans have given the dubious privilege of "liberating" Kuwait. Robert and I have agreed to meet in front of the Meridien Hotel in Kuwait City.

The Iraqis end their occupation with a frenzy of arson, looting, kidnapping and destruction. They position their old Soviet tanks in front of the parliament and the main hotels and fire shells at them. They burn down the national museum, the library of the Seif

Palace and Kuwait's collection of antique wooden dhows. They destroy the emir's Dasman palace with explosives and bulldozers, machine-gun the city's distinctive, Swedish-built water towers. Scores of buildings smoulder. Broken glass is scattered through streets and parking lots. Nearly every shop has been looted.

I ride into Kuwait in a convoy of Saudi and Kuwaiti tanks and armoured personnel carriers. We encounter no mines, no snipers, no burning trenches. Instead, the highway is flanked by thousands of joyous Kuwaitis, some weeping, others dancing. They chant "Allah Akbar", "USA! USA!" and "Thank you, thank you!" They wave so many black, green, white and red Kuwaiti flags that I wonder if they have spent the entire seven-month occupation sewing them in secret.

The overall impression is nonetheless sinister. Gunmen who claim to represent the Kuwaiti resistance prowl the streets and the city feels lawless. The Iraqis set fire to hundreds of oil wells, which burn like orange torches against the black line of the horizon. Smoke from the oil fires blocks the sunlight so it seems like evening at noon. The air smells of petrol. A greasy black film covers everything. "It's like nuclear winter," says the Saudi Public Affairs Officer who accompanies our convoy. "Now that Kuwait is free, it's not fit to live in."

I make my way to the Meridien Hotel for my rendezvous with Robert. The façade has been blown away. Bangladeshi employees living in the basement tell me how the Iraqis parked two tanks in front of the hotel and shelled it. I raise my eyes from my notebook to see Robert standing a few metres away, smiling. We rush towards each other and try to embrace, but our flak jackets clink like medieval suits of armour and we almost fall backwards.

Every Kuwaiti we meet knows of someone who was raped, kidnapped or murdered. In a bungalow used as a torture chamber, wires from a hand-cranked electrical generator are attached to a metal bed frame. The litany of atrocities is long: the Iraqis hanged a nineteen-year-old woman and dumped her body in front of her parents' house after they found two-way radios in her bedroom;

another Kuwaiti woman, who made several trips to Saudi Arabia to deliver information on Iraqi troop movements, had her head staved in with an axe and was shot repeatedly in the breasts and vagina; seven girls were raped and hanged in a schoolyard; eleven men at prayer in the Abdullah Othman mosque were lined up against a wall and shot dead because they refused to be taken to Iraq as hostages. A doctor at the Mubarak al-Kabeer hospital tells us that hundreds of women are seeking abortions after they were gang-raped by occupation forces.

Kuwaiti officials say they buried 2,792 Kuwaiti victims of violent death under Iraqi occupation at al-Riqqa cemetery. The ice rink, which was used as a temporary morgue, still stinks of death. Staff at the al-Sabah and Adnan hospitals say that every corpse in their morgues has been mutilated, some with holes drilled into their heads, shoulders, hands and feet.

The Kuwaitis want revenge. A resistance leader who calls himself Mike tells us about Mustafa al-Kubaisi, an Iraqi-born friend and neighbour who had joined his resistance group. Mike realised that Kubaisi was an informant, so he invited him to live in his house, to keep an eye on him. When Kuwait is liberated, Mike cooks a last meal for Kubaisi, then takes him outside and shoots him in the head. Mike says he knows of at least eighty "collaborators" who have been summarily executed since the Iraqis departed.

Colonel Mustafa Awadi of the Kuwaiti resistance movement takes Robert and me to a school in a housing estate in the suburb of Qurain. Sixteen Iraqi soldiers sit cross-legged on the floor. It is difficult to believe that these frightened, emaciated young men were part of such a brutal occupation force. At his press conferences, General Schwarzkopf told us the Iraqi army was ill-fed and terrorised by execution squads. It was all true. The prisoners have eaten only rice and bread made from sawdust for months. They tell us how the *qwat al-khasah*, a special operations unit, shot dead their twenty-three-year-old comrade Salaam when he tried to desert.

The story of Abbas, the Iraqi soldier who died for a drink of water, stays with me. Under many hours of sustained US bombardment, "Abbas kept complaining that he was thirsty", a prisoner called Mohamed recounts. "We said to him, 'Don't go out. It's too dangerous.' The water was kept in another shelter only ten metres away. Abbas ignored our warnings and a piece of shrapnel hit him in the head and killed him."

Saddam Hussein said he would withdraw Iraqi forces from Kuwait if Israel withdrew from the West Bank and the Gaza Strip. It was cheap posturing, but it struck a chord with millions of Arabs, and led the PLO to support Iraq. Some of the 300,000 Palestinians in the emirate helped occupation forces. A smaller number joined the Kuwaiti resistance.

In the days following the liberation, we hear rumours that hundreds of young Palestinian men are being kidnapped from their homes. So on 3 March, Robert and I go to the Palestinian quarter of Hawalli with Colin Smith from *The Observer*. The neighbourhood looks different from the rest of Kuwait City, poor and low to the ground, built with corrugated steel and cinder blocks, like Palestinian camps in the Levant.

"Death to Palestinian traitors. We don't want them" say graffiti on the walls of Hawalli. We stop a woman in the street, not knowing if she is Kuwaiti or Palestinian. "They are hypocrites!" Massmoa Hassan, a Kuwaiti, says. She raises her voice and shouts at the Palestinians around her. "We went to school with you. We helped you. The PLO donation boxes were filled by us. And you are traitors. Get out!"

Sarah Hamdan Salman, who is Palestinian, is distraught when she tells us how Kuwaiti gunmen blindfolded her three sons, handcuffed them and beat them with their guns before shoving them into the boots of cars. When she reported their kidnapping to the local police station, Salman says that police replied "You are Palestinian" and spat at her.

A Kuwaiti army patrol crosses the marketplace just as a Palestinian boy cycles by. Three Kuwaiti soldiers knock the boy off his bicycle and begin to beat him. Robert and Colin pull the soldiers off the boy. "Help us stop them!" we shout to the US special forces soldiers who accompany the Kuwaitis. One of the Americans stares at us blankly. Another laughs.

"These soldiers were beating a child!" Robert shouts at the Americans. "Do something."

"This is martial law, boy!" the laughing American shouts back. His Humvee drives away, following the guilty Kuwaitis.

I have my notebook and pen in hand. "Lara, get their number. Write down the number of their vehicle!" Robert shouts.

I make a note of the vehicle number, which we take to the US Embassy to make a complaint about the special forces unit. There we meet Fred Cuny, a tall, heavyset, balding Texan in jeans and cowboy boots whose emergency relief consultancy, Intertect, works for the US government, the UN and a variety of non-governmental organisations. Cuny and his employees refer to themselves as "masters of disaster".

Unlike the US military and diplomats, who talk about "Palestinian terrorists", Cuny takes the question of Kuwait's vendetta against the Palestinians seriously. At his initiative, a task force is set up to investigate the disappearances of Palestinians. Andrew Natsios, a former head of the US Agency for International Development, credits Cuny with saving many Palestinian lives.

In Kurdistan the following month, Cuny becomes the driving force behind the expansion of Operation Provide Comfort, the US-led relief effort to help more than two million Kurds who fled into Iran and Turkey when their rebellion failed. We run into Cuny again in Zakho, northern Iraq. "Hey you two, I owe you guys big time," he says, referring to our having alerted him to the persecution of Palestinians in Kuwait.

Cuny tells us that before the liberation, the Kuwaiti government made plans for the mass deportation and execution of Palestinians. In the months following the Gulf War, the Kuwaitis succeed in expelling about 200,000 Palestinians to Iraq, in Red Cross buses.

We see Cuny again two years later, in Sarajevo, where he

fills UN transport aircraft with relief aid and replaces the water treatment plant the Serbs have destroyed. His disdain for bureaucracy is well known. When we ask about EU support for Bosnia's beleaguered Muslims, he replies sarcastically, "The EU? What's that?"

In the early 1990s, Cuny is probably the world's best-known, most charismatic and effective advocate for war victims. His constant presence on the frontier between humanitarian and military intervention leads some to wonder if he is some kind of super-spy. As told in Scott Anderson's book *The Man Who Tried to Save the World*, Fred Cuny and three colleagues went missing in Chechnya in April 1995. The mystery of their death has never been resolved, though they are believed to have been murdered by Chechen or Russian forces.

❦

On 26 February, thousands of Iraqi troops flee Kuwait City in tanks, armoured personnel carriers, ambulances, buses, stolen fire trucks, taxis, limousines, and even in a bulldozer and milk vans. The Highway of Death begins just north of Kuwait City and continues for tens of kilometres, to a hill called Mutla Ridge, where the Americans wait for the retreating Iraqi army.

For four hours, Apache helicopters, A-10 "tank-busters" and other aircraft swoop down on what remains of the Iraqi army, killing some of their Kuwaiti hostages as well. The turkey shoot leaves more than a thousand Iraqis dead, sprawled across the asphalt highway, face down in the sand where they tried to run into the desert, carbonised in their vehicles. It is a massacre. Cheerful Kuwaitis drive up from Kuwait City to take photographs of them.

Strewn among the bodies is a phenomenal amount of loot: Persian carpets, jewellery, kitchen utensils, air conditioners, even Korans. Some of the car radios are still playing when we arrive on the scene of horror. Farther up the same highway, packs of wild dogs feast on Iraqi corpses, gulping down viscera, running across the desert with human limbs in their maws. "So this is Bush's New World Order," Robert says bitterly. He is haunted by the image. "If you'd seen what I've seen, dogs tearing bodies apart in the desert, you would never ever support a war," I hear him tell future lecture audiences.

The US photographer Ken Jarecke takes the photograph that should have symbolised the Gulf War, of an Iraqi soldier burned alive as he tries to climb through the broken windscreen of his truck. The man is transformed into ash and charcoal, the same black and rust colour as the metal truck. His sudden incineration preserves the rictus of death on the Iraqi's face. His right hand clutches the edge of the windscreen.

Jarecke later tells the *The Atlantic* magazine that he could "see clearly how precious life was to this guy, because he was fighting for it. He was fighting to save his life to the very end, till he was completely burned up. He was trying to get out of that truck."

The Observer and the French newspaper *Libération* run Jarecke's photo prominently on inside pages. But neither *Time* magazine, for whom Jarecke covered the war, nor any other US publication, publishes the photo, which comes to be known among photo editors as "Crispy".

Time magazine's spineless, unsigned article about the Highway of Death, written in New York, excuses the slaughter at Mutla Ridge, saying that "many a general has bitterly rued the day he let a beaten army get away to turn around and fight again ... war is hell".

We drive up and down the Highway of Death for days to come, to cover ceasefire negotiations. One begins to recognise specific bodies, loot and vehicles from previous journeys. The Red Crescent and some coalition units start burying the rotting corpses.

Schwarzkopf, Prince Khalid and eight Iraqi officers led by Lieutenant General Sultan Hashim Ahmad are negotiating the terms of the ceasefire in a tent at Safwan, on the Iraqi border, 125 kilometres north of Kuwait City. We stand in front of the negotiating tent at Safwan, within an arm's reach of the generals, watching their arrivals and departures.

Twice during the war, George H.W. Bush had appealed to "the Iraqi people to take matters into their own hands and force Saddam Hussein, the dictator, to step aside". When the Kurds and the Shia Muslims heed the US president's appeal at the end of the war, Saddam Hussein brutally represses their twin uprisings, with the tacit permission of the Americans.

In the ceasefire negotiations at Safwan, Schwarzkopf explicitly gives Iraqi forces permission to use their surviving helicopter gunships. Thus America betrays the Kurds and the Shia Muslims. The rebels are slaughtered in their thousands.

When the Americans and their rich Gulf Arab allies wanted to get rid of Saddam, they dreamed that a Sunni Arab general would stage a coup against him. But under Saddam's reign of terror, the slightest sign of disloyalty, real or imagined, leads to extermination. The last thing the Americans want is an Iraq dominated by Shia Muslims, the largest religious group, allied with Iran. Strangely, they no longer worry about empowering the Shia twelve years later, when George W. Bush's administration effectively gives Iraq to the pro-Iranian Shia.

Like the rest of the press corps, we want to witness at first-hand what the war and the rebellion have done to the biggest city in the Shia south. As I have recounted in the Prologue, some journalists have already reached Basra, and I am under pressure from New York to do the same. We weigh the wisdom of crossing the invisible demarcation line between the US-controlled zone and the rest of Iraq, which Saddam is struggling to keep hold of.

A US unit has parked its tank at a cloverleaf junction on the six-lane highway. We pause to talk to the African-American tank commander. "Just think of it," he says, surveying the dun grey expanse of desert around us. "They call this the cradle of civilisation."

Robert stares a long time at the empty highway to Basra. "I don't like this road," he says. "People go up it, but no one comes back." On returning to Kuwait City, we learn that all forty journalists who went to Basra have been seized by Saddam loyalists. They are sent to Baghdad and expelled a few days later.

While Robert and I ponder the road to Basra, we are approached by three Iraqi soldiers in camouflage uniforms. They walk slowly with their arms held out, to signify that they are not hostile and are not carrying weapons. *Marhaba*, we greet them. They ask for cigarettes. I offer my Marlboro Lights. (Robert never smokes.) In one of the more surreal moments of the Gulf War, the Iraqis ask my permission to move the Soviet-built lorry parked on the gravelly soil a few dozen metres away. Fine with me, I tell them. Let me ask the Americans.

"They can take their crap," the tank commander says. The Iraqis look relieved and drive away towards Basra. Robert and I later wonder if, in our small, inadvertent way, we have aided the suppression of the Shia rebellion.

᠁

Starting with the day of Kuwait's liberation, 27 February, Robert and I spend eleven nights in the International Hotel in Kuwait City. There is no electricity, other than that provided by small generators on the ground floor and in the *Time* photo editor's room. The water tanks are filled every second or third day and run out within hours. We hike up and down twelve flights of stairs to our room and scrounge rations off the military.

We also benefit from the generosity of a Kuwaiti family. On the day of our arrival, a large car pulls up beside us on the road outside the hotel. "Are you journalists?" a Kuwaiti woman asks. "Can you help me find my brother in Basra?"

Salwa and her husband Jassem, a retired Kuwaiti army officer, take us to their home, let us shower and then feed us. Salwa shows me photographs of her brother Faisal, a newspaper editor who is one of several thousand men kidnapped by the Iraqis in the last weeks of the occupation. Most were rounded up as they went to work in the morning, herded into buses and taken to a prison in Basra.

The flood of refugees from the Shia uprising starts the next day: women, children, Iraqi soldiers, foreign workers, all intent on reaching the safety of American lines. Salwa's younger sister Siham joins me and Robert in the hope of reaching Basra or finding Faisal among the human flotsam that flows towards Kuwait's border.

Siham helps us piece together the refugees' hair-raising stories. They speak of thousands of daily executions in Shia towns, of rebels being hanged from the gun barrels of tanks, of bound men lined up on the ground so tanks can roll over them. By the end of April, when Robert and I are in Kurdistan, there are more than 18,000 people living in two refugee camps run by the US military at Safwan.

Siham has left her businessman husband and children behind in London to look for Faisal. She remains cheerful despite her fears for her brother and the grim stories she translates for us. A practising Muslim, she is one of the kindest people I have ever met. She discreetly hands her own coat to a shivering Filipina maid who has been caught up in the cataclysm. She gives food and money to an elderly Egyptian, a former caretaker of a school in Kuwait City who has fashioned a makeshift hut beside the highway to shield himself from the rain. The Egyptian weeps as he tells us how he was kidnapped and taken to Basra. Now the Kuwaitis will not let him return.

Robert wakes me in the middle of the night on 8 March. "They're freeing the hostages! The Iraqis are freeing the hostages," he says. "AP will give us a lift. We're going. Now." There is no time to contact Siham.

A dozen coaches are parked in darkness at the border. The Red Crescent checks the names of hostages against a list. I mount the steps of every coach, peer into the tired, grimy faces of the hostages and shout, "Is Faisal al-Marzouk here?"

A man stands up in the back of the last bus and makes his

way towards me. He is unshaven and wears the clothes he was kidnapped in two weeks earlier. I do not recognise him from Salwa's photographs. "I am Faisal," he says.

"Faisal! I am a friend of Salwa and Jassem and Siham. They are looking for you! They are waiting for you. Come with me now. I will take you to them."

Faisal throws his arms around me, weeping. "No, I will stay with my fellow prisoners. We have to be processed. Please tell my family I will be home today."

A few hours later, I spot Siham in the crowd of journalists in front of the generals' tent at Safwan. She has hitched a ride up from Kuwait City. "Did you hear about Faisal?" I shout as I run towards her. I can tell from her puzzled expression that she has not. "Faisal is free! I saw him! Faisal is free!" I shout. Siham throws her arms around me, laughing, crying and shrieking with joy.

The television cameras rush towards this show of emotion, then quickly lose interest. The Red Cross takes Siham and me back to Kuwait City. I attend the Marzouk family's celebration feast that afternoon. Siham's goodness, and Faisal's safe return, are a drop of happiness in an ocean of misery, but they illuminate the end of the war for me.

ॐ

Up to two-thirds of Iraq's 3.5 million Kurds are believed to have fled to neighbouring Iran and to the high mountains on the border with Turkey, to escape Saddam's vengeance for their failed rebellion. Television pictures of Kurdish children dying of hunger and exposure provoke an international outcry. American and British leaders are criticised for abandoning the Kurds.

"I don't recall asking the Kurds to mount this particular revolution," Prime Minister John Major snidely tells ITN on 4 April 1991. Robert is furious. For months to come, he repeats Major's quote, imitating the Tory leader's whiny voice.

In late April, the US and UK mount a month-long airlift,

headquartered on the plain in the northern Iraqi border town of Zakho, to drop food, water, tents and blankets to the Kurdish refugees who are dying in the mountains. Robert and I fly to Ankara and Diyarbakir, in south-east Turkey, en route for Zakho. The majority of Diyarbakir's residents are Kurdish, many of them sympathetic to the separatist Kurdistan Workers' Party or PKK, which Ankara considers to be a terrorist group. Diyarbakir is a tense place at the best of times.

Robert brings along a book on Armenian history, and is delighted when he finds this quote by Winston Churchill about Diyarbakir: "The dogs are black, the walls of the city are black and the hearts of the people are black."

We hire a driver and head for the Iraqi border. The hotels are mostly filthy truck stops, and they are all full. A priest we meet in a restaurant gives us a note to recommend us to his parishioners in an ancient Syriac Christian village. It is late at night. Our driver is attempting to negotiate the rutted mountain track when we are blinded by a spotlight. Armed men are running towards us. "Turn off the headlights. Turn on the ceiling light," Robert orders the driver. He does so and gets out of the car with his hands in the air.

The gunmen are Turkish special forces. Robert jumps out of the car and shakes the officer's hand. "Do you *know* about this part of Turkey?" the officer asks, in English, alluding to the "Kurdish problem". We continue on to the village.

Knowing Lebanese Christians, I have imagined a monastery with whitewashed rooms and vaulted ceilings at the end of our long trek. The home of the parishioners turns out to be a small, unventilated room above a stable, which one reaches by ladder. The family sleep lined up on straw mattresses on the floor. We share no common language – they speak Aramaic, the language of Christ – but make us understand we are to squeeze in among them.

"We always sleep outside at home," I say repeatedly in several languages. I finally convince them to allow us to sleep on the adjacent wooden terrace. They drag out a mattress and piles of blankets. I can smell and hear the livestock beneath us. Robert and I sleep soundly under the stars in the wilds of Turkish Kurdistan. I am awoken in the morning by a chicken walking over me. The family serve us mugs of scalding tea; thick, spongey bread cooked in a stone oven on the terrace; and boiled eggs. I realise it is my thirty-fourth birthday, and I am happy.

Robert produces a Garfield the cat birthday card. It reminds me of the hostages in Lebanon, because Terry Anderson's eldest daughter, Gabrielle, likes Garfield and Robert often posts such cards to her in Japan, where she lives with her mother.

We find American soldiers – some of whom we recognise from south-eastern Iraq – setting up tent encampments around Zakho. They have food and supplies aplenty, but no refugees. The US has imposed a no-fly zone over northern Iraq and has banned Iraqi troops from the protected zone.

Saddam regards the entire country as his personal property. He has several palaces in Kurdistan and is determined to regain control of the area. Out of respect for Iraqi "sovereignty", the Americans agreed to allow policemen to stay. So Saddam sends hundreds of policemen – in fact soldiers – into Zakho in anticipation of the Kurds' return. Hundreds more *mukhabarat* or secret police pretend to be Iraqi civilians. They follow us around Zakho and hover within earshot when we attempt to interview local residents. Even the US soldiers are spooked by the gun-toting "policemen". The Americans hear shooting at night and stay in their encampments. The Kurds have experienced a dozen years of chemical attacks, rape, torture and murder at the hands of Saddam's henchmen. They refuse to come down from the mountains while Saddam's forces remain in Zakho and other Kurdish towns.

Robert and I commute for two days and nights between Zakho and the Turkish town of Nusaybin, where we have found a hotel room. As I mentioned in the Prologue, I call the *Time* magazine news desk from the PTT office on the Habur Bridge between Iraq and Turkey. They tell me that my visa has come through for

Baghdad. My first trip to Kurdistan has barely started before it is over.

Robert and I drive the 285 kilometres back to Diyarbakir. We find a room at the Hotel Büyük Kervansaray, which fulfils my dream of white walls and vaulted ceilings. Conditions are rudimentary, but I am enchanted by this converted medieval inn with arched arcades. It is packed with journalists covering the Kurdish story. We compare notes over meals in the courtyard restaurant. I have to wait for a flight to Ankara, so Robert and I do something unusual: we take a day off. When Robert dies in 2020, I ask myself what was our happiest day. I remember the 28th of April 1991.

I can always find a reason to be unhappy. My widowed mother, handicapped sister and fundamentalist Christian upbringing. The Holocaust. The tragedy of the Palestinians. Arabs living under cruel dictatorship. The cavalier way my own country bombs civilians. Existential angst. The simple fact that, as Camus wrote, "*Les hommes meurent et ils ne sont pas heureux*" – men die and they are not happy. I tend to complain about early mornings and late nights, grotty hotels and filthy toilets, stroppy editors and the stress of deadlines. "Life is *good*, Lara. Life is a gift," Robert insists when he sees that little black cloud forming above my head.

There is usually an explanation for unhappiness, if only *le vague à l'âme*, whereas happiness is something of a mystery. On that sunny spring day in Diyarbakir, we ask the hotel to prepare a picnic lunch which we later consume on the grass beneath the city's fourth-century Roman walls, overlooking the Tigris. They are the widest, longest defensive walls in the world after the Great Wall of China, and are built of volcanic basalt stone. As Winston Churchill wrote, and to Robert's delight, they are black. I am not sure if this really was my happiest day. Memory embellishes. But on 28 April 1991, I feel loved, our life is filled with adventure, and that is enough.

En route for Baghdad via Ankara, Beirut and Amman the next

day, I find a small piece of lined paper from a reporter's notebook in my bag. It reads: "Diyarbakir 29/4/91, My Darling, this is just to tell you that I love you more than ever. You are always with me and I am always with you. From your adoring tigre."

Robert keeps our room at the Kervansaray so he can accompany US military relief flights taking off from the Turkish airbase there. On 29 April, the day I leave for Baghdad, he is shunted by mistake onto an Apache helicopter filled with CIA men bound for a refugee camp at Yasilova, high in the mountains on Turkey's border with Iraq. When the chopper lands, he learns that American agents have been working with a unit of British Royal Marines there for the past week, in the hope of stopping the depredations of their Turkish NATO allies.

"The Turkish soldiers have been stealing the refugees' food and blankets, so we had to stop this and we've been standing off, locked and loaded, ever since," Surgeon Lieutenant Peter Davis of the Royal Marine Mountain and Arctic Warfare Cadre tells Robert. The British want to evacuate all 3,000 refugees from the camp, but the Turks refuse to let them fly out.

The British and Americans would rather load supplies back onto a Chinook helicopter than allow the Turks to seize any more donated aid. For once, the British are happy to have Robert as a witness. "The Turkish soldiers here are shit," an angry British captain tells him. "They take whatever they want. One of them said to me: 'It's better to starve the Kurds – that way, we can control them'."

Robert's story appears on the front page of *The Independent* the following morning, 30 April. Two plain-clothes Turkish policemen in black leather jackets call at the Kervansaray that evening to take him to the police station. He is questioned until 4.45 in the morning about his alleged defamation of the Turkish army. If convicted, Robert risks up to ten years in prison. But faced with his devastating evocation of the army's "betrayal of the principles of Mustafa Kemal Atatürk", the Turks prefer to deport him.

By mid-May, we are both back in Beirut. We want to return

to Kurdistan, but Robert cannot go through Turkey. Thus begins one of our more incredible journeys.

The Kurds live astride four countries: Iran, Iraq, Syria and Turkey. They do not recognise the borders that separate them from their fellow Kurds. Robert knows how bad Syria's relations with both Iraq and Turkey are, and that Syrian military intelligence cultivates warm relations with the Kurds of north-eastern Syria to needle the Iraqi and Turkish authorities.

Robert correctly surmises that Syria is the surest way for us to reach Kurdistan. The Syrian information minister, Mohamed Salman, tells us to take a bus 680 kilometres to Qamishli, on Syria's border with Turkey. We are to go to the Hedaya Hotel and ask for Colonel Mohamed Mansour, the head of Syrian army intelligence in the area.

At dawn on 25 May, a plain-clothes Syrian agent drives us from the Hedaya to the banks of the Tigris. A man rows across from the Iraqi side to fetch us, his oars lapping gently in the water. The scene is idyllic, but my mind is racing, considering everything that can go wrong. I feel confident I can swim across the Tigris if the boat sinks. Only the loss of my Toshiba laptop would be irreparable.

Kurdish Peshmerga fighters wait for us on the opposite shore. One points at my computer, which I wear the way they wear their assault rifles, strapped diagonally across my chest. "*Sahafiya Peshmerga,*" he says, laughing. Guerrilla journalist. He has understood that language is our weapon.

For the next ten days, Robert and I live almost like refugees, sleeping in the tents of various relief groups, hitching lifts by road and helicopter to the far-flung villages and towns of Batifa, Sersink and Amedi.

In Dohuk, 60 kilometres south of Zakho, we visit a large, two-storey stucco villa with rose bushes in the front garden. Until the Peshmerga and local inhabitants stormed it a few days earlier, it was *mukhabarat* headquarters. A thick steel door to the right of the villa opens onto a damp staircase leading to the dungeon where Saddam's secret police kept the pretty young Kurdish women they had kidnapped. "This is where they raped women," Tassin Kemek, a local Peshmerga leader, tells us. Stained mattresses, dirty blankets, women's clothing and piles of excrement are scattered through the cellar, which is divided into small cells and a few larger rooms.

The Kurdish women left messages on the walls of their cells. "I am going to die. Please tell the others," one wrote above a drawing of a rose. A woman called Nadira wrote: "This is my fate." Another young woman pencilled a self-portrait in a high-collared blouse, showing her long hair and big eyes. "We found three naked bodies with their hands bound," Kemek says. "The youngest was only twelve years old."

That afternoon, we interview US General Jay Garner, commander of 15,000 coalition soldiers in Operation Provide Comfort. We will meet Garner again, in the immediate aftermath of the 2003 Iraq war, when he will briefly head reconstruction efforts in Baghdad.

Garner makes it clear that peace between the Kurds and Saddam is Washington's strategy for ending the crisis. America's Turkish allies do not want any more Kurdish refugees, and the US would like to abandon the costly rescue operation. "The Kurds were dying four hundred a day in the Turkish mountains," Garner says. "They weren't Turkish citizens so something had to happen. Now their own leaders are close to signing an agreement with Saddam."

The Iraqis and Peshmerga have fought each other to a standstill. They have no choice but to make peace, for the time being. In late April, the Kurdish leader Jalal Talabani – who will in 2005 become Iraq's first post-Saddam president – travelled to Baghdad with the leaders of three other Kurdish groups, to the relief of the Americans. All four kiss the dictator who has gassed and massacred their people.

The Americans want the Kurds to come down from the mountains and inhabit the refugee camps US troops have built on the lowlands. To this end, the Americans have expelled most of the fake policemen we encountered in Zakho. The strategy is beginning to work. "We never signed up to be a North Iraq security force," Garner says. "I don't think the Kurds will go back to the mountains unless they're under attack. And if they are, that's a problem for the United Nations."

We hear similar rhetoric four days later from General Colin Powell, at the airport which Saddam built in Sersink so he could visit his hilltop palace. Powell is already beginning to talk like the Secretary of State he will become a decade later. He studiously avoids the name "Saddam Hussein" and speaks of "the Iraqi government". The murderous regime that invaded Kuwait has apparently been transformed into a legitimate body. The man Bush regarded as "worse than Hitler" has become the least bad of bad choices, for the time being.

The Kurds know better. In a dramatic reversal of the familiar cry of "Yankee, Go Home", they demonstrate in front of US military installations chanting "Stay, stay". A few hundred UN guards are supposed to replace the 12,000 US troops in Operation Provide Comfort. The Kurds have no confidence in the UN.

"If the Americans go, we will go with them," a Kurdish refugee called Zuleikha Mustafa Ahmad tells me in the tent she inhabits in Zakho with her four surviving children and her in-laws. They had fled a previous refugee camp when the Peshmerga rose up in March, and spent 35 days in the mountains. "Even if the United Nations stays here, we will still go with the Americans, because only America is merciful," Zuleikha says.

Saddam violated all previous agreements with the Kurds. To hear Zuleikha's tragic story is to understand why the Kurds cannot trust Saddam. The mother of six children was married at age fourteen and looks far older than her twenty-five years. As he was beaten and dragged away by Iraqi secret police in Dohuk in August 1988, Zuleikha's husband, Musa Issa Haji, shouted to her: "Take care of my children. If they kill me it doesn't matter, as long as my children are living." Now he visits her in her sleep, not to comfort but to reproach her. "You didn't take care of your children. That is why they died," he tells her.

Musa's disappearance was part of Saddam's Anfal campaign, which retook large parts of Kurdistan held by the Peshmerga. The Iraqis used chemical weapons to depopulate the area, destroyed 4,000 villages and moved in Arab settlers. The Iraqis are believed to have executed 8,000 Kurdish men in Anfal, including Zuleikha's husband. Kurdish leaders say Iraqi forces buried most of the 8,000 men alive, some with their heads above ground so the mass graves could be found later.

The nerve gas came soon after the mass executions. The Kurds would go out into the countryside each morning before the aerial bombardments started. Zuleikha and her children were on a hill about a kilometre from their village when Iraqi aircraft flew over. "We smelled something strange coming with the wind. It looked like smoke, and it had a nice smell, like medicine. The small children's eyes watered. Many who were nearer died."

Zuleikha's two youngest sons, Sarbaz, aged four, and Saleh, one, suffered diarrhoea and vomiting after the gas attack. They turned black in hospital and died later in a refugee camp. She would not be able to find their graves now.

Zuleikha is one of the saddest people I have ever met. When her daughter was born eight months after Musa was taken away, she named the little girl Dilmun, Kurdish for sad heart. "I am living just to raise my children, that is all," she tells me.

ℬ

Baghdad airport is closed because of economic sanctions, so the only way to reach the Iraqi capital is to fly to Amman, stay overnight in a hotel, and hire a four-wheel drive vehicle for the trek across the desert. Eastern Jordan looks as if some divine entity emptied millions of lorryloads of stones there. One half-expects to see John the Baptist wandering in animal skins, or Satan taunting Christ to transform stones into bread.

Aside from queuing at the Jordanian and Iraqi border posts, there is nothing but ugly, flat, dun-coloured monotony for another ten hours. The highway is Iraq's only link to the outside world and it is busy. Three hundred lorries ferry supplies from Amman to Baghdad each day. A comparable number carry bartered Iraqi petrol out of the country.

By chance, I meet the UN special representative for Iraq, Berndt Bernander, as I am checking into the Al Rasheed Hotel on 2 May 1996 and invite him to dinner. I don't know yet that everyone changes money at black-market rates, so the meal costs *Time* magazine more than $700 at the official rate. It is money well spent, since Bernander invites me and Lilli Gruber, a flamboyant Italian television journalist and future member of the European Parliament, to join him for an all-day helicopter tour of southern Iraq, with stops at the provincial capitals of Basra, Kut and Amarah.

Thanks to the UN trip, I am able to see the damage done by the bombers I watched taking off from Bahrain and Saudi Arabia, and by the Shia uprising. We fly low over desert that looks like the surface of the moon, crisscrossed by thousands of berms and trenches that are cratered by innumerable bombs. In Basra, the great rusting hulks of Iraq's merchant navy list at the quayside in the Shatt al-Arab River, next to luxuriant palm groves. It's an image worthy of a García Márquez novel, magical realism in the Persian Gulf. The ships have been grounded since Saddam invaded Iran in 1980.

Pedestrians try to keep their balance as they cross rivers on pontoon passageways. Parallel to them, steel reinforcement rods protrude from the broken stubs of concrete that were the original bridges. I try to distinguish between the destruction wreaked by the coalition's aerial bombardment and that done by automatic weapons and tank fire during the uprising. Provincial governors complain bitterly. In Kut, the governor of Wasit Province hands me a white photo album with "Memory of Wedding" embossed in gold on the front cover, filled with snapshots of bomb damage. The lack of potable water is the biggest problem, because the coalition bombed pumping stations. Iraqis are drinking from irrigation ditches and rivers. Typhoid, dysentery and cholera are spreading.

Officials have banned black flags and the distribution of paper death notices, in order to make the scale of Shia deaths in the uprising less noticeable. The consequences of the rebellion are nonetheless visible. Hundreds of Shia women wait outside Basra's main prison. They raise crossed wrists when we drive past, to signal the incarceration of their men.

Since the war ended, Saddam has visited the Sunni Muslim Baathist heartland only. At a rally in Mosul, he repeatedly fired a pistol into the air. The footage is shown over and over on Iraqi television.

On my way to Baghdad, I dined with a British expert in Amman who told me that Saddam's downfall was imminent. It doesn't take long to realise he was wrong. The tyrant remained firmly in power for another twelve years. I will hear similar mistaken predictions of the fall of Syrian President Bashar al-Assad from French diplomats in Damascus in 2006, and from most of the Syrian "experts" when the civil war starts in 2011. It is hard to kill an Arab dictator.

Saddam's regime is striving to restore a semblance of normality in Baghdad, where there is water, electricity and endless traffic jams. The coalition destroyed several bridges over the Tigris, and quite a few government buildings, but damage is less dramatic than in the south. Lorries from Amman have filled shops with food that is plentiful but too expensive for most Iraqis.

Every Thursday night, there are dozens of wedding parties at the Al Rasheed Hotel. My colleagues claim the *mukhabarat* have placed cameras inside the television sets at the foot of each bed, and that they can watch newlyweds on their wedding nights. Saddam's Iraq is a country of spies and informants. The sense of being under constant surveillance can be unnerving. I throw a blanket over the television in my room, in case the camera story is true.

The inhabitants of most Middle East countries are reluctant to talk to foreigners, but only in Saddam's Iraq have I seen people recoil in terror when I try to speak to them. In a hospital in Basra, I ask a mother who sits beside her dying infant what happened when the war ended. "She cannot answer a question like that with all these people around," the government interpreter says to me. "Look at the pain in her eyes and you will see the answer."

I visit Saddam City, the Shia slums of Baghdad. An Iraqi army source tells me that during the war the army cordoned off the suburb and ransacked every house for weapons, killing 200 people in the process. When I ask the headmistress of a girls' school an innocuous question about everyday life in Iraq, she replies: "Go away. It is dangerous for us and it is dangerous for the school."

Attempting to glean information about anti-Saddam demonstrations which took place in Baghdad at the time of the Kurdish and Shia uprisings, I try my luck with a Baghdad taxi driver. "You cannot ask such questions in this country," he says. "If I talk to you, the police will come and..." He slices a finger across his throat.

The ministry of information tells us we are free to work without government "minders", to go anywhere we want to in Iraq. We know it won't last, so Trudy Rubin of the *Philadelphia Inquirer* and I set off with a driver on 6 May for the Shia holy cities of Najaf and Karbala. We ring the bell outside the home of Grand Ayatollah Sayyid Abul Qasim al-Khoei, the spiritual leader of the world's Shia Muslims.

Khoei's son opens the gate a few inches. "Go away, please," he whispers. He is trembling. But other journalists interviewed the Ayatollah, we say. "Yes, and after they left, the police came and it was worse... Please go away and don't come back. Ten of our family and dozens of my father's followers are in prison."

I am not sure which of the Ayatollah's two sons I spoke to that day. One son, Mohammed Taqi al-Khoei, dies in a suspicious late-night car crash on the road from Karbala three years later.

Abdul Majid al-Khoei is shot and hacked to death near the Imam Ali shrine in Najaf on 10 April 2003, the day after the fall of Saddam Hussein.

The Shia imams Hussein and Abbas were killed at Karbala in 680 AD. The 1991 uprising echoes that first great battle between the two main factions of Islam. Shia rebels murdered those associated with Saddam's regime as mercilessly as the regime murdered them. The rebels hanged dozens of government officials from chandelier hooks in an anteroom of the shrine to Imam Abbas, and from lampposts outside the shrine to Imam Hussein. When they retook the city, the Republican Guard found piles of severed heads in the library next to the mosque of Imam Ali. "Death to Saddam Hussein" was written in blood on the library wall.

The Republican Guards who fired tank shells at the gold-domed mosques are now garrisoned in the anterooms of the shrines. They greet Trudy and me cheerily. We pick our way through the debris carpeting the esplanade. It seems absurd to care about material destruction amid so much human suffering, but I cannot help noticing the broken pieces of exquisite, hand-painted Islamic tiles that litter the ground. A solitary woman in black robes walks past us, carrying groceries in a string bag. She lifts her skirts with one hand to negotiate the rubble. There are holes in her dusty black shoes. Tears flow down her cheeks.

On the way back to Baghdad, we stop to visit the ruins of Babylon. During the war with Iran, Saddam portrayed himself as the reincarnation of Nebuchadnezzar II, the sixth-century BC King of Babylon. Saddam built a kitsch, Disneyland-style version of the ancient city, in yellow brick trimmed with bright blue and gold. He had every brick stamped with the words: "In the reign of the victorious Saddam Hussein ... the rebuilding of the great city of Babylon was done in 1987." The ruins are empty, overgrown with weeds and inhabited by lizards.

I pay my first courtesy call on Naji al-Hadithi, former professor of English literature at Baghdad University, deputy minister of information and editor of the *Baghdad Observer*, the English-language propaganda sheet that is so bad that Robert always jokes that he wants to buy it so he can shut it down, along with the *Syria Times* in Damascus.

Naji is an affable, distinguished-looking man who speaks near-perfect English. Over the years, Robert and I will meet him many times. Each visit is the same. Naji plays Beethoven very loudly on the stereo. When one asks an awkward question, he looks pointedly at Saddam's portrait on the wall opposite and nods, as if to say, "Ask him", or "He is listening".

Naji is the subject of much gossip among journalists. One story says that he was called back from his post at the Iraqi embassy in London after two of his brothers were arrested for plotting against Saddam. Some say his brother, or brothers, were executed. He allegedly told the dictator, "If he betrayed you, *Raïs* (President), he deserved to die a hundred times". Others say Naji is a CIA agent, the Americans' mole in Baghdad.

Two years later, Robert and I will invite Naji, his wife and their four children to dinner in the garden restaurant of the Palestine Hotel. When his family get up to serve themselves at the buffet, Naji seems to confirm that he is Saddam's hostage. "One wants to do something for these children… They make sure the whole family is never outside at the same time," he says to us softly.

Naji is appointed Saddam's foreign minister in 2001. He uses a different version of his name now, Naji Sabri. As foreign minister, he lobbies Russia, China, India, Iran and the UN on behalf of Saddam, in the hope of preventing the 2003 invasion of Iraq.

When the 2003 war starts, Naji dons the olive-green uniform worn by Saddam's cabinet ministers. He greets me and Robert warmly on his arrival at a press conference. His performance is full of bluster and loyalty to the dictator. It is the last time we see him. Though Baghdad and the highway to Amman are under continuous bombardment, Naji somehow makes it to Damascus, then Cairo. US networks later report that he gave the CIA information about Saddam's weapons programmes. After the fall of Saddam, Naji reportedly established a consultancy firm in Qatar. I wonder how the CIA could have infiltrated the government of such a brutal and paranoid dictator. I also wonder what happened to Naji's wife and children. And how he himself survived.

ℱ

For the rest of the world, the Gulf War ended in the spring of 1991. For Iraqis, it continues in the form of hunger and impoverishment, sporadic cruise missile and air strikes by the US and UK, and an epidemic of cancer, which may be caused by the Gulf War coalition's use of depleted uranium weapons.

In June 1993, Bill Clinton orders the launch of twenty-three Tomahawk cruise missiles from US ships in the Persian Gulf and Red Sea on Iraqi intelligence headquarters in the Mansour district of Baghdad. Eight civilians are killed, including a much-loved Iraqi painter, Leila Attar, and her husband. Clinton says he has "compelling evidence" that Iraqi intelligence plotted to assassinate former President George H.W. Bush when he visited Kuwait two months earlier to receive thanks for ending Iraq's occupation of the emirate. Robert later attends the appeal trial of thirteen men convicted of planning to kill Bush. He finds the evidence unconvincing.

Abu Khaled, a gallery owner who worked with Leila Attar for twenty years, prints 6,000 copies of a poster saying "The Americans murdered Leila Attar". When I leave Iraq six days after the 1993 cruise missile attack, the immigration officer looks at my passport and sneers. "USA," he says. "Did you go to Mansour?" Before I can tell him "Yes, I saw the damage done by the cruise missiles. I wrote about the civilian victims", he spits on my passport.

In October 1994, the Clinton administration says Iraq is building up troops on the Kuwaiti border. We rush to Baghdad again, arriving bleary-eyed from the overnight journey to see the crisis dissipate as suddenly as it had started.

Robert and I make the twelve-hour trek from Amman to Baghdad again on 22 February 1998, to cover the latest showdown between Saddam and UN weapons inspectors. This time it is about the United Nations Special Commission's right to enter Saddam's palaces. The US has amassed 30,000 servicemen, two aircraft carriers, eighteen battleships and 176 aircraft in the Persian Gulf, and threatens to attack Iraq. The *New York Times* predicts that a four-day bombardment will kill 1,500 civilians.

Before leaving Amman, we load the four-wheel drive vehicle with bottled water, fruit, biscuits and processed cheese, in case we have to cover another Gulf War. Highway robberies have become so common that it is no longer safe to make the journey at night. Our driver points out the stretch of road where a Jordanian diplomat was recently robbed and shot dead.

Seven years of economic sanctions have transformed Iraq into a nation of beggars and thieves. On arrival in Baghdad, a pack of street urchins try to tear off the reporter's bag I wear slung across my chest. Robert helps me fight them off. Every day, beggars materialise out of nowhere, barefoot and clad in rags. A woman, old man and child peer through our car window when we slow to enter traffic on the Qadisiya Highway. Years later, I think of them when I see Picasso's painting "The Tragedy" in the National Gallery in Washington. They raise hands to their mouths, to show they are hungry. In Rasheed Street, a little girl pounds on the taxi window with a grimy fist. I lower the glass to slip her a 250 dinar note, worth about ten cents. A dozen children swoop down on her, knock her to the ground and fight for the money. The dinar is so devalued that the few shops and restaurants that remain open weigh piles of banknotes rather than count them.

UNICEF says a quarter of Iraqi children under age six – one million children – are malnourished. And 330,000 of them suffer from wasting malnutrition, which causes spindly limbs and swollen bellies. Child mortality has increased eightfold compared to pre-Gulf War statistics. In May 1996, CBS *60 Minutes* anchor Lesley Stahl asks Madeleine Albright, then US ambassador to the

United Nations, "We have heard that half a million children have died [because of sanctions]. I mean, that's more children than died in Hiroshima. And, you know, is the price worth it?"

"I think this is a very hard choice, but the price, we think, the price is worth it," Albright replies.

In Basra in February 1998, we watch women in black chadors and children in rags picking through rubbish piles in the Shia slum of Dour She'oun, searching for anything that can be eaten, burned as fuel or sold for a few dinars. The sun bleaches everything to a dirty, pale grey. On the periphery of this wasteland stand rows of breeze-block and corrugated steel shacks. Fetid troughs of frothy green sewage flow down the alleyways between the hovels.

Thirty-three-year-old Sundus Abdel-Kader shows me two cellophane baggies in the folds of her chador. They contain a few hundred grams of sugar and flour. "I am going to make cake. We will have cake and tea for dinner. Nothing else," she says. "This cost 750 dinars, the most my husband can earn in a day."

Sundus has four children. All of them are hungry. The family of six were given 250 grams of mutton during Ramadan the previous month, the last time they tasted meat. A girl breaks away from a crowd of playing children and runs to us. "This is my daughter, Roula. She is eight years old," Sundus says. The little girl smiles with bright eyes and I tell her mother that she is pretty. Sundus's gentle face breaks into a proud smile. She hesitates. "Roula is my healthiest child. Take her with you. Please take her with you to Europe. She will be better off there."

I glance at Robert. He knits his brow and shakes his head almost imperceptibly, as if to say, "Don't even think about it." You know a country's situation is truly desperate when people try to give you their children. Haiti and Iraq are the only places where this has happened to me.

Sundus's neighbour breaks in. "No, take my children. Take mine instead." She shoves a piece of fading cardboard at me. It is written in English by a French or Italian doctor and says that one of the woman's children died of muscular dystrophy. Now two others suffer from the genetic disease. "When are you going to lift *al hisar*?" a third woman pleads. *Al hisar*, the sanctions, is a word known to every Iraqi. It means "encirclement" as well as "embargo" and accurately conveys their feeling of being surrounded by a hostile world.

UN resolutions say that Iraq must destroy all weapons of mass destruction for sanctions to be lifted, but the Clinton administration keeps raising the bar. Washington has extended requirements to include respect for human rights and the departure of Saddam Hussein.

The February 1998 crisis is the worst in seven years. UN Secretary General Kofi Annan travels to Baghdad to negotiate with Saddam and his foreign minister, Tariq Aziz. Annan defuses the situation. Robert and I admire his dignified calm at his Baghdad press conference. We imitate Annan's Ghanaian accent with affection and make him a hero of our unpublished children's book, *The Adventures of Mus and Malv*.

We call on Denis Halliday, the UN Humanitarian Coordinator for Iraq. Halliday, who is Irish, will resign seven months later, after a thirty-four-year career at the UN, saying he can no longer be complicit in what he calls "genocidal sanctions" and "the collective punishment" of the people of Iraq.

The Clinton administration thinks sanctions will force the Iraqis to overthrow Saddam Hussein. On the contrary, Halliday tells us; sanctions have increased dependency on the regime, because the population rely on the government for the little food and clothing they receive. Saddam and his entourage are not affected by sanctions, but ordinary Iraqis suffer terribly. "When people are hungry, they are not interested in changing the system," he says. "They are interested in survival."

The oil-for-food programme that Halliday administers generates only $78 per Iraqi per year for food and medicine, he tells us; "very small money". On Halliday's initiative, the Security Council has just agreed to double the amount of petroleum Iraq is allowed to sell.

Cancer patients are dying for want of medicine, so Halliday enlists the help of a colleague at the World Health Organization to obtain medicine from Jordan and Turkey for four children on the leukaemia ward of Saddam Hussein City Hospital. "You cannot get involved with people in their thousands," he says, "but I got involved with those four kids." He took presents to the hospital for them at Christmas and learned that two of the four had already died.

The following day, we go to see eighty-one-year-old Sohad Munir Abbas, the widow of an Iraqi diplomat whom we know through friends in Beirut. Sohad lives with her sister Naira in a simple but tasteful villa on the banks of the Tigris. Their home is an oasis of culture and tranquillity. We call on them every time we visit Baghdad.

Over coffee at Sohad and Naira's, we begin to realise the extent of the cancer surge. "It would not be an exaggeration to say that 40 per cent of Iraqis have cancer," Naira says. "She has breast cancer," she adds, pointing at another guest called Murtaza. "Her husband and brother and a cousin died of cancer last year."

Murtaza is dressed in black, including the turban she wears to conceal her head, which is bald from chemotherapy. "Five people in my family have died of cancer," she says. "I don't know what is causing this. We think it's the bombs the Americans dropped in the Gulf War."

Murtaza's brother in Canada and sister in London sent her the $1,000 she needed for cancer treatment in India, the only country to which Iraqis can travel without a visa. "Imagine, we were a rich country and our relatives have to send us money! We used to send money to them." Now she cannot afford to travel to Amman for follow-up treatment.

At the Mansour Paediatric Hospital in Baghdad and the Saddam Teaching Hospital in Basra, we meet heroic, despairing doctors and relatives, and dozens of patients who have been condemned to die by sanctions and contamination from Gulf War weapons. The coalition fired tonnes of depleted uranium, which is used to harden armour-piercing projectiles. When the shells explode, uranium is dispersed, contaminating the target and surrounding area.

Five-year-old Latif Abdul Sattar plays with a fire truck on the floor of the Mansour Hospital corridor. The little boy has no hair, following two rounds of chemotherapy for non-Hodgkin's lymphoma. His father, Abdel Sattar, has already spent 300,000 dinars, the equivalent of 100 months of his salary as a hospital administrator, on treatment. Latif's mother sold her jewellery and the family's linen. "I have seen families sell everything in their house, even their beds," Dr Ali Ismail says. "And then the child dies anyway... In Europe or America, patients with this type of cancer are 100 per cent cured. I would rate Latif's chances of survival at 50 per cent, depending on the availability of drugs."

Robert, Alex Thomson of Channel 4 and I travel to Basra, because the largest proportion of cancer victims come from south-eastern Iraq, the battle zone in 1991. There is standing room only in the waiting room of Dr Jawad Kadhim al-Ali, the chief cancer specialist in Basra. Dr Ali, a slightly built man with thinning hair and a droopy moustache, is a member of the British Royal College of Physicians. He is treating 765 people for cancer, quadruple his caseload before the Gulf War.

Fawzia al-Bader, a fifty-one-year-old Shia Muslim teacher, pulls up her blouse to show us the vertical scar on the right side of her chest, despite the presence of western men and Alex's television camera, as if her mutilation made traditional modesty unnecessary. "Four years ago, they removed my right breast," Bader says. She has suffered three relapses and pulls down her collar to show us a recent incision on her neck, where more tumours were removed. "I have pain here now," she says, holding a hand to her left breast. Dr Ali says Bader's double cancer is unusual. He is seeing breast cancer in women younger than age twenty.

Bader knows she is going to die. The fate of her two young sons is her greatest worry. "I am thinking all the time about what

I can give them to eat," she says. "Please help us. We are human beings. We have a heart. We have families."

Dr Ali believes depleted uranium contaminated the region's water, fish and vegetables. "There were big tank battles just 25 to 30 kilometres south and west of Basra," he says. "The wind blows from that direction over the city." We visit the farms to the south-west, on the road to Safwan, where peasants with leathery skin and bare feet harvest lush red tomatoes, onions and garlic. We ask an old man in a flowing robe if he knows anyone who has cancer. "My daughter-in-law, Amal Hassan Saleh, died fifty days ago from stomach cancer. She was twenty-one," he says. "We have many cases of cancer here; it started three or four years ago."

During the 1991 war, media referred to the destruction of Iraq's infrastructure as a strategy of "bomb now, die later". They did not know how true it would prove to be. While we are visiting the cancer wards of Baghdad and Basra, the British Gulf Veterans' and Families' Association reports that at least thirty British veterans of the 1991 war have died of cancer. A coalition of US veterans' groups says it believes that 40,000 American servicemen were exposed to depleted uranium dust on the battlefield.

Uranium appauvri: la guerre invisible (*Depleted Uranium, the Invisible War*) by Frédéric Loore, Martin Meissonnier and Roger Trilling, published in French in 2001, quotes three reports commissioned by the US military which link depleted uranium to a risk of cancer. Yet the US used depleted uranium weapons again in Kosovo in 1999. The book's authors further discovered that uranium at three US plants which produced depleted uranium was contaminated with highly radioactive elements, including plutonium, because the US Department of Energy had in the 1950s decided to reprocess spent fuel from military nuclear reactors. The hundreds of tonnes of DU fired in Iraq and Kosovo were not so "depleted" after all. Pentagon spokesman Kenneth Bacon acknowledged the plutonium contamination to Roger Trilling in January 2001.

Robert's photograph of five-year-old Latif Abdul Sattar appears across seven columns in *The Irish Times* and becomes the symbol of the fundraising campaign launched by *The Independent* on behalf of the Iraqi children. *Independent* readers contribute $250,000 for cancer drugs and medical equipment to be sent to Iraq.

The UN says the medicine will have to be cleared by the sanctions commission, and this could take time. Robert tells them he will deliver the medicine "whether [they] like it or not". He obtains clearance in twenty-four hours. Robert returns to Baghdad in October 1998 with a refrigerated lorry carrying 5,195 kilos of medical cargo.

Margaret Hassan, the Irish-born director of the children's charity CARE in Iraq, helps organise distribution of the medicines in Baghdad, Basra and Mosul. When Saddam Hussein's office delays granting permission, Hassan appeals to the dictator. She was, Robert writes in 2008, "a proverbial tower of strength, and it was she – and she alone – who managed to persuade Saddam Hussein's bureaucrats to let us bring the medicine into Iraq".

The fundraising campaign for the Iraqi cancer children is the only time I remember Robert crossing the line between chronicling the misery of war victims and actively attempting to help them. It does not bring him peace of mind.

"At last, it seemed, we could *do* something, rather than just write angry articles about the plight of these pariah children," Robert writes in *The Great War for Civilisation*. "But could we? Were we going to save lives, or merely prolong suffering?" Latif Abdul Sattar, whose sad eyes and bald head touched the hearts of *Independent* readers, died six weeks after we met him in the children's hospital in Baghdad, six months before Robert arrived with the drugs that might have saved him.

The fate of Margaret Hassan, whom Robert meets through the same story and who becomes his friend, is also a source of great sorrow. Hassan was born Margaret Fitzsimons in Dalkey, County Dublin, where Robert and I had our home. She met and married

Tahseen Ali Hassan, an Iraqi engineering student, in London in 1972, moved to Baghdad and took Iraqi citizenship. This kind, brave woman, who spoke out against UN sanctions and did so much for the people of Iraq, would be kidnapped by men wearing police uniforms on 19 October 2004. Her kidnappers sent three successive videos to the Arab satellite channel Al Jazeera. In the first video, Margaret begs Tony Blair to withdraw British troops from Iraq. Al Jazeera refuses to broadcast the last two: a forced, false confession by Margaret that she "worked with the occupation forces", and the grisly scene of a man shooting a blindfolded woman in the head.

Robert asks the permission of Margaret's widower Tahseen to watch the videos and write about it. No group ever claims responsibility for her murder, and her remains are never found.

VII

The Eyes of a Shark in Water

Hostage is a crucifying aloneness. It is a silent, screaming slide into the bowels of ultimate despair. Hostage is a man hanging by his fingernails over the edge of chaos, feeling his fingers slowly straightening. Hostage is the humiliating stripping away of every sense and fibre of body and mind and spirit that make us what we are. Hostage is a mutant creation filled with fear, self-loathing, guilt and death-wishing. But he is a man, a rare, unique and beautiful creation of which these things are no part.

Former Irish hostage Brian Keenan, at a press conference in Dublin on 30 August 1990, six days after his release from captivity in Lebanon.

The longest-held British hostage, John McCarthy, is freed on 8 August 1991, after more than five years in captivity. McCarthy carries with him into freedom a sealed letter from Imad Mughniyeh, the leader of Islamic Jihad, asking United Nations Secretary General Javier Pérez de Cuéllar to negotiate the release of the remaining dozen western hostages in Lebanon.

When McCarthy is released, I am in Algiers, working on a story about the rise of the Islamic Salvation Front. Robert sends a fax from Beirut to the El Djazair Hotel. "Darling – Don't know if you've finished your end but I think you should head back to Beirut as soon as you can – 1) to be with your Bobby – 2) because the story is getting fairly dramatic."

Robert has waited seven years to cover the end of the hostage drama. Though we've been distracted by the Aoun wars and the Gulf War, hostages have remained a priority. Exchanges of prisoners and bodies are an integral part of the dénouement. On 11 September, Israel frees fifty-one Shia prisoners from Khiam, the prison then run by Israel and its so-called South Lebanon Army militia allies, and returns the bodies of nine Hezbollah fighters. The British hostage Jack Mann is released on 24 September. The glacier is melting.

In the late summer and autumn of 1991, the Middle East harbours illusions of change. George H.W. Bush and his Secretary of State, James Baker, organise the Madrid Peace Conference in the mistaken belief that they can persuade Israel to give up the land it illegally occupies in exchange for peace with Syria and the Palestinians. The Soviet Union is collapsing, leaving Syria's Hafez al-Assad eager to cosy up to Washington. Assad's participation in the Gulf War coalition has won him US gratitude and carte blanche in Lebanon, where General Michel Aoun is evicted from the presidential palace. Even Iran, under President Hashemi

Rafsanjani, is seeking respectability. The hostages have become an embarrassment to Hezbollah's mentors in Tehran and Damascus.

Sheikh Mohammed Hussein Fadlallah, the spiritual leader of Hezbollah, is fond of calling Lebanon "a lung through which Iran breathes". The vivid, creepy metaphor is one of our favourite quotations. As revealed by Bob Woodward in his book *Veil*, the CIA planted an enormous car bomb in Beirut's southern suburbs in 1985, in a failed attempt to assassinate Fadlallah. It killed eighty people, including Jihad Mughniyeh, a brother of the Islamic Jihad leader Imad.

Terry Anderson is kidnapped by Islamic Jihad eight days after the CIA bomb. Anderson might have been kidnapped anyway, but as the years pass I increasingly see events as part of a causal chain. Nothing happens in isolation. *Al damm bejeeb damm.* Blood begets blood.

Hezbollah radicals owe a debt of gratitude to Hojatoleslam Ali Akbar Mohtashemi, the leader of the anti-western faction in Tehran who founded the Party of God when he was Iran's ambassador to Damascus. But Mohtashemi's power is waning, and Hezbollah know they need Tehran to survive.

Robert and I interview Sheikh Abbas Musawi, Hezbollah's leader, on 24 September. He calls the twin suicide bombings that killed 299 US and French servicemen in Beirut in 1983 "the great achievement of Hezbollah in this period" because "it evicted America and the Multinational Force from Lebanon". Musawi's statement is the first Hezbollah claim of responsibility for the bombings, tantamount to the admission that Hezbollah and Islamic Jihad, which staged the attacks, are one. "There is one organisation, and the different names are a mirage," says M., a Shia Muslim contact who is one of our best sources on hostage matters.

A photograph of President Rafsanjani, the reformist president who has sidelined Mohtashemi, sits on Musawi's desk, in seeming contradiction to the Hezbollah leader's tough rhetoric. Hezbollah is beginning to transform itself into a political party which eventually will have cabinet ministers and deputies in the Lebanese parliament. It is not there yet.

M. is a classic Lebanese middleman. A Shia Muslim with a swarthy, pitted face and deep-set eyes, he keeps a small, windowless office in a fashionable part of West Beirut. M. does not seem religious. He is not bearded and he wears gaudy print shirts. His attractive wife is not veiled. He is "close to Hezbollah", he often tells us, but he is "not a Hezbollah member". M.'s contacts range from Shia extremists to Syrian *mukhabarat* to members of the Arab and western establishment. We're not sure if M. is merely a clearing house for information, redistributing news and observations among the many people he talks to, or perhaps some kind of spy or negotiator.

In any case, M. has never given us wrong information about hostages. Sometimes it is just a snippet, at other times an important prediction. When he doesn't know, he says so. We often sense he knows more than he is telling.

One autumn day in 1991, M. suggests we might want to cover the International Conference for the Support of the Intifada in Tehran. It's the Islamic Republic's way of opposing the upcoming talks in Madrid, and of asserting Iranian influence in the region. M. gives us the name of the man to see at the Iranian embassy for our visas.

On 19 October, Robert and I register for the three-day conference at the Esteghlal Hotel – a Hilton before the revolution – in affluent north Tehran. An Iranian woman in a chador and *magneh*, the cowl-like headdress that ensures one's hair and neck do not show, pulls me aside. She is tall and, despite the yards of fabric wrapped around her, strikes me as a coquette. Pointed shoes with bows and kitten heels peek out from under her chador, worn over thick, knitted tights. She has a mischievous smile and long eyelashes. I will call her Roya, the name she chooses for herself years later when I interview her about changing attitudes towards the revolution.

"I am very embarrassed to have to tell you this," Roya begins.

She is an employee of the Ministry of Culture and Islamic Guidance or Ershad. "But some of the men here, the, uh, organisers ... well they are unhappy about your dress."

"But I'm wearing a headscarf. My hair is covered."

"Your dress is too short, and one can see through your stockings," Roya continues. I look down. My loose black dress reaches mid-calf. My tights are ordinary black nylons. I find it hard to believe anyone could find my appearance suggestive. But this is not about modesty. It's not even about religion. It's about power, humiliation and intimidation. I go to a nearby shop and purchase the ugliest, longest, baggiest, black sack-like covering I can find. The Iranians call this smock-like outer layer with buttons down the front a *manteau* or *uniform.*

My problems with the dress code are not over. The conference organisers portray the attendance of foreign media as a sign of Iranian influence abroad, so they want to put foreign journalists on television. Robert and I decline to be interviewed, politely at first. A television crew follows us around the hotel conference centre, to the point of harassment. I become annoyed and, to the horror of the television journalist, begin to tear off my headscarf so they will stop filming. "You cannot do that here! This is an Islamic country," he shouts.

"You would have thought someone had thrown a naked woman into the hotel foyer!" Robert laughs when we're alone in our room.

At the beginning of the year in Saudi Arabia and Iraq, we had seen and heard the most important members of the Bush administration. Now the entire leadership of the Islamic Republic parade past us: the Guide, Ayatollah Ali Khamenei; President Rafsanjani; Foreign Minister Ali Akbar Velayati; Ahmad Khomeini, the son of the late Ayatollah Ruhollah Khomeini, considered to be particularly anti-American. Khomeini urges delegates to the conference to "decide behind closed doors how much arms and ammunition the Palestinians need, and the Iranian armed forces and Revolutionary Guards will do their best".

We run into M. in our hotel lobby. "Look what I've bought," he boasts, unwrapping finely wrought silver picture frames, mirrors and figurines from the bazaar. "Aren't these exquisite?" he sighs. "Persians are so much more refined than the Arabs!" Almost in the same breath, M. asks, "Would you like to interview a member of Islamic Jihad?"

Islamic Jihad? We are stunned. Until that moment, it has never occurred to us that one might seek an interview with the group and live to tell about it.

When Terry Anderson was kidnapped, one of his employees in the AP bureau gasped, "Please God, don't let it be Islamic Jihad". In the 1980s, Islamic Jihad wrote the playbook for Islamist extremism. It bombed US embassies in East and West Beirut and in Kuwait, the French embassy in Kuwait and the US and French military bases – whose destruction Abbas Musawi has just claimed for Hezbollah in that interview with Robert and me. Islamic Jihad bombed a restaurant frequented by US servicemen in Spain, a synagogue and airline offices in Copenhagen. It claimed responsibility for the assassination of the president of the American University of Beirut, the murder of two exiled Iranians in Paris, and a US Navy diver whose badly beaten body was thrown onto the tarmac of Beirut airport during the hijacking of TWA flight 847.

And Islamic Jihad still holds most of the remaining western hostages in Lebanon, including Terry Anderson. Its communiqués swear that "*not a single American or French will remain*" in Lebanon. It has already killed more than 350 people and will kill another twenty-nine at the Israeli embassy in Buenos Aires the following year, in retaliation for Israel's assassination of Hezbollah leader Musawi.

"Would you like to interview a member of Islamic Jihad?" M. repeats while Robert and I draw up a mental list of the group's crimes. "Yes, of course," Robert says. He wants to ask about Terry.

A few hours later, M. and Roya, the young woman from Ershad who scolded me over my "bad hijab", accompany us to the hotel where we are to interview the Islamic Jihad member.

"She's pretty hot," M. says in a most un-Islamic remark when Roya is out of earshot.

Roya likes showing off her excellent English and does most of the talking. Robert and I are certainly a change from the Iranians she usually spends time with. She can be cheerful and friendly one moment, filled with venom the next. "Do you like living in Beirut?" Roya asks. Yes of course, we reply. "I lived in Lebanon for two years," she volunteers. It turns out Roya was the Islamic Republic's equivalent of a missionary, sent to spread revolution. In southern Lebanon, she lived on the front line of Israel's war with Hezbollah. She witnessed guerrilla raids and Katyusha attacks, but also the young men dragged off for torture at Khiam prison and the indiscriminate bombardment of Shia villages. "I think the Americans and Israelis have no humanity," she says.

We meet the Islamic Jihad member in a dingy room on an upper floor of another hotel in north Tehran. There are five of us in addition to the interviewee: Roya and M., Robert and me, plus a fourth man, of whom more later.

"I am Imad Mughniyeh," the world's most wanted assassin, bomber, hijacker and kidnapper announces proudly, holding out his hand. Robert tries not to wince at Mughniyeh's prolonged, vice-like grip. As a woman, I am spared the handshake. We are the only western journalists to have interviewed Mughniyeh, except for those who met him while they were his prisoners.

Mughniyeh lays down the ground rules for the interview. We are not allowed to name him in print, but we may quote him as a member of Islamic Jihad, and we must not say that we interviewed the unnamed extremist in Tehran. Sixteen and a half years later, on 13 February 2008, a Lebanese friend rings to tell me that Mughniyeh has been assassinated in Damascus. I call Robert in Beirut, who hasn't heard yet. We agree that Mughniyeh's death frees us to identify him and describe the circumstances of our meeting.

"In the name of Allah, the Most Beneficent, the Most Merciful..." Mughniyeh begins by reciting the first verse of the

Koran, which, chillingly, is also the first line of Islamic Jihad's claims of responsibility for hostage-takings and suicide bombings. He speaks slowly, as if dictating a communiqué. "The West's only concern in Lebanon is the supremacy of Lebanese Christians and the security of Israel," he says. "There is an American plan to eradicate Islamic existence and resistance to Israel in Lebanon."

Roya takes notes on a letterhead notepad crested with a Kalashnikov raised above the name of Allah, Hezbollah's logo. In the time-lag while she writes down Mughniyeh's words for translation, I study the man at the top of the United States' most wanted list. Mughniyeh takes an apple from a platter of fruit on the table, peels it and cuts it into quarters. He is of stocky build and short to medium height, with brown hair and a beard. Mughniyeh looks so ordinary that at the time of his assassination in Damascus, his neighbours reportedly mistook him for the Iranian embassy's driver.

Islamic Jihad kidnapped and murdered William Buckley, the CIA station chief in Beirut, in 1984/85. Buckley is the second CIA station chief to fall victim to Mughniyeh, after Robert Ames, the agency's Near East Director, who was killed in the 1983 embassy bombing. Mughniyeh sent videotapes of Buckley's interrogation to the CIA, according to the *Washington Post*.

Mughniyeh seeks to justify his treatment of Buckley on the grounds that he was "de facto president of Lebanon, and not Amin Gemayel". At the time, Gemayel used the mainly Christian Lebanese army to round up Muslim militiamen and civilians. "One of the main roles, let us say the primary role, of the CIA station in Lebanon was to plan the protection of Gemayel," Mughniyeh continues. Buckley's remains would be found in a bag by the roadside in Beirut's southern suburbs.

Until now, the meeting is more a monologue by Mughniyeh than an interview. Robert finally manages to place our first question. "My best friend, Terry Anderson, is held by Islamic Jihad. When will he be freed? What can you tell me of his circumstances? Would you allow me to see him?"

Mughniyeh mocks our impatience. The crisis in Lebanon is ending, he tells us, thanks to UN intervention. "There are no obstacles at the moment towards resolving the problem of the hostages. It won't take long. But," he warns, "a partial solution will only solve the problem of present detainees." In other words, if Israel takes more Lebanese prisoners, Islamic Jihad will abduct more westerners.

"We treat him better than you treat yourself," Mughniyeh says of Anderson.

Robert and I glance at each other. We consider protesting but think better of it.

Through seven years of captivity, Anderson is held in airless, windowless cells scarcely wider than a grave, where he cannot stand to his full height. He survives extremes of heat in summer and cold in winter, battles mosquitoes and other insects, wears the same clothes, year in, year out, sometimes only underpants and socks. He is blindfolded and chained and given ten minutes each day to go to the "toilet", a filthy hole in the ground. When hostages are allowed to bathe, they are forced to share the same water and towel. They survive on bread, tea, cheese and rice.

Robert has a habit of repeating the best quotes from the films we see and the interviews we do, out of the blue. Henceforward, "We treat him better than you treat yourself" is a staple of his repertoire, a byword for blatant falsehood.

"Do you feel anything for the suffering of the hostages you are holding?" I ask.

"My feeling towards the mental pain of Terry Anderson is the same as my feeling towards the Lebanese hostages in Khiam, with the exception that the Lebanese hostages go through both mental and physical torture," Mughniyeh replies.

The message is clear. Every evil act Mughniyeh commits is retaliation for barbarous acts by the US and Israel. Action, reaction. To our surprise, Mughniyeh admits that "taking hostages is wrong. It is an evil." But, he adds, "it is the only choice. There is no other option. It is a reaction to a situation that has been imposed on us." Mughniyeh harks back to the 1982 Israeli invasion, the thousands of Lebanese imprisoned by Israel in the Ansar camp, the tens of thousands of civilians they killed. He brings up Iran Air flight 655 too, "filled with innocent men, women and children. The US government didn't admit to having done wrong ... They did not even pay the families of the victims."

For four years, Robert and I have done our utmost to elude Islamic Jihad, and here we are in Tehran, sitting a couple of metres from the group's founder. Imad Mughniyeh is Islamic Jihad. Islamic Jihad is Mughniyeh. I wonder if the irony is lost on him. Our safe conduct hangs by the thread of his will. He could kidnap us, even here, though the fact that he is trying to wind up the hostage saga mitigates against that possibility.

AUB president David Dodge was kidnapped from the campus of the American University in 1982 and taken to Iran. Journalists have been arrested in Tehran and thrown into Evin prison. We have decided to trust Imad Mughniyeh and the Islamic Republic. Terry Waite trusted Mughniyeh too, and paid for it with four years of captivity.

In the event, our interview on 20 October 1991 is more chilling than frightening. We do not ask Mughniyeh why he has not kidnapped us in Lebanon. Perhaps it is better not to tempt fate. Robert does not ask Mughniyeh if it was his gunmen who pursued him through the streets of Ras Beirut in November 1984. In *Pity the Nation*, Robert speculates that Mughniyeh wanted to show us, two westerners, "that he was a human being rather than the 'terrorist' portrayed by his American and Israeli enemies".

During the interview, I silently recall the hijacking of Kuwait Airways Flight 422, which Robert and I covered in Algiers three and a half years earlier. The hijackers demanded the liberation of seventeen members of the Shia Dawa party from prison in Kuwait. Mustafa Badreddine, Mughniyeh's first cousin and brother-in-law, was one of the Dawa 17. Their freedom was a constant demand of Islamic Jihad until the remaining prisoners escaped when Iraq invaded Kuwait in August 1990.

Mughniyeh's eyes impress me most. I have never seen eyes like his, dead eyes, with no light in them. I recall the Kuwait Airways flight attendant describing the hijacker who held a gun to his face in Algiers in 1988: "Have you ever seen a shark in water? The eyes, exactly. They have no expression. A cruel face and very steady hands," he said. That night in Tehran, I feel certain Mughniyeh was the hijacker.

The day after we interview Mughniyeh, Israel releases another fifteen Lebanese prisoners, fourteen from Khiam, one from Israel. The US hostage Jesse Turner is freed in exchange.

I use the telephone booths in a wood-panelled room at the Esteghlal to ring my editors at *Time* magazine. I word my sentences carefully and interrupt Paul Witteman, the deputy chief of correspondents, if he says anything that might be misconstrued by eavesdroppers as evidence of hostility or espionage. When I come out of the phone booth, Imad Mughniyeh is standing a few feet away, staring at me with those dead eyes of his. He has listened to my conversation and he wants me to know it. *We vow that not a single American or French will remain on this soil...*

Shia extremists trust me less than they trust Robert, not only because of my nationality. "He understands us better than you do," Roya tells me years later. Robert covered the Iranian revolution, the eight-year "Imposed War" with Iraq. As early as 1977, he met an Iranian fighting on the side of Palestinians in southern Lebanon, who told him he had come to learn. Robert quotes the Iranian gunman in *Pity the Nation*. "We understand a common cause with our Palestinian brothers. With their help, we can learn to destroy the Shah."

I can never equal Robert's comprehension of Lebanon and Iran and the unbreakable bond between Lebanese and Iranian Shia. But for all its flaws, paranoia and mad lashing out, I am fascinated by the Islamic Republic, by the way beauty and finesse coexist with great cruelty. I am saddened by the tormented history of its relations with the US and France, the country of my birth and my adopted homeland. I visit Iran often, with Robert and later alone.

Every chapter of Mughniyeh's life oozes bloodshed. *Live by the sword, die by the sword,* Robert writes when Mughniyeh is assassinated. In addition to the hundreds of people Mughniyeh kills, he and two of his brothers die in three separate car bombings.

Hezbollah says Mughniyeh's cousin and brother-in-law Badreddine, also a Hezbollah commander, and for whom Mughniyeh committed multiple hijackings and bombings, was killed by Sunni extremists near Damascus airport in 2016. Badreddine is long suspected of having organised the killing of the former Lebanese prime minister Rafik Hariri and twenty-one others in 2005.

According to press reports, Mughniyeh's assassination in Damascus was a joint operation by the CIA and Mossad. They put the explosives in the spare tyre on the back of his Mitsubishi Pajero and detonated them by remote control. When he died, Mughniyeh was reportedly working with Qasem Soleimani, the commander of Iran's Quds Force, to attack US forces in Iraq. The *Washington Post* reported that the CIA had a chance to kill Soleimani with Mughniyeh in 2008 but did not do so because it lacked authorisation. Donald Trump ordered Soleimani's assassination in Baghdad twelve years later.

ᵍᵃ

Robert and I talk a lot about the meaning of words. His refusal to use the word "terrorist" creates a semantic dilemma. So what *does* one call a person who uses violence against civilians for political aims? We opt for "militant" or "extremist". Robert refers to his "gallery of rogues". But "rogues" sounds almost affectionate to me, and inadequate for a man like Mughniyeh, or Osama bin Laden, whom Robert will interview three times. "If they had jet fighters and cruise missiles, they wouldn't be suicide bombers and kidnappers," Robert says.

His central argument – that the word "terrorist" is used almost solely for violence committed by Arabs or Muslims – is indisputable. Most of the acts of terror we write about – for instance, the shooting down of the Iranian Airbus; the US bombing of the Amariya shelter in Baghdad; renditions and torture of Arabs by US agents; Israel's massacre of Lebanese refugees at Qana; the slaughter of thousands of civilians in Israeli assaults on Gaza – have been committed by "our" side.

Roya accompanies us to our hotel after the interview with Mughniyeh. "To me he is a hero," she says, starry-eyed. She will soon marry not Mughniyeh but the fourth man at the interview, the Lebanese Anis Naccache.

Naccache's death from Covid-19 on 22 February 2021 frees me to tell the story of our contacts with him as well. Throughout our interview with Mughniyeh, I sense a strong complicity between the three men. In other circumstances, I would assume they went to school together. We can only begin to guess at the dark secrets they share.

Naccache was born in 1951 to a middle-class Sunni family in Beirut. He studied architecture in his youth. Unlike Mughniyeh, who never smiles, Naccache is affable and polished. He too is an ordinary-looking man, stocky, with a round, bald head and a light-brown beard which later turns white. He mocks his own amateurism when describing his attempt to assassinate Shapour Bakhtiar, the Shah's last prime minister, in the Paris suburb of Neuilly in July 1980. He paid for that attack with ten years in a French prison.

Mughniyeh is eleven years younger than Naccache and hails from a poor, southern Lebanese Shia family. Both men began their careers fighting on the side of Yasser Arafat's Fatah against the Israelis.

Robert and I recall dramatic news footage of Naccache with his shirt torn off, handcuffed and writhing like a wounded beast as French security forces marched him away from the scene of his attack on Bakhtiar. A woman – Bakhtiar's next-door neighbour – and a policeman were killed in the attack. A second policeman spent the rest of his life in a wheelchair.

We arrange to meet Naccache for coffee the morning after we interviewed Mughniyeh. He tells us he decided to kill Bakhtiar based on evidence that he was planning "a coup against the revolution", like the 1953 Anglo-American coup against the democratically elected prime minister Mohammad Mossadegh. An Iranian revolutionary tribunal passed a death sentence against Bakhtiar, he says.

Naccache says he did not see Bakhtiar's neighbour, Yvonne Stein. The bullet went through her front door and lodged in her brain. Naccache was still in hospital with wounds to his arm and thigh when he learned of Stein's death. He says now that he felt very badly, because she was innocent. He says he offered to pay compensation to her family and the family of the dead policeman, "according to the principles of Islam".

"Isn't it unusual for a Sunni to ally himself with Shia Muslims?" I ask Naccache. "I hate this distinction," he replies. "We are all Muslims." He chooses to serve the Islamic Republic because he sees it as the only credible counterweight to US and Israeli domination of the Middle East.

In the 1970s, Naccache was the right-hand man to another convert to the Palestinian cause, Ilich Ramírez Sánchez, known as Carlos the Jackal. Together, they took seventy people, including eleven oil ministers, hostage at the OPEC conference in Vienna in 1975. Naccache was twenty-four years old. Three people were killed in that attack.

Naccache and his four accomplices in the attack on Bakhtiar were the most problematic inmates in the French prison system. Eleven Frenchmen were kidnapped in Lebanon between 1984 and 1987, in a bid to obtain their liberation. Seven bombs exploded in the Paris region in 1986 for the same purpose. The attack in the rue de Rennes killed ten people and wounded another 152. The Iranian strategy worked. President François Mitterrand pardoned Naccache and his fellow gunmen in July 1990, fourteen months before Robert and I met him.

Less than three months before our first encounter in Tehran, a second Iranian hit squad succeeded where Naccache had failed, stabbing Bakhtiar and his secretary to death in a Paris suburb. Perhaps that is why Naccache was so cheerful.

When Naccache died in 2021, *Le Monde*'s headline labelled him "the pro-Iranian terrorist". The Syrian news agency Sana called him "a militant and political scientist". On the photo placards carried by mourners at his funeral in Beirut, Naccache wore the black-and-white Palestinian keffiyeh scarf. His casket was covered with the Palestinian and Lebanese flags.

Naccache and Roya lived together in Beirut, Damascus and Tehran. We visited one another occasionally, sometimes in our home, sometimes in theirs. I had to remind myself that this apparently calm, gentle, smiling man was a convicted assassin. Naccache seemed to mellow with age, dabbled in business, established a think tank and appeared often as a commentator on Al-Manar, Hezbollah's television station, and on the pan-Arab news channel Al-Mayadeen. In later years, he wore an un-Iranian suit and tie on television. Though Naccache remained a pariah in France, his crimes appeared minor compared to those of Lebanese warlords.

Naccache seemed amused to see his wife doing frivolous things such as going clothes-shopping with me, an American, in Hamra Street in Beirut. "I thought I hated shopping," Roya tells me when we return home laden with packages one afternoon. "Now I love shopping."

Unlike Roya, my two closest Iranian women friends are from upper-middle-class, non-religious backgrounds, where the revolution is considered to be a catastrophe. They are completely westernised and have become naturalised French citizens.

Roya opens a window onto a culture and mentality that are foreign to me. She tells me how her devoutly religious mother keeps a separate set of dishes for non-Muslim guests, and washes everything they have touched when they leave her home. Roya is devoted to her husband and to the revolution. She is easily offended, and I often feel she misunderstands me, yet over the years I learn a great deal from her.

Roya visits Paris in the late 1990s, after I have moved there to be the *Irish Times*' France correspondent. She and I sit on the outside terrace at Le Cherche Midi, my canteen at the time. She wears not a chador but a light-coloured headscarf and matching, long-sleeved print blouse over a long dark skirt. The French aversion to women in headscarves must be seen to be believed. The normally friendly waiters are so rude that I stop going to the restaurant.

By the mid-1990s, the pattern of events in the Islamic Republic is well established. The election of a reformist president, first Rafsanjani, later Mohammad Khatami and to a lesser degree Hassan Rouhani, inspires hope that Iran will end human rights abuses and resolve its quarrels with the West. But hardliners, chiefly the all-powerful Pasdaran or Revolutionary Guards but also conservatives in the Iranian parliament – the Majlis – stifle freedom of speech, enforce a strict moral code and maintain support for extremist groups abroad. This is a simplified explanation of a situation that is complicated by family loyalties and financial interests.

Eventually a hardliner, the prime example being Mahmoud Ahmadinejad from 2005 until 2013, regains the presidency and undoes his predecessor's achievements. The US does nothing to help reformists prevail and is engaged on a permanent mission to destroy Iran's economy with economic sanctions.

The country is polarised between convinced revolutionaries and more affluent and educated *gharbzadeh* – "those intoxicated by the West". These two Irans hate each other and coexist with difficulty, not unlike the two Americas one saw under Donald Trump.

ℌ

In June 1995, I mark the sixth anniversary of the death of Ayatollah Ruhollah Khomeini by visiting his vast, gold-domed mausoleum. Families picnic on carpets on the floor of the shrine. At random, I choose a woman with small children to interview. She is a housewife called Hafezeh and she wears blue jeans and a bright turquoise jumper under her loosely draped chador.

"I was sixteen when I joined the Revolutionary Guards [in 1979]," Hafezeh tells me. "I used to go out in the patrol car with the sisters [female Revolutionary Guards]. They were looking for women who weren't wearing proper Islamic covering. They threw acid in their faces or said, 'Let me take off your lipstick,' and cut their lips with a razor hidden in a Kleenex."

The government offered Hafezeh and her husband a luxurious villa in north Tehran. "It was incredible ... like a palace. My husband said, 'No, we cannot take it.' But there were many other Revolutionary Guards who drank alcohol and took people's houses. It sickened us, and we both quit. Now my husband is a truck driver. He drives to Germany. When he comes home, I have a bottle of whisky waiting, and we drink it together. I dress like the loose women in Europe for him. I don't think God minds."

The rest of my two-page article is a chronicle of disillusionment in a country where per capita income has fallen to a quarter of its pre-revolution level. I explain how US sanctions are impoverishing Iran. I describe Rafsanjani's difficulties with conservative clergy and the Majlis.

But the Ministry of Islamic Guidance is obsessed with the opening interview with Hafezeh. They summon my interpreter, who confirms that I have accurately transcribed the housewife's words. They berate the interpreter for having translated such scurrilous statements, and demand more information about the interviewee, in the vain hope of identifying and arresting her. In one paragraph, I have managed to violate three taboos: the sanctity of the revolution, the ban on alcohol, and sex. When Robert and I apply for visas to attend the summit of the Organisation of the Islamic Conference in 1997, I learn that I have been blacklisted. All my efforts to reverse the decision fail. I bring it up with Anis Naccache, who rings the consular section of the Iranian embassy. The problem is solved.

In 2006, I cover an international conference in Tehran for the support of Palestine for *The Irish Times*. Just before it opens,

President Ahmadinejad announces that Iran has mastered the nuclear fuel cycle. Iran will conclude a deal with the world's main powers to limit its nuclear programme in 2015, which Donald Trump pulls out of three years later. (As I write this, the Biden administration is engaged in negotiations to resume the accord.)

Ahmadinejad's 2006 statement is a deliberate taunting of the US and Israel. He calls the Nazi holocaust against the Jews a "myth" and refers to the "holocaust faced by the Palestinians". Posters decorating the conference hall are intended to provoke. In one, Hitler gives a Nazi salute beneath an Israeli flag. In another, the Star of David is placed at the centre of a swastika.

General Rahim Safavi, the head of the Revolutionary Guards, threatens to attack US troops in Iraq if the US bombs Iranian nuclear installations. The conference pledges $50 million to help the newly elected Hamas government in Gaza. The final declaration "considers the Zionist regime presently on the soil of Palestine ... has no right of existence".

Anis Naccache is in his element. He bustles around the conference as if he were hosting a social event, playing his role as Iran's link to radical Palestinian movements. He introduces me to Ramadan Abdallah Shalah, the head of Palestinian Islamic Jihad. Shalah speaks English well – he holds a doctorate in economics from the University of Durham – and gives me his justification for the approximately one hundred suicide bombings claimed by his group in the past five and a half years.

"Initially we did not target civilians," Shalah says. "We adopted this policy as a reaction to the killing of our civilians. Our people feel that Israelis must suffer as we suffer. It's not fair for them to live in peace in Tel Aviv, without knowing what Israeli soldiers do to us, while we are suffering in Khan Younis, Rafah and Nablus."

Naccache asks to be quoted as "the coordinator of the al-Amman Islamic Research Centre for Strategic Affairs", though I of course mention that he was imprisoned in France for killing two people and attempting to kill Bakhtiar. I tell him I believe in international law, in UN Security Council resolutions. "UN resolutions and international law are no longer relevant," he says. "After [the 2003 invasion of] Iraq, Guantánamo and Abu Ghraib, nobody can sell us this product any longer."

In June 2014, I am on a reporting trip to Tehran when the Islamic State group, known as Isis, stuns the world by seizing the Iraqi towns of Mosul, Tikrit, Fallujah, Tal Afar and Rawa in just ten days. *The Irish Times* wants an Iranian perspective on the sudden rise of the Sunni extremist movement. The Islamic Republic reacts with relative calm, compared to the hysteria in the West. Tehran is confident that demographics – the Shia far outnumber Sunnis in Iraq – and Iranian power will triumph over Isis.

I attend President Rouhani's press conference, where he predicts that the appeal by Grand Ayatollah Ali al-Sistani in Najaf to Iraqis to take up arms against Isis will lead to the extremists' defeat. A professor at Tehran University and a retired Iranian diplomat provide other insights. But the most exclusive interview on the subject is the one that Naccache arranges, with a man whose full name I do not know, but who says I may quote him as "a senior Iranian military intelligence source who travels frequently to Syria and Iraq". Naccache's source gives me facts and figures of Isis's troop strength and weaknesses. He reveals that Abu Omar al-Shishani, a notorious Isis leader of Chechen origin, has been killed in Mosul.

Without the support of Russia, Iran and Hezbollah, Bashar al-Assad would probably not have survived the civil war that started in Syria in 2011. I believe Naccache helped to coordinate the military alliance between Hezbollah, Iranian Revolutionary Guards and Assad's forces. When Naccache dies, Assad sends a message of condolence to his family, saying that he "spent his life as a resistance fighter against occupation and a defender of Arab causes".

Imad Mughniyeh and Anis Naccache are protégés of Hojatoleslam Ali Akbar Mohtashemi, a founder, if not *the* founder, of Hezbollah, a rival to President Rafsanjani and a leader of the hardliners in Iran. Mohtashemi is reported by western sources, including the *New York Times*, to have played a role in planning the embassy and Multinational Force bombings organised by

Mughniyeh. I request an interview with Mohtashemi for *Time* magazine on the sidelines of the October 1991 Conference for the Support of the Intifada. Robert sits in on the interview, though I am not sure he wrote about it.

Mohtashemi and I face one another from opposite sides of a table in a wood-panelled conference room. He wears wire-rimmed glasses and the black turban of a sayyid or descendant of the Prophet Mohammed. He has a salt-and-pepper beard and is virtually indistinguishable from any number of Iranian clerics.

Before the interview begins, Mohtashemi stares at me in a way that makes me uneasy. He lays his mutilated hand on the table in front of him. When he was Iran's ambassador to Damascus, from 1982 until 1986, someone sent Mohtashemi a bomb concealed in a coffee-table book about the Shia holy places. It blew off two of his fingers and nearly killed him.

Suddenly, Mohtashemi shouts at me: "Did you write this?" With the index finger of his claw-like hand, he jabs a two-week-old issue of *Time* magazine. He opens the magazine to my article about Hezbollah and raises it to show me a sentence underlined in ink. The military wing of Hezbollah "has lost influence with the eclipse of its outside mentor, Iran's former Interior Minister, Ali Akbar Mohtashemi", it says. Eclipse. "Did you write this?" Mohtashemi repeats. I nod. The article also talks about Hezbollah's arrangement of short-term "pleasure marriages" between fighters and the widows of martyrs, but it is my allegation about the diminution of his power that infuriates Mohtashemi.

It is not easy to maintain one's sang-froid while angering one of the most dangerous men in the Middle East. The tension in the room is palpable. I do not attempt to explain my use of "eclipse", but instead change the subject.

What is the importance of the Conference for the Support of the Intifada? I ask Mohtashemi. He has made his point and allows the interview to move on. "In the first decade of the revolution, Iran played a very prominent role in the Middle East," he says. He is probably thinking of his years in Damascus, when he dispatched

Revolutionary Guards to Lebanon to set up Hezbollah. "But in the past two years [i.e. since Rafsanjani's election], Iran's role has greatly diminished. We are ready to bring life back to that role," he says. Mohtashemi has recently regained some influence by becoming chair of the defence committee of the Majlis.

Is it true that he founded Hezbollah? I ask. "I consider Hezbollah my sons, and I will always protect them," Mohtashemi replies, speaking almost tenderly of the group the US and EU classify as "terrorist". Hezbollah kills three Israeli soldiers in southern Lebanon that week.

Mohtashemi was a companion to Ayatollah Khomeini when the founder of the Islamic Republic lived in exile in Najaf and in Neauphle-le-Château, 50 kilometres west of Paris. Mohtashemi was twice imprisoned by Saddam, and also by Kuwaiti and Saudi authorities. Robert further eases the strained ambience by asking a question that the cleric likes, about the effect of those experiences. "None of this hindered or affected my beliefs or my determination and this made me even more resolute in my decision to fight and struggle against the United States of America, Israel and all the other proxy governments and states," Mohtashemi says.

ЯЭ

The only other time I recall feeling as nervous in an interview, I am the interviewee. In the autumn of 2018, I am summoned to an annexe of the French interior ministry in Levallois. I enter through a cage-like, revolving turnstile, turn over my identity papers, am told to turn off my mobile phone and leave it with my handbag in a locker. It is just like entering the protected "Green Zone" in Baghdad.

An intelligence officer comes to fetch me and leads me to a small, windowless room with a table and three chairs, void of all decoration. I am in the final stages of applying for French citizenship. I know quite a few naturalised French citizens. None have undergone similar questioning.

The male officer is the good cop, the female officer the aggressive, bad cop. She wants to know whom I know at the US embassy. The previous press attaché, but he has left now. And that woman who worked with Hillary Clinton at the State Department... I can't remember her name... I met her once at a reception. The woman interrogator says the diplomat's name. Yes, that's her.

Now they want to know about my years in the Middle East. Am I in contact with anyone in the Palestinian territories? In Lebanon? Syria? Iraq? Iran?

I am nervous, not because I have anything to hide, but because I want to be French and I believe my naturalisation is at stake. I almost never sweat, but I feel perspiration sliding down my sides, inside my dress. "Mainly my interpreters," I reply. They want names. My mind goes blank. Kassem and Amjad from Baghdad. Where are they now? Both emigrated to the US, with their wives and children. I wrote recommendation letters for them. Iranians? Do you know any Iranians? Two of my best friends are Iranian, but they are French now. One is married to a French ambassador. "We should meet some time in a café. Some place more relaxed, for a coffee," the good cop suggests.

Only when it is over do I remember Imad Mughniyeh, Anis Naccache, Ramadan Abdallah Shalah and a few others. Perhaps someone in the interior ministry checked my articles online. Or they have intelligence traces. Of course, that was what they were after. I tell a French friend, a civil servant, that I have the unpleasant impression they were trying to recruit me. "You're too old for that!" she laughs. "They want to know if you *are* a spy."

I hear nothing more from the ministry. A few months later, I become a French citizen.

೪ು

Two weeks after leaving Tehran, Robert and I fly to Dublin where he receives a Jacob's Award on 9 November 1991 for his coverage of the Gulf War for RTÉ Radio 1, the Irish public broadcaster. Ireland's national newspaper radio critics choose the winners. At the black-tie dinner, the television journalist Charlie Bird is overheard grumbling, "Did they really have to give it to that Brit?" The remark gets back to Robert and annoys him immensely. He loves Ireland, took risks covering the Troubles in the North, did a doctorate at Trinity College Dublin, bought a house in Dalkey, spends his holidays in Ireland. Robert will become an Irish citizen the year before his death and be buried in Ireland. Yet for a certain type of Irishman, he will forever be "that Brit".

The following week, I go to the US embassy in Ballsbridge to apply for a new passport. Mine has years to run, but I travel so much that each time my passport is opened by an immigration officer, the accordion extension pages, covered with stamps, tumble out. It is getting to be a problem.

I am stunned when the consular officer returns an hour or so later and hands me my passport, machine-punched with holes and stamped "CANCELLED".

I ask for an explanation. He refuses to provide one. I leave the embassy quite shaken. Robert and I remember that he rang the press office at the US embassy in London four years earlier, before I travelled to Beirut with him for the first time. There was some kind of travel ban, the diplomat confirmed. But she didn't think it was enforced, especially not for journalists.

I telephone the *Time* news desk from the cottage in Dalkey. "We'll get the lawyers on it right away. Don't worry," Paul Witteman assures me. The remaining western hostages in Lebanon are about to be released, but I am unable to leave Ireland, unable to do my job as *Time*'s Beirut correspondent. Robert promises to stay with me until my passport crisis is resolved. I know how much he wants to be in Damascus when Terry Anderson shows up there.

We call Robert's solicitor, James Heney. He engages Paddy McEntee, a famous criminal lawyer in Ireland at the time. James, Paddy and I return to the embassy to see the consul, who refuses to allow McEntee to smoke in his office. The consul will not say what I am being reproached for, nor why I cannot be issued with a passport. On the telephone the following day, the embassy offers a one-year, limited-validity passport. "What does 'limited validity' mean?" I ask. "It's not valid for travel to certain places, like Lebanon," the consul replies.

Time magazine's lawyers initially say the Reagan-era executive order banning travel to Lebanon has never been tested in court and is probably unconstitutional. Then word comes back that the State Department will not budge. "I'm really sorry, Lara. There's nothing more we can do," Witteman says. *Time* magazine has dumped me in it, not for the last time.

"Lara can remain in Ireland for as long as she wants to, and after two years she can apply for Irish nationality," an Irish diplomat friend assures us. That's a comfort, but I need to work. My home and job are in Beirut, with Robert. We appreciate the irony of the situation: I must return to Lebanon to cover the release of US hostages, but I cannot do so because I am a hostage of the United States. I have been rendered effectively stateless because of an executive order from a past president which is probably illegal anyway, and which those who have temporarily deprived me of my citizenship will not discuss. I feel this Kafkaesque nightmare is the result of some abstract transgression on my part, that I am being punished for crossing an invisible line between enemy camps, for refusing to take sides in what Robert will later call *The Great War for Civilisation*.

James, Paddy and I return to the embassy a second time. The Americans are more polite now. We assume they have discovered McEntee's reputation as a legal heavyweight. A second man in the consul's office is introduced to us as a political officer. Our suspicion that he is CIA is strengthened when he suggests that I might be able to help them. "Some of our people would like to meet you," he says. The consul fidgets. I smell a rat.

I have been living in Beirut for three years and have just interviewed the head of Hezbollah and a member of Islamic Jihad, to whom the CIA has lost two Beirut station chiefs. I suspect they are starved of information. I have nothing to tell them. Everything I know appears in print. "My client will accept nothing less than the *unconditional* issue of a full-validity passport," McEntee says, as we'd agreed during a brainstorming session around the dining room table the previous evening.

On the morning of 18 November 1991, five days after my passport was cancelled, the consular section rings the house in Dalkey. I can pick up a new, full-validity passport, they say. No explanation is offered. I remain uneasy about the episode and contact a US diplomat who was in consular training with me in 1984. She discovers that I have been put on a watchlist because someone fabricated a story that I used my former diplomatic passport to travel to Lebanon. I will be detained if I travel to the US.

I give Robert my diplomatic passport, which was cancelled – as required by regulations – when I left the State Department. It could not have been used even if such a thing had occurred to me. On a reporting trip to Washington, Robert obtains an appointment with the head of consular affairs and produces the old passport. "It's cancelled," she gasps when she sees it, realising I have been framed. The State Department removes me from the watchlist.

That day in November 1991, Robert and I stop to fetch my new US passport on the way to Dublin airport. Terry Waite, the Archbishop of Canterbury's special envoy and the last British hostage, and Tom Sutherland, the Scottish-born American Dean of Agriculture at the American University of Beirut, are released on the same day. They have been held with Terry Anderson, and Sutherland brings a message for Robert: "Terry wants you to be there."

We wait in Beirut for three weeks, having meals with friends, catching up on administration and remaining on the lookout for the first indication that Terry is about to be freed. We keep our packed bags by the door so we can make a bolt for Damascus at short notice.

The American hostages Joseph Cicippio and Alann Steen are freed on 2 and 3 December. It won't be long now, says M., our link to Islamic Jihad. By the afternoon of the 4th, we are still not

certain, but we leave for Damascus with Abed, our driver. A last
obstacle awaits us: the weather. Snow clouds hang low over the
Mount Lebanon range. We drive into a blizzard. At the ridge at
Mdeirej, a Syrian soldier tells us the road is closed. Robert is close
to despair. Cars and lorries slither across the frozen highway,
become embedded in snowbanks. We put snow chains on our
tyres and plough ahead, wending our way through the traffic
jam, past stranded cars and lorries. We turn on the BBC World
Service. "The American hostage Terry Anderson has been freed
and is on his way to Damascus," the newsreader says.

For nearly as long as I have known him, Robert has done
everything in his power to secure Terry's liberation. "Goddammit!"
he shouts now, banging his fist into the side of the car door and
feeling guilty for wishing that Terry's kidnappers could have held
him for just a few more hours. We spy a Syrian army truck, covered
in snow, coming towards us. "Where have you come from?" Robert
shouts. From Damascus. The road is open. We can make it.

But the logjam of cars is nearly impassable, and Abed does not
want to spend the night in the snow. It is almost nightfall when
Robert and I set off on foot over the Dahr al Baydar pass, the
highest point in the range, after which the highway descends to
the Bekaa Valley. We walk for what seems like an hour, lugging
our bags with our computers, sloshing through ice water, snow
sticking to our eyebrows and eyelashes. For once, I am not
tempted to complain about the hardships of our profession.
Terry's liberation means too much to Robert, and it is a huge
story for my American readers. On the downward slope, a Syrian
taxi driver agrees to take us to Damascus.

We drive directly to the foreign ministry, where freed hostages
traditionally make their first appearance. To our immense relief,
Terry has not yet arrived. He was still a hostage in Baalbek when
he too heard the BBC announcement, he tells us later that evening.
The Syrians assure us we have time to check into the Meridien
and drop off our things.

We return to wait at the foreign ministry. A door finally opens and Terry walks into the room filled with photographers and cameramen. "Robert!" he shouts, the first word of his press conference. The front rows are packed with journalists and diplomats, but Terry lunges towards Robert and clasps his hand for a long moment of joy. "Incredible," says Robert. They have not seen each other for nearly seven years, since March 1985.

Terry thanks Syria, Iran and the UN for his liberation, and is about to be whisked away to the US ambassador's residence. "Robert, I want to see you!" he exclaims. Robert reaches through the crowd to hand Terry our hotel phone and room number. The embassy calls a couple of hours later, saying they are sending a car for us. Robert usually avoids western embassies, *especially* US embassies, but he makes an exception that evening.

We are ushered into the ambassador's sitting room. Terry, his Lebanese fiancée, Madeleine, and their daughter Sulome, who was born three months after Terry was abducted, sit on a sofa in front of a Christmas tree, grinning with their arms around one another. Terry bounds to his feet and envelops Robert in a bear hug.

Terry has renewed his Catholic faith in captivity, but he still swears like the Marine Corps sergeant he was in Vietnam. "Fisky, you asshole," he says, "didn't you get my warning to get the fuck out of Beirut? We were all waiting for you to join us in our cell. They were after you, I promise you; they asked all about you. They asked me all the time, 'Who is the little Brit with the spectacles who goes to the AP office every day?' I pretended I didn't know you."

In a letter to Madeleine, which she never received, Terry asked her to tell Robert to read Matthew 25:13: "Watch therefore, for ye know neither the day nor the hour ..."

"Jaysus, Terry. I'm glad I didn't get that message!" Robert says. "I would have found it very disturbing!"

In the aftermath of Terry's kidnapping, Robert was afraid Islamic Jihad would use his military record as a pretext for ill treatment, so he tried to keep it a secret. It turns out Terry's young Hezbollah guards were in awe of the man who had served as a marine in Vietnam. They peppered him with questions about it and showed him greater respect than the others.

"You really haven't changed!" Robert beams as he looks Terry up and down.

"I've been in a closet for seven years. Time stopped," Terry replies.

Terry's guards read him passages from the Arabic translation of *Pity the Nation*. He pleaded for the original English version, to no avail. "They loved the part about me shouting at the British officer who called the Lebanese 'niggers'," Terry says. "Thanks, *habibi*! It made them think maybe I wasn't so bad after all."

During Terry's last months of captivity, conditions improved. He lived in a house in Baalbek, was allowed to watch as much Al-Manar television as he could stomach and was given British and American news magazines to read. This is what Imad Mughniyeh meant when he told us: *We treat him better than you treat yourself.*

Terry remembers the two-page piece that I wrote from Baalbek four months earlier, about how the advent of peace in Lebanon and the influx of non-Muslim tourists was creating problems for Hezbollah. The article speculates that American hostages might be held in the vicinity. "So you're the woman from *Time* magazine!" Terry says. "When I read it, I thought you must be with Fisky."

Terry and Robert's reunion that evening, and further meetings in the days that follow, fill in the blanks about Terry's ordeal. Christmas was always the worst time, he tells us. In 1985, he dropped his glasses and the lenses broke, so he could no longer see to communicate with hostages in other cells by sign language. "That was a bad day," Terry says. At Christmas 1987, he banged his head against the wall so hard it bled, because his captors refused to let him write to Madeleine.

Being moved from one prison to another was the hostages' worst nightmare. They were wrapped mummy-like in duct tape and transported in the boots of cars. They were gagged so they could not scream at checkpoints, and nearly suffocated on petrol fumes. They were bruised from bouncing over rough roads.

Terry was held for a long period with Tom Sutherland in the basement of a mosque between Sidon and Tyre. He fed breadcrumbs to a mouse he named Mehitabel. She sat on his shoulder. Their jailers plastered up a hole in the wall and Mehitabel disappeared.

The kidnappers beat the American hostage Frank Reed so badly that he became unhinged. "You're killing this guy. Why are you doing this?" Terry pleaded with the guards. "We got him into our cell, and he'd gone very bad," Terry tells us. "He kept claiming he had a transmitter implanted inside his brain and that he was receiving messages from the American embassy."

Terry was especially close to Father Lawrence Jenco and Reverend Benjamin Weir, with whom he prayed and read the Bible. Captivity forges unbreakable bonds between men who would otherwise not know each other, for example John McCarthy, an upper-class British journalist, and Brian Keenan, from working-class Belfast. Because he learned French at the agricultural institute in Versailles, Sutherland was able to communicate with the French hostage Jean-Paul Kauffmann. Kauffmann later told me he "never met anyone as humorous as Thomas Sutherland. He made me laugh in captivity." Kauffmann taught Sutherland and Anderson the 1855 World's Fair classification of Médoc wines, which remains unchanged to this day.

The ordeal seems to prove Sartre's maxim that hell is other people. Sutherland calls Terry Waite "the bane of our existence". Waite is a large man, and when he moved in a tiny cell shared with other hostages "it was like a goddam herd of elephants", Sutherland says. Other hostages "had a sense of when people needed privacy and didn't want to talk. Waite wanted to talk constantly."

Waite suffered from asthma. His wheezing prevented the others from sleeping. Anderson tried to calm him each evening, keeping up a hypnotic patter of "take it easy, breathe easy, exhale" until Waite fell asleep.

When Waite was united with the other hostages after four years in solitary confinement, he had an insatiable appetite for information. He and Terry Anderson were initially in adjacent cells. Anderson gave Waite updates on the news he culled from radio broadcasts by tapping on the wall. One tap meant *a*, two taps *b*, three taps *c*, and so on. "Didn't that take an awful long time?" I ask Terry. "We had nothing *but* time," Anderson replies.

As a hostage, "you don't 'kill time'", Kauffmann tells me. "Time kills you. That is the great trial – the monotony of days, the time you must fill up. Time is like a giant with a club trying to beat you, and you have to dodge him. When a prisoner resolves the problem of time, he is saved."

The AP reports that at least ninety-two foreigners were taken hostage in Lebanon between 1984 and 1991. Eleven are believed to have been murdered or died of illness in captivity. Some suffered permanent mental or physical damage. Alann Steen has to take medication for the rest of his life to control seizures and blackouts that result from being kicked by guards. Joseph Cicippio's skull is dented from being clubbed on the head. He has a permanent sensation of burning in his fingers and toes which were frostbitten when he was chained to a balcony one winter.

Each man found his own mental tricks for survival. Several kept diaries which were confiscated by guards. In addition to practising his faith, Anderson wrote poetry and invented games. He made an ersatz chessboard, a deck of cards, rosary beads. Kauffmann imagined the wines he would drink, the cigars he would smoke. Keenan decided to become his own self-observer, "letting madness take me where it would as long as I stood outside it and watched it", he wrote in *An Evil Cradling*. Before he was paired with McCarthy, Keenan invented a companion, based on the seventh-century blind Celtic harpist Turlough O'Carolan.

The loved ones waiting on the outside were perhaps the greatest incentive to hang on. Terry had Madeleine and Sulome. To the annoyance of western governments, who feared they were driving the price up, the hostages' loved ones campaigned for their liberation. Robert and I were close to Jean Sutherland, who stayed in the house she shared with Tom on the AUB campus for the six and a half years of his captivity. It was a ten-minute walk from our apartment on the Corniche, and we often dropped by to say hello. Jean is a cheerful, no-nonsense professor of English from Colorado. For years, she felt guilty for having hired Brian Keenan to teach at AUB. If we asked her how she kept going, she invariably replied, "I have high hopes and no expectations... Tom and I are like one person. When he comes out, all that time will be telescoped into one day."

Robert secretly hopes that Terry will forego the usual "debriefing" by US agents, the drugs and sessions with shrinks at the US base at Wiesbaden. If Robert were in the same position, he would never consent to such a procedure.

That night at the US ambassador's residence in Damascus, Terry asks Robert to fly with him, Madeleine and Sulome to Wiesbaden. Robert decides to take a commercial flight with me instead, to spare me from travelling alone, but also because he doesn't want the Syrians to record him boarding a US military aircraft. He can't help remembering that Terry Waite repeatedly accepted helicopter flights from Lieutenant Colonel Oliver North, the point man in the arms-for-hostages Iran Contra scandal. That may be one of the reasons why Waite was kidnapped.

Again, Robert's sacrifice for me turns to his advantage. On the flight to Frankfurt, we find ourselves sitting next to Giandomenico Picco, UN Secretary General Javier Pérez de Cuéllar's representative who has negotiated the liberation of nine British and American hostages over the preceding seven months. We are bound for Wiesbaden, to continue our coverage of Terry's liberation. Picco is heading for Bonn, to negotiate on behalf of the last two westerners held in Lebanon, the aid workers Thomas Kemptner and Heinrich Struebig.

Picco is a tall, elegant Italian who earlier helped negotiate the Soviet departure from Afghanistan and the ceasefire that ended the Iran-Iraq war. He grants us an exclusive interview on the plane.

Pérez de Cuéllar described Picco as "an unarmed soldier of diplomacy". Picco entitled his 1999 memoir *Man Without a*

Gun: One Diplomat's Secret Struggle to Free the Hostages, Fight Terrorism, and End a War.

While negotiating for the hostages held by Islamic Jihad, Picco travelled repeatedly with Syrian *mukhabarat* to the Lebanese border, where he was met by Hezbollah men in a black Mercedes. He was then driven, with a cloth bag over his head, sometimes in the boot of the car, to the Bekaa Valley or southern Lebanon. Picco accepted these measures to show his respect for the security of the kidnappers. He will not name names, though we are certain he negotiated with Mughniyeh, whom we interviewed so recently in Tehran. "I met with them alone, and always at night," Picco says. "We met many, many times." Picco was aware, of course, that Terry Waite was seized in similar circumstances. "Either you are afraid or you are a fool," he says.

Picco succeeds in freeing Kemptner and Struebig six months later. They were held by Abdul-Hadi Hamadi, the security chief of Hezbollah, whose brothers Mohamed and Abbas were imprisoned in Germany for murder and kidnapping.

Picco's determination to address both sides of the conflict is the key to his success. In late 1991, he obtains the liberation of ninety Lebanese held by Israel and Israel's militia allies in the South Lebanon Army. At the ceremony for Kemptner and Struebig at the Lebanese foreign ministry, he tells us he is committed to working for the freedom of all people held without due process in the Middle East. These include about 200 Lebanese still held by the SLA at Khiam prison, thirty Arabs held inside Israel, four Israelis missing in Lebanon and at least eight SLA militiamen.

Picco foresees the transformation of Hezbollah into a political party. The kidnappers "come out more credible, because they have been part of negotiations in which they kept their word", he says. "They can join in politics. If it can be proven that things can be done through negotiation, then the appeal of violence will diminish."

For the British and American public, the hostage saga was about westerners cruelly deprived of their liberty. Picco is fighting an uphill battle to get the world to recognise that there is more to it than that. "This began not as a story about just ten or eleven westerners, but about several hundred people," he says. "It is a serious moral and political commitment. There are a lot of things left to do."

Picco was an assistant secretary general of the UN when he left to establish a private consultancy group in 1994. In 2018, I was saddened to learn that he had been institutionalised after being diagnosed with Alzheimer's disease the previous year, at the age of sixty-nine. "The process of deterioration was shockingly swift. It seemed like one minute, Gianni was his usual charismatic, suave, articulate self; the next, he was unable to finish sentences," Sulome Anderson wrote on her fundraising website, "Helping the Man Who Saved My Father". Despite two decades working for the UN and several corporate directorships, Picco had ended up in what Anderson called "the abysmal conditions of a state nursing home". Teresa Norris, a nurse, realised the stories he told her were not tall tales or delusions. She contacted Picco's friends and moved him to a more comfortable setting. By June 2021, Anderson had raised more than two-thirds of the $60,000 it takes to maintain Picco in a private nursing home for one year.

ℐə

August 1996

Terry Anderson lives in upstate New York, where he writes a newspaper column and hosts a radio talk show. He is about to start teaching journalism at Columbia University and is an active member of the Committee to Protect Journalists. He has returned to Beirut with Madeleine and Sulome, to make a documentary for CNN.

When Terry was kidnapped in March 1985, he and Madeleine lived in the third-floor apartment above the flat that Robert and I occupy. We celebrate not only Terry's deliverance but the fact that, with the exception of Israeli-occupied southern Lebanon, the civil war seems to be over.

In the old days, Robert and Terry had a ritual of popping champagne corks into the palm tree at the corner of the building. It was good luck to lodge the cork in the heart of the palm fronds, a feat Terry accomplishes without difficulty, to the delight of Sulome, now aged ten. She is a serious, bookish child who sits engrossed in my copy of Edith Hamilton's *Mythology: Timeless Tales of Gods and Heroes*.

Ronald Reagan's travel ban is still in force, in theory, and I cannot resist asking Terry if he has sought a waiver. I quote his answer in my last article for *Time* magazine: "I do not believe the State Department has a right to restrict Americans from going to any country the US is not at war with," Terry says. "I am perfectly willing to go to court over it if they want to."

Terry says the travel ban was declared because Americans "are bad losers". He goes on to explain: "We got burned here, like we did in Vietnam, like we did in Cuba. It seems to me we hold a grudge for a long time."

Terry gives us a signed copy of his book about his captivity, *Den of Lions*, in which he affectionately describes Robert's rapid-fire speech and perennially smudged eyeglasses. To my delight, Robert begins washing his glasses every day.

On the night before his abduction, Terry and Robert had an intense discussion in our very building about what to do if gunmen tried to kidnap them. "I don't think we should let ourselves be taken, in any circumstances," Robert said with a determination that never faltered.

"Don't be a fool," Terry replied. "They've got guns. If you fight, you'll just get killed. Go along. At least you'll be alive."

Terry's presence in our home with his wife and daughter seems to vindicate his decision. We open *Den of Lions* to find his handwritten inscription. It says: "See – I was right!"

VIII

The Black Decade

The war dug.
What it dug:
A black tunnel.

Black dunes.
Black sand.
Black moon.

What remained of it.
A black thought.
And it came.

A black war.
And which left again.
A black wave.

Mohammed Dib, from "The War"

Kouba, Algiers, 9 August 1991

A seemingly endless sea of bearded men dressed in the fundamentalist uniform of the *khamis* converges from every direction for Friday prayers. This is the mosque where Ali Belhadj, the fieriest sheikh of the Islamic Salvation Front, used to preach. Belhadj is mouldering in prison now, with the movement's other leader, Sheikh Abassi Madani.

The Algerian regime blames the Islamic Salvation Front for rioting in June which led President Chadli Bendjedid to postpone parliamentary elections. The movement calls itself by its French acronym, FIS, which is ironic since its adherents reject the French language. Though the FIS remains legal pending elections rescheduled for December and January, 6,000 of its members have already been arrested.

I wear a calf-length blue shirt dress with long sleeves and a headscarf, despite the heat. To avoid problems, I've brought a man from the FIS office with me. *Time* magazine has dispatched photographer Barry Iverson from Cairo to take pictures for my story. Barry is a gentle soul who was badly wounded by an Israeli shell during the 1982 invasion of Lebanon. His wife Nihal is Egyptian. Barry and I work well together.

The graceful white mosque with its blue-patterned tiles cannot contain the thousands of men who have risked arrest to make this show of piety and strength. The prayer-goers unfurl small rugs in the garden around the mosque and on surrounding roads, then prostrate themselves towards Mecca, feet tucked beneath their bodies and foreheads pressed to the ground.

"The Algerian people are Muslims," says the voice booming from the loudspeaker on the minaret. "The police who prevent people from coming to prayers are not true Muslims." I turn to look at the policemen in riot gear and sunglasses behind us. They clutch assault rifles and stare impassively at the multitude. The preacher grows more strident. "The government ruined this country. It is the people who suffer from the economic crisis. The government claims it is Muslim, but if it is, why won't it proclaim sharia? The people of Algeria want an Islamic state. They should be allowed to choose this freely."

Popular support for the FIS has grown steadily since the army killed about 500 people in nationwide riots in 1988. The fundamentalist party won an overwhelming victory in municipal elections in June 1990, the first free, multi-party vote since independence in 1962; and it would certainly have won the first round of parliamentary elections in June if *le pouvoir* had not postponed the vote.

Le pouvoir, the power, is the Algerians' word for the murky clique of army generals, family clans and profiteers who have misruled the country for the three decades since independence. Though three-quarters of the country's 26 million citizens were born *after* the 1954–62 war, *le pouvoir* continues to base its claim to legitimacy on having won the struggle against France.

The month before I arrive in Algiers, the FIS uses a laser device to write "Allah" on the clouds overhead during an open-air rally in Bab El-Oued. Many FIS voters believe they have witnessed a miracle.

While we listen to the sermon at Kouba mosque, an army unit moves into the square between us and our car and driver. On our way back, a soldier asks to see our papers, then demands Barry's film. "You cannot do that!" I tell the soldier. "We are accredited journalists." The soldier holds out his hand. Barry winds the spool and gives it to him. You don't argue with a man holding an assault rifle.

Suddenly I recognise a familiar face across the square. I have not seen General Fodil Cherif since the murder of Lebanese President René Moawad in Beirut nearly two years earlier. Cherif had given us a lift to Moawad's election at a disused airbase on

Lebanon's northern border with Syria on 5 November 1989. We talked for hours in the car, and met again by chance on the scene of Moawad's assassination seventeen days later.

One sometimes sees photographs of Algerian generals at ceremonial occasions. Lined up like the members of a South American junta, they are moustachioed, overweight and drip gold braid and medals. Not Fodil Cherif. He's a general from Hollywood central casting: clean-shaven, with steel-grey hair and Ray-Bans, fit in his olive-green fatigues and black army boots.

The state's war with Islamic fundamentalism is just beginning. The term *éradicateur* has not yet come into common usage. Cherif will be a leading *éradicateur*. When he tracks down and kills the head of the Armed Islamic Group, Antar Zouabri, a decade later, Cherif strikes the pose of a victor and smokes a cigar, standing over Zouabri's body. Cherif believes so strongly in eradicating Islamic fundamentalists that he will retire early rather than accept future president Abdelaziz Bouteflika's policy of "reconciliation".

"General Cherif, remember me? Lara Marlowe. My husband Robert Fisk and I met you in Beirut, when you were in charge of Lakhdar Brahimi's protection."

"*Qu'est-ce que vous faites là, avec ce foulard?*" (What are you doing here, with that headscarf?) Cherif sneers. He spits out the words *là* and *foulard* to show his loathing for the place – Kouba, a FIS stronghold – and my head covering.

I tear off the scarf and shake Cherif's hand, all the while hoping that FIS militants will not record the moment and assume I am a collaborator of *le pouvoir*. Once I have removed the offending piece of cloth, Cherif flashes a white-toothed grin and continues chomping on his chewing gum. "Of course I remember you," he says.

"General Cherif, your soldier just took our film," I say. "Can we have it back, please? We really need it."

Cherif promises to return our film, just not right away. He gives me a telephone number, allegedly at the defence ministry, which I call many times. Once or twice, I reach a person who sounds like a cleaner, who understands neither French nor my Lebanese Arabic. Usually the phone rings with no reply. We never get our film back. I have an unpleasant suspicion military intelligence may be using Barry's photographs to catalogue FIS supporters.

Two years after bringing an end to Lebanon's civil war, Lakhdar Brahimi has returned to Algiers as foreign minister. I haven't seen him since he left Robert and me at Taif airport in Saudi Arabia, after we flew with him to the peace conference there. I request an interview through the foreign ministry and Brahimi invites me to breakfast at Djenane El-Mithaq, the sumptuous gardens and residence where the government receives foreign guests. Over croissants and coffee, he rails at those western media who suggest that Algeria is about to follow Iran, that Algeria will become the first Arab country to complete an Islamic revolution.

Iran is not Arab, and it is Shia, not Sunni like Algeria, Brahimi argues. He claims Algeria has no tradition of radical Islam and martyrdom. The rise of the FIS is the result of an economic crisis and thirty years of one-party rule by the Front de Libération Nationale, the FLN. Things will improve once the transition to democracy and a free-market economy gets underway. Brahimi states categorically that "there is no likelihood of our becoming an Islamic republic".

Time magazine increasingly allows me to write my own articles, but editors in New York still leave their fingerprints all over my copy. When my article is published, I discover that World editor Johanna McGeary has tacked this phrase onto the beginning of my story, contradicting my interview with Brahimi: "Ominously recalling Iran in the months before Ayatollah Khomeini's revolution…"

In the summer of 1991, the FIS is still a legal political party with a headquarters in downtown Algiers. I go there to pick up its programme and interview party workers. If the FIS takes over, it promises to ban alcohol, segregate men from women and impose sharia. When I ask to buy a copy of Algeria's constitution in a nearby bookshop, the salesman pointedly hands me a Koran.

A debate rages over whether fundamentalist Islam should be allowed to come to power through democratic means. If elections go ahead that winter, secular opponents of the FIS predict that "it will be one man, one vote, one time". There is already talk of banning the party. "If they exclude us, we will go underground and it will be much harder for them to control us," Youssef, a chemistry teacher and FIS militant, tells me.

The FIS wins 188 of 231 parliamentary seats in the first round of elections on 26 December 1991. I return to Algiers on 9 January 1992, this time with Robert, with the intention of covering the second round, which is scheduled for 16 January.

At Friday prayers in Kouba on 10 January, we notice that a lot of worshippers wear pakols, the rolled Afghan hat typical of the mujahidin guerrillas who defeated the Soviets. Hundreds of aspiring Algerian jihadists learned to fight there, and the government has begun arresting those who come home. Four years later in Afghanistan, Robert will converse in French with an Algerian bodyguard to Osama bin Laden.

Robert's three interviews with bin Laden are in a sense the result of this trip to Algiers. I have coffee one morning with a bright, articulate Saudi colleague who has, like us, come to write about Algeria's "democratic process". He speaks enthusiastically of a new religious leader whose sermons are stirring fervour among Arabs. The journalist is Jamal Khashoggi and the preacher is Osama bin Laden. Jamal covered bin Laden's jihad against the Soviets in Afghanistan, when the CIA and Saudi royal family still supported bin Laden.

I tell Robert the story and introduce him to Jamal, who will accompany Robert on his first interview with bin Laden in Sudan in 1993. I regret not having joined them. The mere thought of "selling" the story of yet another Islamist preacher to my editors at *Time* magazine, and especially of fighting to preserve the integrity of my copy, wearies me in advance.

Robert sees every event in the Arab and Muslim world through the prism of history, and Algeria is petrified in its own

Robert's first foreign holiday, in 1956, was a trip to World War I battlefields with his parents. Here he is with his father Bill, who pretends to read Le Figaro.

The first photograph of us together, taken by a stranger in Central Park on 15 November 1987.

*In December 1987, Robert kept his promise to take me
for a camel ride in Egypt if I came to live with him.*

*With Juan Carlos Gumucio, boarding the Middle East Airlines
flight from Beirut to London in December 1987.*

We made a ritual of drinking
champagne in the Wicklow mountains
on Christmas morning.

August 1988. I am nervous because the
Phalange have threatened to shell the
Lebanese parliament to stop the
presidential election.

The Sleit building on the Beirut
Corniche, where Robert and I lived
together for eight years, and where
he spent most of his forty-five years
in Lebanon.

At the wedding of friends in Beirut,
with AP driver Hussein Kurdi,
January 1991.

*In the BBC office in Sarajevo, September 1992.
I dived under the desk moments earlier when a
shell exploded outside.*

*Our Beirut cat Walter was
an endless source of affection
and amusement.*

Prime Minister Rafik Hariri proved to be a loyal friend to both of us.

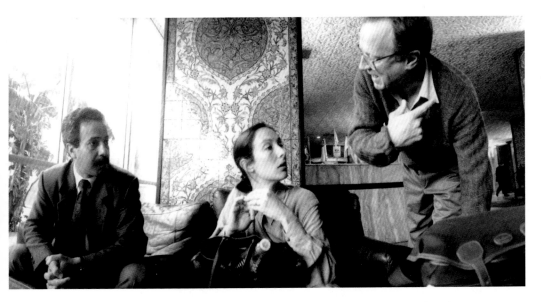

Robert and me with a plainclothes Algerian army officer in the El Djazair Hotel, photographed by Michael von Graffenried, March 1995.

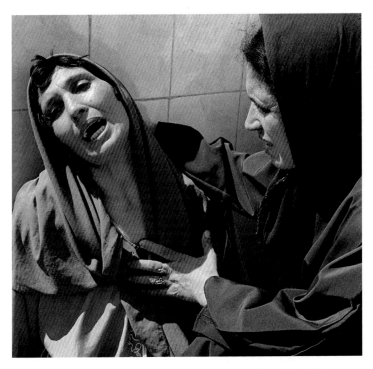

This picture of a grieving woman, taken by AFP photographer Hocine Zaourar, came to symbolise the agony of Algeria's Black Decade.

In the ruins of Baalbek with a Lebanese gendarme, July 1995.

At our post-wedding brunch in London, 14 February 1997.

history. In Algiers, the 1954–62 war with the French is ever-present, far closer than thirty years. We take advantage of the Muslim weekend to visit the basilica of Notre-Dame d'Afrique, overlooking the Bay of Algiers, and the nearby Cimetière Saint-Eugène, where Robert transforms the tombstone details of long-dead French colonialists into a parable of lost *Algérie française* for his newspaper.

The beauty of Algiers, with its lush gardens and white buildings spilling down the hillside to the Mediterranean, belies the horror of the dark decade that is beginning. No wonder the French made Algeria a *département* of France and fought so hard to keep it. France's ambassador to Beirut, René Ala, had told me the previous year, "*Mais, Madame, l'Algérie est la chair de la France!*" But Madam, Algeria is the flesh of France!

The attachment of some older French people to Algeria remains visceral. My close friendship with the French academician Michel Déon and his wife Chantal, who lived for forty years in the west of Ireland, will be all but destroyed by articles I publish in 2015/16 in *The Irish Times* about long-past French atrocities in Algeria. Chantal's father was a colonel during the Algerian war. To his dying day, Michel believed in *l'Algérie française*.

Yet if I feel at home in Algiers and Beirut, it is because of the imprint the French left there. In both capitals, landmarks often have two names, pre-independence French and Arabic. Algiers's main thoroughfare, the rue Didouche Mourad – formerly rue Michelet – could be the boulevard de Cimiez in Nice. With its arcades and wrought iron balconies, the rue Larbi Ben M'Hidi – formerly rue d'Isly – reminds me of the rue de Rivoli in Paris.

Robert blames colonialism for adulterating the true nature of Algeria and Lebanon and for dividing their peoples. He mocks the Gallic mannerisms of Maronites and French-speaking Algerian intellectuals. In Saudi Arabia and Kuwait, I did not want to be cast by him as an apologist for war in the Gulf. In Algeria, I do not want him to brand me a neocolonialist.

Yet having aspired to Frenchness since childhood, I see the

Algerians' command of the French language as, in the words of the Algerian writer Kateb Yacine, *un butin de guerre*, a spoil of war. There is something serendipitous in the way that I, an American born in California, can form an immediate bond with French-educated Lebanese or Algerians.

In Robert's opinion, colonisation debilitated Algeria, turned it into a cheap imitation of France that cannot find its own identity. "Look at this breakfast tray," he says in the morning at the Hotel El Djazair. "You would think you were in a hotel in Paris, except that the croissants taste like cardboard, the orange juice comes from a tin made in Italy and the coffee has no taste at all."

Even the Valentine's Day card which Robert buys in the El Djazair shop the following month looks like a relic of 1950s' France. *Ni vous sans moi ni moi sans vous*, neither you without me nor me without you, is printed next to a watercolour painting of two red roses. "To the woman I adore, my beautiful Lara I love you – your Bobby," he writes inside.

The words are reassuring, for our relationship seems to be losing in romanticism as it gains in journalistic prowess. In Algeria, we make a particularly efficient team. I feel a real affinity for the country, and my fluency in French means that I contribute more than usual. I translate complicated passages of interviews for Robert, schedule most of our appointments and maintain contacts and friendships in Algiers, which I visit more often than he does.

Robert, too, appreciates what he calls the magnetism of Algeria. "It's like a place you know from a previous life," he says. "It reminds me of my first visit to France with my parents in 1956." With reason. After independence, the corrupt *pouvoir* siphoned off most of Algeria's wealth. So, aside from a few monuments to the revolution and 1970s' Yugoslav-style monstrosities like the Hotel El Aurassi, the capital was preserved as it was under the French. The nineteenth-century architecture, old jalopies, faulty plumbing, even the railway stations and corrugated steel railway carriages, remind Robert of the French provincial cities he came to know in the 1950s.

Hotels help to shape my memories of the wars we covered together. The Méridien, Dhahran. The Holiday Inn, Sarajevo. The Majestic in Belgrade. The Palestine in Baghdad. In Algiers, it will be the El Djazair, with its Moorish façade and blue-tiled foyer. Every day on the way to the restaurant, we pass a bronze plaque in three languages which says: "Dwight D. Eisenhower, Commander in Chief of the Allied Expeditionary Forces in North Africa, maintained his headquarters in this room from November 1942 to December 1943".

The El Djazair, the former Saint Georges, is an important part of that "place we know from a previous life". We return to it as if to a haven, after interviews with torture victims and harrowing journeys in armoured vehicles with masked special forces soldiers. Little matter that the restaurant food makes you ill and one sometimes fears having one's throat slashed in bed at night.

Monsieur Mouloud, the concierge, is always there, lugubrious in his grey suit, wedged between an orientalist painting and the massive green malachite reception desk. He whispers titbits of news, furtively, like Peter Lorre as Ugarte in the 1942 film classic *Casablanca*. Furtive like many of his compatriots, secretive and evasive, beaten down by 132 years of French rule and thirty years of FLN dictatorship, embarking now against his will on another nightmarish adventure. For the generals – among them Fodil Cherif – decide to "suspend the democratic process". They force President Chadli Bendjedid to resign on the night of 11 January 1992, and replace him five days later with Mohamed Boudiaf, a seventy-two-year-old hero of the 1954–62 war who has lived quietly in Morocco for twenty-six years, running a brick factory.

A tall, bald man with hollow cheeks, Boudiaf is one of the nine founding fathers of independent Algeria. He has an unimpeachable record as a war hero, having served six years as a prisoner of the French. In the 1960s, he refused an offer from Colonel Houari Boumediene to lead a figurehead civilian government under military control. We don't understand why he accepts a similar pact now. Unlike fellow revolutionaries who are tainted by corruption and misrule, Boudiaf has earned an honest living in his Moroccan exile.

At a press conference at the presidential palace in February, Boudiaf talks in oxymorons: "The halting of the electoral process was made necessary in order to safeguard democracy," he says. "The state of emergency has nothing to do with any restriction of fundamental freedoms."

We are in Moscow six months later, when Boudiaf's bodyguard, Second Lieutenant Lambarek Boumaarafi, fires two bullets into Boudiaf's head and a third into his back while the president is delivering a speech in Annaba. At first, everyone assumes that Boumaarafi is a closet fundamentalist, like Khalid al-Islambouli, the Egyptian army officer who assassinated Anwar Sadat in 1981. Then, as often happens in Algeria, contradictory information seeps out. Boudiaf's anti-corruption campaign had resulted in the arrest of a retired army general and a prominent businessman linked to former president Bendjedid. Rumour has it that Boudiaf started secret negotiations with moderate FIS officials. His widow says she does not believe "for a single moment" that the FIS murdered her husband.

જી

Sheikh Abdelkader Hachani, the acting leader of the FIS and the architect of the party's election victory, calls a press conference on 15 January 1992, three days after the declaration of martial law. "We won the election, and they stole it," a bodyguard to Hachani tells me. "They will pay for it – in heaven and on earth."

Hachani is upstaged by Amar Brahmia, the long-distance track coach to Algeria's national athletic team, who recounts that he has just been released after being detained and beaten at the defence ministry for having attended a FIS rally. "They threatened to rape my wife if I told anyone what happened," Brahmia says. "I am telling this to the press so that Algerians will know what sort of people are in power."

A week later, Hachani is arrested on the orders of the defence minister, General Khaled Nezzar, for appealing to army conscripts to rise up and overthrow the government. He will spend five and a half years in Serkadji prison. When he gets out, he negotiates a truce between the armed wing of the FIS and the army. Hachani is shot dead in a dentist's waiting room in Bab El-Oued in November 1999. No one is sure if he was killed by fundamentalists more radical than him, or hardliners from the military who want to foil attempts to make peace.

Prime Minister Sid Ahmed Ghozali bans all political speeches and demonstrations at mosques. Extremists nonetheless continue to gather at places of worship. The "Afghans", former combatants in Soviet-occupied Afghanistan, congregate at the so-called Kabul mosque – real name Salaheddin – in the poor seafront quarter of Belcourt. Robert and I go there at prayer time one cold winter evening. By the light of street lamps, we see hundreds of men, many dressed in Afghan costume, their eyes ringed with black kohl, pouring out of the mosque.

The most fierce-looking "Afghans" refuse to talk to us, but we persevere until a thirty-two-year-old biologist called Akli agrees to sit with us in a grimy café where we drink mint tea from chipped cups. Akli prays five times a day at the Kabul mosque and is convinced that Algeria will soon be an Islamic republic. "The Islamic *sahwa* [awakening] started here in the 1970s, in the cafés, in the streets, even in bars," he says. "It filled a void in Algerian society. We will succeed because God is with us."

Algerian women stand to lose most if the FIS comes to power, and many are frightened. I wear a shawl wrapped around my head and Akli thanks me for what he calls my "modesty". I ask him why he thinks so many Algerian women fear the prospect of an Islamic republic. "The women who don't want Islam are our sisters," he replies, "but we think they are sick. They are culturally alienated. They need re-education."

Such retrograde views are standard fare among Islamists. In a 1989 speech, FIS leader Abassi Madani said a woman need leave home only three times in her life: "when she is born, when she is married, and when she goes to the cemetery".

The situation deteriorates rapidly. Dozens of imams are arrested. A gendarme is assassinated. In the early hours of 14 February, Algerian paratroopers fire rocket-propelled grenades into a house in the Casbah, killing five men. The Casbah is a thousand-year-old citadel composed of mosques, dilapidated Ottoman palaces and humble wood and mud-brick dwellings. It has grown organically, like barnacles on a rock. The maze of narrow alleys, ancient, overhanging houses and steps leading in every direction is a thief's or an assassin's dream. With Algeria hovering on the edge of chaos, it feels like a death trap. Robert and I go there to find the house of Bouznad Hadi, the grocer who was burned alive with four fellow Islamists on St Valentine's Day 1992.

Such scenes will become all too familiar: the weeping women and curious onlookers in the alley outside, the jagged hole at the point of impact, the charred furniture and angry relatives. One of them says he is Hadi's cousin, and leads us up the dark staircase by torchlight to the room where the men died. Two had been wounded at a demonstration, the cousin says. We suspect they were wounded not at a demonstration but in the fatal ambush of six policemen in the Casbah the week before. At least one of the attackers was reported to have been wounded.

The bearded men in the ruins of Bouznad Hadi's house have the fierce, hard look of insurgents who have been driven underground. They tell us the army attacked the house to avenge the killing of fifteen soldiers at Guemar, near the Tunisian border, the previous year. Now they too want revenge.

A man in the crowd leads us a few hundred metres deeper into the warren of wood and clay structures, to another house. This is the place where the FLN fighter Ali Ammar, better known as Ali la Pointe, hid with three comrades in October

1957. The Italian director Gillo Pontecorvo filmed the last scene of his masterpiece *The Battle of Algiers* in this house, which has become a museum. In 1957, an informer betrayed the guerrillas to French paratroopers, who offered them the chance to surrender. But in an act of heroism known to all Algerians, Ali la Pointe refused, for fear he might talk under torture. The paratroopers blew up the house, killing twenty people, including la Pointe. For our anonymous guide in February 1991, the parallel is obvious.

In May 1993, Robert is busy shooting a three-part television documentary with director Mike Dutfield, entitled *From Beirut to Bosnia*. It will be shown on British Channel 4 and Discovery Channel in the US. I return alone to Algiers. It is the first time I use the words "civil war" in print to describe the Algerian conflict. About 1,000 people have been killed since the elections were cancelled and the FIS was banned. Thousands of FIS members are imprisoned in desert camps. Those still free have created a guerrilla group calling itself the Armed Islamic Movement or MIA – its French acronym. (The name will change yet again, to Army of Islamic Salvation or AIS.)

Twenty thousand soldiers are deployed at entry points to the capital and across the city. You see them patrolling streets in armoured vehicles, perched in tank turrets and manning sandbagged machine-gun nests. Police conduct nightly raids in pro-FIS neighbourhoods, and blow up more houses suspected of sheltering guerrillas. At former FIS mosques, government-appointed imams weep when they pray for peace.

Henceforward, fear is the only emotion shared by all Algerians. Few civilians venture out at night because militants disguised as police or soldiers erect *faux barrages*, fake checkpoints, where they steal cars and in some cases kidnap or murder suspected supporters of the regime. Policemen, like the Islamists they are tracking, are afraid to sleep in their own beds. Hooded informers accompany gunmen on killing missions. Security forces infiltrate Islamist groups. Duplicity and confusion reign. The great newspaper columnist Saïd Mekbel, who will be murdered in December 1994, popularises the expression *Qui tue qui?* Who is killing whom?

Les Palmiers is an Islamist stronghold at the heart of what is known as the "triangle of fear". The neighbourhood stinks of sewage and rotting garbage and is raided often by police because it is known to shelter MIA guerrillas. In Les Palmiers, an unemployed young man called Ramadan gives voice to popular hatred. "This government has pushed people to take up arms," he tells me. "They are thieves, bloodsuckers, vampires. Anyone who works with them deserves to die."

I travel to Les Eucalyptus, a slum just east of Algiers, where the family of Karima Belhadj are mourning the pretty twenty-year-old secretary for the Police Welfare and Sports Association. The previous month, Karima earned the sad distinction of becoming the first female "martyr" of the 1990s' civil war. Karima was one of only 8 per cent of Algerian women to hold a salaried job. She supported her parents and five siblings on a monthly salary equivalent to 150 euro. She fell in love with the bus driver who drove her home from work. They were engaged to marry, and Karima spent evenings embroidering clothes for her trousseau.

When Karima steps off the bus on 6 April 1993, a boy from her neighbourhood points her out to six waiting assassins. The boy has been paid a few dinars to betray her. One man grabs Karima by the hair and pulls her down. A second fires a pistol into her abdomen and head. Karima's brother Reda runs into the street when he hears the shooting.

"She was lying on the ground with her eyes open and a hole in her forehead," Reda tells me. "Blood was flowing out the side of her head. She said, 'Take me to the hospital. I want to live.' Those were her last words."

I have coffee with Omar Belhouchet, the director of *El Watan* newspaper. Belhouchet's name appears on a list of thirty French-speaking journalists condemned to death by fundamentalists. He has already survived the first of two assassination attempts, and his wife has just suffered a nervous breakdown. Belhouchet could easily move to Paris, but he stays on. Why? I ask. "Because journalism is still the most beautiful profession," he replies, as if the answer were obvious. I think of Robert, refusing to leave Beirut when the threat of kidnapping scared everyone else away. I question my own commitment.

In Algeria in the 1990s, clothing and language mark one's belonging to what the fundamentalists call the *hizb fransa*, the party of the French. The conflict in Algeria is in part about language. Arabic was almost lost under French rule, so the victorious FLN imported Arabic teachers from Egypt and Syria in the 1970s and 1980s. Algerian secularists say many of the Arabic teachers belong to the Muslim Brotherhood and blame the official policy of *Arabisation* for the flowering of fundamentalism. Hypocritically, the elite continue to educate their children in French schools.

On the morning of 26 May 1993, the award-winning author and newspaper editor Tahar Djaout, aged thirty-nine, is shot twice in the head at point-blank range in the parking lot of his apartment building at Baïnem, in the western suburbs of Algiers. I go there and see pools of blood where he fell. I then go to the hospital where Djaout is dying. His desperate colleagues wait in the corridor outside his room, talking of forming their own armed group.

"We cannot continue allowing ourselves to be picked off one at a time, each waiting his turn, burying our friends. I'm afraid for everyone who thinks in this country. We intellectuals may be doomed to extinction," Djaout's friend and colleague Abdelkrim Djaad tells me. They founded a weekly together earlier in the year. Its title is *Ruptures*.

Djaout dies after six days in a coma. The writer Mohammed Dib calls him and other slain intellectuals "martyrs to the French language". A FIS newsletter denounces Djaout's "communism and visceral hatred of Islam", but his killing is attributed to a new, more virulent movement, the Armed Islamic Group or GIA.

Its leaders are believed to be veterans of the war in Afghanistan, like those we saw at the Kabul mosque.

The slogan inscribed on the GIA's communiqués is "no agreement, no truce, no dialogue". The GIA uses kidnapping, assassination and bombings to achieve its goal of creating "an atmosphere of general insecurity". It massacres civilians, wiping out whole villages. It also targets Islamists from other groups and is responsible for most of the murders of at least 118 foreigners in Algeria during the 1990s. Twenty years before Isis takes over large swathes of Iraq and Syria, the GIA makes beheading its signature method of killing, calculated to create maximum horror.

Time magazine has assigned an Algerian photographer to work with me. He takes me to the tiny village of Ain Sheik, 120 kilometres south-west of Algiers, where he has family ties, to write about the murder of "Moustache" Kechroud, an ageing farmer and veteran of the war of independence who was recently killed by Islamists because he refused to turn over the shotgun he had kept since his years in the resistance.

Polygamy is still common in the Algerian countryside and Moustache lived contentedly with his two wives and their fourteen children. Aliya, the older wife, was tortured by the French when Moustache joined the guerrillas in 1954. "In those days, we only wanted to be free," she says; "not to turn Algeria into an Islamic State." Aisha, the younger widow, expresses the incomprehension of many civilians caught between the army and the fundamentalists. "We fasted during Ramadan and gave to charity. What is this new Islam they want to force on us?"

The constitution of Algeria begins with the first words of the Koran, and the founding document declares Islam to be the state religion. The national flag is emblazoned with a crescent moon, the symbol of Islam. Yet fundamentalists accuse the FLN of betraying what they claim was an Islamic revolution.

There is a macabre sense of déjà vu about the insurrection, three to four decades on. Then, as now, fighters called themselves mujahidin or holy warriors, and the dead are given the status of martyrs. The rebels of the 1990s denigrate the leaders of the regime as *Harkis*, Muslim Algerians who fought on the side of the French. The government uses the same torture methods the French used against the FLN. It jails Islamists in Serkadji prison at the top of the Casbah. The French built Serkadji in 1856, called it Barberousse and locked up FLN members there.

Not all Islamist sympathisers are poor. Benyoucef Benkhedda, the first prime minister of independent Algeria, runs a pharmacy in the middle-class neighbourhood of Hydra. Benkhedda was twice imprisoned by the French and later fled through the sewers of Algiers to avoid arrest by General Jacques Massu's paratroopers. He co-founded the government newspaper *El Moudjahid*, played a part in the establishment of the country's main trade union and in the writing of the national anthem. As prime minister of the provisional government, he completed independence negotiations with the French, but he was rapidly pushed out of office by more vicious politicians, who later placed him under house arrest.

When I first meet him in May 1993, I find Benkhedda to be a courtly, modest but embittered seventy-three-year-old gentleman living quietly with his wife and sons. He has co-founded a party called El Oumma, meaning the Islamic nation, whose objective is to restore the Islamic principles that were declared at the outset of the 1954 insurrection. When the word "Islam" is later banned from political discourse, Benkhedda co-founds another party with the aim of denouncing the regime's human rights abuses.

Each time I talk to Benkhedda, I feel I am touching Algerian history. I later introduce him to Robert, and they hit it off. The ageing politician knows that the regime would not hesitate to harass or imprison him, and he does not want to be quoted in our articles. But he is an invaluable contact who repeatedly puts us in touch with survivors of the regime's torture chambers. Benkhedda dies in February 2003, just short of his eighty-third birthday. Much later, one of his sons falls victim to the brutality that the ageing independence fighter helped to reveal. In March 2019, Hassan Benkhedda, aged fifty-six, attends one of the mass rallies organised by the Hirak movement to protest Bouteflika's bid for a fifth term as president of Algeria. "Boutef" has been in power for twenty years and has been incapacitated by a stroke since 2013.

The interior minister says Hassan Benkhedda, son of Algeria's first prime minister, died of a heart attack during the demonstration. Hassan's brother Salim, a cardiologist, tells *El Watan* newspaper that the dead man had returned to their mother's house in Hydra – the house where Robert and I so often talked with their father – and was taken away by police and *baltaguia*, Arabic slang for thugs used to attack opponents of the regime. The family later find Hassan's body in the morgue of Mustapha Hospital, where Salim practises medicine. Salim says Hassan's corpse has multiple fractures to the skull and body. The family's lawsuit for wrongful death is dismissed by an Algiers court.

By 1993, death threats have become a daily occurrence in Algeria. Secular Algerians and foreigners receive in their letter-boxes razors, bits of sackcloth and the kind of soap used to prepare corpses for burial. An anonymous phone caller tells a doctor I interview, "Your shroud is almost ready".

Malika, my closest Algerian friend, is a dentist whom I met when we sat together on a flight from Paris to Algiers. She receives a handwritten letter. "In the name of God, the most merciful," it begins in Arabic, then switches to French: "You are being watched. Dirty whore. No work ... No more police." (Malika counts policemen among her patients.) Soon afterwards, a man puts a knife to her throat in broad daylight on a busy downtown street and drags her into a doorway. She thinks her life is over. He takes her identity papers and lets her go.

At the end of October 1993, the GIA releases a French woman hostage, a consular officer. They give her a letter warning all foreigners to leave Algeria by 1 December or be killed. More than 4,000 foreigners flee the country in November. Foreign companies take down their signs. Anti-fundamentalist death squads dump the bodies of three kidnapped Islamists in Kouba. One of them is the brother-in-law and close friend of imprisoned FIS leader Ali Belhadj. The "Organisation of Young Free Algerians" tortures to death an Islamist professor, then circulates a tract threatening fundamentalists: "You will pay the price for supporting those who have spilled Algerian blood," it says. "An eye for an eye, a tooth for a tooth."

On 31 January 1994, Robert and I attend the swearing in of yet another Algerian president, the retired army general Liamine Zéroual. Robert carries the camera tripod for a French cameraman, Olivier Quemener. The following morning, we come downstairs in the El Djazair to learn that Quemener has been assassinated. He went out early to film at the top of the Casbah, near Serkadji prison. A man stepped up to him and fired a bullet into his head. Olivier was thirty-three years old. He is the twenty-seventh foreigner to be murdered in Algiers since 1993.

There are perhaps a dozen French journalists in Algiers to cover Zéroual's inauguration and a "national dialogue", which is aborted when most of the political parties boycott it. We join their discussion in the hotel lobby. The French embassy wants to take us all under armed escort to the airport for the next flight to Paris. We could go with them. Robert and I discuss it alone in our room. We thank our colleagues for the offer but decide to stay on.

Two days later, we interview nineteen-year-old Mohamed in a safe house in Algiers. Mohamed attended madrasa and preached in a mosque until police came for him in the middle of the night in the autumn of 1993. "They blindfolded me and took me straight to a torture room," he says, describing a cold dungeon, several floors below ground. "They stripped me naked. There was a manhole in the floor. They kept dunking my head in the sewage." Like a professor I interviewed the previous year, Mohamed is waterboarded and asked repeatedly: "Where are the weapons?"

This torture technique, which creates the impression that one is drowning, is called *la baignoire* (the bathtub) in French, waterboarding in English. It was used by the Gestapo during the Nazi occupation of France, by the French during the Algerian war, and now by Algerians against Algerians. The CIA will use it widely against Arab detainees after 9/11.

Mohamed is taken to the basement of the Châteauneuf police school, where he is tortured on his feet with an electric taser gun. He is moved again, to the central commissariat near the Air France building in downtown Algiers. There he sees five dead people, "two hanging from the ceiling, the other three … burned to death with blowtorches".

A cellmate called Sid-Ahmed Shabla tells Mohamed that the police tortured and raped his mother in front of him. "I was outside the room when they did this, and when his mother came out, she was naked and covered in blood. She told us to be brave, to hang on."

Mohamed's hands and feet are bound and he is placed on the cement floor, on his stomach. His head is smashed onto the floor until his teeth break. Mohamed tells police that his brother is fighting with the "resistance". When they bring his brother in, Mohamed breaks down in tears, saying, "It's not true. I only said it because of the torture."

Mohamed's brother weeps and says, "May God forgive you." The torturers break the brother's ribs and let him go.

After forty-five more days, this time in a dark, rat-infested cell in Serkadji prison, Mohamed is acquitted and released. He lives in hiding "because death squads are going around killing everyone who comes out of prison".

⁊ə

In July 1994, seven Italian sailors have their throats slit while they are sleeping on their boat, the *Lucina*, docked in the port of Djendjen, near Jijel, 350 kilometres east of Algiers. The boat is carrying a cargo of semolina, to feed the Algerian people. The extremists consider all *roumi*, their term for foreign Christians, to be legitimate targets.

Robert and I adopt Beirut-like habits. I wedge a chair under the doorknob in our hotel room at night. If someone comes into the room while we are sleeping, at least we'll be woken and have a fighting chance. I could pass for a fair-skinned Algerian, so I sit beside Omar, our driver, in the front seat of his taxi, wearing sunglasses and a headscarf. Robert sits in the back, holding a newspaper in front of his face. When we arrive for an appointment, we rush through the front door of the building. If the door is locked and our host keeps us waiting, we curse and anxiously watch the street.

The risks we take are carefully calculated, and include an occasional meal at our favourite restaurant, El Djenina, down the hill from the El Djazair. We know the armed guard outside the front door probably could not save us, but when it is open, the Djenina is one of few respites from watching what feels like the collective suicide of a country. The décor is a replica of an Ottoman palace. I enjoy talking to the owner, the tough, Algerian widow of a French paratrooper. She serves Algerian specialities like *chorba*, *bourek*, couscous and tajine.

Albert Camus's unfinished autobiographical book *The First Man*, published in 1994, is such a moving account of his childhood in Belcourt – the neighbourhood where we visited the Kabul mosque – that I persuade Robert and my friend Malika to go there with me. Omar the driver stands watch. Constantly looking over our shoulders, we are able to enter the small, two-room apartment where Camus was raised by his grandmother and deaf mother Catherine, a Spanish-born cleaning lady.

Places, I believe, have a soul, and I cannot help feeling a sense of Camus's presence in the empty apartment. The communal toilet is on the landing and the only water tap is in the courtyard below, just as Camus described it. Robert takes pictures for the article I never find time to write.

By March 1995, 40,000 Algerians have died in the first three years of the civil war. A thousand are meeting violent deaths each week. The sixty-nine journalists who have been assassinated represent only a tiny fraction of the war's victims, but their murders attract a great deal of attention. The killing of Saïd Mekbel, the editor-in-chief of *Le Matin* newspaper and a brilliant columnist, leaves such a deep impression on me that I enlarge his last column, published on 3 December 1994, frame it, and hang it on the wall of my office in Beirut. Mekbel's column was called *Mesmar J'ha*, "the rusty nail", which was a satirical nickname for former president Chadli Bendjedid. It was witty, eloquent and terrifying, and I made a point of reading it every morning when I was in Algiers. In his last column, published on the day of his death, Mekbel describes an Algerian journalist as "this thief who slinks along walls to go home at night ... this father who tells his children not to talk about the wicked job he does ... this man who makes a wish not to die with his throat slashed..."

In 1998, I meet Mekbel's son Hafid by chance at a demonstration in Paris. I make an appointment to interview him and his French mother, Marie-Laure. Hafid recounts how his father went with a colleague from *Le Matin* to the Marhaba Pizzeria, 40 metres from the newspaper office, for lunch. "He was careful. He never sat with his back to the door," Hafid says. The killer was a well-dressed young man, an habitué of the restaurant, so no one tried to stop him when he approached Mekbel, pulled out a pistol and shot him twice in the head.

Mekbel's staff raced across the street from the newspaper office. One of them described what he saw: "In the back of the restaurant, sitting behind the table, still holding a knife and fork in his hands, his head leaning slightly forward, as if he were looking at the food on his plate, Saïd was still breathing. I told him, 'Saïd, hold on. We're taking you to the hospital.' I reached out to caress his hair but pulled my hand back, covered with blood."

Mekbel's unfinished article for the next edition of the newspaper is found on his desk. It begins: "I would really like to know who is going to kill me. But is that what I'd like to know first? Because there may be more important questions. For example, how will I be killed? And this other question: Why will I be killed? When will I be killed?"

The GIA claims it murdered Mekbel because he was an "infidel", but his widow and son say they don't know which side in Algeria's civil war killed him. Mekbel's column savaged the regime and fundamentalists alike. The government is so discredited, and so eager to attribute atrocities to the Islamists, that many Algerians believe the security forces assassinate and massacre so the population will turn against the insurgents. A report published by the Paris-based Reporters Without Borders in March 1997 suggests that the government may have ordered the murder of at least four prominent journalists, including Djaout and Mekbel.

One often hears allegations that the *Sécurité Militaire* has heavily infiltrated the GIA, or even that it created the extremist group. "Everything is infiltrated, everywhere," says a plain-clothes army captain who befriends Robert and me in March 1995. "Fourteen of my military classmates have been assassinated. Someone in the military tipped off the terrorists. When I leave my office in the defence ministry, I don't tell anyone where I am going."

During the same trip, Robert and I obtain permission to spend several days with a special forces unit of the gendarmerie, the masked commandos known as "ninjas", after the feudal Japanese warriors who were immortalised in Yugoslav comic books. Between patrols, the commander of the unit, who asks to be identified only as Major Mohamed, has long chats with us in his office at the gendarmerie barracks in El Harrach. When we are on the road, he is as tense and alert as an animal, both hunter and hunted. In his office, Major Mohamed is relaxed. He makes coffee, plays old rock-and-roll records on a turntable and sits back with his army boots on his desk.

The GIA is by far the strongest group, Major Mohamed says. The rebels started out with hunting rifles, but now they fight with Czech and Israeli automatic weapons they have smuggled across the borders from Tunisia and Morocco. They operate in isolated cells, a pyramidal structure where only the top men know one another.

The GIA maintains a network of spotters throughout Algiers, within eyesight of each other. The spotters use hand signals, sometimes mirrors, never radios. They have shed their beards and the *khamis* and wear jeans, leather jackets and runners. They are indistinguishable from the legions of *hittistes* (in Algerian dialect, someone who holds up a wall) – unemployed young men who stand in doorways and on street corners. GIA spotters wade boldly into slow-moving traffic, peering through car windows in search of government officials, political opponents or foreigners. It is not uncommon for passengers or drivers to be shot in the head.

"If we don't kill them, they'll kill us," Major Mohamed says. "It's kill or be killed." He has grown accustomed to finding severed heads on pikes, bodies strewn along the roadside. Since the GIA started booby-trapping bodies with explosives, no one dares move rotting corpses. We go on patrol with Major Mohamed and his men for three consecutive days, once at night. We travel through the villages and countryside around Algiers in a convoy of four green-and-white Toyota Land Cruisers, past burnt-out shops and supermarkets, a smashed-up school, a gutted factory, and an entire train, charred and twisted on a railway siding. The masked ninjas point their Kalashnikovs out of the open back doors. Young men vanish as we approach them, slipping into shops and houses, racing away down streets. Sometimes the patrol stops and Major Mohamed shouts, "Nobody move. Hands against the wall." The ninjas frisk young men at gunpoint. Some are arrested. We cannot help wondering what happens when we are not there.

On the fourth day, I stay in our room at the El Djazair to write a four-page article for *Time* magazine while Robert and Abbas, the Paris-based Iranian photographer whom *Time* has sent to work with me, go on patrol with Major Mohamed. A few hours later, Robert pounds on the door. "We got ambushed," he says breathlessly. "It's OK. Nobody was hurt. Four bombs. One after the other. They nearly destroyed one vehicle. Come and say hello to Major Mohamed and his men. They're pretty shaken.

Say hello to Abbas." Robert talks even faster than usual, still in the grip of an adrenalin surge.

Major Mohamed has told us how the insurgents fill butane gas bottles with glass, metal filings and explosives, to make bombs which they bury in the roads and detonate under passing patrols. We've seen Hezbollah use these booby traps against the Israelis and South Lebanon Army militia. Later, in Iraq, the Americans will call them IEDs, for Improvised Explosive Devices.

The convoy of Land Cruisers is parked in front of the El Djazair. Major Mohamed shows me the cracked windscreen, the door hanging from its twisted hinges and the fender dangling off the back of the damaged vehicle.

"It happened in a little village called Chaibia, in the countryside near Blida," Robert recounts. "When we drive in, I'm thinking what a pretty place this is, all orange groves and fields of yellow rapeseed. There's no one in the streets and all the windows are open, but it only sinks in later: the GIA warned people. The first explosion is farthest away. It sounds like a tyre bursting behind us. We're getting out of our vehicle when the second bomb goes off, a hundred metres away. Dirt and smoke and pieces of asphalt drop from the sky. The ninjas shoot into the fields. The third bomb is nearer and a petrol cap comes whizzing past my head. 'Get down,' Mohamed yells, and we're lying on the ground when the fourth bomb goes off."

The ninjas are used to roadside bombs, but only one at a time. Four bombs, spaced 50 metres apart, like their vehicles, is an innovation. Robert and Abbas join the soldiers as they uncover the hastily buried wires. The wires lead them across muddy fields to four car batteries on the far side of the railway embankment. "It was a perfect ambush," Major Mohamed says. "We had beautiful luck today." I am glad to have been spared the fright, sorry to have missed the story and grateful that Robert has returned unscathed, all at the same time.

That first week in March, we interview Prime Minister Mokdad Sifi, who gives us a thirty-two-page album illustrated with glossy colour photographs from Algeria's morgues. Severed heads appear on most pages, eyes open, frozen in a terrified stare. Pools of blood fill the stumps of necks on headless torsos. There are bodies of children killed in bombings, reduced to cinders. The only discernible feature on one decayed corpse is the diagonal throat slash from right ear through to the spinal column.

The FIS publishes a similar book in England, showing Muslims murdered by the authorities: a man's body riddled with holes from an electric drill; a young woman covered in blood; a bullet hole in the head of a bald man. The FIS book includes photos of the camps in the Sahara Desert where tens of thousands of militants are imprisoned.

No matter how grisly the photographs and statistics, it is individual cases that stay with you, like the story of Fatima Ghodbane, the fourteen-year-old schoolgirl who is dragged out of class in the village of Oued Djer, 50 kilometres south-west of Algiers, by six GIA guerrillas armed with knives, hatchets and sawn-off shotguns one morning that March.

As Fatima's schoolmates watch, the men bind her hands with wire. One man pulls her head back by the hair and stabs her several times in the face. Then he slits her throat. "This is what happens to girls who go to university," the guerrilla tells Fatima's classmates and teacher, shaking the bloody knife in front of them. "This is what happens to girls who talk to policemen. This is what happens to girls who don't wear hijab." The killers carve the symbol of the GIA on Fatima's hand and dump her body in front of the school gate. Her name, like that of Karima Belhadj two years earlier, becomes synonymous with the horror of Algeria's civil war.

So too do the monks of Tibhirine. On the night of 27 March 1996, seven Trappist monks at Our Lady of the Atlas monastery, in the mountains south-west of Algiers, are abducted by the GIA. For the fifty-six days of their captivity, candles burn in Notre-Dame Cathedral in Paris, to pray for their survival. They are beheaded on 21 May.

Robert and I meet Monsignor Henri Teissier, the Archbishop of

Algiers, six months later. A kind, humble, sad man, Teissier came to Algiers at the age of seventeen and took Algerian nationality at independence. The Catholic church has long understood that Algerians will not convert in significant numbers, he explains. "We created a different church here, Christians at the service of a Muslim society." That is why the slain monks continued their ministry at Tibhirine, providing medical care to wounded soldiers and guerrillas alike.

When the terrible news comes in, Teissier travels to see the monks' severed heads, "on the road to Médéa, just after the petrol station. Three heads were hanging from the tree. The other four heads were lying on the ground, in the grass." He asks to see the monks' bodies. His Algerian interlocutors claim that they are in the morgue at Ain Naadja military hospital in Algiers. Before the funeral, the military weight the monks' coffins with earth. Teissier learns, to his horror, that only the heads were found.

In June 1998, *Le Monde*'s religious affairs correspondent, Henri Tincq, reports that Church officials and former Algerian military officers believe military intelligence played a role in the murder of the monks of Tibhirine. The most charitable interpretation is that the monks were killed during a botched rescue mission, so the military decapitated the bodies in the hope of convincing the world that the GIA killed them.

There are more disturbing theories. A former Algerian officer tells the review *Confluences Méditerranée* that the monks were murdered as the result of a dispute between French and Algerian intelligence agencies. Infiltrators within the GIA, who worked for military intelligence, allegedly wanted to foil negotiations between the French and Islamists. One source says a French official saw the monks in captivity. In any case, the GIA sent an emissary to the French embassy in Algiers with an audio recording of the monks at the end of April. The emissary was never seen again and is believed to have been murdered.

The story is powerfully told in Xavier Beauvois's award-winning 2010 film *Of Gods and Men*. Monsignor Teissier spends the last years of his life campaigning for the beatification of nineteen Catholic clergy who were murdered in Algeria between 1994 and 1996. They include Monsignor Pierre Claverie, the bishop of Oran, whom Church and French diplomatic sources believe was killed by an anti-French faction within the Algerian military. The nineteen are beatified at the end of 2018, two years before Teissier's death at the age of ninety-one.

Two days after we interview Monsignor Teissier, we receive a message from FIS contacts in Europe. They are sending someone to meet us and want our hotel room number. On the night of 3 December 1996, a young man knocks softly on our door at the El Djazair. The tall, clean-shaven youth in stylish clothes reeks of aftershave. He puts an index finger to his lips to signal silence until the three of us are seated on the balcony overlooking the garden. Then he speaks, barely above a whisper.

"You can call me Abu Mohamed," our visitor says. He identifies himself as a member of the Army of Islamic Salvation, the armed winged of the FIS. As is Arab custom, he comes bearing gifts: imported chocolates, a gaudy pop-up card of the Kaaba, the holy shrine in Mecca, and a glittering keychain spelling Khaled, the name of his *emir* or commander.

It seems amazing – and frightening – that Abu Mohamed has walked through the allegedly secure lobby of the El Djazair, under the nose of numerous guards, police and intelligence agents. They probably assumed he was the playboy son of a general. As the Irish revolutionary Michael Collins said, *no one sees a man on a bicycle*.

Earlier that day, someone detonated a home-made bomb on the tracks at Port-Royal metro station in Paris, killing four people. Abu Mohamed says he had no previous knowledge of the attack but that the metro was "a legitimate target" because "France is the cause of everything that's going on in Algeria. It helps the Algerian state ... As for civilians ... when they experience something like this, they are going to avoid taking the Métro. That will create a problem for the government. It's legitimate."

We ask Abu Mohamed why Islamists slash throats and behead victims. The Koran talks about the severing of hands and feet and the slashing of sheep's throats, he says. "It is the best way to come closer to God, to kill a *taghut* [enemy of God]."

And besides, Abu Mohamed continues, bullets are expensive. Of all the blood-curdling things he says, this quote, published by Robert in *The Independent* and by me in *The Irish Times*, creates the most outrage in Algerian media. The government is killing children, he alleges, as if Islamists were not. "If you have someone who is capable of killing five-year-old children, what do you do with him? Kill him with bullets? Bullets are precious to us – they are very expensive. Take a 9-mm Kalashnikov bullet – it's as if you are throwing it away. Anyone who tries to destroy Islam … is a devil. You can do anything to wipe out a devil."

Abu Mohamed says he organised three meetings in the previous six months between AIS and GIA leaders in Chlef, 200 kilometres west of Algiers. They agreed to work together. He distinguishes between what he calls the "bad GIA", which is infiltrated by military intelligence, and the "real GIA", which is now allied with the FIS.

Three passengers were murdered when the GIA hijacked Air France Flight 8969 from Algiers to Paris on Christmas Eve 1994. Seven years before the atrocities of 9/11, the Algerian gunmen intended to crash the aircraft into the Eiffel Tower. But the pilot landed in Marseille to refuel, and French commandos stormed the plane on the ground before it could take off for Paris.

Abu Mohamed thinks it was the "bad GIA" that hijacked the Air France flight – not because innocents were killed, but because they did not kill *all* the French passengers and did not crash the plane. "If they really wanted to hijack the plane, they should have planned it better, and they should have gone all the way. There were French people on that plane, and they didn't kill them. They said they were going to blow up the plane, so why didn't they do it?"

As foreigners and journalists, Robert and I feel doubly

threatened by the GIA. Abu Mohamed tries to reassure us. "You are not in danger," he says. "The only foreigners in danger here are the ones who come to support the government economically." One hundred and eighteen foreigners, including the nineteen Catholic clergy mourned by Monsignor Teissier, have been murdered in three years.

Abu Mohamed says the killing of Algerian journalists is justified. "There was a communiqué by the GIA saying that if a journalist cannot tell the truth, he must stop working. If he doesn't stop, he must die. They have been warned." Since it is impossible to tell the truth under government censorship, there is no excuse for working as a journalist in Algeria, he explains.

The man sitting in the dark on our balcony tells us he is the son of an affluent, devoted Muslim merchant family. A verse from the Koran about God's protection helped him withstand police torture the previous year. "I didn't tell them anything, because if you tell them something, they will torture you more and more until you say something else, and so on until you die."

Abu Mohamed says he has lost 200 comrades in the war, "but it doesn't matter because I know that one day we'll see each other again. For the 200 who were killed, another 600 or 700 have become mujahidin." The fallen insurgents doubtless shared Abu Mohamed's illusions about death and paradise: "The Koran says real martyrs don't bleed very much. When they die, they smell of musk perfume. This is true – the security forces have noticed that sometimes our dead smell of musk. When a martyr dies, he is met in paradise by seventy-two beautiful women."

Another twenty-nine men, women and children are massacred in Benachour and Trab, villages south-west of Algiers, during the two nights that follow our interview with Abu Mohamed. Ten of the victims, including seven women, are decapitated. A seventy-year-old woman is dragged from her bed before she is beheaded. Both hands of a twelve-year-old boy are chopped off. A baby is cut from the womb of a pregnant woman before her throat is slashed.

Unspeakable barbarity has become commonplace in Algeria. The government has armed 200,000 civilian militiamen whom Islamists target for slaughter. The GIA has invented a portable guillotine mounted on the back of a pick-up truck which they drive from village to village. They stuff the mouths of their victims with newspaper before beheading them.

In late 1996, Prime Minister Ahmed Ouyahia says government forces have won and that they are merely fighting "residual terrorism". The slaughter continues. By April 1997, the death toll in the civil war is estimated at 100,000. The guerrillas invent new horrors: decapitation by chainsaw, and dousing civilians with petrol and setting them alight as they try to flee.

The government uses helicopter gunships and bombers against marauding guerrilla bands that move about the countryside, often with captured girls in tow as sex slaves. Survivors of a massacre in the summer of 1997 say Islamists cut open the chests of victims and ate their hearts in front of villagers. One survivor saw a nursing mother plead for the life of her baby. The gunman grabbed the infant and threw it into a pan of boiling water.

Three hundred and ninety civilians are massacred in Rais on 29 August 1997, three hundred in Bentalha during the night of 22/23 September. Both villages are in the eastern suburbs of Algiers.

On the morning of 23 September, Agence France Presse photographer Hocine Zaourar hears about the massacre and drives to Bentalha, which is still on fire and bustling with police and rescue workers. Police turn him around, so he goes to Zmirli Hospital, where he sees a woman collapsing in grief against the wall of a guard post, her head thrown back and her mouth open. A second woman supports her. The women's headscarves and the folds of their clothing, the theme and composition of the photograph evoke Christian iconography: Bernini's Saint Teresa, a pietà by Michelangelo or El Greco. The photograph is published on the front pages of more than 750 newspapers throughout the world. *Le Monde* and *The Guardian* call it the "Madonna in

Hell". Just as Robert Capa's dying Republican soldier epitomised the Spanish Civil War, or the running girl aflame with napalm brought the Vietnam war into American living rooms, Hocine's picture encapsulates the tragedy of Algeria. It wins the World Press Photo Award for 1997.

"I feel very close to these people – and removed from those who aren't living through this," Hocine tells me. Any journalist who has covered a war would say the same.

Nearly a month passes before I can obtain a visa to Algiers and permission to visit Rais and Bentalha. The horror of what happened there is undiminished. Bentalha is a ghost town. I enter a villa on a dusty, deserted street, an unfinished house with a kitsch Moorish arcade on the roof terrace where a river of dried blood clogs the drainage pipe.

Wooden shutters hang charred on their hinges. Black soot climbs the walls like silent screams. The steel gate is twisted and gaping where it was blown open by the killers. The front door stands ajar. I try not to step on the wine-coloured stains that flow down the stairs. Mattresses look like burnt tree trunks amid pools of blackened, coagulated liquid.

In some places the blood is redder, swirled and smeared where bodies were dragged out. Ordinary objects – women's hair curlers, plastic slippers, a melted clock – are scattered over the scene of carnage. Blood is splattered on the wall of the laundry room on the top floor. I meet Boubker Hansali, an unemployed mason, in a nearby house. He takes me to the rooftop where he cowered with his wife and two children through the night of 22/23 September, listening to the screams of his dying neighbours, watching their slaughter by the flames of burning houses. "Thirty-six people died in that house," he says, pointing across the square. "I saw one of my daughter's girlfriends, a girl of twelve, thrown from that balcony, there on the third floor." Hansali starts to cry. He is one of the few survivors to stay in Bentalha, because he has nowhere to go. We see army helicopters hovering like gnats over Ouled Allel to the south-east. We hear the rockets they fire exploding.

Most of the original residents of Bentalha fled years ago, when the area became a rear base for Islamist guerrillas. Refugees from worse areas moved into the abandoned houses. No one is certain who killed them, or why. The military may have done it, to punish the poor for voting for the FIS back in 1991, and for having supported the guerrillas. Several nearby army posts ignored pleas for intervention. The guerrillas may have done it, because they thought the townspeople had turned against them. Most of the killers wore Afghan costume, but some wore army uniforms.

The slaughter is far from over. On New Year's Eve 1997, 412 civilians are massacred in four hamlets in the governorate of Relizane, north-west Algeria. Survivors tell how men carrying walkie-talkies and pickaxes herded whole families into "killing rooms" where they slashed their throats or hacked them to death. Babies' heads were smashed against concrete walls. The slaughter lasted for seven hours.

In late 1997, Robert and I interview an army deserter and two Algerian former police inspectors, one at a time, in the conference room of our hotel in London. We have accumulated hundreds of pages of notes from interviews with torture victims in Algiers. For the first time, we hear about atrocities from the point of view of the security forces. Our sources chain-smoke while they tell their stories. Reda, the youngest and a former conscript, cries. For us, it is like going through to the other side of the mirror.

The defectors describe a Bosch-like hell, in which security forces inject drugs before they set out on killing missions, and professional torturers attack their victims with electric drills and sodomise them with bottles, cables and broom handles.

Reda, aged twenty-three, provides further evidence that the army is responsible for at least some of the massacres. The previous June, his conscript unit went out at midnight with a group of professional soldiers. The conscripts were instructed to wait on a ridge, three kilometres from a village. If they saw flares, they were to intervene. They were not called in.

"The next day, we hear that twenty-eight people have been beheaded in that place. I start to think the soldiers were the killers," Reda says. "Two days later, we are cleaning the barracks and we look through the soldiers' clothes for cigarettes. My friend finds a fake beard in one of the soldiers' pockets. We also find musk perfume like the Islamists wear."

Reda believes the soldiers committed the massacre "to discredit the terrorists". He also believes that the army murdered twenty-six conscripts whose bodies he saw. "They said they died in a gunfight. Maybe they thought they talked too much. We knew they were eliminated."

Reda is training with a commando unit when he and other conscripts are taught to inject each other with a white substance which he says "made me feel like Rambo ... as if you are on the moon, as if you are dreaming. When we killed men, it was like killing cats."

Reda is stationed in Blida, 40 kilometres south-west of Algiers. He recalls a 2 a.m. outing to the nearby town of Sidi Moussa. "We ordered people out of their houses. We stole everything – money, gold. We beat people with our Kalashes [Kalashnikovs]. We took sixteen prisoners."

In the basement of Blida barracks "there was a special room where they tortured, called *al katela* – the killing room," Reda says. "We said, 'You gave shelter and food to terrorists. Tell us about them.' We drilled holes in their hands and bodies with an electric drill. We burned their beards. I did not do it personally. My role was to stand guard."

Reda says prisoners were waterboarded and sodomised with bottles. "In the cells they were stripped naked. It was very cold, and we sprayed them with water ... Three of them died: one when they drilled a hole in his stomach, two others from electric shocks when they put cables in their ears and anuses."

Reda and his unit take the corpses of the dead men back to Sidi Moussa. "If they want to bury them, their families have to pay us 50,000 dinars. We give them sealed coffins that they have to bury in our presence. We tell them their men died of heart attacks, but they know we killed them."

Reda removes a set of false teeth with his tongue to prove his only act of courage. "I hid some bread in my jacket and gave it to the detainees. They found out and four men kicked my teeth in with their boots. They locked me up for a week."

In July 1996, Reda decides to run away, in the midst of a gun battle by the light of street lamps in Blida. "I see eight friends of mine dead around me. The terrorists see me. They know me. Some of them have been friends of mine in Algiers. They shout to me: 'There are many days in the year. We will get you, Reda.' I and three others drop our Kalashes and run." Reda was, he says, "caught between two fires, between the terrorists and the military".

Dalila, a thirty-year-old former plain-clothes police inspector, worked at the Cavignac police station. Her father was a policeman, she tells us detachedly, fingering her thick black chignon. She wanted to be a cop from the age of twelve and joined the police force when she turned eighteen.

"The police don't call it torture. They say, '*nakdoulou eslah*'," Dalila says. "It means 'Our guest is here; we have to treat him well'." Executions take place at 11 p.m., so the bodies can be moved after curfew. Dalila tells her commanding officer, Hamid, that she is troubled by the torture and executions. "He says, 'My girl, you are not made for the police force. If you suspect someone, you must kill him. When you kill people, that is how you get promoted'."

Dalila sees close to a thousand men tortured at Cavignac, in shifts from 10 a.m. until 11 p.m., in the ground-floor garage of the police station. "Seventy per cent of the cops would have seen it. It's the job of the judiciary police, and the other cops join in."

Torture victims are tied half-naked to a ladder. Water is forced through a pipe down their throats. Their bellies swell up. "They kick them in the ribs ... They put them back in their cells covered in blood." When prisoners die, Dalila is ordered to take them to the hospital and say they died in a shoot-out. She has to fill out the death certificates.

Dalila feels sorry for an old man who has been tortured. "His arm is rotting. He has gangrene and it smells very bad. I go to the pharmacy to buy him some medicine. I put penicillin powder on his arm. There are twenty to thirty people in a cell. There are no toilets. It smells like death in there."

A fellow policeman sees Dalila help the old man with the gangrenous arm and reports her. "The commissioner calls me in and says, 'Maybe you will go to prison for helping terrorists.' The man I helped is freed afterwards, which proves he was innocent."

Four young Islamists tell Dalila's mother she has two weeks to hand over her weapon. Dalila flees because she is, like Reda, "caught between two fires"; between the fundamentalists and the regime. She lives in north London, still mourning her fiancé Abdelkader, a policeman who was murdered in 1993, and two close girlfriends who were shot dead a year later. Dalila has nightmares and is under treatment by a psychologist. "My great passion is to see horror movies. It's the only thing that interests me. I want to see blood. I can't sleep in the dark because I am afraid."

In 2001, Éditions La Découverte in Paris publishes *The Dirty War* by former Special Forces Lieutenant Habib Souaïdia. For the first time, an Algerian army officer testifies under his full name and allows his photograph to be published. "I've seen colleagues burn a fifteen-year-old child to death," Souaïdia writes. "I've seen soldiers massacre civilians and claim their crimes were committed by terrorists. I've seen colonels murder suspects in cold blood, I've seen officers torture Islamists to death. I've seen too many things. I can no longer remain silent."

Soldiers were turned into "professional throat-slashers", Souaïdia writes. "I don't see much difference between the behaviour of the terrorists and that of the soldiers ... We brought back the heads of the terrorists we killed. The rest of the body we left for the vultures and wild animals. Our bosses ... often said things like, 'Don't waste a day bringing the bodies back to the command post. Just bring the heads.'"

Souaïdia lists names, dates and locations of atrocities, in the hope they will be used by future war crimes tribunals. After his book, no one can have any illusion about the nature of the Algerian regime. Yet the US makes Algeria a partner in its "war on terror". France and the EU continue to support the regime.

Abdelaziz Bouteflika becomes president in 1999 and remains in office for twenty years at the pleasure of the generals, though he is barely *compos mentis* for his last six years in office. In 2005, Bouteflika holds a referendum on a "Charter of Reconciliation" which pardons everyone, fundamentalists and military alike. The charter refers to Algeria's "national tragedy", not its "civil war", as if the calamity were visited upon Algeria by the gods. General Mohamed Lamari, the chief *éradicateur*, admits that "some excesses may have occurred on the part of individuals".

Up to 200,000 people died during what comes to be known as Algeria's Black Decade. As in Iraq in 1991, everything changed so that nothing would change. The country chooses amnesia over justice. There are no investigations, no trials. The state admits that "about 8,000" people disappeared without trace. The Algerian League for Human Rights and other NGOs say the correct number is 18,000. Those who find loved ones in the photo dossiers published by the government and Islamists can give up the search. The others will always wonder.

IX

The Euphoria of Destruction

I am not ashamed of being,
as you would say,
a barbarian from the Balkans,
home of all that's unclean and stormy.

Desanka Maksimović, from
"Man from the Balkans"

North-western Bosnia, 30 August 1992

Lieutenant Colonel Božidar Popović is proud of his internment camp. The sprightly, middle-aged colonel with a bushy moustache wears a green uniform and V-shaped partisan cap. He swings a walking stick as he leads a delegation of the Conference on Security and Cooperation in Europe (CSCE) around the former dairy farm. "My prisoners love me," the colonel boasts as we walk down the aisles between cattle stalls. "As you can see, everything is according to the Geneva Convention."

Nothing, of course, is "according to the Geneva Convention". These men are civilians, torn from their homes in the prosperous Muslim town of Kozarac. Their emaciated, hollow-eyed faces are etched with despair. They sit cross-legged on bedding on the earthen floor of the barn. God knows what they think of us, inspecting them in the company of their chief tormentor. I desperately wish I could give them some sign of hope.

We have accepted an invitation from Sir John Thomson, a former British ambassador to the UN, to tag along on his two-day inspection of Serb-run prison camps in north-west Bosnia.

"These men are prisoners of war," Popović continues. "We treat them according to the Geneva Convention ... Do you know what jihad is? They are Muslims fighting a jihad." Humanitarian aid officials interviewed all 3,640 internees at Manjača camp and concluded that only four were fighters. Nearly 400 are under the age of sixteen or over the age of sixty.

Colonel Popović leads us to his office in a prefabricated building across from the cattle barn. He begins pouring *šljivovica* plum brandy into glasses. This is our first of many encounters with manic Serb officers who want to share their national drink. Sickened by what I have seen, I slip outside.

When he puts down his glass, Robert writes later, "I looked out the window and I saw lines of men, those poor, defeated souls, tramping grey-faced through the rain back to their cattle stalls". Colonel Popović ends up on a list of war criminals sought by the UN. A Serb contact tells us that he has moved to Switzerland under an assumed name.

Over the next seven years, Robert and I will cover wars within wars within wars in Bosnia, Croatia, Serbia and Kosovo. I am always amazed at the brazen way in which the Serbs carry out their "ethnic cleansing". Robert emphasises the irony of the Serbs' use of the term, which their Nazi enemies coined during World War II. We keep the words signifying mass killings and expulsions between quotation marks, because, as Robert says, "It has nothing whatsoever to do with cleanliness".

On the roads of north-west Bosnia in the late summer of 1992, we drive past hundreds of gutted houses, two-storey villas with smashed red tile roofs. Black smoke stains climb the walls above broken windows. The catastrophe occurred so suddenly that many families left laundry drying on clotheslines. The Serbs demand that Muslims fly white flags to signify that they have no weapons. It is in fact a way of knowing which houses to destroy.

Another 2,000 Muslim men are held at the "open reception centre" at Trnopolje, two kilometres from Kozarac. They sit shirtless under makeshift tents in a parking lot beneath the hot sun. One or two of the prisoners speak English well enough to interpret for the others. They tell us the Serbs killed 5,000 Muslims when they "cleansed" Kozarac three months earlier. Sometimes the Serb gunmen who surround the camp let them return to their plundered and dynamited homes to pick fruit from their gardens.

We find six Serb militiamen lounging in deckchairs and sofas on the lawn of a former Muslim home in Kozarac. They have rifles at their feet and smoke cigarettes while they leaf through comics and pornographic magazines. Twenty-two-year-old

Dragan Zamaklaar wears jeans and cowboy boots. He drags heavily on a Marlboro. Then he starts to cry.

"I feel nothing for the Muslims who lived in the house we have taken," Dragan tells us. "Muslims moved into our house in Kladuša. They killed my uncle last spring. How would you feel if you saw Muslims slit your uncle's throat; if you saw them throw Serb women and old people out of windows?"

This too is a constant of the Yugoslav wars. Every Serb we interview has been wronged: by Muslims, by Croats, by NATO, by Nazis in World War II, by Turks through 418 years of Ottoman occupation. Sometimes I ask a question and begin to write down the answer, only to realise the Serb I am interviewing is talking about something that happened before he or she was born, not in *this* war but the one before, or even the one before that. "I hate history," says a graffito on a wall of the defence ministry in Belgrade during the 1999 war with NATO.

Thousands of Muslims have already been killed in the first months of the Bosnian war, yet I find the regulations issued by the municipality in the village of Čelinac particularly shocking, because they so resemble those enacted by Nazis against Jews. Čelinac is officially off-limits to outsiders, but we are able to enter with the CSCE delegation. Under the "special status" ascribed to them, the Muslims of Čelinac must observe a 4 p.m. to 6 a.m. curfew. They are "not allowed to stay in the street, in restaurants and other public places". They are forbidden to swim in the rivers, fish, hunt, use or drive motor vehicles, convene in groups of more than three, use telecommunications facilities other than at the post office, sell property or exchange apartments without special authorisation. Thirty-four residents listed by name are not allowed to speak to their neighbours or leave their houses.

The hamlet of Cela, population 1,200 Muslims and 500 Serbs, seems to have fared better. Local Serb officials vaunt Cela as a model of Muslim-Serb cohabitation. They even allow residents to take food to their co-religionists at the Trnopolje camp, 15 kilometres away.

Adil Alukic wears a black beret to signify his status as the village imam. "We have made a deal with the local Serb authorities," Alukic tells us. "We will not oppose them, and they will not harm us. They will protect us."

Yet even peaceful little Cela has seen violence. Less than a month has passed since drunken Serb soldiers set fire to the mosque, damaging it slightly. They killed an old Muslim man and threw his body down a well. Of the fifteen Muslims taken away for interrogation, only fourteen returned. Another was sent to Colonel Popović's camp at Manjača. Imam Alukic no longer makes prayer calls from the minaret, and residents have promised to hold no public meetings. "Remember Cela," Alukic implores us as we are leaving.

Robert *does* remember Cela. He returns there a year later while filming *From Beirut to Bosnia*. Robert finds the coffee shop where we interviewed the imam smashed up and overgrown with weeds. The roof of the mosque has been blown off, its walls burned, its carpets stolen. There are fire-blackened pages of a Koran in the rubble. The imam's house has also been burned and looted. His daughter's schoolbooks, signed with the name Halida Alukic, are scattered over the floor. A wedding portrait of Imam Adil and his wife in a melted frame lies among the schoolbooks.

In retrospect, Robert sees *From Beirut to Bosnia*, filmed in Lebanon, Gaza, Israel, Egypt, Bosnia and Croatia through much of 1993, as "a ghastly, unintended but all too accurate warning" of the atrocities of 11 September 2001. Standing in the burnt-out mosque of Cela he asks, "What has the Muslim world in store for us?" He suggests that he ought to end each of his reports from the Middle East with the words "Watch out!" A propaganda campaign by pro-Israeli groups in the US dissuades the Discovery Channel from showing the series a second time.

Inspector Radovan, the Serb policeman who accompanies Robert and his film crew, says he doesn't know what happened to Imam Adil and the Muslims of Cela. Like Zamaklaar, the militiaman in Kozarac, Radovan talks about his own relatives who were murdered by Muslims. "In Cela, there was this euphoria of destruction," Robert quotes Radovan in his report in *The Independent*. Then Radovan makes a surprising avowal for a Serb policeman: "It has been worse in [the Serb-controlled town] Banja Luka. There the police and authorities are behind the violence and the killing of Muslims."

At the beginning of September 1992, *Time* magazine asks me to travel to Pristina to report a story which they entitle "The Fire Next Time", using the title of James Baldwin's 1963 book of essays about race in America. The article predicts that after Croatia and Bosnia, Belgrade will go to war with the predominantly Muslim Albanian province of Kosovo. For once, my editors get it right, albeit six years early.

Robert remains at the Esplanade Hotel in Zagreb while I head for Kosovo with Filip Horvat, the photographer *Time* has assigned to work with me. I tell Filip that Robert and I met a Horvat when we worked in Yugoslavia in 1988.

"Horvat means Croat. It's the most common name in the country," Filip says. "The only one I'm related to is Zelimir, the taxi driver."

"Zelimir drove us from Zagreb to Banja Luka!" I tell him. When Zelimir refused to travel beyond a certain point in Banja Luka because it was controlled by Serbs, Robert told me, "there is going to be a civil war here".

Former Yugoslavia, like Lebanon, often creates such coincidences. Filip, who is tall, balding and very skinny, jokes that he looks like the prisoners we've just seen at Manjača and Trnopolje.

Filip and I fly from Zagreb to Skopje, rent a car and drive up to Macedonia's border with Kosovo, where Serb border guards turn us around. On a second try, we bribe our way through with a carton of cigarettes.

Ibrahim Rugova, the president of the self-declared Independent Republic of Kosovo, tells me, "I opted for non-violence because there has been too much violence in the Balkans. But Serbian ideology is one of brute force. Non-violence may become absurd in these circumstances."

With his spectacles and silk cravat, the French-educated Rugova looks as if he has just arrived from Saint-Germain-des-Prés. He has accurately predicted his own fate, which is to be sidelined by the ethnic Albanian rebels of the Kosovo Liberation Army (KLA) and their thuggish leader Hashim Thaçi. During the 1999 war with NATO, Serb President Slobodan Milošević will bully the weedy Rugova into appealing for an end to the NATO bombardment.

Kosovo Serbs enforce an apartheid regime, under which the two-million-strong Albanian majority are constantly harassed, beaten, jailed and sometimes murdered by the province's 200,000 Serbs. When Albanians declared independence in 1990, the Serbs fired 112,000 workers and the Albanian unemployment rate rose to 80 per cent. We visit a clandestine medical clinic, part of the Albanians' underground network of social services, and an illegal Albanian celebration where participants wear national costume and sing Albanian songs.

Our most telling encounters are with belligerent Serbs. In a bar in Kosovo Polje, I strike up a conversation with a woman who sits drinking *šljivovica* and beer beneath a portrait of Milošević. "Why shouldn't we kill all the Albanians?" she shouts. "Kosovo is ours, and the Albanians have no place here."

Filip points out Vojislav Šešelj at breakfast in the restaurant of the Grand Hotel. (Every large town in Yugoslavia has a "grand hotel". They are anything but grand.) Šešelj, a future convicted war criminal, is a far-right-wing politician who advocates the creation of Greater Serbia through the "ethnic cleansing" of Croats, Bosnians and Albanians from Serb regions of former Yugoslavia. His White Eagles militia are still slaughtering Croats in eastern Croatia. Filip doesn't want to go near him.

I approach Šešelj's table, introduce myself and ask for an interview, while Filip waits at a safe distance. Šešelj, who studied briefly in the US, narrows his eyes and says to me in perfect English, "I hate Americans. I hate journalists."

During the 1999 war, Albanian women will recount being raped by Šešelj's followers in the White Eagles. "If you see these creatures coming out of their shacks, you'd have to be blind to rape them," said Šešelj, who was by then deputy prime minister of Serbia.

Because the Serbian claim to Kosovo is in large part based on the presence of ancient Orthodox monasteries, I want to talk to an Orthodox priest. Filip and I ring the bell at the Orthodox church in Pristina. A man in a black cassock comes to the gate. He identifies himself as Father Miroslav. "Kosovo is the holiest place to an Orthodox Serb, more holy than Jerusalem," he says. "We are ready to die to defend it."

While Miroslav is talking, he studies the face of Filip, who is interpreting for me. He demands to see Filip's identity papers, which confirm that he is Croatian. "*Ustaše!*" the priest yells at the top of his lungs, using the word for a World War II Croat Nazi collaborator. He hurls Filip's ID card as far as he can throw it, and runs to the telephone in the guard post, presumably to call Serb police. The war between Croatia and Serbia is only a year old and will continue for another three years, so it is particularly dangerous for Filip to work in Serb areas. Fortunately, he and I have our bags in the car for the journey back to Skopje. We don't breathe easily until we have crossed the border.

Robert says Yugoslavia brings us luck. Despite the terrible stories we cover, it is true that our plans usually work out there, that we come out each time unscathed. A few days after I return from Pristina, we head for Sarajevo, the besieged capital of Bosnia. *Time* assigns Filip to work with me again. He and I find seats on a Swedish convoy carrying supplies for the UN High Commissioner for Refugees (UNHCR). Robert gets a lift with Christiane Amanpour of CNN.

A month earlier, David Kaplan, an American television producer for ABC News, was killed by a sniper's bullet that struck him in the neck as he rode from Sarajevo airport into the city. It was Kaplan's first day in former Yugoslavia. I think of him as we enter Sarajevo, especially as we race down so-called Sniper Alley, the boulevard that runs from Sarajevo airport through the industrial outskirts of the city and into the Old Town. Robert is waiting for me at the UNHCR base. We are so glad to have been reunited safely that we rush towards each other in our flak jackets and helmets. Eighteen months have passed since a similar reunion in Kuwait City. We have forgotten the lesson. Our flak jackets collide with a thud and we laugh as we almost fall over.

We live at the Holiday Inn, with the entire press corps and the players of the Sarajevo Football Club. The latter are regarded as an asset so precious that they must be protected for the future. In most wars, male television correspondents strut around press hotels like peacocks. In Sarajevo, there are two queen bees: Amanpour of CNN and Kate Adie for the BBC. We dine with them on alternate evenings. I don't recall ever seeing them speak to each other. When someone notes that Amanpour takes off her flak jacket and helmet to go on camera, Adie remarks in her inimitable voice, "I survive".

Because Sarajevo is built in a geographical depression, Serb artillery gunners and snipers stationed on the surrounding heights can hit any location at will. "The Serbs are shooting into a fishbowl," a UN officer responsible for monitoring artillery positions in the hills around the city tells me. Deutschmarks and cigarettes are the only serious currencies. An egg, if you can find one, costs one Deutschmark, 10 per cent of an average monthly salary. Despite their sudden impoverishment and constant danger in streets raked with artillery and gunfire, Sarajevans stoically attempt to continue life as normal.

Robert and I call on the BBC office in the United Nations Protection Force building. The 1992–95 UN force saw its mandate expanded from protecting Sarajevo airport to protecting humanitarian organisations and eventually "safe areas" – a mission it would utterly fail to carry out at Srebrenica.

The "Beeb" have shielded their ground-floor windows with a large iron panel. We are chatting away when a shell explodes in the parking lot outside. It is one of the loudest deflagrations I have ever heard. I dive under a desk, without thinking. Shrapnel clatters against the protective iron panel. When I emerge from under the desk, Robert is there to greet me. The BBC cameraman snaps a photo of us in our flak jackets and helmets, grinning like idiots.

I hire a woman interpreter called Amira, who is so frightened that she makes me afraid. "Be gentle with her," Robert tells me. "Remember, she's been here through five months of siege already. You and I can leave any time we want to. She cannot."

I interview Muhamed Kreševljaković, the mayor of the city, in a tiny cubbyhole office because his normal office has been destroyed by a shell. He has just decided to transform the 1984 Winter Olympics stadium, the symbol of Sarajevo's pride and vitality, into a cemetery for the victims of Serbian shelling and sniping.

About 8,000 people have already been killed in Sarajevo. "We don't have enough cemeteries. What else can we do?" Kreševljaković asks. "In the Dobrinje suburb, people are burying the dead in their gardens. They have to dig graves at night, so the snipers won't kill them."

In every war, I have immense admiration for the doctors who continue to care for the wounded at great risk to themselves: for Amal Shamma in Beirut, for Alija Aginčić in Sarajevo, later for Khaldoun al-Bayati in Baghdad. Six doctors at Kosevo Hospital in Sarajevo have been killed. Direct hits killed one patient and wounded eight others.

"Foreigners have been coming here for five months and gawking at our misery," Aginčić says. "They ask me what we need, and I tell them medicine, ambulances, weapons. But nobody has done anything to help us." My article in *Time* magazine is not likely to change that, I think to myself in silence, feeling hopelessly inadequate. Aginčić is changing the bandages of a twenty-six-year-old tram driver whose right hand was amputated. "I fear we will be a city of maimed people. Some patients would be better off dying. I have a ten-year-old boy here who has no face. He was playing in front of UN headquarters – the kids go there because the soldiers give them chocolate and Coca-Cola – when the shell exploded."

Sarajevo's firefighters are also heroes. I interview Senad Podjorica, aged thirty-eight, in the garden behind the fire station. Eleven of 120 firefighters in his unit have been killed. There are two holes in his frayed blue shirt. "The shrapnel went in here," Podjorica says, showing me the hole on the right side, "and came out here," over his stomach. He received first aid and went back to work the same day.

As we talk, a sniper's bullet rips through the canopy of leaves above our heads. Amira the interpreter and I jump, but Podjorica ignores it. "I am in danger every day from fire, shells and bullets," he shrugs. Like everyone I interview in Sarajevo, the fireman alternates between despair and determination to keep Sarajevo alive.

The siege will last nearly four years and claim 13,952 lives, of whom 2,241 are Serb military. The shame of US and European leaders at having allowed the siege and other atrocities, including the massacre of 8,000 Bosnian men at Srebrenica, will be a motivation for NATO's 1999 war on Belgrade.

The morning of our departure from Sarajevo, Robert and I meet Filip in the lobby of the Holiday Inn. The Serbs have been known to take Bosnian passengers out of UN vehicles at gunpoint, and all three of us are worried for Filip.

"Filip, you look like a victim. Go back to your room and shave," Robert orders my photographer. When we climb into the armoured personnel carrier to begin the outward journey, Robert places Filip at the back of the APC, where it will be hardest for Serb soldiers to see him. I hold my breath when the Serbs open the hatch of the vehicle to inspect the passengers. They wave us on.

Back in Zagreb, Robert writes me a note on Hotel Esplanade letterhead, dated 21 September 1992. "My darling, brave and beautiful lover", it begins. He thanks me for "coming to protect your Bobby in Sarajevo", tells me I am "a trooper" and promises to love me for ever.

ℐⅅ

In May 1994, we fly to Zagreb and Split, then drive to Medjugorje, where the Virgin Mary is said to have appeared to six Bosnian Croat teenagers in 1981. In the midst of the war, the local hotel industry thrives on the custom of UN officers and, incredibly, Catholic pilgrims.

It is after dark when we reach the outskirts of Medjugorje. We are stopped at a checkpoint of the HVO, the Bosnian Croat militia. The gunmen are obviously drunk, and they ask us to share a drink with them. We refuse once, but they insist. Forcing journalists to drink large amounts of *šljivovica* and then walk a straight line is a standard militia joke in former Yugoslavia. We often speculate that the wars would be less savage if the combatants were not plastered most of the time.

We manage to depart amicably after just one drink. "Goodnight, Rapić! Goodnight Lootić! Goodnight, Pillagić!" Robert waves cheerily as we drive away. *Rapić*, *lootić* and *pillagić* are henceforward our private joke terms for armed men in former Yugoslavia. We call restaurants *pectopahs*, because that is what the Serbo-Croatian word looks like to us. We invent pseudo-Serbo-Croatian pet names, "Bobić" and "Larić", for each other. Robert uses Bobić in self-derision; I use it with affection. He quickly abandons Larić, saying I have a beautiful name and that it is a shame to adulterate it.

In nearby Mostar, Robert introduces me to women he interviewed while filming *From Beirut to Bosnia* the previous year. Serbs forces used systematic rape as a weapon of terror. The most conservative estimate of the number of Muslim women raped by Serbs is 10,000, though estimates range up to 50,000. They were imprisoned in hotels and Serb-run detention camps. Robert introduces me to survivors of a Serb rape camp who meet occasionally in a group called Mariam, after the Muslim name for the mother of Christ, to comfort one another.

We pick our way through the wreckage of the Mostar train station, through shoals of broken glass, fallen girders and the torn, bloodstained garments of people killed by snipers and artillery fire. At the end of the street lined with burning rubbish and gutted buildings, we find the small cinder-block house where Ziba lives with her husband and two little boys, as squatters. Ziba and the other women I meet that day were imprisoned in a school gymnasium in the Bosnian town of Kalinovik, where they were repeatedly gang-raped over twenty-six days by Serbs from Šešelj's White Eagles and Arkan's Tigers militia. More than 100 women were held there with their children. "Before the war, our lives were normal," says the leader of the Mariam group, called Munevera. At age thirty-seven, she is the eldest. "We had modern houses, cars, nice clothes."

The Serb police who held the women initially were less cruel than the militiamen. "The militiamen came in groups of twenty or thirty," Munevera says. "They wanted to humiliate us because we were Muslims. They took our jewellery and money. They put our children on tables and held knives to their throats. They starved us. They raped us every day. They came in the morning and evening and raped. They would be drunk, and they did horrible things."

Muslim women were used as human shields on the front line. They were ordered to walk across a suspected minefield and decided among themselves that only childless women would do it. Four women, including twenty-three-year-old Samija, won their freedom by retrieving the bodies of dead Serbs. "The bodies were in pieces – arms and legs," she recalls. "They were decaying, and I had to pick them up. I will have nightmares about it for the rest of my life."

"We didn't wash or brush our hair or teeth. We tried to look ugly so they would leave us alone," says Munevera. "My daughter smeared dirt on my face and matted my hair."

Ziba's little boys were one and a half and two and a half years old. "My nightmare is always the same," she says. "The Serbs tearing me away from my boys, and the boys screaming. I was afraid they would kill them while they raped me. My oldest son is four now, but he remembers everything."

The women never discuss their ordeal with their husbands, because they do not want to upset them. They were freed because the Bosnian Muslim army captured fifty Serbian women to trade for them.

৯৯

Is it wrong to weep for monuments and works of art when humans suffer so greatly? Six months before Robert and I travel to Mostar, the Bosnian Croat HVO fired sixty artillery shells at the city's Stari Most, which means Old Bridge in Serbo-Croatian. Another example of "the euphoria of destruction". The bridge was commissioned by the Turkish sultan Suleiman the Magnificent in 1557. The white limestone half-moon rising above the emerald waters of the Neretva was a thing of beauty, registered on UNESCO's list of world heritage sites.

"In my opinion it was one of the ten most important bridges in the world," a British engineer working with an UNPROFOR unit tells me. We stand on the eastern, Muslim side of the river, our eyes fixed on the jagged stubs and the void between them. "It was an emotional bridge ... a meeting place for lovers," the engineer continues. "The tank commander who did this was a stupid man. He did it to destroy the morale of people."

An old Bosnian Muslim stands nearby in the cobblestone street, also staring at the empty expanse above the river. For seventy-seven years, the bridge was a fixture of his life. He doesn't want to give his name, because he still has relatives on the Croat side of the river. He's been shot by a sniper, has lost his house and suffered a heart attack. "I can no longer hold back my tears," the old man says. "The people are like stray dogs, wandering without direction. It is as if we were drowning."

Watching the video of the bridge's destruction nearly three decades later is still painful, even when one knows that it was rebuilt and reopened in 2004. With each successive explosion, more stones plummet into the river. The battered carcass finally crashes into the Neretva, spewing up a great fountain of water, the victory of ignorance over civilisation.

The Council of Europe coins the term "cultural cleansing" for the deliberate, wholesale destruction of heritage by combatants in the Yugoslav wars. I have written so much about the torture, mutilation and murder of human bodies that it is almost a relief to investigate a different type of war crime, which is in a sense the destruction of souls. I read about the levelling of eighteenth-century Vukovar, attacks on the medieval quarter in Dubrovnik, the incendiary shells that consumed unique, four-centuries-old archives at the Institute for Oriental Studies in Sarajevo, and three million works in Sarajevo's National Library.

I interview experts in Paris, as well as Bosnian, Croatian and Serbian officials. Though the estimates they provide are subject to caution, they give an idea of the scale of the phenomenon: 243 Orthodox and 510 Catholic churches and monasteries and 1,450 mosques have already been destroyed or severely damaged. When warring factions preserve cultural artefacts, it is usually to use them as bargaining chips in future negotiations.

Ferdinand Meder, the director of Zagreb's Institute for the Preservation of Cultural Monuments, tells me he is "protecting" 3,000 pallets of icons and other objects taken from Serb Orthodox churches. He expresses concern about the contents of Croatia's Drniš Museum, in particular the works of Ivan Meštrović, one of Croatia's greatest twentieth-century artists. They have disappeared from the museum, which is in Serb-occupied Croatia, the self-declared Serbian Republic of Krajina.

Robert and I drive from the Croatian capital, Zagreb, across the dormant front line to Serb-held Knin. I ask everyone we meet if they know about Meštrović's works, which are the object of an international search on the part of the Croatian government, Interpol and London's Art Loss Register. Someone, perhaps Alyn Roberts, the affable and well-informed UN press officer in Knin, suggests that I have a look at Knin castle. Robert calls me Sherlock Holmes and accompanies me on my cultural mission.

The keeper of the castle is a tall Serb with a bushy black moustache called Milojko Budimir. Does he know anything about the Meštrović works that went missing in Drniš? I ask. Budimir leads us down a narrow, winding stone staircase to the cellar, opens a door and turns on the light. The scene before me takes my breath away: a large, neo-impressionist, Gauguinesque oil painting of a Croatian folk dance and a superb collection of twenty-five bronze busts, arranged haphazardly on a table and metal shelves. I understand why Auguste Rodin, with whom Meštrović studied in Paris, called the Croatian "the greatest phenomenon among sculptors".

Eureka! I have found the missing artworks. Like his counterpart in Zagreb, Budimir swears he is keeping the treasures to protect them. He promises he'll give them back "when the world recognises the Republic of Serb Krajina". Unfortunately, Budimir adds, "six other Meštrović paintings disappeared in the fighting". He hears rumours that they have been taken to Belgrade, for sale to the highest bidder.

We find a small restaurant with red-and-white chequered tablecloths that evening. The steak and chips are greasy but delicious. I am in a celebratory mood, so we order a bottle of Serbian King Lazar red and admire its splendid label, almost as beautiful as the Ksara '68 labels in Beirut. Except for his Byzantine crown, King Lazar, I note, could be mistaken for Milojko Budimir up in Knin castle. It is a history lesson on a wine bottle. Lazar and his arch-enemy, the invading Ottoman Sultan Murad, both died at the 1389 Battle of the Field of Blackbirds in Kosovo. The defeat remains the cornerstone of Serb identity.

Alyn Roberts agrees to "lend" us his interpreter for the 200-kilometre trek from Knin to Banja Luka, the bastion of Serb nationalism in north-west Bosnia. Ljiljana Matijašević, from Belgrade, is a devout Orthodox Christian and the wife of a retired Serb army colonel. She dresses primly in skirts and blouses and wears her hair up. As a young woman, she spent the Blitz in London and is nostalgic for a time "when Serbia and England were friends". We are charmed by her excellent, slightly dated English.

The Serbs' "ethnic cleansing" of Bosnia continues into its third year, with Serbs controlling 70 per cent of Bosnian territory. We drive through village after village of gutted, ransacked Muslim houses. A few fly Serbian flags, signifying that a Serb family intends to renovate the home. But there are signs of war-weariness. A Serb woman recounts the stories she hears from her brother, who is fighting in the "Bihać pocket" at the north-west corner of Bosnia.

"You cannot imagine how bad it is," the woman says. "They go to the toilet, eat and sleep in the trenches. I wish this war had never started. It is the fault of our leaders. They swagger around like bears, but none of *them* will ever die on the front at Bihać."

The Serb symbol, a cross with the Cyrillic letter "c" in every quadrant, stands for "Only Unity Saves the Serbs" and is scrawled like a signature on many Muslim ruins. Confronted with incontrovertible evidence of atrocities committed by her people, Ljiljana is torn between her Serb identity and revulsion. She is not an alcoholic, but after particularly distressing interviews or scenes of destruction, she tells us it's time for a *šljivovica* stop. In the car, she belts out songs she learned in London. Robert and I sing along, humming the verses we don't know. The three of us drink and sing our way across a large swathe of Bosnia, at the same time horrified and superficially joyous.

When we return to Paris, Robert leaves a cartoon on my desk.

"TRAVEL WITH 'Bobić'! The easy way to enjoy Bosnia!!" it says above a sketch of three characters waving from a moving car. The copyright says "Poglavnik", the World War II title of the Croatian Fascist leader Ante Pavelić.

In Banja Luka, we dine at an open-air café across the street from the ruins of the once beautiful sixteenth-century Ferhad Pasha mosque. The Serbs have destroyed every mosque in the city. In the countryside, we come across three Muslims who have managed to hang on. They are so frightened they do not even want us to print the name of their village. The eldest, a religious leader, remains speechless while tears stream down his face. The youngest lists numerous cases of beatings, murders and dispossession. It is the slave labour that concerns him most now. "There are 15,000 Muslims doing forced labour," he tells us. "They make us clean streets, cut wood, prune trees, pick corn. Lately they are sending more and more men to dig trenches on the front line. Many have been killed."

Nothing ever ends in life. Ljiljana will help Robert in his failed attempt to obtain an interview with the fugitive war criminal Ratko Mladić in eastern Bosnia in 1996. She will be a sort of surrogate mother to us in Belgrade during the 1999 NATO war. There is a certain tension between them, because Robert thinks Ljiljana cares only for Serbs, while Ljiljana thinks Robert is against her people. She also believes he is wrong to put her and me in danger on reporting trips. You have to stop expecting people to be something they are not, I tell Robert. I still ring Ljiljana in Belgrade every year on her birthday.

After Robert's death, I receive several messages from Alyn Roberts, who remembers my late former husband with affection and admiration. He publishes a tribute to Robert in the Belgrade magazine *Novi* and reminds readers that when the Croatian army retook Knin and the Krajina region in "Operation Storm" in 1995, Robert reported on the violation of Serbs' human rights by Croatian forces.

The Dayton Accords, which finally end the Bosnian war in late

1995, maintain the fiction of a single, sovereign state of Bosnia Herzegovina composed of two parts, the Republika Srpska and the Bosniak-Croat Federation. But every component of former Yugoslavia seems doomed to go to war with Belgrade. Attention turns to Kosovo. By the summer of 1998, the Kosovo Liberation Army holds close to one-third of the province. Slobodan Milošević reconquers almost the entire territory, at great cost in bloodshed.

Haunted by their shameful passivity in the face of genocide in Bosnia, western countries pass UN Security Council resolutions, impose sanctions on Belgrade and send observer missions. The massacre of forty-five Albanians in the village of Račak, central Kosovo, in January 1999 convinces most western leaders that they will have to fight Milošević. Negotiations in Rambouillet, outside Paris, end in failure on 22 March. NATO's eleven-week bombardment of Serbia starts two days later.

Robert and I meet at the airport in Budapest on 25 March 1999. We make the 370-kilometre drive to Belgrade on the second night of the bombardment, in a passenger minibus. Our driver keeps a keen eye on the frequent flashes of light as NATO bombs explode on the horizon. Just north of Belgrade, a statue of a fighter-bomber on a plinth seems to surge forward, framed against a wall of orange flames outside Serbia's main airbase at Batajnica, bombed for the second night running.

We ask the minibus driver to drop us off at any hotel in Belgrade. It is late, but both of us write up descriptions of the journey for the front pages of our newspapers. We telephone Ljiljana first thing in the morning. She says she's too old to work with us, but suggests we hire her daughter Maša, whose job as a stewardess for the Yugoslav flag carrier JAT ended when the airline shut down because of sanctions.

Maša is at the same time shy and flamboyant. Her bright red hair is cut pageboy-style and she has long red fingernails. When we meet her, she still dresses like a flight attendant. By the end of the war, her style evolves to late 1970s' British punk. She has Ljiljana's mischievous cheerfulness and flair for drama. On car journeys, she sings the old sea shanty "What Shall We Do with the Drunken Sailor?" instead of Ljiljana's World War II ballads.

The waiter grumbles as he sets a plate of rolls on the breakfast table. "He says, 'You send me missiles, I bring you bread'," Maša translates. "An old Orthodox proverb says that if someone throws stones at you, you should give them bread," she explains. The waiter grumbles again: "He says, 'I am sorry. I hate all foreigners'."

A few hours later, we run into the same waiter. He smiles and holds out his hand to shake ours. "Let's be friends," he says now. Serbs are probably the most mercurial people we have ever known. The next three months are a constant back-and-forth between menace and hospitality, hatred and friendship. "I don't believe you are really journalists," the hotel receptionist sneers. Then he changes his tone and invites us for coffee in the smoke-filled lobby. "Anyone can stay here," he says. "Anyone but Albanians. I loathe them. I cannot believe this kind of people exist."

The US Secretary of State Madeleine Albright and President Bill Clinton are also hate figures. Belgrade television interviews a Serb family who sheltered Albright when she was a Jewish refugee from Nazi-occupied Czechoslovakia in the 1940s. When Clinton appears on the television screen in our hotel restaurant, a second waiter mutters, "I would like to fuck his mother". The night before Serbian state television is bombed, the Košava channel, which belongs to Milošević's daughter Marija, broadcasts a pornographic spoof with Clinton and Monica Lewinsky lookalikes. They imitate the American president and the White House intern by smoking a cigar they have used as a sex toy.

Air raid sirens go on and off so often that most people soon ignore them. In the first four days of the war, Serb claims that more than a dozen NATO aircraft have been shot down are greeted with scepticism. Then the Yugoslav Army Press Centre buses us to a village 40 kilometres north-west of Belgrade, near the Bosnian border.

In Buđanovci, twenty-first-century technology, in the form of an F-117A stealth bomber, crashes into a time warp: a village of six hundred ancient, crumbling houses where peasant women wear headscarves, thick woollen socks and clogs. Prize pigeons nest in rooftops and the locals make *šljivovica* from plum trees in their gardens.

NATO announces that the pilot is "in good shape" and "giving a full account" of what happened. US forces stationed over the border in Bosnia are believed to have spirited him away to safety.

Sixty-five-year-old Milica Lalošević was in her cottage a few hundred metres from the crash site when she heard a terrible racket. "When we went outside, the plane was on fire. The whole of Europe was lit up by the fire," she tells us with the Serb penchant for poetic hyperbole. "If a needle was on the grass, you would have found it."

General Spasoje Smiljanić, the commander of Yugoslav air defence, tells us two days later that the aircraft "flew from New Mexico to rest on our Serbian territory, never to fly again. It is a pity, because if it had come as a friend, it would still be flying."

Robert and I delight in the Serbs' use of imagery, especially animal metaphors: people like stray dogs; leaders who swagger around like bears; fighter bombers transformed into birds...

The plane wreck is a tourist attraction that has fast attained the status of a relic. Serb peasants pile on the back of tractor-pulled wagons to visit the site. Women jump and dance on the aircraft's wing, which lies on a bed of burnt corn husks in a muddy field. The wing looks as if it were made from dull, black linoleum and appears to have been strafed by a Serbian MiG fighter.

Every visitor wants a souvenir of the downed aircraft. Men saw at the wing with knives, fill rucksacks with pieces of cake-like yellow styrofoam. A farmer with a weathered face, missing teeth and dirt-stained fingers pulls a piece of the plane's black coating from his pocket. "I know mechanics and it is very simply made," he boasts. The stealth bomber reportedly cost $45 million. "The US military makes a lot of propaganda about how expensive it is, but it is only because of this material that the plane is invisible," the farmer tells me.

Robert and I settle into life in Belgrade. There are daily visits to the Army Press Centre, where we establish a good working rapport with a plump, outgoing Serb woman with short blonde hair called Vesna. She seems to be some kind of intelligence agent, and because she likes us, she shares information with us. When there is nothing happening at the press centre, Maša, Robert and I go to the foreign ministry, politicians' offices and the daily rock concerts organised on Republic Square. Concert-goers wear T-shirts emblazoned with bull's-eyes and the word "Target?" to express their fear of becoming civilian casualties of the bombardment. "I am not Monika [sic] Lewinsky," says one placard.

The pop singer Svetlana Ražnatović, known as Ceca, is the star attraction. She is married to Željko Ražnatović, the baby-faced Serb militia leader, politician, football club owner, convicted bank robber, assassin and wanted war criminal, better known as Arkan. His Tigers raped and pillaged their way through large parts of Croatia and Bosnia and will soon turn their attention to Kosovo.

The crowd on Republic Square makes a perfect human shield for Arkan. He cuddles his and Ceca's small children in front of the television cameras while she sings. The previous day, his beer-drinking skinhead followers had rampaged down Knez Mihailova, Belgrade's main shopping street, smashing the windows of the French and US cultural centres and daubing walls with crude drawings of sex organs and graffiti about Clinton and Lewinsky.

A couple of months later, Robert and I dine with Serb friends at the Writers' Club in Francuska Street. There is a lot of bombing that night, so the restaurant is nearly empty. The garden restaurant is surrounded by high walls, we reason, so the risk is mitigated. Suddenly, Arkan, Ceca, her sister and their body-guards emerge from the penumbra like an evil omen.

Ceca is a beautiful young woman with long dark hair. She wears a powder-blue trouser suit and glittering jewellery. "Arkan cured her of a cocaine addiction," our Serb friend whispers. "He keeps a close eye on her." Ceca seems to enjoy the public appearance. Arkan sits in the back corner, facing the entry like a cowboy who fears being shot in the back. The couple's bodyguards, in twin skinhead haircuts, black T-shirts and shiny grey suits, sit at the end of their table. A Range Rover with two more gunmen waits in the dark street outside.

I've heard Arkan described as "the most dangerous man in Yugoslavia". He owns a casino, a bakery and an ice cream plant, and is deeply involved with the Albanian and Serbian mafia. His father was a colonel in the Montenegrin secret police and secured for his son a job as a hitman in Tito's intelligence service. Milošević is said to hold Arkan in reserve, in case he needs him. The following January, Arkan and a bodyguard are shot dead in the lobby of Belgrade's Intercontinental Hotel.

A few days after our arrival in Belgrade, the hotel receptionist tells us our room is needed and we must find other accommodation. At first, we think we are unwanted because of our British and US nationality. Then we see luggage trolleys loaded down with polished shoes, whisky bottles and police uniforms belonging to the new occupants. NATO is systematically bombing police and army barracks, so the police and military are moving into hotels.

Western journalists are staying at the Hyatt Hotel across the Danube in Novi Beograd, but Robert and I prefer the old Majestic Hotel in downtown Belgrade, near the press centre and Republic Square. We opt for a room on the second floor, based on the old Beirut principle that lower floors are safer. But the hotel is packed with Serbian families, probably refugees from military barracks. Blaring television sets and screaming children drive us upwards. When the concierge shows us a large top-floor suite with a view over the Danube, we are like newlyweds who have found their dream apartment, notwithstanding the vile smell that comes from the bathroom drains.

The porter who brings up our things takes a long look at the view and predicts that the bridges, where government employees hold nightly "human shield" vigils, will be blown up soon. NATO destroys bridges in much of the country, but spares those in Belgrade. After the war ends, French President Jacques Chirac claims that he vetoed bombing the Belgrade bridges.

Six days after we arrive in Belgrade, Robert receives a phone call telling him that he has won the Orwell Prize for outstanding journalism. Though he receives such honours nearly every year, sometimes several times a year, the novelty never wears off. Robert laughs and cries at the same time, with joy, when he hangs up the phone. I give him a bear hug. The awards protect him from his critics, he tells me. In Knez Mihailova Street, Maša and I find a royal blue and emerald-green striped dressing gown as a congratulatory gift. I can still see Robert wearing it, sitting at his desk in our suite at the Majestic, pounding away on his laptop.

The Army Press Centre takes us to the Sloboda ("Freedom") household appliances factory in Čačak, 160 kilometres south-west of Belgrade, the day after it is hit by seven US cruise missiles fired from Hungarian airspace. It's hard to be upset over a factory that was destroyed without casualties in the middle of the night, but the damage is impressive. The craters are big enough to engulf several houses. The steel girder frame of the factory remains, but its roof and walls have been blown away and there are acres of debris.

My mobile phone rings. It's Tony, the architect in Dublin whom we've hired to renovate the ruin of a house we recently purchased overlooking the sea in Dalkey. There's a problem, Tony says. Irish windows open outward, which means it will be impossible to close the Mediterranean-style louvred shutters we have ordered. No, I protest, I don't want shutters nailed to the outside walls for decoration. Arguing over windows for our home in Dublin from the ruins of a bombed-out factory is one of my more surreal memories of the 1999 war.

Sloboda supplied half the vacuum cleaners, cookers, hairdryers and refrigerators in Yugoslavia. It also made munitions, though the Serbs who accompany us insist the quantities did not justify such destruction. "Boeing makes civilian airliners as well as weapons," one of our Serb minders suggests. We know that is true, from Robert's investigation into the Hellfire missile that destroyed an ambulance in southern Lebanon.

Our scepticism about the purely civilian nature of the target grows when we are ordered away from a plastic ribbon cordon. As we turn to go, a plain-clothes policeman shoves me hard in the lower back.

We are then taken to a "peace rally" at the Zastava car factory, 50 kilometres away at Kragujevac. The factory also manufactures assault rifles and machine-guns, and the workers have "volunteered" to make "a heroic stand against NATO aggression" by occupying it around the clock. We later learn that the civil servants who act as "human shields" on the bridges in Belgrade have been told that they will lose their jobs if they don't participate. I assume the Kragujevac workers are under similar duress. They do their utmost to publicise their sit-in and send messages to Albright and Clinton. NATO bombs the factory anyway, wounding 120 people, on 8 April.

Robert will revisit Zastava in Kragujevac in the summer of 2018, to confront its management with machine-gun manuals from their factory which he found in the ruined offices of al-Nusra and al-Qaeda when Syrian government forces retook East Aleppo. He discovers that in the 2010s, Zastava sold machine-guns to Saudi Arabia which ended up being used by Islamist rebels in civil-war Syria – concrete evidence of Saudi support for jihadist extremists. Follow the weapons, Robert always says. If you don't cut the weapons off, wars will never end.

NATO's bombardment claims more and more civilian casualties. Milošević's earlier wars in Bosnia and Croatia have brought around 300,000 Serb refugees to live in Serbia. The government cynically moves them to deserted army barracks, knowing that these buildings will be bombed. A story told by the head of the intensive care ward in a Belgrade hospital makes a deep impression on me. The previous night, an eighteen-year-old Serb refugee called Boris Grubješić died. The young man was from the Krajina region of Croatia and was so depressed at the prospect of another war that he threw himself from the top of the McDonald's building in Belgrade, breaking his neck and skull.

On 7 April, NATO bombs downtown Pristina. The press centre takes us on a 15-hour return trip coach ride to the capital of Kosovo. We see Serb tanks, armoured personnel carriers and military vehicles buried under stacks of hay and nestled up alongside farmhouses and barns. The farther south we move, the more burnt-out, roofless houses we see, virtually identical to those in Bosnia in the early 1990s. If the KLA attacks our convoy, we are told, we must not panic. For the last hour of the journey, we are accompanied by an armoured vehicle mounted with a heavy machine-gun. Serb forces control the roads, but the guerrillas own the surrounding hills.

Huge flames shoot up from the Beopetrol storage depot on the outskirts of Pristina. Downtown, the post and telecommunications building is still burning, twelve hours after NATO bombed it. Several square miles of the city centre are devastated. At least ten civilians are said to have been killed. The city is eerily empty. Many of its shops have been looted. An old Albanian man in a black raincoat walks down the street, carrying a portable typewriter and a net bag full of clothing. He tells us he is going to live with his sister in Macedonia.

Robert's and my next trip to Kosovo, on 15 April, is a grisly demonstration of twin horrors: the surge in "ethnic cleansing" of Kosovar Albanians by the Serbs, and NATO's bombing of four separate convoys that were taking "cleansed" Kosovars from their homes to the Albanian border. The NATO bombings kill seventy-three of the refugees for whom the Alliance is meant to be fighting.

We are standing by the side of the road, 15 kilometres west of Prizren. Colonel Slobodan Stojanović of the Yugoslav army holds an impromptu press conference beside a bomb crater. Bloodstained clothes and bedding spill off a rusty wagon onto the asphalt. A second wagon and the tractor that pulled it have been blasted thirty metres off the road.

"NATO systematically attacked these convoys," Stojanović says. A few of us turn to see two mud-caked coaches coming towards us. The dark blinds are pulled down, but we glimpse the faces of Albanian women and children peering through cracks, a haunting image of dispossession and forced expulsion.

In the course of our two-day journey through the war zone, I count four such buses, packed with Albanians. On the town square in Požaranje, I see a crowd of about 200 Albanians, mostly women and children, waiting with their belongings. NATO says another 10,000 Kosovar Albanians have been deported in the preceding twenty-four hours, torn from comfortable, European homes to face the hardship of life in refugee camps.

In the most eerie moment of the thirty-three-hour trip, a Serb official boasts that although the Nazis made Belgrade the first "*Judenfrei*" capital in Europe, no Serb ever collaborated with Nazis in the deportation of Jews. As he says this, our coach passes another burning house. All eyes, including the official's, are on the house, yet no one mentions it.

Until now, I have the impression that our Serb colleagues, who never ask a question about the burning houses and coaches packed with refugees, are somehow complicit. Then I notice the tears flowing down the cheeks of the woman journalist sitting beside me. We share no common language, so she scribbles a note. "You will find someone to translate this for you," she writes at the top.

Dear Lara, there are a large number of us who do not accept that the Kosovo/Metohija [the Serb name for south-western Kosovo] problem should be solved this way. Where are the people? Why are their houses and cattle abandoned? Why are they being punished? All the children in the world are the same, they should be allowed to play and laugh. God, when will the innocent stop suffering, regardless of which nation, which religious confession and which race they belong to?

The note is the only expression of remorse I encounter on the part of a Serb throughout the entire war. I would like to think that others felt similar grief but dared not express it. That spring day in the killing fields of Kosovo, a weeping woman journalist restores a shred of Serbia's lost honour.

We visit three sites, spread out over several kilometres immediately south-west of Djakovica. Southern Kosovo is lush and green in mid-April. The mountains in the distance are beautiful. Yet we hear the constant drumming of the bombardment. Funnels of grey-brown smoke scratch the horizon, either burning Albanian homes or NATO targets. We stand in a field littered with carbonised corpses, amputated limbs, clothing and personal belongings. A man's head sits upright in the grass, a handsome, bearded head with long brown hair and large, staring eyes. The Old Testament name Absalom pops into my mind and attaches itself to that image.

A tall Serbian journalist from our group stands in the midst of this carnage, munching crisps from a packet. The *New York Times* correspondent Steven Erlanger, Robert and I exchange incredulous glances. "Massacres always make me peckish," Steven says with black humour.

It is almost sunset, and our Serb minders do not want to risk the long drive back to Belgrade in the dark. We spend the night at the disused ski resort at Brezovica. It is still very cold in the mountains of Kosovo in mid-April, and the hotel has no electricity or heating. Robert and I sleep fully clothed, entwined, with our arms around each other, simply to keep warm. I realise what a long time has passed since we have slept in each other's arms.

NATO initially suggests the Serb Air Force may have bombed the refugees. Robert prowls around the devastated convoys, looking for bomb components. He writes down the serial numbers he finds on pieces of casing and publishes them, under the title "The atrocity is still a mystery to NATO. Perhaps I can help." After five days, US Brigadier General Dan Leaf admits that F-16 pilots dropped nine 500-pound laser-guided bombs on what it calls "mixed refugee and military convoys" in south-western Kosovo on 14 April.

The previous year, Robert and I had reported extensively on the effects of depleted uranium weapons in Iraq. After the 1999 war, NATO admits it has used depleted uranium weapons, but will not say where. Serb authorities advise women to avoid pregnancy.

From the beginning of the 1999 bombardment – which UN lawyers confirm is illegal under international law – Robert calls the NATO emblem the "Death Star". He travels to Brussels to question NATO spokesmen about the use of depleted uranium. As recalled by the former UN press officer Alyn Roberts in *Novi* magazine: "NATO said depleted uranium was harmless, that it was found in trees, earth and mountains. Robert reported it was a lie. Only pure uranium is found in the earth, depleted uranium is from nuclear reactor waste. After the bombing ended, Robert asked NATO for the locations of depleted uranium munitions explosions. He was told details were 'not releasable'."

Robert visits hospitals and bomb sites throughout former Yugoslavia and finds evidence that NATO troops are also dying from unexplained cancers. NATO refuses to give information to Bosnian officials who are investigating an increase in cancer cases. "This is not a scandal. It is an outrage" is the headline of Robert's story in *The Independent*.

☙

We are woken in the middle of the night of 22/23 April by a phone call from Vesna, telling us that NATO cruise missiles have just destroyed the building of state-run Radio Televizija Srbije (RTS), killing at least ten people. When we arrive there shortly afterwards, we see a dead man hanging upside down in the pancaked building, his brains oozing out of the top of his head. The body of the station's make-up artist, a close friend of an interpreter for a British television network, is charred beyond recognition. Survivors moan or tap from beneath concrete slabs. One man can be freed only by amputating his two legs. A limp, dead hand emerges from the rubble.

Tony Blair calls RTS "a recruiting sergeant for Milošević's wars" and a NATO spokesman says it is "the heart of Slobodan Milošević's propaganda machine".

Serb television taunted US and NATO officials. It broadcast Madeleine Albright wearing a Nazi helmet, her face becoming a skull with flames shooting from the eye sockets. In another segment from the *NATO u Blato* (NATO into the Mud) series, Adolf Hitler transmogrifies into Bill Clinton, and Hitler pats a little boy on the head, calling him Javier Solana. (Solana was then head of NATO.)

Yet regardless of its programme content, Robert and I feel there can be no justification for bombing a television station. Both sides are morally reprehensible: the Serbs for forcing journalists to continue to work in a building which they knew was about to be bombed; NATO for bombing a civilian structure they knew to be full of journalists. "Yes, Serbian TV could be hateful, biased … owned by the government," Robert writes. "But once you kill people because you don't like what they say, you have changed the rules of war."

My birthday falls on a Sunday at the end of April, providing a much-needed respite from death and destruction. Ljiljana invites us with Maša for lunch at her modest home on the outskirts of Belgrade. The house is as I imagine a Russian country dacha: ramshackle, with flowering trees in the garden. She serves a delicious home-cooked meal before we speed back to our hotel through the empty streets of Belgrade. Ljiljana presents me with a tiny icon of the tenth-century female Saint Petka of the Balkans. She says Saint Petka specialises in protecting women.

Robert gives me a volume of poetry by the much-loved Serb writer Desanka Maksimović, who died in 1994 at the age of ninety-five. Though *Visions* was published three years before the Yugoslav wars started, every poem seems to foresee the catastrophe. The message in Robert's card goes some way to allaying my fears about his dark mood during the 1999 war: "To my beloved Lara, another place to spend your birthday, but always more love from your adoring husband. As ever, ton tigre."

On 29 April, the nightly bombardment starts earlier than usual, around 10.45 p.m., and continues without interruption through the night. NATO bombs several targets it has already hit repeatedly, starting with the television transmission tower at Avala, in the hills south of Belgrade, where Milošević is rumoured to sleep in his bunker. The twenty-four-storey Palace of the Federation, headquarters of Milošević's political party, is bombed for the third time. The already destroyed interior ministry is bombed again, splitting the charred ruin in two. The foreign ministry, where I called on an official the previous afternoon, is bombed. So is Vračar, the residential district where Robert and I dined earlier that evening.

From our balcony at the Majestic, Robert and I study the red glows dotting the skyline and try to guess what has been hit, a foretaste of Baghdad four years later. We watch the lights of cars that found themselves on the wrong side of the Danube when the bombardment started. They race across the bridges in terrified, accelerator-to-the-floor flight.

Every time we start to sleep, we are woken by more explosions. At dawn, the bombing has just subsided when the earth begins to tremble. Our walls and furniture vibrate in silence. We wonder if it could be the aftershock of a very powerful but distant explosion, then realise it is an earthquake. As they emerge into the light of day, the inhabitants of Belgrade speak of nothing else. Bombing is normal, but an earthquake is an act of God.

We have been under near constant bombardment for five weeks. I am weary, and I must go to Dublin to firm up arrangements for the renovation of our house. I suggest we take a break in Paris and Beirut. Robert agrees, but then blames me when we miss the US bombing of the Chinese embassy in Belgrade, which kills three Chinese journalists, on 7 May. I tell him he could have stayed on in Belgrade without me.

At lunchtime on 12 April, an American pilot fired two missiles at the railway bridge over the Morava River gorge, near the south-eastern Serbian town of Grdelica. The Belgrade passenger train for Thessalonica is on the bridge when the missile explodes. The first missile severs the cable powering the train. The second missile hits the train itself, setting two carriages on fire and plunging two other carriages into the narrow river gorge. At least twenty civilians are killed, some sources say up to sixty.

By the end of April, NATO is bombing Serbia twenty-four hours a day and killing civilians with alarming frequency. On 1 May, NATO bombs the Niš to Pristina bus on a bridge at Lužane, killing forty-six Serbian and Albanian civilians. The pilot waits until an ambulance arrives and bombs a second time – something we often see the Israelis do in Lebanon. The rhetoric of NATO spokesmen is also reminiscent of the Israelis. NATO bombed the *bridges* at Grdelica and Lužane, *not* the train and the bus, we are told; they were merely "collateral damage".

We travel twice to Surdulica, in south-eastern Serbia, after NATO kills large numbers of civilians there. The first time, on 27 April, NATO scores a direct hit on the basement shelter of a cosy villa in Jovanović Zmaj Street. Vojislav "Voja" Milić and his son Aleksandr built the villa with their earnings from the local Zastava windscreen wiper plant and a small grocery store. The Milićs' cellar is large and sturdy, so neighbours send their children there each time air raid sirens go off.

Voja Milić was running home on 27 April when the missile

hit his house. Twenty of the twenty-one people sheltering in his basement were killed, including Voja's wife, son, daughter-in-law, grandchildren and cousins. We see him the following day, an old man with a worn face, wearing a tweed cap and a leather jacket, leaning against a wall, crumpled over with grief. His face is bathed in tears and his blue irises stare out crazily from blood-red eyes. He sobs quietly while officials make speeches in front of his destroyed home. "The first thing he said when they pulled him away from the rubble was: 'Shoot me. Kill me'," one of Voja's relatives tells us. I think of Saadallah Balhas, who lost his family in the 1996 Qana massacre in southern Lebanon.

Robert and I return to Surdulica on 31 May, twelve hours after NATO bombs a tuberculosis sanatorium, killing another nineteen civilians, all patients. Most of them were sleeping in hospital beds when the ceiling and walls caved in on them. "I am beginning to think that Surdulica is doomed," Dušan Petković, the town's English teacher, says. "We have been bombed four times, and this is the second time they've killed twenty civilians."

As we survey the bodies and wreckage, I ask for news of Voja Milić. Townspeople tell me he posts photographs of his dead family members everywhere. He has twice attempted suicide and is kept under permanent sedation by cousins who look after him.

The bombing of the sanatorium has taken the life of a beautiful young woman, nineteen-year-old Milena Malobabić. Her body lies at the end of the row, in sun-dappled shade beneath trees, alongside the corpses of her mother and two brothers. Milena's long black hair drifts over her sadly pretty face and silver hoop earrings. Her blue-green eyes seem to stare out in pain, even in death. She suffered from a broken heart, as well as tuberculosis.

Robert spots a blue notebook lying on the ground, twenty metres from Milena's body. "This notebook is dedicated to Dejan," Milena wrote inside the front cover, entwining her beloved's birth date in 1972 with her own. "If you only knew how much I suffer now," begins the poem she wrote. The first letters of each line form an acrostic of Dejan's name. "Maybe it's wrong, but I want to go back to you. Your Milena still loves you, but I feel my wounds so much. I don't know if I can still kiss you."

We see many other bodies at Surdulica, but it is Voja, the devastated family man, and Milena, the broken-hearted young woman, whom I remember. Robert is moved by Milena Malobabić's death and sad love poem. He refers to it often in conversation.

We try to find an explanation for the NATO attacks. Both times, local Serbs are reluctant to acknowledge that there are nearby military installations. The Geneva Convention, which NATO cites so often regarding the Serbs' treatment of Albanian Kosovars, states that civilians must be protected even if they are near military personnel. When Voja's house is destroyed, an old woman finally admits that "when they aimed at this place, they meant to hit the barracks". The second time, we wander through the pine forest surrounding the sanatorium until we find sixteen foxholes, each big enough for a soldier or two, and two campfires whose ashes are still warm.

The Serb parliament barely reaches the required two-thirds' majority needed to endorse the EU-NATO-Russian peace plan on 3 June. Talks on the implementation of the agreement stall, and NATO continues bombing until 10 June.

Robert and I return to Pristina on 8 June, this time with our Belgrade driver, Goran, and Vesna, the former aide at the military press centre who is now free to work with us. The Serb army officers who escort our convoy of journalists from Belgrade have changed into civilian clothing. We find ourselves in a twilight zone between war and peace, in which Kosovo's Serbs and Albanians rush to complete unfinished business. Some Serbs set revenge fires in Vranjevac, the still-deserted Albanian quarter of Pristina. Others burn their own homes so that returning Albanians cannot move into them.

NATO bombers rumble overhead and gunfire rattles down the empty streets of Pristina. The departure of Serbs from what was their home province begins as a trickle of cars loaded with bedding and household goods. In coming days, the road north is clogged as traffic swells to a chaotic mass exodus of Serb civilians, military and Milošević's purple-clad interior ministry police.

The arrival of NATO troops from Macedonia is repeatedly delayed, first because Russia shocks the US and Britain by dispatching a company of Russian paratroopers from Bosnia to Pristina at great speed, thus beating NATO ground troops into Kosovo. Robert and I stand on the Corso at 1.30 a.m. on 12 June amid a throng of jubilant Serbs. The Russians are cheered wildly by the Serbs, who regard them as fellow Slavs, fellow Orthodox Christians and saviours.

The crisis with Russia forces the US and UK to settle their own spat over whether British troops or US marines should have the honour of arriving first in Pristina. The Russians seize control of Slatina Air Base, which the international Kosovo Force needs for its deployment. General Sir Michael Jackson, the British commander of KFOR, spends two sleepless nights negotiating the terms of the NATO deployment with Russian General Viktor Zavarzin.

We take Vesna and Goran for a last lunch at an outdoor café. The city is in anarchy, but we are reassured by the presence of two uniformed Serb officers. When they get up to go, we are left in the company of Serb militiamen wearing hand grenades and knives on their belts. One has a brandy bottle sloshing in the knee-pocket of his trousers. The others throw back white wine and mineral water spritzers. Two of the irregulars begin arguing in the adjacent parking lot. Bullets smash into the patio floor of the restaurant, so we decide it is time to leave. When we drive past the same place two hours later, we are stopped by gunmen so drunk they can barely stand.

The first soldiers we see on 13 June are Irish Guards, whose armoured fighting vehicles, named Dublin, Drogheda, Dromore, Donaghmore, Derrylin, Donegal and Downpatrick, spread out along the Pristina to Belgrade highway. Thousands of exultant Kosovar Albanians line the road for two kilometres, showering the troops with flowers and sweets and chanting "NATO, NATO, NATO!" Robert and I follow the deployment with Goran and Vesna. Our car has Belgrade licence plates, so we are pelted with pebbles. One hits my cheek, leaving a stinging red welt. I keep the pebble for luck.

We try to enter Vranjevac, but turn back because of shooting on the road ahead. Serb officials tell us later that three Serb soldiers have been shot dead. In an extraordinary sequence of coincidences, we will soon meet the man who ordered the shooting. We will attend the funeral of one of the dead soldiers, 300 kilometres away in northern Serbia, the following week. And nearly twenty years later, the International Criminal Tribunal for the Former Yugoslavia will contact me about the case.

The path to the front door of Zenel Hajdini School in Vranjevac is strewn with rose petals. The red Albanian flag with a black two-headed eagle flies from the roof. We are ushered in to meet Commandant Sali Mustafa, aged twenty-nine. He is a balding man with glasses and several days' growth of beard, wearing a Puma tracksuit and runners. "I am the commandant of guerrilla unit Pristina. We were here during the war because our duty was to fight the Serbs from behind the lines," he says.

Mustafa boasts about his "last action" before Milošević accepted the peace plan on 3 June. "It was in the Vresta neighbourhood that we assassinated Zoran Jovanović Zoki, a high-ranking Serb intelligence officer," he says, dragging on a cigarette. "Serb forces were living on either side of the road, yet we managed to shoot him ten metres from his front door," Mustafa continues. "There were three of us – me and two others. The whole street was full of Serbs. They started shooting from both sides and we escaped through the city sewers."

Mustafa joined the National Movement for the Liberation of Kosovo while studying history at Pristina University. He spent four years in Serb prisons.

The previous day it was Mustafa's men who killed the three Serb soldiers a few blocks from the school where we interview him. He tells us the Serbs were looting Albanian homes and shooting. But, by chance, we meet two British soldiers who were sent to retrieve the bodies. They tell us that the vehicles packed with household goods looked staged, and they believe the deaths were revenge murders. One of the Serbs had the back of his head blown off, another was shot in the chest and the third was so soaked in blood that the British were not sure how he was killed.

It is not clear, I write in *The Irish Times*, whether the KLA are summarily executing Serbs whom they suspect of committing atrocities, or whether they are arbitrarily killing any adult Serb males they can find.

On 19 June, six days after the three Serb soldiers are shot in Vranjevac, and five days after Robert and I interview Commandant Sali Mustafa, the Jeličić family in the northern city of Novi Sad hold a wake for their son and brother, twenty-one-year-old Boban. Dozens of relatives and family friends, including Serb soldiers, drink a toast "to free Boban's soul". Local beggars are invited to the funeral meal of chicken soup and roast meat, set on picnic tables in the driveway.

Boban Jeličić's parents are too grief-stricken to talk, but his brother Zoran, a manager at Novi Sad's open-air market, agrees to speak to us because he wants some trace of his brother to remain. Boban was an army driver. He loved techno music, parties, girls and weightlifting, Zoran says. "The most tragic thing for us is that he was killed after the peace agreement."

As Zoran recounts the circumstances of his brother's death – one of three soldiers shot dead in Vranjevac on 13 June – we realise those were the shots we heard, the men who Commandant Mustafa accused of looting. The desire for revenge is a powerful force in the Balkans, but Zoran Jeličić says he feels only sorrow. "Even if they brought the Albanians who killed my brother and executed them in front of me, it would mean nothing to me, because nothing can bring Boban back now."

In September 2020 I receive a phone call from the International Criminal Tribunal for the Former Yugoslavia in The Hague regarding our June 1999 interview with Commandant Sali Mustafa in Vranjevac. Mustafa has been arrested and taken to The Hague to be tried for war crimes. They want me to testify.

Nearly three years earlier, I had agreed to sign an affidavit saying that I had written the article and believed it to be true. If one advocates international justice, I reasoned at the time, one cannot refuse to cooperate. But the more I think about it, the more uneasy I feel about testifying against Commandant Mustafa. Fewer and fewer people are willing to talk to journalists. If combatants believe journalists are likely to testify against them later, no one will speak to us. Sali Mustafa gave us an interview for our newspapers. He obviously would not have done so if we had told him we would testify against him in a war crimes tribunal. If I interviewed a criminal in Paris or Dublin, I don't think I would take the witness stand against him.

I also feel that NATO and western leaders are responsible for hundreds of civilian deaths in former Yugoslavia, including the seventy-three refugees in the Albanian convoys, the passengers in the train at Grdelica and the bus at Lužane, Voja Milić's family and the patients at the sanatorium in Surdulica. No NATO officer will ever be taken to The Hague.

Because Robert shared the interview with me, and because I suspect the Tribunal has approached him as well, I write to him a few weeks before his death asking for his thoughts. My letter was in his stack of unanswered mail when he died. One night a few months later, I open *The Age of the Warrior*, a collection of Robert's essays. "To beloved Lara – without whom this book could not have been written!" he wrote on the title page when it was published in 2008. I open the book haphazardly, the way one sometimes opens a Bible or a book of poetry, and my eyes fall on this chapter title: "Should journalists testify at war crimes trials?" His essay expresses the same reservations I outlined in my letter to him. "If we ever have an international court to try all the villains, I might change my mind," he concludes. "But until then, a reporter's job does not include joining the prosecution."

※

On our last day of reporting together in Kosovo, Robert and I drive alone to Prizren, Djakovica and Peć, to take stock of the twin catastrophes of the NATO bombardment and Serb "ethnic cleansing". We see terrible destruction. Albanian survivors tell us stories of cruelty and murder, of people burned alive in their houses, of children being shot. We arrive in Peć before the Kosovo Liberation Army, just in time to see the last Serb looters departing.

The journey has taken longer than we anticipated. Robert is nervous that we might run out of petrol, and we don't relish driving back in the dark. We can take a shortcut to Pristina, but it means passing through countryside that we believe is held by Serb irregulars. Three days earlier, two German journalists from *Stern* magazine were shot dead at a checkpoint in this part of western Kosovo. The Germans reportedly told the men who stopped them that they were looking for mass graves.

After much reflection, Robert and I decide to take the more dangerous shortcut, rather than drive at night and risk running out of petrol. We come around a corner to find a checkpoint manned by gunmen wearing black ski masks and brass knuckledusters on their hands. "These must be the guys who killed the Germans," Robert gasps. A gunman walks up to the car window. "*Dobre dan*," good evening, Robert says cheerily, as if everything were normal. We hold out our Serbian press accreditation, from the Army Press Centre in Belgrade, annotated by a Serb colonel to say that we are "following the realisation of the implementation of the peace plan".

This part of Kosovo is lawless, but we have made the right gamble. The hooded gunman feels some vestige of loyalty to Belgrade. He waves us through, and we drive off into the sunset, towards Pristina, Belgrade, Budapest, Paris and Beirut, immensely relieved to be alive.

X

Peace is the Continuation of War by Other Means

I saw my children scattered like dead sheep around me.

> Lebanese farmer Saadallah Balhas, who
> lost thirty-one relatives, including his wife,
> children and grandchildren at Qana.

When General Aoun is driven out of the presidential palace in Baabda and the western hostages are freed at the end of 1991, I want to believe that war in Lebanon is over, at least except for the south. One would so like to freeze history and write: *and they all lived happily ever after.*

Robert and I receive so many invitations to dinner with academics, diplomats and Lebanese leaders – including to an *iftar* (the meal breaking the Ramadan fast) with Hassan Nasrallah, the head of Hezbollah – that we cannot accept them all.

We work hard, too, making repeated trips to Algeria and former Yugoslavia as both countries disintegrate into civil war. At Christmas 1993, Robert proudly screens his three-part television series, *From Beirut to Bosnia,* for Patrick Keatinge, his wife Sue and me in the cottage in Dalkey. Patrick, a professor of political science at Trinity College Dublin, supervised Robert's doctoral thesis on Irish neutrality during World War II. Sue designed the interior of the cottage in Dalkey and the house we built later overlooking the Irish sea.

My editors increasingly treat me as a "fireman" war correspondent. Every time Bill Clinton threatens Saddam Hussein, they send me on the long, overland trek to Baghdad. They ask me to cover the deployment of US marines to Mogadishu at the end of 1992. I eat camel meat at the Sahafi Hotel and clutch my reporter's bag to my chest as Somali children try to tear it from me. Journalists circulate in Mogadishu in "technicals", pick-up trucks mounted with machine-guns. I accompany marines on their overnight "humanitarian" mission to famine-stricken Baidoa. I amaze myself by writing a two-page article without being able to read what I am writing, after the Somali sun burns the liquid crystal screen of my Toshiba.

Mogadishu is a tough assignment, and *Time* rewards me by

making me a permanent staff correspondent. I am nonetheless annoyed at the saccharine title that is chosen in New York for my piece – "The Gift of Hope" – and the caption "Building trust" under a photograph of a marine with Somali orphans. I manage to inject a note of scepticism with quotes from a survivor of the October 1983 US marine bombing in Beirut. They read like a premonition of the Black Hawk Down incident, when nineteen US soldiers will be murdered and dragged through the streets of Mogadishu the following year.

In April 1993, my editors send me to the Azerbaijani capital Baku, to cover Armenia's seizure of Nagorno-Karabakh. I am dispatched to Goma, Zaire, for the exodus of Hutus following the Rwandan genocide in the summer of 1994. I dread the urgent, last-minute requests from New York and the mad scramble for the airport. Robert is an invaluable help at such moments, calling airlines, booking flights and making me laugh. He slips into my shoulder bag a small photo album in an envelope marked "not to be opened by Lara until she is having breakfast on the plane". It contains one photograph of Robert and five of Walter the cat, then a dozen pictures of our newly redecorated Beirut apartment. The captions read: "When far from home ... remember that your lover loves you ... that your friends remember you ... and that your home is waiting for you..."

When Robert travels and I stay in Beirut, he often sends red roses from the florist in Jeanne d'Arc street back to the apartment with Abed. I keep a little pile of the business cards inscribed with "I love you. Ton Tigre" which he has the florist pin to the cellophane holding the bouquets.

The cat is an endless source of affection and comic relief. One night in the autumn of 1991, kidnappers issue a statement saying they are about to free an American hostage. We work late and are about to go to bed when I realise I haven't seen Walter for some time. After a long search, I hear faint mewing. Walter had jumped into the back of the filing cabinet drawer before I closed it without noticing she was inside. The poor puss has bloodied her paws trying to claw her way out. We frame a watercolour painting by Robert's mother Peggy, showing a cat's paw emerging from a filing cabinet drawer marked "Hostages".

During the 1993 onslaught which Israel calls "Operation Accountability", the devastated villages of southern Lebanese look as if they have been draped in cobwebs. These are in fact the wires of countless guided missiles. Robert brings a segment of wire home and leaves it on his desk, with the vague intention of sending it to the *Independent*'s defence correspondent, Christopher Bellamy, for further examination. I arrive home one afternoon to find Walter choking and frothing, with the missile wire sticking out of her mouth. Her elderly vet, Dr Masri, stares at the cat and shakes his head. "I've seen cats do everything imaginable, but never in fifty years have I seen a cat eat a missile wire," he says. If it doesn't come out quickly, Walter will die of metal poisoning. Masri shoots liquid paraffin down the back of her gullet with a syringe. Walter races around the apartment as the malodorous wire emerges from the other end.

The funniest Walter incident occurs when Robert and I return from a day of reporting in southern Lebanon. I am in the kitchen preparing dinner. I hear Robert shriek. In a scene from a Tom and Jerry cartoon, a mouse tears past me at high speed, followed by Walter. The mouse makes it to safety beneath the electrical generator on the kitchen balcony. Robert arrives seconds later. "I was coming out of the bathroom when Walter dropped her mouse in front of me," he explains, laughing. Walter has a collection of toy mice made of rabbit fur, which she fetches like a bird dog when we toss them. "I picked it up by the tail and was about to throw it. I was thinking, 'My, this one is well made' when I saw its little trotters thrashing about. It was *real*!"

In August 1993, I am working on a story about Islamic radicals in Khartoum. The reporting is going well and I am dismayed when *Time* tells me to break off and go straight to Jerusalem, because the PLO and Israel have concluded a secret peace deal in Oslo. By chance, Robert is in Cairo and he books my onward flight from Egypt to Israel, which is impossible to do from Khartoum. He joins me at the King David Hotel in Jerusalem two days later.

Once the flurry of news subsides, I propose a story with the working title "Family Saga", about the Kawash family, Palestinians from Galilee who have been scattered between northern Israel, Lebanon and Jordan since the 1948 Arab-Israeli war. My editors enthusiastically approve of my idea.

Robert is extremely sceptical about the agreement, but I interview the three branches of the family, in the Mieh Mieh refugee camp near Sidon, southern Lebanon, in Amman, and in the Arab village of Deir Hanna, Galilee, without preconceptions, in a genuine desire to find out how a typical Palestinian family feels about the Oslo Accords.

The refugees in Lebanon have led a hard and violent life. They invest no hope in the Oslo Accords because the text abandons the refugees' "right of return" as defined by UN General Assembly resolution 194. "All the Arab kings and leaders were liars. They never kept their promises, and Yasser Arafat is with them now," Mohamed Kawash, aged seventy-eight, tells me in Mieh Mieh. "I wish I had died fighting in 1948."

The Kawashes in Amman have fared better. They are Jordanian citizens. One brother is a retired Jordanian army general. "In Jordan, I had a good education, a clean house with heating and air conditioning, and good healthcare," says thirty-five-year-old Bassam Kawash. Jordan gave citizenship to more Palestinians than any other Arab country. The Lebanese government refused to do so, out of fear that it would destroy the fragile balance between religious communities.

Bassam Kawash studied catering in England and manages his father Naif's Orient Restaurant. "It's finished. It's history," Naif mutters when I ask about Mirun, the family's native village in Galilee. But when we sit down alone at a corner table, the old man lifts his glasses to wipe away tears. "Ah Mirun, Mirun, Mirun… I cannot forget you," he sighs, as if lamenting a woman loved beyond reason.

Naif was thirty-one when he left Mirun during the 1948 war. He tells his grandchildren it was paradise on earth, a place of fresh milk and honey and roses in profusion. Leah and Moshe Deri, the kindly caretakers of the Jewish shrines there, lived in friendship with their Arab neighbours. There were groves of apricot and olive trees, lentils and tobacco crops, all watered by natural springs flowing down to Lake Tiberias. Each evening the livestock came back from the meadows, and the wheat harvest was a time of celebration.

In northern Galilee, as in Lebanon, the peace agreement evokes more fear than satisfaction. "We are afraid the world will wash its hands of us now," says Mohamed Abbas Kawash, aged sixty-five. His forty-year-old son, Faraj, agrees: "They are trying to divide Palestinians into three categories with this agreement," he says. "The refugees from 1967, those from 1948 and the Palestinians in Israel, but we are all one people."

Mohamed Abbas and his brother Said take me to Mirun, the village from which they were expelled, and which every Kawash longs for. Outside the graceful Ottoman stone house where both men were born in British-mandate Palestine, we are approached by Rabbi Haim Levy from Morocco. The Kawash brothers back away fearfully while I converse in French with Levy. It is Saturday, the Jewish Sabbath. "You must not write in your notebook. You must not take photographs. This is a holy day, and this is holy ground. It is forbidden," Levy tells me and photographer Barry Iverson. In Roman times, he notes, Rabbi Shimon bar Yohai, a Talmudic sage, sought refuge in the village the Israelis call Meron.

"What happened to the Arabs who lived here until 1948?" I ask the rabbi.

"This land was given to us by God 2,000 years ago," he replies. "There were never any Arabs here."

Time's World editor Johanna McGeary wants "Family Saga" to be a good-news story about the Oslo Accords. She asks me to rewrite it several times. "But that's the point," I tell her. "Oslo turns Palestinians in the West Bank and Gaza into policemen for the Israelis. It doesn't help the Palestinians in the diaspora." The story of the Kawash family means a lot to me. It is never published.

In July 1994, *Time* asks me to go to Yemen. It is a daunting prospect, since one must first travel to Djibouti and then hire a boat to cross the Bab-el-Mandeb strait to Aden. Robert volunteers to go with me. We find the Yemeni embassy in Beirut in a shambles of overturned furniture and scattered documents. Embassy staff divided along civil war lines and fought one another, a male consular employee explains. He wears only a piece of cloth wrapped around his waist like a skirt. He puts a visa with Robert's name in my passport, and a visa with my name in Robert's passport. We point this out, but the Yemeni waves his hand in the air and says it doesn't matter. By good fortune, the Korean dictator Kim Il-Sung dies and *Time* cancels the story before we depart.

Beirut remains our home base and refuge. The boutiques are stocked with fashions from Europe, and my *Time* salary enables me to splurge on clothes. Our favourite restaurants are called Blue Note, Al Dente, Rabelais, Le Retro, Rigoletto and Vieux Quartier. Babylone, the first restaurant on the former demarcation line, is all the rage. Women in stiletto heels walk with difficulty through rubble to reach the front door. The B018 nightclub opens at Karantina, site of the 1976 massacre of 1,500 Muslims, mostly Palestinians, by the Phalange. Now Lebanon's youth dance, literally, on the mass grave. There's a frantic desire to believe that peace has returned, though it hasn't really. Post-war Lebanon is boisterous and wants to forget.

Enter Rafik Hariri, the multi-billionaire philanthropist and banking and construction magnate who bankrolled the 1989 Taif peace conference. Hariri is the son of a citrus farmer from Sidon. "I was born in a modest house, into a modest family," he tells me when I interview him for *Time* in January 1993. "Each of us loved the others, but I was not satisfied with our situation. I was sure that I had to do something to change it. I never dreamed I would reach where I am now. I still think that I am in a dream."

This childlike wonderment is one of Hariri's most endearing characteristics. His Rabelaisian appetite for everything – food, property, banks, radio and television stations, power – is intriguing and almost frightening. He has a throaty laugh and is as much at ease with farmers from remote villages as with world leaders. In 1992, Hariri's fortune is estimated at $4 billion. He owns homes in Beirut, Damascus, Jidda and Riyadh, Paris, London, Monaco and New York. He owns a yacht and private jets.

Like many Lebanese Sunnis, Hariri emigrated to Saudi Arabia to seek his fortune. He was a mathematics teacher when he left home at age twenty-one in 1965. He studied accountancy and worked for the French construction firm Oger, which he eventually bought out. His big break came in 1977 when King Khalid urgently needed hotel rooms for an Islamic conference in Taif. Hariri built the Intercontinental Hotel there in six months. Other contractors said it was impossible. The royal family are grateful, and Hariri becomes one of the principal builders of the kingdom's palaces, hospitals, hotels and schools.

But Hariri doesn't forget Lebanon. He spends $150 million to build a state-of-the-art medical centre at Kfar Falous, southern Lebanon. The Israelis destroy it in the 1982 invasion. He contributes $87 million annually to Lebanese charities, including the financing of 15,000 university scholarships for Lebanese of all faiths.

Hariri draws up a $2.65 billion plan to rebuild downtown Beirut, the former front line. In exchange for their stake in the city centre, 127,000 landlords and tenants are offered half-ownership of a property company called Solidere. The other half will belong to Hariri and investors, with individual holdings capped at 10 per cent of the total.

Architects' impressions of the new Beirut show skyscrapers lining an avenue wider than the Champs-Élysées. Supporters say it will be Manhattan on the Mediterranean. Opponents call it Haririgrad. Robert and I argue with a friend of ours, an economics professor at the American University of Beirut, who claims the project will double Hariri's fortune.

"Hariri is too big for Lebanon," the professor says. "If he were operating in the US, the country is so big that it could absorb him. That is not the case here... What kind of blackmail is this? Hariri says, 'Either I come in and do it like this, or it doesn't get done'."

"I've spent most of my adult life watching men destroy Lebanon," Robert tells the professor. "For once, somebody wants to rebuild it, and the rest of you are complaining."

The professor grudgingly admits that Hariri's ambition is not so much to make a killing as "to go down in history as the man who saved his country".

The concept of conflict of interest does not exist for Hariri. "You're prime minister of Lebanon and the biggest stakeholder in a private company that is rebuilding the centre of the capital," I say to him. "You own four newspapers, two television stations and a radio station, and you say there's no conflict of interest?"

"Are you going to argue that the prime minister should be a poor man?" Hariri shrugs off the question, claiming to have put his vast wealth into a blind trust.

Hariri is one of few Lebanese politicians who have never commanded a militia. He has no blood on his hands and is too rich to be corrupted, but that doesn't prevent him from corrupting others. Tales of his largesse are legion. A colleague from Lebanese television tells me that Lebanese journalists received $25,000 each in envelopes from Hariri at the Taif peace conference. Abdul Halim Khaddam, the Sunni vice-president of Syria who is in charge of policy in Lebanon, is a close friend of Hariri. Khaddam's son is one of Hariri's business partners.

An impeccable source confirms that Hariri financed Jacques Chirac's 1995 presidential campaign. The friendship between them is nonetheless genuine. In October 1996, Chirac travels to Damascus, Jerusalem, Amman and Beirut. I cover his trip for *The Irish Times* and witness their complicity at first-hand. At the French ambassador's residence in Clémenceau, West Beirut, Chirac and Hariri are as gleeful as old school chums. For years after Chirac left office in 2007, suffering from incipient Alzheimer's, Hariri's son Saad lent Jacques and Bernadette his luxurious apartment on the Quai Voltaire in Paris.

"The past is past," Hariri insists. His optimism, his belief in the transformative power of business and his perennial willingness to start over are catalysts for change in post-war Lebanon. In many ways, life improves. Each time Abed speeds through the slick new traffic tunnel beneath roads where we endured countless hours of gridlock, Robert and I laugh and say, "Thank you, Sheikh Rafik!" We adopt the affectionate title used by Hariri supporters in jest. In person, we always address him as Mr Prime Minister.

Hariri's detractors say his reign is a throwback to nineteenth-century American robber barons. He makes a great deal of progress rebuilding Lebanon's infrastructure, but does little to restore the Lebanese state. Everything is privatised, including telephones and rubbish collection. The country never enjoys round-the-clock electricity, because the rich own private power generators. There is almost no investment in public education or national healthcare and welfare systems. Beirut in the Roaring Nineties is an unregulated, capitalist jungle where the rich get richer and the poor grow poorer. The war had fostered a sense of solidarity among neighbours and within communities. Even that is lost now. "*Ya ma kan ahla ayam al harb*!" Oh, but it was beautiful in the days of the war, say some Lebanese, including our beloved interpreter, Imad Saidi.

Hariri becomes prime minister for the first time in October 1992, in the wake of bread riots sparked by the plummeting Lebanese pound. He will serve as prime minister for an aggregate of ten years between 1992 and 2004, twice resigning due to political disputes with Syrian-backed stooges. Under Hariri's rule, downtown Beirut is partially rebuilt and the currency stabilises at 1,500 Lebanese pounds to the dollar.

Hariri several times invites Robert and me to lunch at his palace in Koreitem, West Beirut. His conversation is entertaining and informative, as long as he is off the record. When one turns on a tape recorder, he freezes and answers questions in monosyllables, particularly sensitive questions regarding the 40,000 Syrian troops still in Lebanon and their protégés in Hezbollah.

"Isn't it dangerous for the stability and future of Lebanon to ride solely on one man?" Robert asks Hariri.

"So keep me alive," the prime minister replies.

I dwell on the topic in my *Time* interview, noting that strong-willed Lebanese politicians usually end up being assassinated. "I believe if my life is finished, it will be finished," Hariri says. "*Maktoub*. It is written."

Despite his feigned fatalism, Hariri devotes considerable resources to ensuring his own survival. In 1992, he spends $2 million to have blast-resistant armoured plating and bullet-proof glass installed in the prime minister's office in Sanayeh. He pays forty bodyguards and buys four armoured Mercedes with smoked-glass windows. Even the Lebanese soldiers who ride shotgun in Range Rovers interspersed through his motorcade do not know which vehicle he travels in.

The threat derives from Hariri's Saudi affiliation. He has spent more than half his life in Saudi Arabia, speaks with a Saudi accent and holds dual Saudi and Lebanese nationality. Rivalry between Sunni and Shia, between Saudi Arabia and Iran, is already tearing at the fabric of post-war Lebanon. Yet Hariri insists he is not King Fahd's man. "I am not here on a Saudi mission," he tells me.

Rick Hornik, *Time*'s deputy chief of correspondents, rings me in January 1995. "Congratulations," Rick says in a jovial tone. "The *Time* Newstour is coming to Beirut."

Each year, *Time* invites the eighty richest men in the US to play pretend journalists for a week. The magazine charters a jet and flies them around the world, stopping in several cities where it has bureaux.

"But you cannot come to Beirut," I protest. "There's a ban on US citizens travelling to Lebanon."

"Don't worry about that," Rick says. "We've got lawyers working on it."

For the next nine months, I do my normal reporting job, and the work of two male correspondents who have left Cairo, while organising a two-day Newstour stop in Beirut for *Time* brass and their retinue of millionaires. I reserve the Summerland Hotel for two nights and write a personal cheque for $25,000 to charter a plane from Cyprus to Beirut, since US aircraft are not allowed to land at Beirut airport. I organise a group interview with Sheikh Mohammed Hussein Fadlallah, the spiritual leader of Hezbollah, to take place at his home in the southern suburbs. I schedule visits for ten groups of eight millionaires with Palestinian families who lost relatives in the Sabra and Chatila massacres and write up their stories in an elaborate briefing book. I recruit drivers and interpreters and buy replicas of Roman oil lamps as gifts for the participants.

Receiving millionaires is right up Hariri's alley, and he embraces the project wholeheartedly. When *Time* executives fly in on a private jet from New York in July 1995 for a dry run of the Newstour, he invites them to lunch at his Koreitem palace. Robert and I take the executives to the Chouf mountains for a meal with Walid and Nora Jumblatt, to the ruins of Baalbek and for dinner with the men in charge of the reconstruction of Beirut. We are mortified when a *Time* vice-president gropes the wife of a Solidere executive at table in the Rabelais restaurant.

The final event of the Newstour is to be a banquet for 500 people in Koreitem. Hariri sends out engraved invitations a few weeks before their scheduled arrival on 7 October. Everything is ready.

Time's managing editor, Jim Gaines, rings me just before D-Day. "I'm really sorry, Lara, but we can't come to Beirut," he says. "The Clinton White House refuses to waive the travel ban. The participants are spooked, and a lot are backing out."

"But you promised," I say, in shock. "Rick said the lawyers were taking care of it. You can't do this... I quit."

"I knew you'd say that," Jim replies. "Listen, you are going to write a cover story with everything you were going to tell the Newstour. Instead of sharing it with eighty men, you'll share it with *Time*'s twenty-five million readers."

I ring Hariri and ask to see him first thing the next morning. Robert tries to console me, but I am distraught. After a sleepless night, I go to the prime minister's office in Sanayeh to tell Hariri that *Time* has cancelled the Beirut stop on the Newstour. I half expect him to be angry, but Hariri pats my forearm in a comforting gesture. "Don't worry, Lara. It doesn't matter," he says.

I remember the story told by Issa Goraieb, the editor of *L'Orient-Le Jour* newspaper. He once asked Hariri how he put up with so much abuse in parliament. "I lost a son in a car crash in Boston, a big, handsome, intelligent boy," Hariri replied, alluding to the death of his third son, Houssam, in October 1990. "When something like that happens to you, smaller things don't matter." Houssam Hariri was studying mathematics at MIT. He and his brother Bahaa were racing their twin Porsche 911s on Jamaicaway when the crash occurred.

I take up Gaines's offer to write a cover story instead of resigning. *Time* sends photographer Tomas Muscionico from New York and we fill a nine-page spread on the rebirth of Lebanon, including two pages on Palestinian refugees and a one-page interview with Fadlallah. After putting the story to bed on 4 November 1995, Tomas, Robert and I are enjoying a celebratory dinner when we hear joy-shooting on the Corniche. The Israeli Prime Minister Yitzhak Rabin has been assassinated.

Our cover story is postponed repeatedly, first because of the killing of Rabin, once for an exclusive article about a "revolutionary" no-fat potato chip. I pester editors relentlessly. It is finally published in January 1996, but in the international edition only.

Hariri's press secretary in Paris, Rima Tarabay, has been

a friend since her days as a militiawoman in Samir Geagea's Lebanese Forces. After I leave *Time* for *The Irish Times*, Rima proposes a meeting with Hariri almost every time he visits Paris. She meets me at Hariri's mansion on the Place d'Iéna, the former home of Gustave Eiffel, with an amazing view of the Eiffel Tower. In February 2001, Hariri tells me he has been inspired by the example of Ireland's booming "Celtic Tiger" economy to lower Lebanese income and corporate tax rates, as well as social charges.

The meetings with Hariri tend to be repetitive and I am not particularly keen, but I continue to go out of friendship for Rima and Hariri. "Where have you been? We miss you in Beirut, Lara!" Hariri says.

In December 2001, Hariri is one of the first people to telephone Robert when he is badly beaten by Afghan refugees on the border with Pakistan. "I'll send my jet to Quetta for you. Pervez Musharraf is a friend of mine. I can get landing permission and you will be in the American University Hospital tomorrow," Hariri says. Robert declines, because he thinks journalists should not accept gifts from prime ministers. After the US invades Iraq in 2003, Robert occasionally calls on Hariri at Koreitem. Hariri pumps him with questions about what is going on in Iraq.

I see Hariri for the last time on 5 January 2005. This time the interview is anything but boring. Hariri is bubbling with political intrigue and tells me he is about to publicly join the anti-Syrian opposition. He refuses to accept Bashar al-Assad's reappointment of Émile Lahoud as Lebanese president. The previous summer, Assad rang him on the telephone and said, "I alone have the right to choose the president of Lebanon. No one else has the right to do it." Assad threatens to "break Lebanon over [Hariri's] head" if he resists. Rostom Ghazale, who has replaced General Ghazi Kanaan as Assad's henchman in Lebanon, is extremely rude to Hariri.

Hariri further enrages Assad by secretly using his influence to push for the French and American-sponsored UN Security

Council Resolution 1559, which demands an end to Syria's tutelage over Lebanon.

Then a car bomb nearly kills Marwan Hamadeh, a close friend to Walid Jumblatt and Hariri. "Did the Syrians blow up Hamadeh's car?" I ask Hariri. "At the very least, they let it happen," he says. "At the most, they ordered it." In October 2004, Hariri resigns as prime minister and begins moving his Mustaqbal (Future) movement towards the anti-Syrian opposition. Hariri believes the loose grouping will gain a majority in upcoming legislative elections. "The ground is shifting. Syrian power is crumbling," he says.

Hariri has a naïve belief that George W. Bush is working for the good of Lebanon and the region. "The Americans have told the Syrians that if there is violence in Lebanon, they will be held responsible," he says. "The US ambassador to Lebanon says [the Syrians] must leave quietly, in an orderly fashion. It is a dream, but it will come true." Hariri thinks Bush will broker a just peace between Israel and the Palestinians, and between Israel and Lebanon. He is entranced by the mirage of a revitalised Lebanon as the future financial centre of the Middle East. Many Lebanese share his dream. "Bush feels these people [in Assad's regime] are working against his big project. He wants to give Lebanon as an example. It will work."

Hariri does not want to be quoted on any of this. He does not even want me to mention in print that I have seen him. "I trust you, Lara," he says. "Don't betray me." He suggests I ring Walid Jumblatt and Samir Kassir, an editorial writer at An Nahar newspaper. "They will tell you the same thing," he says.

I have known Jumblatt for more than twenty years. Samir often appears on a political talk show on the French channel TV5 with me, so both are at ease giving me telephone interviews. I publish an article in The Irish Times about how Syria is losing its grip on Lebanon.

When I interview him in person in Mukhtara two months later, Jumblatt predicts his own murder: "Somewhere, on the road to Beirut, or I don't know where, there will be unknown individuals, men of the shadows, waiting in ambush to spray me with bullets or detonate an explosive charge ... That is what is going to happen ... In Beirut, they can blow up my house. Here it is more difficult, though they could try aerial bombardment ... Their only argument is assassination."

Jumblatt's life alternates between obeisance to and rebellion against the Assads, *père et fils*. Fate imposed this game of Russian roulette on him; he didn't choose it. Somehow he survives.

I see Kassir during the same March 2005 reporting trip to Beirut. A cheerful, charming man with a salt-and-pepper beard and easy laughter, Kassir is organising mass protests to demand the withdrawal of Syrian troops from Lebanon. In repeated articles in *An Nahar*, he names Syrian generals who are interfering in Lebanese politics and denounces the repression of the opposition in Damascus. When Kassir turns the key in the ignition of his Alfa Romeo sports car on the morning of 2 June 2005, the bomb under his car seat explodes. Horrific though Kassir's murder is, it is a mere footnote to the Valentine's Day massacre.

On 14 February 2005, I come out of a session at the Académie Française in Paris and turn on my mobile phone. Robert has rung me a half-dozen times. Before I can call him back, the phone rings again.

"Hariri has been assassinated. Hariri is dead. A massive car bomb," he says. "It happened in front of the St George." I know the place exactly. Robert and I used to swim at the St George every morning. The hotel remains gutted from civil war days, but the pool and outdoor restaurant thrive.

"I was outside the Spaghetteria and there was this wall of white light and a huge blast." Robert talks fast. "I see people falling to the ground on the Corniche. I run towards it and everything is in flames. More than twenty cars burning, with people inside them. I see a big man lying on the ground, a blackened corpse. His socks were on fire. Hariri. It was Hariri. God, Lara, it was terrible."

Robert is in shock, and so am I, standing on the Quai Conti. I feel sorry for him, wish I could put my arms around him. Before we say goodbye, I add, almost as an afterthought, "It's our wedding anniversary." We have been separated for three years. "I know," says Robert. "I thought of it too."

I call Rima Tarabay, who is devastated. President and Madame Chirac are with Hariri's widow Nazek in the mansion on the Place d'Iéna, she tells me. I ring the *Irish Times* foreign desk. "I did the last interview with Rafik Hariri before he was assassinated," I tell deputy foreign editor Evelyn Bracken. "He told me Assad threatened him. How much space can you give me?"

Few doubt that Assad's regime is behind the killing of Hariri and the twenty-one people who died with him. The massacre triggers mass protests which force the Syrians to withdraw their troops from Lebanon – the very result Hariri sought, and which Assad hoped to avoid.

The UN sets up a special tribunal to prosecute Hariri's assassins. The court case lasts for eleven years and costs more than $800 million. Five Hezbollah militants are indicted, including the group's military leader, Mustafa Badreddine, Imad Mughniyeh's cousin and brother-in-law.

When the alleged co-conspirators are charged in 2011, the Hezbollah leader Hassan Nasrallah says the authorities will never catch them: "They cannot find them or arrest them in thirty days or sixty days, or in a year, two years, thirty years or 300 years." As recounted in Chapter VII, Badreddine dies in Damascus in 2016. The other four alleged co-conspirators are tried in absentia in 2020.

Salim Ayyash, a mid-level Hezbollah operative, is found guilty of conspiracy aimed at committing a terrorist act, committing a terrorist act by means of an explosive device and the intentional murder of Hariri with premeditation by using explosive materials. Charges against the others are dropped for lack of sufficient evidence. No one knows where Ayyash is. There will never be justice for Hariri, though it is widely believed that the Valentine's Day atrocity was a joint mission by Syrian military intelligence and Hezbollah.

Hariri's assassination freezes France's relations with Syria, until Nicolas Sarkozy succeeds Chirac. In September 2008, Sarkozy flies to Damascus with the same delusion that Chirac once harboured, that he can tame Bashar al-Assad.

Presidents Sarkozy and Assad hold their final press conference in the palace on the hilltop overlooking Damascus which Hariri built on behalf of King Fahd as a gift to Assad's father, Hafez. At the end of the press conference, Assad and foreign minister Farouk al-Sharaa see off Sarkozy. I am on deadline and rush after them in the hope of finding a lift to the hotel. I am halfway down the vast corridor when I see Assad and Sharaa walking straight towards me. Sharaa recognises me and holds out his hand to shake mine. Assad does the same. *Forgive me, Sheikh Rafik*, I think to myself. *I have shaken the hand of your assassin.*

Five years after Hariri's murder, Rima Tarabay asks me to participate in a commemoration at the Institut du Monde Arabe. Jacques Chirac, no longer president, sobs like a baby for his slain friend.

During the "Grapes of Wrath" offensive in 1996, Israel destroys most of the infrastructure that Hariri so painstakingly built. I interview his sister, Bahia, a member of the Lebanese parliament, and his niece Ghena in Sidon. "If my uncle saw this [Israeli bombardment], it would break his heart," Ghena says. During the 1996 onslaught which included the Qana massacre, an Israeli general said he would "smash Hariri's dream".

Dr Ghassan Hammoud, a friend of the Hariri family and the owner of Sidon's best hospital, recalls touring the battered city with Hariri in 1982. "It was terrible for him," Hammoud tells me. "He was very sad and he said, 'When it's over, I am going to rebuild everything.' … This time, there is no one like him… They destroyed everything he built. It is as if the Hariri era never existed."

೪೨

Beirut, 10.30 a.m., 11 April 1996

All the telephone lines go dead at the same time, without explanation. Israeli Apache helicopters swoop in from the sea and fire Hellfire missiles at Hezbollah targets in the southern suburbs. It is the first time the Israelis have struck the capital since 1982, and the first major Israeli assault on Lebanon in nearly three years.

Israeli commanders imitate US officers in Saudi Arabia in 1991, releasing black-and-white videotapes of pilots' crosshairs locking onto targets, followed seconds later by explosions. "Surgical strikes", we are told. One of the missiles blows chunks of concrete out of a hospital parking lot across the street from the Mickey and Minnie Mouse Nursery. Another hits a BMW on the highway north of Sidon, killing a twenty-seven-year-old woman.

Israel names this assault on Lebanon "Operation Grapes of Wrath". Its purpose is allegedly to end Hezbollah rocket attacks on northern Israel. The Lebanese say Israel started it, by killing two Lebanese men building a water tower in the village of Yater, just north of the Israeli-occupied zone of southern Lebanon. Hezbollah fires twenty-eight Katyusha rockets at Qiryat Shemona. Then a Lebanese boy is killed by a roadside bomb on the edge of the Israeli-held zone. Hezbollah says there are Hebrew markings on the bomb fragments, and it fires another thirteen rockets, injuring thirty-six people in Qiryat Shemona. Prime Minister Shimon Peres is in the midst of an election campaign and needs to appear tough, so he launches airstrikes across Lebanon, prompting the predictable Hezbollah rocket fire into northern Galilee.

Robert and I are about to leave for Washington for the presentation of the Johns Hopkins SAIS-Ciba Prize for Excellence in International Journalism which he has been awarded for his reporting from Algeria. We cancel the trip.

Israel orders civilians to leave homes in the south, then bombs petrol stations and civilian traffic, making it almost impossible for them to do so. About 400,000 inhabitants of southern Lebanon nonetheless manage to flee. Most go to Beirut, but 5,000 seek refuge in nearby compounds of the United Nations Interim Force in Lebanon, UNIFIL.

On 13 April 1996 an Apache helicopter, like those that attacked the retreating Iraqi army in Kuwait, fires two US-made Hellfire missiles at an ambulance that is evacuating fourteen civilians from Mansouri, 8 kilometres north of Israel, to the relative safety of Tyre. Mansouri has run out of food and is under heavy bombardment. Its inhabitants are obeying the Israeli order to depart.

One Hellfire fails to explode. The other goes through the back door of the ambulance and kills two women and four girls. Robert interviews the survivors of the attack, as well as a Lebanese camerawoman for Reuters who happened to be present at an abandoned UN checkpoint when the ambulance was hit and filmed the attack. The blast throws the ambulance twenty feet into the air and lodges it in the living room of a house.

Israel admits that it fired the missiles at the ambulance, but claims that it was owned by a Hezbollah member, and that it was carrying a Hezbollah fighter – none of which is true.

Those killed are Mona Jiha, aged twenty-seven, her three daughters, Zeinab, nine, Hanin, five, and baby Mariam, two months. Mona's aunt, Nawkal, aged sixty-nine, and niece, Huda, aged eleven, are also killed. Abbas Jiha, Mona's husband, a farmer who works as a volunteer ambulance driver, is at the wheel of the ambulance. He has already made two trips carrying wounded people into Tyre that morning. The ambulance is the communal property of the village, paid for by expatriate Lebanese.

Captain Mikael Lindvall, a Swedish spokesman for the UN force, gives Robert a piece of the Hellfire missile casing engraved with codings. Some of the codes have been chiselled off, so Robert tells the Fijian battalion of UNIFIL that he wants the codes from the second, unexploded missile when they dig it out. Lindvall stops the Fijians sending the entire missile – defused, one hopes – to our apartment in Beirut.

Through military contacts and with the help of *Janes Defence Weekly*, Robert determines that the missiles were manufactured by Rockwell, which has since been taken over by Boeing. He tells me he intends to "confront the armourers with the consequences of their profession".

As recounted over twenty pages in *The Great War for Civilisation*, Robert's contacts at Beirut airport allow him to carry the piece of missile casing on a flight to Paris. He knows it will be impossible to take it to the US in hand luggage or checked baggage, so he asks Amnesty International, which has reported on the ambulance atrocity, to airfreight the shrapnel to Washington DC, where Robert is reunited with it. He then takes a train to Duluth, Georgia, where he has scheduled an interview with three executives from the Boeing Defense & Space Group. The head of public relations is there, along with two retired US officers who served in Vietnam, one a colonel. They think Robert is writing a piece about the performance of Hellfire missiles in the Middle East, and boast about its precision.

Robert takes the Hellfire shard out of his bag and sets it down on Boeing's polished conference table. He tells the executives how, when and where it was used, and the Israelis' explanation. "Yeah, well it's a Hellfire. We all know that," the PR man says, adding, "I'm getting a little uncomfortable." The colonel is angry. "This is so far off base, it's ridiculous," he says.

"Is this some kind of crusade?" one of the executives asks. *The Independent* uses the question as the headline for Robert's article. Robert reminds them that he is talking about the killing of two women and four little girls, by one of their missiles. He also gives them photographs of the victims' bodies. "Whatever you do, I don't want you to quote me as saying anything critical of Israel's policies," one of the executives says twice.

After the story is published, Robert receives a letter from a European missile technician who says he can tell from the NATO stock number that the Hellfire "was exported from US stocks and given to the Israelis covertly". The technician is wary of telephone taps and warns Robert that the two of them risk being charged with compromising NATO security. I am by now living in Paris for *The Irish Times*, so I organise a lunch between Robert, the whistle-blower and his wife at the Lutetia Hotel. Robert returns to our apartment in the rue du Cherche-Midi and tells me what he has learned. Coding on the missile cladding indicates that it is the property of the US Marine Corps, not Israel.

Robert begins a second round of investigations. Neither the State Department nor the Pentagon responds to his questions, but a spokeswoman for the Marine Corps rings his hotel in Washington and tells him, "We don't like our missiles being used to attack kids". She sends a car to collect him and bring him to a marine base, where he is received by seven men in civilian clothing. They confirm that up to 300 Hellfires were shipped to Saudi Arabia to be used by marines against Saddam's occupation forces in Kuwait in 1991. One hundred and fifty-nine of these were fired at the Iraqis. When the conflict ended, the remaining Hellfires and other ordnance were dropped off in Haifa port for the Israelis, as part of a secret deal under which Israel agreed not to retaliate for Iraqi Scud attacks during the 1991 war.

Everything is connected in the Middle East. I recall the exchange I witnessed between the journalist from New York and a Marine Corps officer on the airbase in Bahrain, on the first morning of the 1991 Gulf War. "Israel is being attacked and they're not allowed to defend themselves," my colleague complained. "They'd better not retaliate, because the Israelis make trouble all over the Middle East and we're tired of cleaning up their shit," the officer fired back.

Nor are the Hellfires an isolated incident. Robert uncovers cases of tanks and armour, a squadron of aircraft, anti-tank cluster bombs and artillery shells that have been rifled from US stockpiles and given to Israel without traceability or accountability.

❧

18 April 1996, Qana, southern Lebanon

Robert and I spend the morning driving across the war zone with a convoy that is ferrying rations to UNIFIL posts. Israeli jets drop three bombs near our convoy. While travelling, we learn that an Israeli F-16 has bombed a house in Nabatiyeh, killing Fawzieh Al-Abed, aged forty, seven of her children, including her four-day-old baby daughter, and the fiancé of Fawzieh's eldest daughter.

We unload food with soldiers from the Irish Battalion for the orphanage in Tibnin and head back towards Tyre with Irish Commandant Eamonn Smyth. It is just after two in the afternoon when we leave the village of Hinniyah. We hear outgoing mortar fire from beyond the ridge to the north. A few minutes later, the air pressure changes as incoming artillery fire passes over our heads. "This is Fijibatt," says a voice on the UNIFIL radio transmitter. "Our headquarters is under fire. We have taken six rounds." He wants UNIFIL headquarters in Naqoura to tell the Israelis to stop shelling, which it does, but the shelling continues.

Minutes pass, during which the air pressure fluctuates each time another shell explodes. The voice returns. "They have hit Fijibatt headquarters... The rounds are coming in here now... We have casualties... One of our main buildings in Fijibatt has been demolished."

Fijibatt's radio goes dead. A Lebanese army liaison officer stationed in the house across the street from Fijian headquarters comes on the frequency, his voice breaking with fear and emotion. "The people are dying here!" he shouts. "We hear the voice of death. Do you understand?"

When we arrive at the gates of the Fijian battalion headquarters a few minutes later, blood is flowing down the asphalt driveway. I try not to step in it, but there is blood everywhere. Pools and rivers of it. And human flesh. An evil giant has run amok in a butcher's shop and thrown viscera and limbs and escalopes in every direction. Two buildings are on fire. Smoke and a pungent odour of roasting meat fill the air. We see charred bodies through the flames. The mind tries to register that this is the smell of humans burning in the battalion's conference room where they had taken refuge, but the mind recoils, rejects this information, then recommences in the vain attempt to process it.

UN soldiers and rescue workers work frenetically to sort the living from the dead. They run down the incline, taking care not to slip in the red viscous liquid, carrying the wounded to ambulances that scream up the 12 kilometres of road from Tyre. The blue helmets place the dead in rows beside the pathway and cover them with blankets. They wear rubber gloves to collect organs and body parts which they place in black plastic bin bags. Some of the soldiers are crying.

Burnt hands and feet protrude from under the blankets. In the smouldering ruin of the officers' mess, a Fijian soldier holds a baby aloft in one hand. Its head has been sliced off diagonally, the work of a proximity shell, an anti-personnel weapon designed to explode high above ground and create amputation wounds.

I recognise a cameraman from Lebanese television, a big, burly figure whom I've often seen at press conferences. Two colleagues struggle to carry him out of the compound, propping him up beneath his arms. He is not physically wounded. He has lost his reason. I see Hassan Seklawi, a Lebanese press officer with UNIFIL, crying on the shoulder of Captain Lindvall. "Look at my shoes!" Hassan screams in horror. "I am standing in meat."

Every minute or two, Robert and I exchange glances. We cannot believe what we are seeing. I sense that Robert fears I too will crack up. Be a camera, be a machine, I tell myself. Write it down. Don't think now. Just record it. My notebook and pen are a lifebuoy in a swamp of agony and death. I cling to them desperately, an automaton that writes down every detail. Absurdly, I keep remembering the Bible story from childhood, of Christ changing water into wine. Here, in Qana.

The walkway past the burning conference room is patterned with blood-red shoeprints. The concrete walls of an old building are still standing, though artillery shells have shredded the roof into pieces. We find a sinuous path between bodies and come upon a kneeling woman with her arms wrapped around a man's torso. "*Abi, Abi*," she wails, rocking back and forth. "Father, Father." The dead man looks to be in his fifties, with greying hair. An arm and shoulder have been cleaved away in a straight line, again the signature of a proximity shell. The wailing woman tries to hold together the pieces of his body.

"I am beginning to wonder if the Israelis are truly evil," Robert says in the midst of this bloodbath. Though I often hear him criticise Israel's actions, this is the only time I hear him blame Israelis as a people. He says it with a kind of amazement that human beings can inflict such unspeakable suffering on others. In his lifetime, Robert covers five Israeli wars in Lebanon: in 1978, 1982, 1993, 1996 and 2006. I cover the last three. All these wars, like Israel's frequent assaults on the Gaza Strip, are characterised by the huge disproportion between Arab and Israeli casualties, and total disregard for the lives of civilians.

We telephone our respective news desks, standing inside the battalion headquarters while the drama welters around us. The Fijian blue helmets are dazed by the catastrophe that has befallen their compound, but at the same time galvanized by a sense of urgency, to save anyone who can be saved. Bearded men rush into the disaster zone, searching for wives and children. We hear screams of loss and angry curses. "America gave Israel the weapons to do this. Americans are dogs!" one man shouts.

News of the massacre is just beginning to reach our bosses via the wire agencies. London and New York are preoccupied with the eighteen Greek tourists who have been murdered outside their hotel in Cairo that morning. A Palestinian gunman shot them in the mistaken belief that they were Israelis, in protest at the bombardment of Lebanon. This is worse, we tell our editors. This is more important. As the gravity of the massacre becomes known, our mobile phones ring almost continuously, especially Robert's, for days and nights. Every radio and television station we have ever spoken to is on the line. Robert is angry but he never loses his sang-froid. He ceaselessly recounts what we have seen, for days, weeks, months, and years.

Abed the driver waits for us at UNIFIL headquarters in Naqoura, 103 kilometres from Beirut. "Drive fast, *habibi*," Robert says. He needn't ask. Two Hetz-class Israeli gunboats lurk offshore. They are shelling the highway and we are virtually the only motorists. We reach the oil refinery at Zahrani, just south of Sidon, when the first artillery shell explodes behind us. It was here, I remember, that my colleague Barry Iverson from *Time* magazine nearly lost his leg in 1982. Another shell explodes ahead to the right. "I think they're firing at us," Robert says. "Faster, *habibi*." Abed floors the accelerator.

Images of the immediate aftermath of the massacre play over and over in front of me for weeks, as if a visor transformed into a video screen hangs low over my forehead. The videotape plays in a loop, whether my eyes are open or shut. It is there when I wake up in the morning, when I shower, eat, dress, work, and go to bed at night. After Qana, no other story seems worth telling. But it is a story almost too terrible to tell.

The experiences of those trapped inside the compound during the bombardment are infinitely worse than any trauma we might suffer as journalists. Survivors tell of people running in every direction, colliding with one another, of throats slashed by shrapnel, a sibling's face cut off and burned, of animal shrieks silenced by more incoming shells. A man is tossed tens of metres into the air. His head detaches and lodges in a burning tree. Some refugees can no longer distinguish between the living and the dead. Parents carry children with no heads or limbs without realising they are lost for ever. The Lebanese liaison officer across the street sees a throng of horribly wounded people stampede through the compound gates, some trying to run on bleeding stumps of missing feet. A Fijian soldier's arm hangs by a piece of skin.

Hamida Deeb hugs two small nephews to her chest then sees them "fly away in pieces, and with them my right arm and leg".

She lies beneath a tree. Burning leaves fall on her wounds. She loses twenty relatives.

Nayla Berji loses sixteen family members, including her father Abbas, two brothers and their wives. When she tries to lift her father, his intestines spill out. "Those people were very, very dear to me," she says, lying in her bed in the Jabal Amel Hospital in Tyre. "When I saw them like that, I cannot tell you what I suffered. What I have seen and what I experienced – I tell you; it has ruined the rest of my life."

Saadallah Balhas is also hospitalised at Jabal Amel. The fifty-six-year-old farmer remembers me from three years earlier, when his right leg was crushed in Israel's "Operation Accountability". In 1993, Balhas recalls, we took his picture. "My wife Zeinab was standing beside me," he says.

Balhas recently underwent a bone implant operation to repair his wound from the previous war, so his leg is in a plaster cast during "Grapes of Wrath". His children carry him into the conference room when the shelling alarm sounds. Close to forty relatives squeeze in around Balhas: his wife Zeinab, their eight sons and six daughters. The eldest son, Ali, is there with his wife Zohra and their five children. Balhas's two brothers, a sister-in-law, their children and grandchildren are with him.

A proximity shell explodes above the wooden roof of the conference room. "There was a terrible explosion, and the first thing I felt was hot, wet liquid all over the right side of my face," Balhas says. "There was a great flash of fire and I was burning. There was no space between the sound of the explosions. There was blood, so much blood, running down my face. I pushed the blood away with my hand and wiped my hand on the mattress. Everyone was shrieking and dying."

A second direct hit on the conference room destroys its corrugated steel walls and sets fire to wreckage and people. Balhas's right eye is blown out of its socket. With his remaining eye, he tries to see through the smoke and flames who is alive. He shakes his children. "I was crying so much and each one I shook, they didn't move. I saw my children scattered like dead sheep around me."

In all, 106 Lebanese civilians are slaughtered at Qana, fifty-two of them children. Robert has seen thousands of corpses since he began covering the Troubles in Belfast in 1972. He believes we should be loyal to the dead. "I've learned not to be afraid of dead people," he says. "I tell myself that they would want me to be there, that they'd invite me in and offer me a cup of tea if they could. I publish their names whenever I can, because to say someone's name is to make them immortal, if only for a moment."

Israeli Prime Minister Shimon Peres claims Hezbollah fired Katyushas from within the Fijian battalion headquarters. It is a lie. In his report to UN Secretary General Boutros Boutros-Ghali, Dutch Major General Franklin van Kappen establishes that Hezbollah fired mortars from several hundred metres away from the compound.

Through his binoculars, the Fijian captain on guard duty saw the bearded guerrillas fire the mortars. He knew there would be Israeli retaliation. Over a loudspeaker, the Fijians told their 150 soldiers to put on flak jackets and helmets and move indoors the 600 refugees who were living in their compound. "Our bunkers were for 150 men and we pushed 400 people into them, maybe more," the battalion commander, Colonel Wame Waqanivavalagi, tells Robert and me. "There was no more room." Hundreds of people ran into the compound at the last minute for protection, so it held well over 800 civilians when the seventeen-minute bombardment started.

Survivors of the massacre and UN personnel saw a miniature Israeli aircraft hovering overhead before and during the bombardment. The Israelis categorically deny that they had aircraft of any description above the compound, but witnesses describe to us the drone's high-pitched whining noise, the way it trailed grey smoke. Israeli drones are spotters for artillery and helicopter gunners, and they are a common, if ominous, sight over southern Lebanon. The technical abbreviation for the unmanned air vehicle is MK. To reassure children, parents call the drones by the familiar name Um Kamel – Um like M, but meaning "mother", and Kamel, the boy's name. Saadallah Balhas remembers seeing the MK around all morning, along with a helicopter. UN observers record the presence of two helicopters, and a high-altitude AWACS reconnaissance aircraft.

Robert is obsessed with rumours of an amateur video taken during the bombardment. He and Abed drive to southern Lebanon almost every day so Robert can question UN soldiers and officers about it. "If we can show the drone was there, it proves the Israelis are lying," he says.

We return to Qana to cover the burial of the victims on 1 May. "You are damned for ever, Israel," says a banner flying over the ceremony. The bodies are wrapped in white shrouds in open caskets which are passed above the heads of the crowd. There's a terrible, sickly sweet smell of decaying corpses. Each coffin is placed in a concrete and brick niche in the hastily built memorial adjacent to the Fijian battalion headquarters. Robert and I talk to a Fijian peacekeeper who has seen the video but cannot remember the details. Robert gives the soldier his card and begs him to call if he learns anything more about the video.

Two days later, Robert's mobile rings. A man dictates a set of map coordinates and says twelve noon. Robert and Abed drive south at great speed. A Norwegian soldier from the UN's Force Mobile Reserve is waiting for Robert.

"I've got it! I got the video!" Robert exclaims when he bursts into our Beirut apartment a few hours later. He rushes to the video player and slides the cassette in. Taken from a nearby UN position, it clearly shows the MK drone and a helicopter flying overhead while the compound burns. We hear the voice of Commandant Smyth on the recording, relaying the message over the UN network, saying "Fijibatt headquarters is under fire". The camera zooms in on the burning conference room.

"Fortunately, the soldier made a copy of the video before

he gave it to van Kappen," Robert says excitedly. "He was told not to talk to anyone about it. He tossed the envelope with the cassette onto the front car seat. Before he walked away, he said, 'I have two small children, the age of the children who died at Qana. This is for them.' It was one of the bravest things I ever saw a soldier do."

Robert works like a man possessed, writing three pages for the next day's *Independent*. The newspaper publishes a front-page story under the title "Massacre film puts Israel in dock" and distributes free copies of the video and still photographs showing the drone over the burning compound to all media who request them, free of charge.

Forcing the UN to release the van Kappen report, which it had kept secret, is one of Robert's greatest achievements. Without his persistence, the truth about the Qana massacre might never have been known. Boutros-Ghali later tells us that Washington had him sacked as UN secretary general because he allowed the report to be published.

The report notes that "in response to repeated questions, the Israeli interlocutors stated that there had been no Israeli aircraft, helicopters or remotely piloted vehicles in the air over Qana before, during or after the shelling". It refers to the drone's "real-time data-link capability". In other words, the Israelis watched the massacre as the artillery shells exploded. The massacre was "unlikely" to have been an accident, van Kappen concludes.

Israel admits that the drone was present only after Robert publishes the video story. Then they state that it was not watching Qana but "was on another mission". The phrase immediately enters Robert's and my lexicon of absurd quotations. Israel makes two other patently false claims: that the drone arrived only after the bombardment, and that the Israel Defence Forces were using a faulty map which showed Fijian battalion headquarters to be elsewhere.

The recording of Commandant Smyth relaying the radio message proves that the bombardment was still going on. The

Israelis' claim that they did not realise Fijian headquarters was there, and that they did not know the compound was sheltering hundreds of refugees, enrages UNIFIL.

"It's been there for eighteen years!" Captain Lindvall says. "The Israelis rely very heavily on accurate mapping," says Timur Goksel, the political adviser to UNIFIL. "They use aerial photographs and mark every house on their maps." The Israelis claim they stopped shelling two minutes after UNIFIL contacted them. UNIFIL says the shelling continued for another fifteen minutes. "We made the effort to make them stop, but they kept firing," Colonel Wame tells us. Three UN positions fired red warning flares, to no avail.

Van Kappen reacts with hurt feelings to Israeli accusations of anti-Semitism. "I've heard that some Israelis think this is an anti-Jewish vendetta," he tells one of my colleagues at *Time* magazine. "My wife is Jewish. I am not anti-Israeli. When I went there, I believed the Israeli army – a few shells had just overshot." After ten minutes on a rooftop at Qana, van Kappen adds, "I knew I was in deep shit. This was not a simple overshoot."

In the course of the investigation, it emerges that Hezbollah fired the mortars at an Israeli raiding party that was laying mines north of Israel's self-proclaimed "security zone" and deep inside UNIFIL's area of operations. The raiding party called for fire support, whereupon the Israelis shelled Qana. The first shells fell on the cemetery from which the mortars were fired, but the gunners then shifted their targeting hundreds of metres to the Fijian battalion headquarters where the refugees were sheltering.

Soldiers from the unit that fired the thirty-six artillery shells give an interview to the Israeli weekly *Kol Ha'ir* which is published on 10 May 1996. "Soldier A" says the unit's battery commander "told us that we were firing well and we should keep it up, and that Arabs, you know, there are millions of them".

"A few *Arabushim* died, there is no harm in that," says a man identified as "Soldier T". *Arabushim* is a derogatory Hebrew term meaning "a bunch of Arabs". No Israeli is ever disciplined for the massacre. Robert writes about the *Kol Ha'ir* interview. I offer an article to *Time* magazine, but they are not interested.

The Qana massacre is a turning point for me. The editing process is particularly difficult because my editors are, as usual, afraid to criticise Israel. My eyewitness account of the immediate aftermath of the bombardment is placed across the bottom of two pages. The Israeli writer Amos Oz is given considerably more space for his hand-wringing essay questioning what his country has done.

In *Time*'s system of multiple edits, copy is sent to correspondents for "comments and corrections". I correct the number of dead at Qana, but the text comes back to me repeatedly, still saying that "at least seventy-five" people have been killed. On Saturday morning, two days after the slaughter, I telephone World editor Johanna McGeary in New York to ask why she has not corrected the fatalities figure. "We always use the lowest estimate," she says. "AP said 'at least seventy-five'."

"That was right after the bombardment on Thursday, Johanna," I say. "The figure has gone up since. Believe me, more than a hundred people were killed there."

"I think I'll stick with seventy-five," she replies.

I go over Johanna's head and call Joe Ferrer, the editor of *Time*'s international edition. "Joe, Johanna will not correct the casualty figure in the Qana story."

"I'm not going to get involved in a dispute between a correspondent and an editor," Joe says.

"This is not a dispute," I say firmly. "If you will not believe your Beirut bureau chief, call UNIFIL spokesman Captain Mikael Lindvall and he will tell you *officially* that more than a hundred people are dead."

When *Time* magazine arrives in Beirut on Monday morning, the number of dead has been corrected, but the caption under the photograph accompanying my eyewitness account says, "A child, who had been caught in the crossfire at Qana, lies dead on a hospital floor in Tyre."

Crossfire? There was no *crossfire* at Qana. I fought tooth and nail to maintain the integrity of my reporting, only to see my editors invent "crossfire" at Qana. The subtitle on *Time*'s cover story, written in New York, is: "Israel stands tough after a disastrous error". *Error?* My editors have automatically accepted Israeli assertions that the bombardment was not deliberate.

Three weeks later, the title on *Time*'s article on the van Kappen report, again written in New York, is "Anatomy of a Tragedy". *Tragedy* – like a natural disaster or an act of God? If anyone else had killed 106 civilians, the headline would surely have read "atrocity", "massacre" or "war crime". The subtitle is a question: "Did Israel unwittingly shell a UN base in Qana?" *Unwittingly.* "A disturbing investigation is hotly disputed" the subtitle continues. The conclusions of an investigation by a major general from a NATO country for the UN secretary general are *hotly disputed*.

I am willing to risk my life on important stories, but I refuse to continue to do so for a magazine that distorts the truth. I start looking for a new job. Six months later, I begin work as the *Irish Times*' Paris correspondent. Robert and I plan to commute between Paris and Beirut. Although covering France is my primary responsibility, *The Irish Times* allows me to continue reporting important Middle East stories. It is a huge relief to work for a serious newspaper which has the courage to print my copy as I write it.

XI

The Depth of Love

saying again
if you do not teach me I shall not learn
saying again there is a last
even of last times
last times of begging
last times of loving
of knowing not knowing pretending
a last even of last times of saying
if you do not love me I shall not be loved
if I do not love you I shall not love

the churn of stale words in the heart again
love love love thud of the old plunger
pestling the unalterable
whey of words

terrified again
of not loving
of loving and not you
of being loved and not by you
of knowing not knowing pretending
pretending

Samuel Beckett, from "Cascando"

Robert used to tease me for starting sentences with the words "My fear is…"

My fear is… that no matter how I tell this story, I will tell too much and too little, that it will seem self-indulgent, that it will blow the drama of a personal sorrow out of proportion. There are, after all, far greater tragedies than another failed marriage. Would it be more dignified to say, like Jane Eyre to Rochester, that I have no tale of woe?

But if I do not tell this story, this book will not make sense. If Robert's and my life together was such a great adventure, readers will ask, why did we not stay together?

Am I revisiting the past to liberate myself from it? There ought to be a statute of limitations, a time beyond which wounds heal, the end of the prison sentence. Some episodes remain too painful – or too damning – to write about.

How I wish someone had given me the following advice in 1992: if you have the good fortune to find true love, cherish the person, be faithful. Infidelity is not a gag in French *théâtre du boulevard*. Cuckolded spouses and lovers hiding in cupboards are not funny. I curse my fickle heart.

I do not want to be defined, by myself or by others, as the repudiated wife of Robert Fisk. Though we both suffered, I am not a victim. Robert and I both had a life and loves before and after we were together. I got over it, went on to do other things. I have had a good life regardless, in large part because of what he gave me and taught me. For this I remain immeasurably grateful.

After forty years of journalism, I ought to be able to write this story. Robert is the person I know best. I could portray him convincingly as a villain or as a saint. He was neither, or perhaps both. He was immensely human. I am trying to be fair to him. I do not want to sully his reputation. I want to find words, as Philip

Larkin wrote, *not untrue and not unkind*. That is why this is at the same time the most difficult and the easiest part of our lives to write about. Difficult for the obvious reasons, and because many of my questions remain unanswered. Easy, because I know this story by heart.

༄

Paris, 30 March 2000

Robert takes the taxi directly from Roissy airport to the Cherche-Midi restaurant. I know the instant he walks in. That confident stride, despite the weight of the shoulder bag, computer and briefcase. He is suntanned and lean and fit and happy. He is the young man I met in Damascus in 1983. He is in love with someone, and it is not me.

When Robert sits down, his eyes avoid mine. He chatters about Taliban schools and obtuse Pakistanis. He talks about work, nothing but work, journalism, projects. At one point he snaps at me, something to do with Tony the architect whom we hired to rebuild the derelict house we purchased in Dalkey. After dinner, I help him carry his belongings back to the apartment.

When we get in the lift, I start crying. "What's wrong? What's wrong?" Robert says, pretending he doesn't know.

We go to bed. I awake after an hour or two and go to look for his briefcase in the next room, the one I gave him several years earlier for Christmas. I find sacred religious medals embossed with Mary, Mother of God, given to him by an Irish reader. There's a black-and-white photograph of me, taken in New York in 1987. I am about to stop looking when I happen upon a receipt: "Paid to interpreter in Pakistan for nine days, £650". It is signed by her.

Neither of us comes out of this well. There is no dignity in snooping in your spouse's briefcase. And hiring one's mistress at the expense of one's newspaper is also dodgy, though I have no doubt that they worked hard.

I sit on the sofa, weeping. Robert gets out of bed and comes to me and says, "Oh, Lara, Lara, what's wrong?"

"You know what's wrong," I say.

"What is it? Do you think I'm having an affair?" I am surprised by his directness. He must realise, as I do, that we can no longer elude the subject.

"Yes. I know you are."

"What makes you think so?"

"I know you are."

"Who do you think it is?"

"I know who it is…" I say her name. My pessimistic, fatalistic streak tells me from that night that he will end up with her in the house we so painstakingly built together.

"How do you know it's not someone else?" Robert asks. Then he denies it, repeatedly.

I am annoyed by his denials. "Don't ask me how, Robert, but I know. I swear on the soul of my mother that you were with her in Pakistan." My mother is only fourteen months dead. Robert drops the denial.

"*You* had an affair!" he shoots back with venom.

৪৯

I did – in Lebanon in the aftermath of the civil war, when *le tout Beyrouth* wanted to forget the bad years and wallow in luxury and pleasure. He was older, long separated from his wife, suave, and spoke perfect French. Like Robert, he knew many things; just not the same things Robert knew. He pursued me assiduously for months. I was flattered by his attention.

My liaison continued on and off for two years. On 9 March 1994, Abed takes Robert to Beirut airport and returns to the apartment with two dozen red roses and the habitual card saying, "I love you Lara. Ton Tigre." I have behaved shamefully, but suddenly I am filled with remorse. It is Robert I love; Robert I want to spend my life with. I call the other man to say I cannot attend the classical concert he has bought tickets for that evening. I cannot see him any more. I never speak to him again. If I am strong enough to do this, I tell myself, I can stop smoking. I give up a three-pack-a-day cigarette habit that same day.

ജ

Now Robert asks me how the affair ended. "Thank God I sent you those roses!" he says on that sleepless night in Paris. Two months later he will say, "I wish you had left me for him," which is devastating.

The boil has been lanced. Upset as I am, we are strangely close, the closest we have been in a long time. We sit together on the sofa, our arms around each other, both weeping and talking softly until dawn. "I feel so close to you now," Robert says. "We must try to tell each other everything."

"We may never be able to talk like this again," I say. "This moment will pass."

Robert tells me he knew about my affair from the beginning. "I saw it happening. I felt powerless to do anything." He pumps me with questions about the where and when of it. Like an idiot, I tell him the truth, not foreseeing that his anger will extend to objects and clothing he associates with his former rival.

I ask a lot of questions about her, but he is evasive. The little he does tell me pours salt on the wound. They intend to make a documentary together about the Armenian Holocaust. She recites Persian poetry to him. They lingered for hours in an antiquarian bookshop in Peshawar where she chose a rare edition of a book about the British in Afghanistan as a gift for him. In refugee camps, poor, uneducated Afghans "looked at her as if she were a queen. She gave away all her money." She is always positive and cheerful. In sum, perfection.

And she is sixteen years younger than me, about the age I was when Robert met me in Damascus. Middle-aged men leave their wives every day for what Robert calls "cuties". Though there may be an element of that – after all, Robert is only human – I would like to think that we are more than a cliché. I nonetheless prepare a pat reply for future inquiries: *He traded me in for a more recent model.* It's not even funny.

From the outset, Robert establishes a symmetry between our two affairs: the age difference; the deceit; how the wronged party suffers. Our mutual infidelities become a weapon of mutually assured destruction.

ഇ

There can be no excuse for what I did, but there are extenuating circumstances. When I stumbled, Robert and I had known each other for nine years, had lived together for five. Our work increasingly took us to different destinations. I was often alone in Beirut.

Though we eventually marry, once we begin living together he never again speaks of a desire for children. On the contrary; when we visit the homes of friends with children, he is horrified by the noise and disorder, by the way infants clamour to be the centre of attention. On the rare occasions when I try to broach the subject, he says he has often seen children drive a couple apart. I am far from certain of wanting children myself, but I am hurt by the fact that he will not discuss it.

There is something else, more impalpable and which it is unfair to hold against him, since these are also Robert's admirable qualities. My sister in California, who will later divorce, complains that her husband never talks. "Robert never *stops* talking. Consider yourself lucky!" I tell her. I am increasingly exhausted by Robert's *intensity*, by his unrelenting absolutism and simmering anger. Am I unfaithful because he is angry? Or is he angry because I am unfaithful? Had I resisted temptation, would we have stayed together? Or does he dredge up my transgression as a pretext for having an affair he would have had anyway? Did we lose the lightness of spirit and good humour of our first years together because of my infidelity? Or was I unfaithful because we had lost those precious ingredients?

I suspect Robert of having had an affair with Isabel Ellsen, the French photographer who worked with him in the Saudi desert in 1991. He was with Isabel again, for several days and nights in Syria, reporting a story on the Turkish genocide against the Armenians, when my own affair started the following year. When he went to Jerusalem soon after, I felt certain he was with her. I called the King David Hotel and asked to speak to Isabel. The operator said she was out.

I take the operator's response as confirmation that Isabel is indeed staying at the same hotel as Robert. I confront him, on the telephone to Jerusalem, in tears. He swears Isabel is not with him and that he checked with the switchboard operator who says a Swede called Elson has a room there. "My poor Lara," Robert says. "I can only imagine what pain you must be in to believe something so silly."

When we started living together, I had asked Robert how he managed to maintain love affairs with several women at a time. "Lie, lie, lie," he said, laughing. Adamant though he is, I am never certain he is being honest.

In October 1994, I invite Isabel to dinner at our apartment in Paris. There are five of us at table, including Robert. I ask visitors to write in a leather-bound guest book that Robert gave me for Christmas. "Lara & Fiski," Isabel begins her inscription. "Thank you for taking me as 'your photographer', Robert, you really 'made' it with me, and you Lara, you're the woman in the middle of it, wich [sic] means you're the heart of it... Love to both of you. Isabel Ellsen."

"What does this *mean*?" I ask Robert when our guests leave. "You *did* have an affair with her, didn't you?" Again, he denies it.

Either Robert was unfaithful first and lied, which would assuage my guilt but dent my faith in his integrity, or I carelessly broke the heart of the best man I have ever known, forfeiting my only chance of a happy marriage. I am not sure which is worse.

It is so important for me to know that several years later I invite Isabel to lunch. I explain that Robert and I have separated, that it really doesn't matter now and I will not hold it against her but I must know: did she have an affair with my husband?

Isabel throws back her head and emits a theatrical, howl-like laugh. "Nev-air!" she shouts in a strong French accent. My heart sinks, because I can never be certain. Isabel dies of a stroke in her home in 2012, at the age of fifty-four.

ᴥ

When the US embassy in Dublin confiscates my passport in late 1991, Robert says, "We've got to get you another nationality." We discuss the possibility of marriage. We consult a London lawyer who says we would have to live in the UK for five years as husband and wife before I would be eligible for British citizenship. That is impossible, so we abandon the idea for a while.

Five years later, Robert decides he wants to marry me, for love. Heather Kerr, manager of the *Independent* foreign desk, books a ceremony at the register office in Ealing, West London, for 14 February 1997.

We spend the eve of our wedding at the Hyde Park Hotel in Kensington, where we slept the first night of our new life together in 1987. I still have a receipt for £55 for "One tied posy, white Dutch rose (bridal arrangement)" from the florist in Knightsbridge where Robert orders a bouquet for me. We dress up in our best clothes and meet Heather and her husband, the *Independent*'s defence correspondent Chris Bellamy, at the register office. We say our vows and exchange the rings we have been wearing for years. "I hope you will be very happy together," the registrar says. "In fact, I believe that you are *already* very happy."

Heather serves us champagne brunch at their home after the brief ceremony. She or Chris takes one of my favourite photographs. Robert and I look into each other's eyes with joy and complicity as he draws me towards him for an embrace. No matter what happens, I think, I will have known what it is to marry a man I love deeply. We fly to Dublin that evening. Through the rain-streaked window of the taxi, I see a beautiful blonde woman whose arms are filled with red roses at a bus shelter in Blackrock. I do not know why, but I never forget that image.

At this point, the fictional ending would say, "And they lived happily ever after in Dalkey, County Dublin", but the collapse of our marriage teaches me how dangerous it is to think that one has *arrived*, that no arrival in life is permanent. As Louis Aragon wrote:

> *Rien n'est jamais acquis à l'homme Ni sa force*
> *Ni sa faiblesse ni son cœur Et quand il croit*
> *Ouvrir ses bras son ombre est celle d'une croix*
> *Et quand il croit serrer son bonheur il le broie*
> *Sa vie est un étrange et douloureux divorce*
> *Il n'y a pas d'amour heureux...*
>
> *Mon bel amour mon cher amour ma déchirure*
> *Je te porte dans moi comme un oiseau blessé...*
>
> (Nothing ever definitively belongs to man Neither
>   his strength
> Nor his weakness nor his heart And when he thinks
> To open his arms his shadow is that of a cross
> And when he tries to embrace his happiness it shatters
> His life is a strange and painful divorce.
> There is no happy love...
>
> My beautiful love my dear love my tearing apart
> I carry you in me like a wounded bird...)

Everything seems perfect for a few months after our marriage, though the late summer of 1997 is a hard slog. Diana, Princess of Wales, is killed in a car crash following a week that sees a papal visit to Paris and the worst massacres so far of the civil war in Algeria. I have just arrived in Dalkey for a long summer holiday with Robert. *The Irish Times* rings before dawn. Robert books my plane ticket while I shower and dress to take the first flight back to Paris. Once coverage of the Princess of Wales's death subsides, we travel to Algiers together for a productive week in October. On 26 November 1997, we celebrate our tenth anniversary together with a champagne and foie gras breakfast in Beirut, followed by a trip to the ruins of Baalbek.

Both our mothers are suffering from Parkinson's disease and their illness hangs over us. We are in the cottage in Dalkey in January 1998 when my sister calls to say that my mother, Jean, is dying. Robert books flights and later argues with Air France when it loses my frequent flyer upgrade. He slips a card into my handbag as I leave for Los Angeles. "Lara, my angel," it begins. "I love you so much and I feel so sorry for you this morning, I'm very happy I knew your Mum (*my* Mum-in-law...). But this card is also to remind you of the wonderful life we have together and to tell you that you are the *most* wonderful, *most* beautiful lover and wife that any man could have."

やう

I tease Robert about his "fan club", the hundreds of readers who send him letters and invite him to give lectures. He spends evenings and weekends replying to every letter. One fan launches a website to his glory. There's a woman in Manhattan who clips newspapers for him, and another in Wisconsin who organises lecture tours in America. Proud as I am of my husband, the fan club makes me feel somehow excluded, as if he no longer belongs to me. My unease is well founded. She comes from the fan club.

In 1997, Robert receives a screenplay based on his Lebanon book, written by a journalism student in north America. "It's not bad," he tells me. "She has clearly understood that you and I are together."

"It's obvious," I say. "The book is dedicated to me."

The following December Robert and I are in Tehran. Mohammad Khatami, a kindly, open-minded intellectual theologian, has been president of the Islamic Republic for six months. I decide to write an article about Khatami's efforts to encourage Iranian filmmakers. The phone rings in our room at the Homa Hotel. It is her.

Robert grows animated, insists that I talk to her for my article about Iranian cinema. She gives me several contacts for my story. Robert explains that she is close to the family of a prominent Iranian director. I've been vaguely aware that he's struck up a correspondence with her, but I'm surprised that she knows where he is staying in Tehran. We are busy working and I try to forget it.

In May 1998 an American colleague at *Time-Life* puts me in contact with a German doctor who says he has proof that the US military are testing chemical weapons on prisoners. It seems a far-fetched story, not the sort that *Time* or *Life* would touch, but outrageous things have been known to happen. The German says it is dangerous to discuss it on the telephone. Robert and I decide to go and see him in Spain. *The Irish Times*, to its credit, is willing to send me on the story.

We meet the German and his girlfriend in Reus, near Barcelona. We've been journalists long enough not to judge them by their late 1960s' hippie appearance, but it takes only a few minutes to realise that the German's documents on University of Paris and White House letterhead are crude forgeries. We tell the "doctor" – in fact a failed medical student – that we know he is lying, and he admits it. Robert not only invites him and his girlfriend to dinner but arranges to meet them for breakfast the following morning. Back in our hotel room, we argue.

"Why did you invite them to dinner?" I ask harshly. "He wasted our time and our newspapers' money. He's a loser, and dishonest into the bargain. Did you really have to do that?"

"I feel sorry for him. I'm interested in the way his mind works," Robert says.

"I know you're always on the side of the underdog, but this guy is not a persecuted victim. He's a crook."

Robert shrugs and sulks. I refuse to join them for breakfast the following morning. I sense there is something else lurking in Robert's conscience. He seems alienated and cannot stop talking about the journalism student, the one who sent him the screenplay and who recently organised a lecture by him at her university. She will organise several more Fisk lectures in the autumn. I ought to worry, but I don't want to believe he would fall in love with a student, not even a mature one. In retrospect, the trip is a turning point in our marriage.

In September, Robert's mother Peggy is dying in Maidstone. He does not want me to go with him to see her. "You'll be emotional. You'll cry. It will make it harder for me," he says. "I love Peggy too," I insist when Robert is leaving for Maidstone. "You have no right to exclude me. I am coming with you." Two years later, he tells me the real reason why he didn't want me to accompany him to Maidstone. He feels I betrayed Peggy when I was unfaithful to him.

After Bill Fisk retired, Peggy, who was twenty-one years younger than her husband, found an escape from her cantankerous husband through her work as a magistrate, her painting classes and garden. She adored Robert, their only child, and was a loving and affectionate mother-in-law to me.

Each time we leave to cover a war together, my own mother cries and carries on, to such an extent that I stop telling her where we are going. By contrast, Peggy says cheerfully, "How interesting! Now do be careful and come back and tell me all about it."

There is a Peggy expression for every occasion, and we start many a sentence with the words, "As Peggy says..." Setbacks are greeted with the phrase "It's all part of life's rich tapestry". Playing with Walter the cat, we say: "Little things please little minds". On being shown a less than successful attempt at fashion, art or architecture: "At least they tried." Peggy's phrase "mutton dressed as lamb" is the perfect commentary on overdressed, over-made-up Lebanese ladies, though Robert and I amend it to "mutton dressed as mutton".

Peggy dies on 10 September 1998, three days after we arrive in Maidstone. Her sister, Auntie Bibby, is, like me, unwanted by Robert at her bedside. "You were the apple of your mother's eye," Bibby says to Peggy, who is unconscious, minutes before the death rattle.

I surmise that cheerful, vivacious Peggy Barbara Rose was her mother's favourite daughter. After inspiring jealousy in her sister, Peggy is the object of decades of Oedipal rivalry between Bill and Robert, who later calls her "a flame of optimism in my young life". Peggy is not beautiful – she bears a passing resemblance to Margaret Thatcher – but Bill is a jealous husband. He punches the mayor of Maidstone in the jaw when he flirts with Peggy at a city council dinner.

We stay on in Maidstone to prepare the house for sale. I sort all the furniture, household goods and clothing. Robert is interested in his father's library only. A few nights after Peggy's death, I remark softly that he hasn't cried, and that it cannot be good for him. I mean it as an expression of sympathy, but, like so many of the things we say to each other over the coming four years, my meaning is distorted. Robert accuses me of saying that I loved Peggy more than he did. He explodes, yelling and beating his fists on the rose chintz wallpaper. He runs down the stairs, out of the house into the dark Kentish countryside. He doesn't come back for more than an hour.

Robert channels his grief into a journalistic investigation, calling associations of families of victims of Parkinson's disease in London and New York. From their statistics he concludes that western governments "prefer missiles to medicine". By his calculation, they spend more on weapons every five minutes than in a year on Parkinson's research. "If resources had been better spent, Peggy would not be in that coffin," he says in an angry oration in Barming church. He is right, of course, but the ladies from Peggy's painting class and bridge club look stunned. In his prayer, the vicar "commit[s] this anger to God".

A month before Peggy died, we moved out of Robert's lovely cottage in Sorrento Road, after swapping it for a dilapidated, uninhabitable house with spectacular sea views. For sixteen months while we renovate the house, we stay at a luxury bed and breakfast when we visit Dalkey.

I notice that the footprint of the house on the architect's plan resembles that of an Ottoman mansion in Lebanon. Robert and I comb salvage yards in Beirut for arched tracery windows, marble columns and iron shutter holders in the form of Ottoman figurines. I help a mason place the exquisite tiles I have brought back from Algeria, Iran and Iraq onto the walls of the entry, garden stairs, bathrooms, gazebo and kitchen. Robert spends his inheritance on the house, but most of the effort is mine; a gift of love to him and to our future.

But the renovation, at the height of the Celtic Tiger boom, is often fraught. Robert fears the architect, builder, engineer and workmen will walk off the site if we create trouble; they have plenty of work elsewhere. We order seasoned oak floors. I arrive for a site meeting to find them installing narrow pine boards instead. Delays and cost overruns pile up. Robert and I vent our frustration on each other. When we finally move in at the end of 1999, Robert says he hates the house, that he misses his cosy cottage. The lies we tell ourselves, the lies we tell each other, are taking a toll. We both suffer from psychosomatic ailments.

For the millennium New Year's Eve we invite Robert's oldest friends from his youth as a reporter in Belfast and their spouses: David and Pat McKittrick, Conor and Zhanna O'Clery, Olivia O'Leary and Paul Tansey. The evening seems to lift Robert's spirits.

In January 2000, she visits Robert in Beirut. He tells me she is staying at a hotel, that I needn't worry. I have tried to ignore his budding relationship with her for more than two years, but now alarm bells really are ringing, more so when Robert tells me that Abed the driver and Imad the interpreter say she is 'a cutie'. When Robert goes AWOL in Pakistan in March, for the first time in the thirteen years we have lived together, I feel certain that he is with her, which brings me back to the beginning of this chapter.

§⸜

Robert often says that people who live in war-torn countries are *invisibly mutilated*. In different words, he tells me that he has been mutilated by my crass infidelity. "I can't get over it. I won't get over it," he says.

"But my affair ended six years ago! Yours is ongoing."

It is an objection that I raise often, but Robert is deaf to it. In a letter from our home in Dalkey dated January 2002, he explains with more nuance why he cannot let go of my betrayal. He says he experiences time as a continuum, not something that passes. That is why he still feels exactly as he did when he first came to Lebanon at the age of twenty-nine. He tells me he remembers every detail of my arrival at Heathrow in 1987, how he was too nervous to drink coffee, and gave great consideration to how far he should stand from the exit, "how I felt when you put your arms round me. Such joy."

But for the same reason, he continues, "because time is a continuum" his pain has remained fresh, "as if its cause was yesterday". He says he was gradually broken by despair, that time has no healing power for him, that his sadness became addictive.

For years I tormented myself. Should I confess? Should I not? Would it heal a wound, or drive him away? I am stunned that he could keep this hurt inside him for eight years without confronting me. We are so very different; I could not remain silent for even one night. "Why didn't you say anything?" I ask.

With the exception of two trial separations in 2001, we continue to see each other for another nine years after the great unravelling, until he remarries. Our correspondence in 2000–2002 includes twenty letters by Robert and at least twelve letters and poems written by me. Rarely has the implosion of a marriage been so well documented.

In Robert's first long letter, after a terrible, terrible scene in our Beirut apartment on 17 May 2000, he writes how strange it is that two people who loved each other so much can so misunderstand and hurt each other. He claims he still truly loves me. "It's as if the depth of love and experience of love over the years has a kind of ghastly counterbalance in pain and hurt." He has not forgotten a moment of the two months since I confronted him over his affair, and knows how wounded I am.

Robert begs me to believe that he has never deliberately tried to hurt me, least of all out of some desire to balance the pain he felt in the past. "I had no way of comprehending it, let alone resolving it," he says of my infidelity. "I have told you so many times what it felt like. The most searing, fearful pain and anguish I have ever felt in my life. My angel, the most precious human being whom I lived for, was sharing everything with someone else."

Robert says he is crying as he writes the letter. He tells me that he decided the only way to keep me was to remain silent. He often felt that he did not have the courage to continue, and it drove him a bit mad.

By 2000, I have returned unscathed from a dozen wars, but this is killing me. Why does infidelity hurt like the breaking of bones? I am amazed by women who put up with wandering husbands: Hillary Clinton, Bernadette Chirac, innumerable French women. How do they deal with such pain?

Robert wants me to be friends with the new woman. In April 2000, she stops in Ireland on her way back from Pakistan and suggests coming to our home to tell me that she has no intention of stealing my husband. *No way*, I tell Robert. *You'd better not bring her here.*

Not long after, I sit in a café in Monaco with a freelance cameraman, waiting for President Mary McAleese to emerge from lunch with Prince Albert. I do not mention my troubles, and am surprised when the cameraman tells me, on the verge of tears, that he was happily married with children until he fell in love with an aid worker he met on a story in Africa. "You can't help it when it happens to you," he says. "It's like an accident." His wife is understanding and puts no pressure on him. Why can't I be like the cameraman's wife? I wonder. I run into him a few years later at a conference in Paris and ask what happened. He ended his affair and stayed with his wife.

I find myself in the impossible position of striving to be sweet, loving and seductive when I am angry, heartbroken, fearful and insomniac. I understand now why Robert's behaviour was so erratic in the 1990s. When I tell him that I cannot bear it, when I beg him to choose between us, he says angrily: "You had two years. I am being propelled down a path that I have no particular desire to go on, in which I must start making decisions." He says he has never thought of leaving me, or of not living with me in the home we built together. "Suddenly the issue has become larger than I ever thought it should be."

Our marriage is collapsing. Normal life – and journalism – continue. On the morning after our sleepless night in Paris, Robert's foreign desk calls to say there has been a clash between Israelis and Hezbollah in southern Lebanon. Can he file? We haven't finished breakfast, but Robert rings Beirut and UNIFIL headquarters and hammers away on his portable computer while my life crashes around me.

We are scheduled to fly to Dublin that same day. Robert is giving a lecture at the National University of Ireland at Maynooth. I am scheduled to talk to the Irish UN Association. I muddle through with great difficulty. When my talk ends, Sue Keatinge, the friend who is helping me decorate the house, says, "You look like you are going to break into a thousand pieces".

When he leaves to deliver a series of lectures in the US the following day, Robert gives me a copy of Alain de Botton's *How Proust Can Change Your Life*. "Dalkey, 5/4/2000. To my darling Lara – the most beautiful and gentlest lady, I love you always. De ton tigre," he writes on the title page. I am infuriated by the contradiction between Robert's messages and actions, by the constant fluctuation between love and recrimination. It is a measure of his cussed strength of character and power of persuasion – and my weakness – that he convinces me that *I* am the guilty party. I am the one who begs for forgiveness.

When I think back on those months of despair, when we both wept repeatedly through terrible scenes, I am surprised at how little of our turmoil showed. We were like people stricken with a serious illness who prefer to ignore it and go about their daily business. We continue to invite friends and contacts to our homes in Beirut, Dublin and Paris. My photo albums are filled with happy, posed shots, my clippings files are fat with the articles I write as if everything were normal, though I feel I am dying. No one outside knows what goes on in a marriage. *Be kinder than necessary, for everyone you meet is fighting some kind of battle.*

I blubber over pizza with a friend in Paris on my birthday, by which time Robert is in the west of Ireland, with the younger woman. Friends save my life, particularly Margo Rietbergen, the wife of Henk Werner, who was a student at Lancaster University with Robert. We spent our first New Year's Eve in 1987 at their home in Groningen. Margo listens on the telephone from the Netherlands for countless hours. The best advice comes from Lisa Perrine, my oldest friend, during a late-night call to California: "Don't drink. Exercise."

Others are less helpful. "It serves you right," shrugs Nicole, my surrogate French mother from my days as a student in Paris. The unkindest cut comes during a lunch with Thierry, a journalist from the judiciary press with whom I have covered many stories. "A fifty-four-year-old bloke who's bonking a twenty-seven-year-old girl?" he says, almost in admiration of Robert. "No way he's going to give her up!"

We agree to spend three months together, during which time Robert promises to have no contact with her. I tell my editors only that I need to spend time with my husband. There is plenty of Middle East news for us to cover. In May, the Israelis pull out of southern Lebanon after twenty-two years of occupation. In June, Hafez al-Assad dies in Damascus.

Concern about our beloved cat Walter, who has stopped eating, has temporarily replaced my obsession with our troubled marriage. Walter's old vet, Dr Masri, is at a loss to help her. If Walter dies, I tell Robert, it will be a bad omen for our marriage. Nonsense, he says. He makes a one-day return trip to Roissy in business class with Walter in a cat carrier at his feet. I meet him at Terminal 2 and take Walter directly to a veterinary clinic in the Marais. It turns out she is suffering from heart disease. She has a stroke in the clinic and has to be put down.

I take Walter's ashes to Beirut three days later. Robert and I scatter them on the Mediterranean, from the rocks below the Corniche. We have line of sight to the balcony sofa where Walter sat for much of her life, watching Lebanon parade past her.

Hardened war correspondents that we are, we weep profusely as Robert reads my three-page tribute to Walter out loud. It begins, "We will never know another cat like Walter. We will never forget you." I recount plopping down on the bed one afternoon facing Walter and looking deep into her eyes.

You stared back into mine, and there was so much understanding, so much humour and complicity in your eyes that I knew then we would always be special friends. I wondered if in some way you weren't my counterpart, a sort of animal extension of Lara. I don't think I ever told Robert about it. It was our secret … I always knew that it wasn't Mustafa's apartment, nor *The Independent*'s, nor mine and Robert's. It was, as Robert often said, your home, and you let us live there. It will always seem empty now, without your gentle, playful presence, sharpening your claws on the chair arms, sleeping in the basket under the bed, on the stack of *L'Orient-Le Jour*s … Unlike our friends and relatives, unlike Robert and me with each other, you never hurt us. Robert used to say there was not a mean bone in your body. Forgive us if we somehow transmitted our grief and lost innocence to you.

Six months later, Robert and I spend a last, tearful New Year's Eve together at our house overlooking the sea. I have just adopted Spike, like Walter a striped tabby. "Where is your cat? You should be with your cat!" Robert says animatedly at midnight. He thrusts Spike into my arms. The message, I think, is that Spike will replace him. I resent it at the time, but later realise that Robert is right. I can live without a man. A cat is indispensable. Spike stays with me for twenty years, until his death in Paris, three months before Robert's passing.

ℬ

Long before the crisis in our marriage, I know how unforgiving Robert can be. Now *I* have joined the ranks of the unforgiven.

When his father, William, is dying in 1992 at the age of ninety-three, Robert refuses to go to the nursing home to see him. He has never forgiven Bill for sending him to boarding school, tearing him away from his pampered life, from tea and toast in bed in the morning in his room under the eaves at Fairlight, the Fisks' neo-Tudor villa in Rectory Lane, Maidstone. At Yardley Court, he was subjected to early wake-up calls, cold showers and sadistic prefects. During holidays he cried and begged not to be sent back. Bill would have none of it. "We've got to make a man out of you, fellah," he said. Robert recounts in *The Great War for Civilisation* how Bill bullied him and Peggy. When we argued, nothing enraged him more than to be told he was acting like his father.

Thirteen years after Bill dies, Robert softens his cruel assessment, dedicating *The Great War for Civilisation* to Bill and Peggy, "who taught me to love books and history". But it was Bill, far more than Peggy, who loved books and history. Robert praises his authoritarian father for having sneaked a camera into the trenches of World War I, in violation of regulations. Bill refused to head a firing squad that executed an Australian soldier who got drunk and murdered a French gendarme. It was, Robert said, "the finest act of his life". This act of insubordination prevented Bill from joining the Gurkhas and becoming a regular officer. He taught himself accountancy instead.

Robert develops what he calls *scunners* against people he suspects of insulting or betraying us. In 2000, when he is interrogating me about my long-dead love affair, he wants to know which friends I talked to in the early nineties and what advice they gave me. I tell him their names, and that most confessed to having been unfaithful to their husbands. None of them told me to stop it. Robert will not forgive them either. "You wasted a lot of time with stupid people. We must start a new life without the old anniversaries, without the old friends," he tells me. He wants, I write in my diary then, "a clean slate, the Khmer Rouge, Year One of the revolution".

Robert's estrangement from his Beirut *compañero* Juan Carlos Gumucio, over a silly incident of machismo, is saddest of all. In the autumn of 1991, Robert and I meet Juan Carlos for lunch at Uncle Sam's restaurant near the American University of Beirut. Juan Carlos and his then wife, Agneta Ramberg, have a toddler called Ana Céleste. Like many new parents, JC advocates parenthood with missionary zeal. Two years earlier, when we had moved into Juan Carlos and Agneta's old apartment in the Sleit building, he presented us with a Bolivian stone, carved in the shape of an Incan head and wrapped in brightly coloured yarn. He told us she was a Mama Qucha and that she would bring us fertility. "It worked for me and Agneta," JC boasted. Robert rolled his eyes.

After a few beers over lunch in 1991, Juan Carlos tells me: "You won't be a real woman until you've had a baby." I don't like it, but Robert is enraged. He harps on about it for days. A few nights later, Juan Carlos shouts at our second-floor window from the street below. He wants to come up for a chat. Robert tells him to go away. Robert says JC drinks too much, which is true. But the thing that irks Robert most is JC's little lecture about the necessity of motherhood. I am happy to ignore it, but Robert is determined to cut JC out of our life.

Not long afterwards, in one of their last conversations, JC tells Robert "I lost my family", meaning that his marriage to Agneta has broken up. Robert mocks JC in private. "What does he *mean*, 'I lost my family'? They were killed in a plane crash?" Robert asks rhetorically, showing not the slightest sympathy. The last time I see JC, in Belgrade during the 1999 NATO bombardment, he approaches us at an outdoor café and obviously wants to sit down. Robert is extremely cold to him and JC slinks away like a whipped dog.

At the beginning of March 2002, my telephone rings in Paris. Robert is sobbing. I have never heard him so distraught. I let him talk uninterrupted, in a sort of stream of consciousness. "JC committed suicide six days ago and I have been very upset," he says. "He was alone in a house near Cochabamba and had – of course – been drinking and felt miserable and then shot himself. I've spent hours this past week sitting on the balcony – that place of memory and pain – and crying. I remember the good days when he was my *compañero*, when he protected me in Beirut during the kidnap years, how he'd meet me at the airport and smuggle me into the city and how proud we were of ourselves for staying on when everyone left." Those were, Robert concludes, "blithe and oddly happy years of innocence amid danger".

I desperately wish I could hug Robert and comfort him. I do not tell him how terribly sad it is that he could not find it in his heart to forgive JC for what was, after all, a minor offence, before this happened, but I think it. He could not forgive Juan Carlos. Now he cannot forgive me.

Robert publishes an obituary of Juan Carlos in *The Independent* in which he describes him as "a big man with the energy of a hyperactive puppy dog and a deceptively mild, bland humour that concealed a dark understanding of his colleagues' weaknesses".

I think a lot about Robert's expression, "blithe and oddly happy years of innocence amid danger". I might say the same of Robert's and my shared past.

ℒℷ

Having done the right thing by ending my affair in March 1994, I naïvely assume that all will be fine now. But Robert is increasingly moody. He broods for days at a time, sullen and taciturn. I suspect it is because I had an affair, but I dare not ask him. I tell myself that Robert has seen too many terrible things, that he works too hard.

My memories of us as a couple in the mid-nineties are tenuous. I remember the stories we reported together – southern Lebanon, Algeria, Yugoslavia – better than I remember our conversations or lovemaking.

Perhaps it is a mistake for me to move to Paris in October 1996, but I am desperate to escape from *Time* magazine. I want to work for *The Irish Times*. It is possible that I want to escape from Robert's moods too.

We continue, at huge expense, to commute to see each other every two to three weeks. We talk every day, usually several times a day. We often go on stories together. There are enough good days for me to ignore the *froideur* between us. Robert still writes "kisses for Bobić" on my grocery lists. He leaves cartoons of Walter and our plush toys, Mus and Malv, on my desk, and showers me with cards and gifts, including fine jewellery from Weir's on Grafton Street in Dublin at Christmas. Robert tells me that he worships me, that I am like a religion for him. "I will never let you down," he promises over and over.

Even during my visits to Beirut in 2000, when our marriage is deeply troubled, he slips me a note saying "You are beautiful" at a Red Cross dinner, sends me roses with a card professing love. No wonder I am confused.

Then in March 2002, Robert retroactively disavows the countless declarations of undying love that he has made over the preceding decade. He speculates that I want to hear him say again that he will never leave me or let me down. "Those words, I think, were burned on my own particular funeral pyre ten years ago," he writes. He says he could say them again "if we can find a new way to start a new life". But you *continued* to say those words throughout the last decade, I want to scream. I believed them. That is why I stayed with you. Was it all a lie then?

We act out the same scenes over and over in 2000, 2001 and 2002, as if we are locked in an existentialist play. Robert and I both say we love each other and want to remain married. Sometimes I start the fight, by bringing up his affair with the younger woman. Other times, Robert goes on the offensive, chipping away at my composure, saying, "How *could* you? What were you thinking? Didn't you think about the consequences?" I torment myself with the same questions.

My faithlessness has become the focus of Robert's anger, like the Israelis, the Americans, *le pouvoir* in Algeria, the Serbs. There are tearful scenes in Beirut and Bcharré, northern Lebanon, in Damascus, Paris, Geneva and Dublin, an international roll call of heartbreak. He says I use Isabel Ellsen as an excuse. I say he uses my affair as an excuse. "I'm not saying it's *because* you were unfaithful, but it made it *easier*," he says.

෯෨

Our Beirut apartment has no central heating and is cold and damp in winter. In the mid-1990s one of our favourite pastimes on winter evenings is to rent a video film classic from Smith's grocery store and eat dinner in bed, under piles of blankets, with a portable gas fire blazing in the corner and Walter sleeping at the foot of the bed. It may be my guilty conscience, but the theme of wronged husbands seems to come up often. Robert is particularly taken with *Colonel Chabert*, in which the eponymous character, played by Gérard Depardieu, comes back from the Napoleonic wars to learn that his wife, played by Fanny Ardant, has given him up for dead and remarried.

Robert takes *War and Peace* with him on the long journey to interview Osama bin Laden. I imagine him lying on the bed of his ground-floor hotel room in Jalalabad, immersed in the lives of the Russian aristocracy as Napoleon's troops invade Russia. There's a tap at the window. Bin Laden's men, come to take Robert to their master for an interview in a cave.

War and Peace "is a novel about marriage", Robert tells me when he finishes recounting his trek to see bin Laden. He clearly identifies with Count Pierre Bezukhov. Does he take me for Natasha Rostova, the naïve young woman who is led astray by an unscrupulous lover, or for Hélène Kuragina, Pierre's wanton wife? Both, I suspect. When he says he blames "someone else", not me, I am Natasha. When he repeats, "How could you? How could you?" I am the viperous Hélène.

For my part, I find a parallel in the life of the French World War I hero, Georges Clémenceau. "Father Victory" was a lady's man who was credited with many romantic conquests, yet the original *tigre* was vengeful when his pride was wounded.

Clémenceau lived in the US for four years in the 1860s and married one of his students, Mary Eliza Plummer. They moved to France where Mary gave birth to three children. She and the children stayed in Clémenceau's home town of Nantes while he pursued his career as a newspaperman and politician – and numerous extramarital affairs – in Paris. When Mary complained about his absence, Clémenceau accused her of being "jealous and exclusive".

But when Mary commences an affair with her children's tutor, the fury of *le tigre* knows no bounds. He has her followed. A police commissioner catches Madame Clémenceau and her lover *en flagrant délit d'adultère*. Adultery carries a two-week jail sentence in late-nineteenth-century France. Clémenceau has his wife imprisoned for a fortnight, stripped of her French nationality and deported to the US. He retains custody of the children. In front of them, he burns his ex-wife's letters and photographs, and breaks the marble bust of her on the mantelpiece, so they will have nothing to remember her by.

Obviously, Robert's treatment of me is mild by comparison, but I wonder if my husband and the World War I hero share more than a nickname. Some accounts say that in old age Clémenceau expressed remorse for his cruelty to Mary.

ॐ

Almost from the beginning of our life together, I am concerned by the extent to which work dominates everything. "Sometimes I wonder if we don't have too much journalism woven through our love," I say in a telex conversation between me in Beirut and Robert in Bahrain following Saddam's invasion of Kuwait in 1990. He agrees that "journalism creeps through our love too much". As long as it takes second place, he says, he can live with it.

It is typical of the melding of our work and marriage that even at the height of our conjugal crisis, Robert feels it necessary to fax me NATO spokesman Mark Laity's complaint to the editor of *The Independent* about his reporting on the use of depleted uranium munitions in former Yugoslavia, along with his own five-page retort.

After a year of emotional turmoil, I suggest a trial separation. We do not talk for a month, during which I fill a 200-page diary. On a Saturday morning, for no apparent reason, I draft a letter to the other woman, in jest, to myself, with no intention of sending it. I begin by asking her to give Robert back to me.

But if you must take him, don't expect it to be easy. You will never have a real holiday with him. He will never learn to help with housework or choose clothes that match. He tells me that you don't care about clothes, but be careful. He hates trousers on women, and baggy things. When he has to wear a tie, he tugs at his collar as if he were choking … If you take him, I am sure that you will work together … Don't expect to have a life outside journalism, but the life you will have will be amazing. There can be nothing in the world as exciting as a voyage of discovery with my Robert.

We are extremely fortunate to love our profession, I write to Robert as our discord drags on into a third year. "And I dare say that without it we both would have gone mad. But every time we talk now, we talk about work. It would be very easy to slip into the old habit of being better colleagues than lovers. A marriage must be more than a newspaper partnership."

Al-Qaeda suicide hijackers crash civilian airliners into the World Trade Center, the Pentagon and a field in Pennsylvania four months after Robert tells me the marriage is over – a declaration he reverses by the end of the year. My personal grief seems infinitesimally small compared to events of earth-shattering proportions. Yet the attacks seem somehow connected to me and Robert, to the years we spent in Palestinian refugee camps, under Israeli bombardment in southern Lebanon, on military bases in Saudi Arabia, following the trail of US depleted uranium munitions across Iraq, meeting Islamic fundamentalists in Beirut, Baalbek, Tehran and Algiers.

By 11 September, Robert and I have had no contact for two months. Watching on television from Paris those poor souls clinging to window ledges, then dropping into the abyss as the building disintegrates, I am certain that he feels the same dismay and instinctive understanding of what has happened as I do. America responds to the attacks with a cry of: "Why do they hate us?" Robert and I have seen the reasons.

For the first time in months, I do not think of Robert and his mistress when I wake up on 12 September. Before I open my eyes, I see smoke billowing up from steel and glass towers, tiny figures jumping because they prefer smashing into the ground to incineration. They plummet down behind my eyelids like black commas, falling, falling. Then the structure rips through the blue morning sky, vertically, from top to bottom, a masterpiece of evil genius.

Not since Qana has my mind replayed images of horror, though the scale of bin Laden's atrocity dwarfs the slaughter of the 106 Lebanese. In the grey Paris morning, I see the nightmare in every pair of eyes, as if the universe has been deluged with fire and ash, as if all has changed for ever.

The entire world is an eyewitness. I have nothing to write, and I feel useless. Robert, I know, will not be useless. He is never at a loss for words. No matter where he is, he will write volumes. Sure enough, I hear him on *Europe 1* radio station. *Le Monde* publishes an entire page by him about his meetings with bin Laden.

Partly to escape the barrage of Fisk commentary, I ask my editors to send me to Afghanistan, where the 9/11 attacks were planned and where bin Laden is hiding. There is, I know, a risk of running into Robert and her, but I am willing to take it. Once I've obtained an Afghan visa, I fly to Tashkent, travel overland to Dushanbe, take a helicopter to Faizabad and drive south across the wilds of Afghanistan in a clapped-out Lada with two French journalists. I report for a month from behind the lines of the Northern Alliance while the US bombs the Taliban into submission before sending in NATO troops.

When I return to Paris in late October, there are posters for a film by an Iranian director, starring Robert's mistress, on every bus hoarding. I couldn't have made it up, I tell myself. On my first night back, I have dinner with my surrogate mother Nicole. She produces the latest issue of *Télérama* magazine to show me an article about the Iranian-made film. She suggests I would find it interesting.

"That's her. That's Robert's girlfriend," I tell Nicole. She "walked up the red carpet at the Cannes film festival like a star", says *Télérama*.

A few days later, I have lunch with a contact at the foreign ministry who has just seen the same film. "You know, the actress looks a bit like you!" she says.

"Funny you should say that." I pause for dramatic effect. "My husband just left me for her."

I need another war to escape to. At the beginning of December, I ask *The Irish Times* to send me to Gaza to cover the latest Israeli assault on the enclave. I have developed a sixth sense about the proximity of things having to do with Robert. When I go to the Al Deira Hotel to put my name on the waiting list for rooms, I notice a guestbook lying on the reception desk and know instantly that he is there, though it was unlike Robert to sign guestbooks. I page through it from back to front and sure enough, there on the first page is Robert's entry.

The following September, I am in a bookshop in Sligo when I know before seeing it that a copy of *Pity the Nation* is within reach. I take the book down from the shelf and open it gingerly. It still says, "For Lara." She cannot take that away from me.

David Shanks rings me in Gaza from the *Irish Times* foreign desk to tell me that Robert has been beaten up in Pakistan. He reads me the wire copy, which says Robert's car broke down on the road between the border city of Quetta and Charnan, and that he was stoned by up to a hundred people.

I weep in my hotel room, thinking of Robert's pain, of his wounded body, of which I know every centimetre. I want to call the *Independent* foreign desk, leave Gaza and go to him. But he told me our marriage was over. She must be with him, no doubt working as his interpreter.

On the morning I leave Gaza, I pack my bags and sit down at the desk in my hotel room to write to Robert:

Beloved Robert. I love you. I miss you desperately. I shall put this message in a bottle in the sea, in the hope it finds its way to you. If it washes up on the rocks below our apartment in Beirut, you must return to me. Your Lara

I put the note in an empty mineral water bottle and screw the cap on, then wander along the rubbish-strewn beach in Gaza. The sea is filled with sewage and detritus. I throw the bottle as far out as I can. Then I tell myself: *you really have seen too many Hollywood movies.*

Robert breaks the silence in a letter from our home in Ireland ten days after the attack. He tells me about the beating and complains of headaches, memory lapses and diminished sight in his right eye. He says he cannot bear the thought of spending Christmas in the house we built "when the light of that day which was always so precious to us – you – has been replaced only by memories of the hopes and joy we felt when we first spent Christmas together in Ireland". He says he thinks of me always with gentleness, never with anguish or pain.

Robert rings me on the night of 3 January 2002, the first time we have spoken since the previous July. "Do you think we could live together and make a new life?" he begins. I burst into tears and say, "Yes, yes." The immediacy of my answer seems to frighten him. "Don't answer now," he says. "Let's think about it for two or three weeks. If we tried to start over again and it didn't work, I think I would hang myself." Already it feels like a cruel joke. *Let me torture you a little more, my darling.*

Robert talks a lot about the attack in Pakistan, asking me repeatedly if I have read his account in the newspaper. His editors thought it very suspicious. Why did the attackers take his contacts book and not his passport or money? He thinks western and Pakistani intelligence services may have been involved. After all, he was the only journalist to interview Osama bin Laden three times, and the attack occurred not long after the atrocities of 9/11. "They obviously thought I would try to get to bin Laden," he says.

I remember Robert's contacts book, a soft burgundy leather

Filofax that I bought for him at the *papeterie* in the rue du Four. It held hundreds of names and telephone numbers, crammed in, filling the margins, in various colours of ink, in tiny writing. I imagine it discarded in a pile of refuse by the roadside in north-west Pakistan. Or being pored over by intelligence agencies.

"They broke my glasses. I'm still using the cheap substitutes I bought in Quetta," Robert continues. I offer to buy him new glasses in Paris. Our optometrist will have his prescription on file. He doesn't seem interested. He tells me how Rafik Hariri called him and offered to send his private plane. Hariri asked a lot of very pointed questions, he says. He wondered if someone told him what to ask. Robert would not go to hospital in Pakistan, refused injections and stitches, because he did not trust the Pakistani doctors. He went back to the village where he was attacked and found one of the men in a CD shop and tried to interview him, but the man wouldn't talk. Then he flew back to Beirut where our interpreter Imad took him to see several doctors.

Robert says he knew I was in Gaza because an *Observer* correspondent, "a disgusting person", said to him a couple of days after the attack that by an extraordinary coincidence he had spoken to a friend in Gaza City who was in the hotel room "next to your ex-wife whom you have repudiated".

Robert keeps telling me that he longed for me to call or come to him after he was hurt. "I lay on my bed with my head covered in bandages, my hair stuck to the pillow with blood, I wanted you to call me. I waited for that call. I waited and waited and when the phone rang I had an absolute conviction it was you." It was his mistress, wanting to make certain he was getting proper medical care, he says. "But it was you I was waiting for and I sank back onto my pillow in disappointment."

It seems a tragic misunderstanding, a lost opportunity to restore our marriage. Robert says that when I was supposed to visit our home in September he went there and waited for me, that he'd strewn roses from the gate down the drive into the house. And I cancelled my trip to Ireland and went to Afghanistan instead. Pat, who looks after the house, forgot to tell him.

"Why didn't you call me?" I cry. "You told me last summer that our marriage was over. You knew I thought you were with her." Robert doesn't answer. He says he faked my signature on his Christmas cards.

"Why are you pretending that we are still together, when you told me our marriage was over?" I ask. Again, he doesn't answer.

Robert picks me up at Dublin airport when I visit him nine days later. As soon as we arrive at the house, he sits down at the kitchen table and begins telling me again about the attack in Pakistan. He fetches his newspaper story for me to read. I stare at the front-page photograph. Robert's head is wrapped like a mummy's. Blood seeps through the bandage. I see the distress in his eyes, a sort of mad hurt and surprised disbelief that a conflict he is covering has finally wounded his body.

"They hit me with rocks in their hands, they wanted to kill me," Robert says, his face contorted with pain. He cannot talk about the beating without crying. If he had not fought back, he says, they would have killed him.

Five years later, Robert recounts the attack in detail on the BBC's Desert Island Discs programme. He has thought a great deal about it since recounting it to me on the telephone and in the kitchen in Ireland. His tone is more detached. He begins by scolding Kirsty Young, the presenter, for calling his attackers "a mob of people from Afghanistan, refugees".

"I hate that word 'mob'," Robert says. "They were refugees whose families had just been killed in a B-52 American air raid. I was the first westerner they saw." He recounts "bashing them, just like in the *Boys' Own* paper", crying all the while because he hates violence and would never want to hit anyone, anywhere. His attackers fell back and an imam, a religious man, led him away.

Young comments that the thing which seems to have affected Robert most was when he had to hit them. If his family had been torn to pieces by an American bomber, "I'd have done the same as they did. I'd attack Robert Fisk. Of course I would," he says. Young asks if he forgives his attackers entirely. "It's not about forgiveness. This is a war... This is something that was inevitably going to happen if my car broke down, as it did, in the wrong place."

The attack fans Robert's long-smouldering depression. He writes to me in March of his foreboding. First he is almost beaten to death in Pakistan. Then the American journalist Daniel Pearl, who with his wife had been very kind to Robert after he was beaten, has his throat cut in front of a video camera. Then Juan Carlos takes his own life. "What in God's name, I have been asking myself, have we done to deserve this?"

Our letters ought to help us find a way out of the labyrinth we are lost in. Instead, we begin to argue about language. After our weekend in Ireland culminates in yet another terrible scene, he reproaches me for twice failing to say the word "beloved" before his name in a phone call. He objects to what he calls my "new vocabulary" which he says included the words estrangement, cruelty and reconciliation. In a different context, he would castigate colleagues for using words like *terrorism* and *collateral damage*.

In retrospect, Robert writes, he understands how things had come adrift the previous weekend. We were searching for two different things, he says. He wanted to seek a way of starting a new life with me, while I, his "beloved Lara", thought we were going to start it. I had laughingly agreed that two phrases in my letter, *since Thursday night I have suspended all unkind thoughts* and *at this moment I am filled with goodwill* "sounded a bit like one of those ominous Israeli-Palestinian ceasefire announcements".

Robert's letters contain beautiful passages, as well as recriminations, which is part of the reason the break-up takes so long. After that weekend, he writes to me sweetly, saying that it was not a failure, because we had seen one another again after a seven-month separation.

"Instead of a distant, almost ghostly, pained Lara, there she was with her lovely soft eyes and all the habits I remember so well." He remarks on my silence when I was upstairs while he remained in the ground-floor sitting room. "You are a very quiet person, you move softly and gently, soundlessly, and I must have spent weeks of my life in various homes searching for Lara," he writes. Years earlier, we invented a two-tone flute-whistle to find each other at home. "How I smiled when I realised I couldn't hear you moving," Robert writes. "And how happy I was when I saw you moving silently across the landing."

We continue to share the house, though our visits rarely coincide. In August 2002, Robert writes to thank me for the book I left on his desk for his birthday, congratulating me for finding a gift that combined three of his great interests: painting, World War I, "and yes, a whole series of *locomotives à vapeur*".

Robert has always hated what he dismisses as "psychobabble". He rejects my plea for "a mediator, an intercessor, someone who can help us to reach a shared vision of us and what has happened". He says he trusts no one else, only himself and me. At this point, our marital crisis has been going on for two and a half years, but he still wants to believe that if we could prove our "respect and honour for each other" we could go to Saint-Sulpice and light a candle together "and our new life would begin".

It becomes more and more difficult to reconcile Robert's romanticism with his erratic behaviour. At one point, he calls me in Paris to tell me he has thrown his wedding ring into the sea. I am understandably distressed. A few days later, he reproaches me for my reaction, saying he had wanted to explain how upset he was, and I accused him of trying to punish me. "My poor Lara was back in 'victim' mode and your poor Robert, already depressed enough, had the plug pulled on him." He says I ought to have told him that I could imagine the torment he must have felt to have done such a thing.

Robert often alludes to Winston Churchill calling his own depression his *black dog*. Robert's black dog lingers for years.

I'm not sure he ever shook it off. When *The Great War for Civilisation* is published in France in the autumn of 2005, he tells Gilles Anquetil of the *Nouvel Observateur* that writing it has been "a profoundly depressing experience ... I ask myself if the Middle East – this region where I have been allowed to work for more than a quarter of a century – has not been a curse. Today I find it more and more difficult to see dead people all the time ... I ought to be used to it, and yet I find it more and more difficult to bear."

Robert still says he loves me and wants us to get back together, which is also what I want, but we find it impossible to be together peacefully for more than a few hours. Sooner or later, he reverts to his pain at my betrayal a decade earlier, and I demand to know where things stand with the other woman. We cannot help ourselves.

"Like you, I think that what has happened to us is the most tragic event in our lives," Robert writes to me on 18 December 2001. "And I ask myself how such sorrow can be visited on two people who shared and loved each other so much."

Our repetitive cycle of letters, phone calls, reunions and tearful scenes has become what the Irish would call a head wreck. I write to Robert on 22 December 2002 that "we are stuck in a rut where both of us are determined to be right. You constantly go back over the past, zeroing in on something I've said or written and proving with Cartesian logic that I had a warped perception and was unfair to you." I perpetuate the dispute by responding to his accusations, "when all I want is for us to stop this nonsense, hold you in my arms, begin planning our New Life ... To put it bluntly, you've been jerking me around all year, and I am weary of it."

Our vocation as journalists has often strained our union. But at the end of the day, it enables us to salvage a deep friendship and platonic *amitié amoureuse* from the wreckage of our marriage. "I've volunteered to go to Baghdad," I write to Robert in September 2002. The US-led invasion appears imminent, and

Irish Times foreign editor Peter Murtagh is eager for me to get going. "I still cannot believe the US will do this insane thing," I add.

Two months before the start of the Iraq War, Robert writes to me from London. He has been going back and forth to America every few weeks, lecturing against the war. Two thousand people attend each lecture. "I spoke to 32,000 people in a fourteen-day trip last month," he writes, "I think for the first time in my life – though the cause may be futile – I am actually doing something to stop a war."

I am having difficulty obtaining a visa through the Iraqi embassy in Paris. Robert enlists his friend Laith Shubeilat, a prominent Jordanian Islamist politician who has influence with Saddam Hussein's regime, to help. Around the time I tell Robert that I want to step off the marital roller coaster, he and I start making plans to cover another Gulf War together.

XII

A Licence to Kill

In the streets of Baghdad the war caught up with me
I could not see; she lent me a torch
I was forsaken; she betrothed me to the fallen
When I returned, footless, from days that exhausted my
   wandering
The pen smiled at me, dragging my body from the field of
   battle
Obscuring disembodied heads on either side
So that I walk upright, without limbs, in an interminable,
   never-ending Baghdad

Siham Jabbar, "In Baghdad"

16 March 2003

Robert and I board Royal Jordanian flight 1736, the last commercial flight to land at an airport called Saddam Hussein International. George W. Bush's ultimatum to Saddam and his sons Uday and Qusay – to leave Iraq *or else* – will expire on the morning of 20 March. We have not heard such dire predictions of chemical and biological warfare since the 1991 war.

The Bush administration accuses Saddam of hiding tonnes of VX nerve agent and anthrax spores. The US has just tested a 9.5-tonne bomb in Florida called a Massive Ordnance Air Blast or MOAB. It spreads inflammable fog over its target, then sets it alight for an explosion as powerful as an atomic weapon, killing everything within 500 metres. We have packed chemical weapons suits and goggles, flak jackets and helmets; risible protection in the face of such destructive power.

Saddam's claim that he has no more weapons of mass destruction is subsequently proven true. But Bush and British Prime Minister Tony Blair, widely referred to as "Bush's poodle" in the Middle East, have based their *casus belli* on non-existent WMDs. They say they'll retaliate with tactical nuclear arms if Saddam uses the mythical weapons. "Can you believe it?" I say to Robert as we settle into our airline seats. "The Pentagon is threatening the most intense, sustained bombardment in modern history, and airport security just confiscated my *fingernail clippers*!"

We are in a cheerful mood during the ninety-minute flight, despite the doom-laden ambience and the fact that Iraq has always been one of the most difficult countries to work in. Thanks to Robert's friend Laith in Amman, we got our visas in time. We made the last flight, and we are starting another adventure.

We discuss sleeping arrangements in Baghdad and decide to

rent separate hotel rooms. *Keep your bolthole*, an Irish girlfriend in Paris advised me while I was packing. "Should we tell people we've split up?" I ask tentatively. "No," Robert replies. "It will get back to the sleazebags in the ministry of information and they'll be all over you." If anyone asks why we have two rooms, we decide to say it's because we each need our own space to write in.

At the end of 2002, I thought there was a tacit, mutual acceptance that the love affair we started nineteen years earlier in Damascus had worn itself out. Yet a kind of ambiguity lingers. Neither of us is certain if our marriage is over or merely on hold. It may be easier to say, like the Bolshevik general Strelnikov in *Dr Zhivago*, "the private life is dead" than to dwell further on the breakdown of our marriage.

During the flight I read a French magazine article comparing Saddam to the Soviet leader Joseph Stalin, whom he admires and imitates. Saddam read biographies of Stalin when he was in prison in the 1960s. Neither dictator ever knew his father. Their mothers both worked as maids. In a photograph of Saddam as a small boy, he has the hard face of a street urchin who is beaten by his stepfather, steals eggs and chickens, sells watermelons to feed his family, and stones stray dogs for fun.

"*Dernier métro!*" Robert says to our friend from *Paris Match*, Patrick Forestier, as we disembark in Baghdad. Patrick makes Robert's *bon mot* the opening line of his book *Hôtel Palestine*, which is published later the same year. Like the other colleagues we see every day for weeks to come, Patrick mistakenly assumes that we are back together. "When storm winds blow, they team up like two birds in cold weather," he writes quaintly.

Baghdad airport is staffed by wolfish Saddam lookalikes determined to extort a last buck before the curtain falls. "Locusts," I write in my notebook, recording the bribes I will later claim on expenses: $20 to avoid the AIDS test; $20 to get my satellite telephone through customs; $20 to have my passport stamped; $20 to soldiers guarding the exit.

The information ministry, which Robert refers to by the

Orwellian title "ministry of truth", dictates that journalists live in the Palestine Hotel. Formerly part of the Méridien hotel chain, its décor was frozen in the 1970s by war and sanctions. Balancing the knowledge that satellite telephones work better higher up against the probability that we will have to walk up and down stairs, we take adjacent rooms on the eighth floor. Robert's courtesy in taking the room next to the lift shaft soon becomes irrelevant, since the lifts are usually out of service and explosions wake us every hour.

Colleagues report seeing an armoured Mercedes with tinted windows drive into the car park beneath the Palestine Hotel. There is a disturbing rumour that Saddam and/or high-ranking members of his regime are sheltering in the basement, using the international press corps as unwitting human shields. US military intelligence must share this suspicion. If the Americans think Saddam is there, we wonder if they will bomb us. After all, they have warned all journalists to leave Baghdad.

UN personnel and diplomats evacuate the country. Baghdadis who have the means to flee have already done so. Some of those left behind purchase chemical suits and gas masks. The government distributes six months' worth of food rations. The vast majority of the city's inhabitants simply wait, apparently accepting the idea of their own annihilation with weary stoicism.

We spend three full days before the war starts calling on Iraqi friends and contacts and stocking up on supplies. We buy matches and candles, a camp stove for my room, tinned food, biscuits, cases of mineral water and toilet paper. Robert writes about it in a column and we laugh at a letter from one of his readers about the toilet paper: "Mr Fisk is obviously expecting a long war."

The first airstrike, on a disused farm on the outskirts of Baghdad, takes place at 5.30 a.m. on 20 March, an hour when street lights are still reflected in the muddy waters of the Tigris. The explosions sound like distant peals of thunder. Air raid sirens howl, and the rat-a-tat-tat of anti-aircraft artillery continues for half an hour. Robert taps on my door. We share Nescafé and biscuits and listen to the BBC World Service against the auditory backdrop of Iraqi anti-aircraft artillery, barking dogs, chirping birds and the muezzin's call to prayer. The early morning episode is so brief and inconclusive that many people seem unsure that the war has started.

Personnel from the ministry of information have moved into the Palestine Hotel, because they feel safer surrounded by journalists. Ministry staff have an insatiable appetite for bribes. When they are not extorting money, they are making unwanted advances to unattached women journalists. We find their presence at meals, and that of more than 200 journalists, claustrophobic. Added to that, the Palestine's menu offers mainly pasta and rice. So we make the restaurant of the Al-Fanar, a small hotel 300 metres away, our canteen. It is inhabited by Iraqi families who have fled homes close to military positions, anti-war protestors and freelance journalists too poor to afford the Palestine.

The Al-Fanar is unusually busy on the evening of the 21st. A handful of male journalists from the Palestine are drinking beer and talking loudly. They don't seem to notice the silent stares of the Iraqis around them. The restaurant's plate-glass windows are crisscrossed with masking tape, to hold shards of glass in place if windows shatter. The waiter brings two steaming bowls of *mouloukhiya*, overcooked chicken floating in a green-brown broth. We are about halfway through the meal when the bombing starts.

From the corner of his eye, Robert thinks he glimpses the form of a long, dark whale streaking through the open space between the Palestine and the Al-Fanar. The restaurant falls silent, except for the loud whoosh of the cruise missile, which explodes with a deafening crash across the river. An incandescent, yellow-orange blob expands and glows in the night. Chairs and tables are knocked over as screaming diners scramble for an inner room. The air pressure changes constantly as more explosions follow, in what sounds like a chain reaction. Bubbles of flame envelop the opposite bank of the Tigris.

"Let's go outside to see what's happening!" Robert says. He senses my hesitancy and holds out a hand. "C'mon. They won't hit this side of the river. They know the journalists are here." I don't think he believes what he's saying, but I follow him anyway. Several Iraqi men hover in the doorway, pleading with us to stay inside. Robert ignores them.

Outside in Abu Nawas Street, the corniche along the river, advertising hoardings and eucalyptus tree branches crash to the ground. We hear the shriek of more cruise missiles, like the sound of tearing fabric. Everything shakes and swirls, as if in a hurricane. I find it difficult to keep my balance. Iraqi anti-aircraft artillery spouts fountains of red light, adding to the din. The explosions continue unabated, but a lighter, more delicate sound can be heard *sotto voce*: broken glass falling onto balconies and pavements.

We go back into the restaurant to fetch our shoulder bags, throw a few thousand-dinar banknotes on the table, then run through the underground car park to the entrance of the Palestine. Dozens of people mill in the lobby, listening to the explosions with anxious faces. With each detonation, the seventeen-floor structure shakes. We are amazed that the electricity is still on, and take the lift to the top of the building.

Dozens of photographers and cameramen are lined up on the roof, facing the Tigris, filming the ribbon of molten light across central Baghdad. Saddam's monuments to himself appear even more grandiose when they are burning. Fire shoots up from the ramparts of a huge, flat-roofed, pyramidal building. Saddam's Republican Palace, built by King Faisal II in the 1950s, was the dictator's favourite. Now its curved colonnade, topped by bronze busts of Saddam, is engulfed in flames. The monuments are surrounded by lush gardens and I think momentarily and absurdly of the Mayan ruins that I visited on the Yucatan Peninsula in what seems a lifetime ago, on my thirtieth birthday.

The scene is worthy of Hollywood, produced with American tax dollars for the precise purpose of creating Shock and Awe. It has been willed by US Defence Secretary Donald Rumsfeld, a proponent of the doctrine of rapid dominance, as taught at the National Defence University in Washington DC.

The US fires 320 cruise missiles at Baghdad that night. The violence of the barrage is at the same time beautiful and utterly terrifying. Because we cannot see the Kitty Hawk-class aircraft carriers or the B-52 bombers from which the missiles are launched, the spectacle feels more like a natural disaster or an act of God, a simultaneous earthquake and volcano.

"It's *Götterdämmerung*, the twilight of the gods," Robert murmurs. More prosaically, I think of *Star Wars*, then recall my late mother's belief in Armageddon, the battle at the end of the world. (A month after the war, I will spend five days in Ireland, alone. On a walk down to Killiney Bay, I surprise myself by bursting into tears at the sight of a red-breasted robin. I assume it is an after-effect of the violence I witnessed in Iraq. I did not realise I was such a tender flower.)

The images are broadcast around the world, but Robert and I have front-row seats for the live performance. If there are any humans under the deluge across the river, they are surely dead. Robert seems mesmerised by the staggering display of US power. I can almost see his mind working, composing his front-page, eyewitness report as he watches the conflagration. *We are the superpower. This is how we do business. This is how we take our revenge for 11 September*, he writes later.

Mohsen, the number two at the ministry of information, runs around the rooftop screaming impotently that it is forbidden to take pictures or videotape. The Iraqis suspect some journalists are acting as spotters for the US military, and that the images could help the Americans improve their targeting. But the ministry's authority evaporates the moment the first cruise missile explodes. On the Night of Shock and Awe, the necessity of obtaining pictures outweighs everything, even the danger of expulsion.

Photographers and cameramen will be whipped back into line in the coming days. On 30 March, the day after the ministry is finally bombed, its director, Odey al-Tahi, announces new restrictions.

For the last ten days of the aerial bombardment, photographers and cameramen are allowed to film only from the second-floor terrace on the eastern side of the hotel, which has limited visibility.

I am distracted by a tussle at the edge of the roof, between the award-winning American photojournalist James Nachtwey and Mohsen, who demands that Nachtwey remove his camera from a tripod. Nachtwey argues. In a burst of fury, Mohsen pushes Nachtwey's valuable equipment over the edge and into the void. On a ministry bus tour a few days later, Nachtwey tells me that he retrieved the camera from a ledge several floors down. It still worked, a great advertisement for Canon.

Journalists are supposed to use their satellite telephones at the ministry, not in the hotel. Until the Night of Shock and Awe, we pretend to comply, carrying equipment back and forth. Richard Downes from the Irish public broadcaster RTÉ has built a plywood shack adorned with a large Irish tricolour on the ministry rooftop. He kindly lets us use his satphone until I finally get mine working, with the help of colleagues. From then on, I file Robert's and my copy from my hotel room balcony.

Mohsen doesn't stop with Nachtwey's tripod. As the bombardment begins to subside, he stalks the hotel grounds, looking up to pinpoint the balconies and floor numbers where he can see illegal satellite dishes. The next day he confiscates them all, then collects record-breaking bribes for their restitution.

The ministry assigns a mild-mannered "minder" called Abbas to Robert and me for the first ten days of our stay. Abbas despises the regime and feeds on the words of Radio Kuwait. "When will the Americans get here?" he asks eagerly every morning. "Fish" is Abbas's code-word for *mukhabarat* or secret police. We ask him to take us to the home of Sohad and Naira, ageing Iraqi sisters who have become dear friends since the previous Gulf War. Abbas refuses to wait for us outside. "Yellow, hateful fish," he announces, referring to a nearby intelligence building. "Please, Mrs Lara, let me leave now. I have a wife and children."

Abbas has an entrepreneurial spirit. In the last week of the bombardment, when there is no electricity and the Palestine Hotel stops all maintenance, he inveigles female relatives to wash journalists' laundry, and acts as the agent for a man who charges $5 for a symbolic effort at cleaning hotel rooms. The laundry comes back in a damp heap. I manage to identify Robert's and mine, but other correspondents spend days swapping ill-fitting clothing.

Once the bombing starts, Abbas begins making excuses to avoid outings in Baghdad. On a particularly bad day, when the Americans are pounding government ministries with cruise missiles and precision-guided munitions, Abbas turns round in the front passenger seat, and I see that his face is bathed in tears. Robert and I are relieved when he goes to work for a television network.

We then hire Ra'ed, a big, louche figure who has been hanging around the ministry press centre, listening in on journalists' conversations. Ra'ed is the nastiest interpreter/fixer/minder I have ever encountered, but he offers the advantages of excellent English and brazen self-confidence. When he tells me he's a colonel in the *mukhabarat* and shows me the revolver in the glove box of his car, I know we are not going to like him. I come to hate his loud, synthetic shirts, bossiness and habit of sucking air through his front teeth during bombardments. My Arabic is just good enough to catch him distorting translated quotes in interviews to make them more favourable to the regime.

Strange as it seems, the Iraq War is almost the honeymoon that Robert and I never had. It is without joy or sex, but we find each other's presence comfortable, companionable and reassuring. We have reached an armistice in the love wars that caused us both so much pain, through an unstated agreement to avoid taboo subjects. Robert never tells me what happened with his mistress, but gives the impression that she is no longer in the picture. He tells me about a young French woman he met recently in Bosnia and took to southern Lebanon. "She is married and there's a big difference in our ages," he says sorrowfully. "It reminded me of someone else, a long time ago." That is his only allusion to my past affair.

Robert and I are almost inseparable in our self-contained, journalistic bubble. He is more sociable than I am in this war zone, making the daily rounds of wire agencies and television networks to make sure we don't miss any stories. That frees me to concentrate on reporting, and on keeping us fed and laundered. We share the cost of the driver and minder, discuss stories and the people we meet, sit together on the ministry's bus tours of bombsites and hospitals and take all our meals together, usually in my room. "The two of you used to walk through the hotel lobby as if no one else existed," a friend who covered the war for a wire agency comments after Robert dies in 2020.

The Iraqi government has ordered all bakeries to remain open and provides them with daily deliveries of wheat flour and oil, so we always have fresh Arabic bread. We buy tins of hummus and the eggplant purée *moutabal* from the Cortas factory in Beirut. This makes me smile, because we ate Cortas tinned mezze during the 1989 Aoun war, when I visited the shell-damaged plant for an article for the *Financial Times*.

We save tap water in empty mineral water bottles so we can wash and flush toilets when there is no water. Once the hotel cleaners stop coming, I sleep in one twin bed, then the other, so the sheets feel less gritty. Then I turn the sheets over.

I sometimes suspect that Saddam's regime has taken lessons from Milošević in managing media coverage, though the Iraqis are more oppressive than the Serbs. Almost every day, they take busloads of journalists to see bombed infrastructure such as telephone exchanges, and wounded civilians in hospital. We pass coaches identical to the ones we ride in, filled with Iraqi soldiers. I repeat the secular prayer I said in Serbia and Kosovo: *Please don't let the American bombers mistake us for a troop bus*. As in former Yugoslavia, some correspondents ask their news desks to alert the Pentagon that a busload of western journalists is travelling to such-and-such a place. Robert and I think the warnings are pointless. We will soon be proven tragically right.

Just as reporters in Belgrade were accused of supporting

Milošević's "ethnic cleansing" of Kosovar Albanians, the Iraq hawks now consider us to be stooges for Saddam. The British Home Secretary, David Blunkett, accuses media in Baghdad of reporting "from behind enemy lines". But journalists "embedded" with US and British forces are arguably under more censorship than we are. We move around the city and talk to civilians, attend press conferences, read Iraqi newspapers and watch Iraqi television. If the regime tells the truth – and it occasionally does – we report it. When it lies, we mock their propaganda.

More than any other time in my life as a journalist, I feel that I am working to the best of my abilities, and that experience in Beirut and Belgrade had prepared me for this war. I have learned to sublimate whatever fear I feel, to focus all my energy on reporting. "You are writing well," Robert tells me one evening. "How do you know – you're not reading my copy?" I reply. He says, "I can tell."

Though I win three press awards at other times for other stories, 2003 is the only year I really care about such honours. Robert and I are both disappointed. "Nobody won an award for the invasion of Iraq," he later consoles me. "I didn't either. It's still too controversial." He reminds me how opponents of the war were maligned before the invasion. It takes years for the world to realise what a criminal blunder George W. Bush and the neocons committed in invading Iraq.

ℬ

Our one social event of the war is a happy evening in Channel 4's suite, at the invitation of Lindsey Hilsum and her cameraman/producer and partner, Tim Lambon. We print journalists are often stunned by the means at the disposal of our television colleagues. Lindsey and Tim have installed a proper cooker in their suite, and it feels like a home. A stereo plays Beethoven. They even serve French red wine with the omelette.

Shortly after the "liberation" of Baghdad, Lindsey and Tim

visit US marines billeted in one of Saddam's former palaces in the Sunni neighbourhood of Adhamiyah. In the short lapse of time while Channel 4 is there, a marine sniper perched on top of the arched gateway to the palace opens fire on two cars. He kills two civilians, including a neighbour who comes out on his balcony to discover the cause of the shooting, and wounds five others. One of the wounded is a little girl, six-year-old Zahra. At Tim's insistence, the Americans transport her to Kuwait for life-saving surgery.

The Iraqis burn tyres and petrol-filled trenches in the hope of confusing American missile guidance systems. The smoke mixes with desert sandstorms, turning Baghdad into a sinister twilight zone where men wrap keffiyehs round their faces to breathe and cars use their headlights even at midday.

One week into the war, the Americans manage to bomb two markets in as many days in the poor neighbourhoods of Ash-Shaab and Shu'ala, killing seventy-two civilians. The atrocity in Ash-Shaab makes a particularly deep impression on me, in part because it happens in the midst of a sandstorm. As I stand beside the missile crater, dirty raindrops, saturated with smoke and desert sand, leave brown stains on my clothes and notebook.

Ash-Shaab is a working-class neighbourhood of car repair garages and spare parts shops. In the aftermath of the US Air Force missile strike on late morning traffic, the victims' blood swirls in sickening pools with oil and automotive fluid from the mechanics shops. The explosions crumpled up a dozen cars like aluminium foil and hurled them asunder. Car engines, sheet metal riddled with shrapnel holes, plastic chairs and wire cables are scattered over hundreds of square metres. Abu Taleb Street looks like the scene of a plane crash.

We find Hisham Danoon, the building supervisor, cowering in the dark entrance to the Nassiya Shameli apartments, too frightened to step into the netherworld outside. "Four men died right here, in front of this building," says Danoon. "I came out. They were cut into pieces." He nods at body parts overlooked by rescue workers. "That was my friend Tahar," he says. The hand is yellowed, doubtless by tobacco. Its fingers are curled and it is crimson at the wrist where it has been severed. I think of a chicken chopped into pieces by a butcher's cleaver. A little boy tugs me by the arm and points to a viscous, grey-white mound between two shards of corrugated steel roofing. "That is Tahar's brain," Danoon says. "We did nothing. We are innocent. We are peaceful people. Why are they doing this to us? What does Bush want?"

A mother and her three children died in one charred vehicle. Other fatalities include a mechanic, two restaurant workers, the owner of an electrical shop and the neighbourhood beggar. "How can the Americans accept such things?" asks Mustafa Ali, a colleague of the slain restaurant workers. "They say they want to help the Iraqi people, and they are attacking us."

When the Americans kill large numbers of civilians, the military briefers in Doha and some of our colleagues in Baghdad often make excuses for them. Invariably, someone suggests the deaths may have been caused by an Iraqi anti-aircraft missile that fell back to earth and detonated, not a US weapon. "Must we always blame 'them' for their own wounds?" Robert asks.

After the airstrike on Ash-Shaab, a journalist says he saw a Scud missile launcher in a side street near the scene of the carnage. Another western reporter sees tracked artillery near the Shu'ala market, where fifty-five people die. One weighs the weapons sightings against the testimony of a shaken teenage boy who stands in a crater in the midst of devastated market stalls: "We found a woman's body on the roof," he says. "We found a head with no body."

Scud missile launchers and tracked artillery seem to be legitimate targets. The presence of Iraqi weapons – like that of Serb military in civilian areas four years earlier – is meant to justify the airstrikes. But the laws of war forbid attacking civilians, even if they are near military installations. Can there be legitimate targets in an illegitimate war, waged without a UN mandate?

As we drive around the city in our own car and during the ministry's bus trips, Robert sees everything. He nudges me gently, points with a finger held low and close to his body and whispers, "There, behind the bushes, anti-aircraft artillery," or "There, at the end of the street, Soviet-made armoured personnel carrier."

Saddam has predicted that the siege of Baghdad will be "another Stalingrad", like the 1942/43 battle where the Soviets annihilated the German 6th Army. Robert has brought William Shirer's *The Rise and Fall of the Third Reich* to reread in Baghdad. So, for a piece I've offered to *The Irish Times*, I quiz him during a bus trip about similarities and differences between Baghdad and Stalingrad.

As we drive out of Baghdad on the morning of 2 April, I see white flames shooting like lizards' tongues from the barrels of anti-aircraft artillery in a palm grove. The anti-aircraft artillery makes a *pop, pop, pop* sound. Men stand in the doorway of a nearby grocery store, pointing to the sky and the US bomber that the gunners are trying to hit.

The Iraqis take us 100 kilometres south, to Hilla, near the ancient city of Babylon, where sixty-one people have been killed and 200 others wounded in three days of cluster bomb attacks. The wounded moan and writhe in their hospital beds, their faces pocked with hundreds of tiny pieces of shrapnel. Saddam's psychopathic son Uday has predicted that the wives and mothers of US servicemen will "weep tears of blood". That day in Hilla, I see an Iraqi woman weep tears of blood. She is Samira Murza Abdel Hamza, a forty-eight-year-old housewife. Shrapnel has lodged in both her eyes, turning them bright red. Fragments of metal pierced her chest and knees.

In room after hot, airless room in Hilla hospital, wounded Iraqis with drips in their arms, some with plaster casts on their limbs, stare at us with glassy, pain-filled eyes. Five-year-old Houda Nasser stands beside the bed of her ten-year-old sister Miriam. The gash on the right side of Houda's head is still bleeding. Her black hair is matted with the sticky liquid. Miriam has a patch over her right eye after an operation, and bomb fragments in her waist and thigh. They were playing in front of their house when the cluster bombs exploded.

Cluster bomb containers are dropped by parachute and open in flight to release thousands of bomblets that detonate in the air or land as unexploded mines. Their use against civilians is strictly forbidden. A comprehensive ban against the use of cluster bombs will take effect in 2010, but the US refuses to be a party to it.

All eight members of Mohamed Moussa's family have been wounded by cluster bombs. "Some of the bombs are still in our house, unexploded," he says. "They look like bunches of grapes, white and silver. Each bomb has a thread on it, and when you touch it, it explodes."

A hospital employee opens the door to the refrigerated unit where they've stored corpses from three days of US bombardment. The bodies are piled one on top of the other, two or three deep. The refrigeration has broken down and the sight and stench are overwhelming. I look at only one cadaver before turning away. Decomposition has turned him black and swollen. He looks like a golliwog, the grotesque, racist caricatures of Africans which have become unacceptable in America, but which I remember from childhood.

The day after our trek to Hilla, the Americans shoot their way up Highway 1 to the outskirts of Baghdad. In confusion reminiscent of the Russians' arrival in Pristina in 1999, the Americans claim to have taken Baghdad airport while the Iraqis insist they have regained control of it. Information Minister Muhammad Saeed al-Sahhaf, nicknamed "Comical Ali", is all bluster at his 2 p.m. press conference. The Americans "are not even 100 miles from Baghdad", he says. "They are on the move everywhere, a snake moving in the desert." An hour later, the BBC reports that "some units" of the US 3rd Infantry Division "are reported to be taking up position on the edge of Saddam Hussein International Airport, west of the city".

We challenge Sahhaf. If he is telling the truth, why not take us to the airport? "Do you really think this is a good idea?" I ask Robert as we head off on the 25-kilometre jaunt. Exploding cluster bombs ripple across the horizon. "These guys from the information ministry don't want to die either," he says with a laugh and a shrug.

At international arrivals, we are greeted by Captain Faris Rajah, a giant of a man with a black moustache and beret, twirling a Kalashnikov as if it were a pencil. "There are no Americans here, no British," he says. "Only Iraqis. Come in."

"The Americans haven't come here; they will not come here," boasts the director of the ghost airport, Moaffak Abdullah Jabbouri. The airport looks undefended, I remark to Jabbouri. "I cannot answer this question," he says. We return to the Palestine Hotel, and I file a jokey story about looking for the phantom US army in arrivals, departures, the first-class restaurant and the airport shops.

The battle for the airport – the beginning of the end of Saddam's control of the capital – begins at nightfall. Judging from the scenes at Yarmouk Hospital the following morning, it was fierce. For the first time, the Iraqis show us their military dead and wounded. Officers want it to be known that the army is fighting.

The Fedayeen Saddam ("Saddam's Men of Sacrifice"), a volunteer militia founded by the dictator's son Uday, muster the strongest resistance to the invasion. They wear a black and gold patch etched with Saddam's profile on black clothing. At Yarmouk Hospital, we watch three of the irregulars stagger into the hospital, two of them propping up the third. They lay their wounded comrade on a hospital bed and pull off his boots. A nurse opens his blood-soaked shirt. Nearby, two doctors lean over the chest of another fighter wearing a regular army uniform. A Republican Guard with red braid hanging from his epaulette is wheeled down the corridor, one trouser leg cut off so doctors can attend to his leg wound. Everywhere we look there are open, untreated wounds. We pass the health minister, Dr Omid Midhat, in the hospital lobby. "We have many victims from the airport and nearby," he says. "Most of them are wounded by cluster bombs, so the wounds are terrible."

The battle for Baghdad lasts five more days. The Americans

stage "probing missions" deeper and deeper into the western, mostly Sunni, part of the capital. On 5 April, Ra'ed, the secret police colonel, drives Robert and me to the front line in south-west Baghdad. Lesson from Beirut: no seat belts, so you can jump out of the car if it is hit. Keep the windows down to avoid being lacerated by glass as well as shrapnel, and so you can hear how far you are from explosions.

We find Iraqi soldiers setting up an anti-tank gun at an intersection. T-72 tanks, armoured personnel carriers and jeeps trundle past. American Apache attack helicopters have just visited, strewing the boulevard with overturned military vehicles that look like scorched insects. A charred BMP armoured personnel carrier lies at the base of a blackened palm tree. Two burnt-out Iraqi army trucks still smoulder. Amid hundreds of Iraqi soldiers sheltering next to walls, riding in the back of open lorries, we see ragged men pulling wooden handcarts piled high with bodies. A pick-up truck, its back gate open, drives by with four militiamen perched on the sides, guns pointed outwards. The bed of the truck is layered with bodies, two deep, under blankets. Black army boots and a naked foot stick out.

US forces arrive in central Baghdad on the morning of 7 April, announced by the racket of F-18 bombers, A-10 "tank-busters", also known as "warthogs", and small arms fire. The Americans are taking over the presidential complex. They will turn it into the Green Zone, their occupation headquarters.

As on the Night of Shock and Awe, the journalists in the Palestine Hotel have front-row seats. Watching through binoculars and camera lenses, we see about thirty Iraqi soldiers flee their bunkers and artillery emplacements to run along the bottom of the river embankment. Bradley armoured personnel carriers take position above them. An Iraqi wearing only white underpants and a vest appears to have been caught sleeping. Another limps as he runs. Several throw themselves into the Tigris. Most raise their hands in surrender.

Kindi Hospital has become the main emergency hospital for

Baghdad. It admits fifty wounded civilians the same morning. Three are dead on arrival. We stand by the bedside of two-year-old Ali Najha, who is covered in blood and bandages. An older man explains that Ali's mother, father and four siblings were killed when US forces fired on their car as they tried to flee the capital. A young man, a relation, jumps up from Ali's bedside, cursing. "What do you want? Can you bring his father and mother back from the dead? Get out! Get out!"

In the parking lot, a Shia woman in a black chador sweeps down on us like a crow. "My son, my son has just been martyred," she screams. "He was only twenty-two. He wasn't even married." She runs from one person to another, clutching at our clothing, saliva foaming at the corners of her mouth, unhinged by grief. "I want a flag! I want a flag to bury him in! A flag or a banner!"

Western television networks are broadcasting footage of marines showering in Saddam's marble bathrooms with gold-plated taps, lounging by his swimming pool and descending his spiral staircase. The complex has been bombed so many times that it is amazing to see the interior of the palace intact, with crystal chandeliers still hanging from the ceilings.

The battle for the future Green Zone continues all day, shaking the capital with shell explosions, filling the sky with smoke and dust and the smell of gunpowder. Comical Ali Sahhaf's impromptu press conference is nearly drowned out by the sound of artillery fire. "There are none of their [American] troops anywhere in Baghdad," he insists.

Sahhaf is particularly enraged by a report on the Qatari network Al Jazeera that the Americans have seized his ministry and the Al Rasheed Hotel. He organises a coach to take journalists there, to debunk the story. He is right about the information ministry. The Americans may have reached the bomb-damaged building earlier in the day, but we find it swarming with Fedayeen Saddam militiamen. They smoke cigarettes and clutch rocket-propelled grenade launchers. Bundles of trumpet-shaped grenades emerge from rucksacks on their backs, like baguettes in a French bakery.

The strip of boulevard leading to the Al Rasheed has the sinister, abandoned look of a demarcation line. The bus driver takes the narrow lane behind the foreign ministry instead, in the hope of reaching the back of the famous hotel. Shooting breaks out and a field gun in front of us fires orange-flamed volleys over our heads, towards the river. The driver turns so sharply that journalists are thrown across the aisle and the coach nearly topples. We head back for the east bank of the Tigris at speed. It is our last sortie with the ministry of truth.

We are woken early again the next morning by heavy machine-gun fire and low-flying F-18s. They are bombing and strafing Iraqi forces on the far side of the Jumhuriya Bridge. A-10 "warthogs" join in the fray, whinnying like horses. Two M1A1 Abrams tanks inch onto the bridge and begin lobbing shells into east Baghdad, our side of the river. Tareq Ayoub, Al Jazeera's Jordanian-Palestinian chief correspondent in Baghdad, is recording an eyewitness account of the battle from the roof of Al Jazeera's building on the Tigris. A US aircraft swoops low to fire a rocket at him, killing Ayoub and wounding his Iraqi cameraman Zuheir. The network, the most watched in the Arab world, says it received assurances from the US government that it would not be attacked.

Robert and I have not yet learned of Ayoub's death. "It's pretty noisy out there. Maybe we should watch it from my balcony?" I suggest, knowing Robert will want to go out. "C'mon, Lara. What are we here for?" he replies. On a high-speed, 30-kilometre tour of the city with Ra'ed, we dodge panicked motorists, circumvent makeshift barricades and watch Fedayeen Saddam gunmen slink along walls towards US forces.

As we drive down Sa'adoun Street on the return approach to the Palestine, we hear an explosion. Coming out of the underpass, we see a little cloud of smoke drift past the hotel. Passers-by point at a gaping hole on the 14th and 15th floors. Sahhaf is holding forth on the driveway in front of the hotel. "We have surrounded them in their tanks," says Comical Ali. The Americans will be "burned in their tanks, flattened, destroyed".

At that moment, Jérôme Delay of the AP and Jean-Paul Mari of the *Nouvel Observateur* rush out of the hotel, shouting to clear a path through the crowd, a look of sheer agony on their faces. They carry José Couso of the Spanish channel Telecinco in a blood-soaked sheet. Couso's stomach has been blown open. Jérôme and Jean-Paul lay him down in the back of an estate wagon which takes the wounded journalist to hospital. Jean-Paul will spend much of the year drawing up an in-depth report on the killings for Reporters Without Borders, entitled *Two Murders and a Lie*.

Taras "Sasha" Protsyuk, a Ukrainian cameraman for Reuters, was killed by the tank shell that hit the Reuters bureau. He was the father of a nine-year-old boy. Couso dies that night. Samia Nakhoul, a Lebanese-Palestinian journalist for Reuters and friend of ours from Beirut, is the most severely wounded of several other journalists. She is taken to three emergency rooms in the search for a brain scan. In the first emergency room, Samia learns that Taras, with whom she has covered the war, is dead. That night, on the eve of the fall of the regime, she decides to risk brain surgery in Baghdad.

Robert and I follow the trail of blood to the Reuters bureau. Slightly wounded journalists sit on the beds, in shock, caring for their own cuts and bruises. The office is a shambles. Taras's camera lies in a puddle of blood and broken glass on the edge of the truncated balcony, the tripod snapped like sticks of kindling.

Less than two hours after the attack, General Buford Blount, commander of the 3rd Infantry Division, whose Alpha 4-64 armoured company fired the lethal tank shell, says his men were targeted from the hotel by snipers, and that sniper fire ceased as soon as the tank retaliated. General Blount is lying. Journalists have been vigilant to ensure that no weapons entered the Palestine Hotel. More than 200 people are witness to the fact that not a single shot was fired from the hotel. There was a long lull before the tank fired at it.

Journalists are proven right by the videotape recorded by France 3 television. It shows the tank sitting on the bridge for four minutes of total silence before the turret moves to aim at the hotel and spits out an orange bubble of flame. The artillery shell traverses the 600 metres between the bridge and the hotel in two seconds. The image shakes violently on impact, to the sound of the explosion, followed by falling plaster and cement. Hervé de Ploeg, the France 3 cameraman, runs to the Reuters bureau and films the blood and devastation. I show his videotape in a talk about the Iraq War at the Kate O'Brien literary festival in Limerick in 2004. I forewarn the audience that the images are extremely violent. No one budges, but when I show the video, a woman leaves the auditorium in tears and several people complain.

Like Al Jazeera, journalists living in the hotel forwarded the building's map coordinates to the Pentagon and received assurances it would not be attacked. The whole world knew that the Palestine Hotel was media headquarters, but somehow General Blount failed to pass the information down his chain of command.

The following day, the US military says mortars were being fired from the *area* of the hotel, and that Iraqi "spotters" were using high buildings to watch US troops. Sergeant Shawn Gibson, the African-American soldier who asked permission from his company commander to fire the shell, says he saw a man with binoculars on the balcony. A report issued by the Pentagon four months later transforms Gibson's mention of binoculars to "a hunter-killer team".

On 12 August 2003, the US army issues a statement saying that firing a 120-mm high-explosive tank shell because Sergeant Gibson saw the glimmer of a camera lens was "a proportionate and justifiably measured response ... fully in accordance with the rules of engagement". Six months after the journalists are killed, I ask Lieutenant General Ricardo Sanchez, commander of US forces in Iraq, why soldiers who kill Iraqi civilians and foreign journalists are invariably cleared of wrongdoing. "Young soldiers on the ground have to make decisions," he replies. "When they feel threatened, they always have the right to shoot." But everyone in Iraq feels threatened, all the time. US rules of engagement are, in the words of Amnesty International, "a virtual licence to kill".

☙

Ra'ed shows up late for work on 9 April, the day of *al-Suqut*, the fall of Saddam. "I was almost martyred twice," he pants. "I nearly drove into three American tanks near Yarmouk Hospital, and four more in Haifa Street."

US forces are about to take over the entire capital. There are gun battles in the streets, and much of Baghdad is under artillery bombardment. Robert and I ask Ra'ed to take us to a hospital, any hospital, for every place is on the front line now. We shout at him when he tries to drive us into no man's land on Haifa Street, with Iraqi barricades at one end and US tanks hulking menacingly at the other, because he wants to take bread to his sister.

The ground floor of the Adnan Khairallah annexe of Saddam Medical Centre is named after Saddam's cousin and brother-in-law, whom the dictator allegedly had eliminated in a helicopter crash. On the day the regime falls, the hospital is, after Qana, the most nightmarish scene I have ever witnessed. US forces on the far side of the river keep lobbing shells onto the hospital grounds, because it is located opposite the defence ministry and the army has hidden armour in the oleander shrubs outside. Each time a shell explodes, patients shriek. As we survey the ground-floor entry hall, Robert murmurs, "Jesus, Lara, it's the Crimean War."

Before us lie scores of burned, weeping, groaning and dying Iraqis. Blood pours from the throat of a man undergoing an emergency tracheotomy on a trolley. An orderly pushes a pool of blood across the floor with a mop, as if it were soapy water. The body of a half-naked, corpulent, middle-aged man is flayed by fire and riddled with shrapnel. He has been lathered in white burn cream, accentuating his ghoulish appearance. We see him heave forward, almost to a sitting position, then fall back with a thud, dead. A nurse draws a white sheet over him.

The hospital's director, Dr Khaldoun Brahim al-Bayati, is the heroic captain of a sinking ship. His supply of water, bandages, drips and antibiotics is nearly exhausted. "We're running out of everything. The morgue is full. We bury bodies in the hospital garden every time there is a let-up in the bombardment," he says.

Dr al-Bayati's house was destroyed in the war. He does not know where his wife and little girls are. He has barely slept for six nights, since the battle for Baghdad started. "I have twin daughters," he says, holding a hand flat to indicate their height, his voice cracking. "I told them I might not see them for a time, that I had a humanitarian mission."

Ra'ed interrupts our conversation. "Doctor, I think I have high blood pressure. Could you check it?" he says. I give Ra'ed the evil eye, but our egotistical minder doesn't notice. A flicker of ironic resignation passes over al-Bayati's face. As a hospital director in Baghdad, he must have met many secret policemen. An aide brings a blood pressure monitor. "It's a little high," the doctor tells Ra'ed. "It's the stress, isn't it doctor?" Ra'ed says.

Dr al-Bayati accompanies us to the exit, stopping to comfort a nurse who sobs on a bench. He opens the door slightly, as if to test the weather outside. "Go, quickly," he tells us.

We find dozens of "Arab volunteers" – Algerians, Jordanians, Palestinians, Syrians – sitting cross-legged under the portico of the Palestine Hotel, begging for food and water. Saddam Hussein said he had thousands of Arab fighters ready to commit suicide in "martyrdom missions" against US forces. Now their Iraqi officers have abandoned them, and they are hemmed in by the advancing Americans. While we talk, a US aircraft drops a gravity bomb a few hundred metres away. The crowd scatters, but the Arab volunteers do not flinch. They have seen worse in combat. "Another Arab defeat," an Algerian tells me sadly. "If God is on our side, why does this always happen to the Arabs?"

On the day Saddam's regime falls, no one imagines that these men will fill the ranks of the Sunni extremist groups: al-Qaeda in Iraq, al-Nusra and Isis. George W. Bush's invasion of Iraq is already creating monsters. When I hear of jihadist atrocities in coming years, I often think of their famished, beaten faces on the day of The Fall.

The Americans are coming. The news ripples through the crowd outside our hotel. The Arab fighters disappear before the marines arrive there an hour or two later. Ra'ed asks to be paid. We are free of our minder, free of the regime. He leaves a note at the reception desk a few days later, asking for a letter of recommendation. His is the only request for a reference I have ever ignored.

The Americans are coming. We can see the US armoured column advancing down Yasser Arafat Street from a distance. It makes me think of an ancient caravan, with supplies strapped onto the sides of sand-coloured armour instead of camels. The first tank gunner I speak to is from Bush's home state, Texas.

A few minutes later, I ask Corporal Christian Rojas, a nineteen-year-old from Georgia, to recount his day to me. "We've just been clearing, ma'am," Rojas says. What does he mean by "clearing"? I ask. "Firing tank shells and heavy machine-guns." At buildings or people? "At people," Rojas replies in a neutral tone. "What *kind* of people?" I continue. "Some were civilians. Some were in uniform," he says.

The next day, Robert and I visit yet another highway of death, at the Doura interchange, five kilometres south of Baghdad. The highway is strewn with rotting corpses and destroyed civilian vehicles – a bus, a taxi, a Mercedes, a Mustang. One red car has been nearly vapourised. Half a leg, with a shoe on it, is all that remains of its occupant. The form of a naked woman – her clothes were burned off – lies face down in a destroyed pick-up. Her body looks the consistency of charcoal. The figure beside her can barely be recognised as human.

Lindsey Hilsum's report on the marine sniper's victims in Adhamiyah showed how carelessly Americans shoot at civilian cars, from the beginning of the invasion. They will continue to do so through seven years of occupation, because they regard every motorist as a potential "terrorist".

Some of the dozens of fatalities at Doura may have been killed in an airstrike. Most were fired on by the Abrams tanks and Bradley fighting vehicles that now hold the interchange. Captain Dan Hubbard of the 3rd Infantry Division's Task Force 315 gets out of his tank – named "Rhonda Denise" after his wife – to tell us what happened. His unit was ambushed by men firing rocket-propelled grenades on the morning of 6 April. "When we seized this interchange, we had to stop traffic to hold the ground ... Ninety per cent of the vehicles turned around when we fired over their heads."

A large proportion of the tens of thousands of Iraqi civilians killed by US occupation forces are shot dead at checkpoints because they did not heed warning shots. The following year, I am nearly killed in the same way. There is shooting as I approach a line of US marines near Fallujah, but I do not understand that it is meant to warn me and continue walking towards the Americans. Then I hear shouting and turn to see the frantic gesticulation of my driver and interpreter, who are waiting a hundred yards behind me.

"The Red Crescent has been contacted. They will take care of the bodies," Captain Hubbard says. The bodies have been rotting in the sun for four days already. "Move along. All these people will be taken care of," Robert mutters, quoting one of his favourite lines from *Dr Zhivago*, when Czarist troops slaughter Bolsheviks in a Moscow street. He is disgusted by an "embedded" journalist from NBC News who wears US military uniform and comes out to explain his version of the massacre to us, using the word "we" as if he were a soldier.

Columns of sand-coloured US Humvees roll past the charred and bloated bodies at Doura. The Americans seem affected by a kind of disconnection, as if they have been programmed not to link cause and effect. Over the coming months and years, I am amazed to hear US officers talk about their "humanitarian mission" in Iraq, as occupation forces not only prove incapable of running the country but step up arbitrary searches, arrests, imprisonment, torture – remember Abu Ghraib – and killings.

ༀ

On the afternoon of 9 April, the Palestine Hotel and its environs are a chaotic throng of US military, poor Shia, journalists who covered the war *in situ*, and "embedded" journalists who have rolled in with the invasion forces. Robert and I fear the hotel will be looted, so we hide thousands of dollars above the aluminium slats in the false ceilings of our rooms. In the event, the mob merely rushes into the lobby and smashes framed portraits of Saddam, watched by a weeping Sunni woman.

To prevent "terrorists" entering the hotel which they themselves attacked twenty-four hours earlier, the Americans quickly set up a security system. For a week after the "liberation" of Baghdad, they accept not only the press badges they issued in Kuwait City but also the laminated press cards we obtained from the fallen regime.

On Firdos Square, I run into Goran Tomašević, the Pulitzer Prize-winning Serb photographer for Reuters whom we've known since Belgrade, and who was a close friend of Taras Protsyuk, killed by the US tank shell the preceding day. "Goran, I am really, really sorry," I say. He does not speak, but there are tears of impotent rage in his eyes.

Also on Firdos Square, I interview Sergeant Leon C. Lambert from Colorado, the US marine at the origin of what comes to be the iconic image of the fall of Saddam. "I asked my executive officer if we could tear down the statue," Lambert tells me a little later, basking in his fifteen minutes of fame as the wrecker of Saddam Hussein's statue. Lambert's commanding officer initially says it is "up to the Iraqi people", not the Americans, to tear down the statue. "We gave them the rope and they tried for about forty-five minutes, but they were unsuccessful, so they asked our battalion commander and he told us to assist the Iraqi people," Lambert says.

The Bravo Company, 1st Tank Battalion has carefully preserved a US flag taken from the Pentagon on the day of the attacks in 2001, like a relic from the crusades. "The flag! The 9/11 flag!" a soldier yells before the statue is toppled. Sergeant Lambert chooses a corporal from New York to cover the head of the statue with it. "Do you really think Saddam Hussein did the 9/11 attacks?" I ask Lambert. His response speaks volumes about America's muddled, simple-minded motives in overthrowing Saddam to avenge 9/11. "In my opinion, if you support terroristic activities, then you support 9/11," he replies.

Using the boom of Lambert's M88A1 Hercules tank retriever as a ladder, Iraqis place a cable around the neck of the statue. The M88 lurches forward and the statue leans, creaks, breaks at the knees and falls slowly. Under the benevolent eyes of the US marines, the mob whom Lambert refers to as "the Iraqi people" stamp on the statue, hack off its head and drag it around the square with a chain. The fall of the statue is witnessed by only a few hundred Iraqis. Most of Baghdad's five million citizens are cowering in their homes, without electricity, bracing themselves for the anarchy to follow.

While television cameras film the destruction of Saddam's statue, "the Iraqi people" – the swarm of looters who followed the US caravan in from the Shia slums – get to work. The first looter I see is a teenager in a grimy tracksuit pushing a medical X-ray machine down the pavement. Soon there are legions of them, invading government ministries, embassies, UN offices. They load down cars, lorries, motorcycles, even donkey carts with armchairs, sofas, coat stands, lamps and desks. In the looted office of Odey al-Tahi, the lecherous director of the ministry of information, journalists find smashed on the floor al-Tahi's photograph of himself with Saddam. In his open desk drawer sit a comb, a mirror and a blister-pack of Viagra with two tablets missing.

The ministry of education is typical of the concrete monstrosities that Saddam commissioned from Yugoslav architects in the 1970s. Shia Muslim families strip it, taking even the electric cables and water pipes. The thieves establish a guard post at the entry. They allow looters to pass, occasionally confiscating a piece of booty for themselves. But when Robert and I try to enter, one of the "guards" blocks our passage. "Get the hell out," the man says. His comrade points a revolver at us and stares with stupid, mean eyes. "*Tamam, tamam, tamam.*" OK, guys, we're going, Robert says, lifting his hands up and down in unison in a calming gesture as we walk away, backwards, until we reach our taxi. Other journalists are less fortunate. Several are beaten and robbed of money, cameras and satellite telephones.

The looters rapidly understand that the Americans will not intervene. In the beginning they are only the poor. Then the middle classes join in the sport of emptying the villas abandoned by Saddam's acolytes and family. They steal fluorescent light fixtures, washing machines, even kitchen sinks. There are traffic jams in Jadriya, home to many of Saddam's relatives and cronies. We see a stolen double-decker bus, filled to the hilt with loot. A well-dressed lady stands on a lawn in the same neighbourhood, guarding the white satin living room set she has chosen. A man with two refrigerators stands in the driveway. Both wait for accomplices to pick them up with their booty.

Assad, a black stallion that belonged to Saddam's elder son Uday, is led away from his stable. We see two handsome hunting spaniels, white with russet spots, running alongside a plunder lorry, one tied with a leash, the other following its mate. "Those are Uday's dogs!" our driver exclaims. A video of Uday hunting with his dogs has been shown many times on Iraqi television.

At the German embassy, men, women and children walk out shouldering coffee tables, sofa cushions and desk drawers, trampling the German and EU flags underfoot. Robert saves an EU flag. I salvage the blue-and-white UN banner from UNICEF's pillaged office.

In a foretaste of the civil war precipitated by the invasion, neighbourhoods are already barricading themselves and raising vigilante groups to protect them against marauders. Hospitals are ransacked by men wielding guns and knives. The International Committee of the Red Cross reminds the US and UK that they are required by the Geneva Convention to protect civilians and essential services such as hospitals. Washington shows its priorities by protecting only the oil and intelligence ministries.

Donald Rumsfeld criticises the press for using words like "anarchy" and "lawlessness". The US Defence Secretary shrugs off the looting, which he portrays as a sign of newfound freedom. "Freedom's untidy," Rumsfeld says. "Free people are free to make mistakes and commit crimes and do bad things. They're also free to live their lives and do wonderful things." He compares the wholesale pillaging of Baghdad to past unrest in US cities. "Think what's happened in our cities when we've had riots and problems and looting. Stuff happens!" Iraq's post-Saddam ambassador to Washington, Rend al-Rahim Francke, blames the US failure to impose order for the subsequent debacle. "When people started looting and the Americans just watched, what it did was legitimise lawlessness. 'It's OK. No problem.' And we are still suffering from it now."

In the Shia slum of Saddam City, where goats feed on burning rubbish and broken sewage pipes flood the streets, Robert and I find much of the loot from central Baghdad. Stolen buses are parked in front of shacks. Balconies overflow with booty. The grounds of al-Sajjad Mosque look like a junkyard, with plundered goods sorted by type. There are stacks of dental equipment, still in cardboard boxes, air conditioners, tyres, 50kg sacks of sugar, sofas, chairs and refrigerators.

Gunmen pull up looted chairs so that Sheikh Arif Jassim Ali al-Saadi, a local religious leader, can talk to us. "I am collecting all the looted goods here, for safekeeping, for distribution to the people," Sheikh Arif says. "It was not theft," he insists. "The government prevented people having these things; they deprived us." The neighbourhood, he informs us, has been renamed Sadr

City on that very day, in honour of the Shia leader Mohamed Bakr al-Sadr, who was executed by Saddam. Even Sheikh Arif keeps forgetting and calling the slums Saddam City.

In the evening we stand on my balcony at the Palestine Hotel and count the huge bonfires, more than a dozen, raging across Baghdad. Who is lighting them, and why? And why do the Americans do nothing?

Robert reveres books, to such an extent that he can be furious if someone bends the corner of a page as a place-marker or breaks the spine of a book by bending its cover. He is particularly enraged by the destruction of Iraq's cultural identity. First the antiquities in the Archaeological Museum are destroyed. On 14 April, we hear that the Iraqi National Library and Archives are on fire. The inferno is still burning when we arrive. We find a singed folder on the ground, part of the archives of the 1932–58 Hashemite monarchy. It contains handwritten letters between Ottoman rulers and the court of Sharif Hussein of Mecca, the man who revolted against the Turks at the behest of Lawrence of Arabia. Robert takes the file to the royal Hashemite archives in Amman.

As we leave the National Library, we hear shooting down the street. Flames shoot up from a large building; a new fire, one of many in central Baghdad. This time it is the Islamic Library, part of the Ministry of Religious Affairs, with a precious collection of ancient Korans. We go to the US Civil Affairs Unit at the Palestine Hotel and give them the precise name and location of the burning library. A US officer goes on the radio, saying: "There's a guy here who says there's some Biblical library on fire." The Americans do nothing.

Robert and I visit a torture villa in the Baghdad neighbourhood of Kadhimiya. Under Saddam, every district had a little walled villa like this, the local headquarters of the *mukhabarat*. Six days after The Fall, visitors wander through the house as if it were a tourist attraction. Some of them search through filing cabinets and documents scattered on the floor for a trace of a disappeared loved one. The windows are covered with paper and posters of sports heroes, to hide the torture sessions from the outside world. Up to three large hooks are anchored in the ceiling of every room.

Mohamed Aish Jassim has returned to the villa to see where he was tortured. "I was a policeman," he explains. "On 26 April 2002, I got drunk and I insulted Saddam Hussein. They brought me here, and an officer named Amar al-Issawi had them tie my hands behind my back with electrical wire. They winched me up to the hook by my hands, until my shoulders were breaking."

Our taxi driver is reluctant to drive into the General Intelligence complex at Mansour, Saddam's equivalent of the CIA. "Saddam isn't dead yet," the driver explains. "Before, if you so much as looked at the gate, they'd arrest you." Even the looters picking over the intelligence headquarters seem nervous. The vast main building has been flattened by US airstrikes, but the cosy, holiday village-style bungalows where Saddam's chief torturers lived are intact. "This was the place of greatest evil in all the world," says a former nuclear scientist who has, like us, come to explore the abandoned complex. There are black plastic bags filled with shredded documents, but also bales of documents which the intelligence bureaucracy did not have time to destroy. We find an essay in English on Samuel Beckett's *Waiting for Godot*, written in the school for children of secret policemen.

Robert is the bravest person I know. He has built a career on fearlessness in the face of kidnappers, gunmen, bombers and critics. But he is terrified of dentists. Around the time the regime falls, he begins to suffer from toothache. The pain grows worse daily, and with it, Robert's mood. His colleague Phil Reeves, Jerusalem correspondent for *The Independent*, brings a gallon bottle of gin from Amman, which Robert drinks at night in lieu of painkillers. After dinner one night, he falls into a gin-induced stupor on one of the twin beds in my room. I cannot wake him, so he stays there all night, snoring. It is the last time we sleep in the same room.

"There must be dozens of US and British army dentists in Baghdad," I tell Robert the next morning. "I am sure they are well-trained. Let me find one for you. I can't stand to see you suffer." But Robert is also the most stubborn person I know. There is only one dentist he trusts, in Beirut. By 17 April, a month and a day after we took the last Royal Jordanian flight to Baghdad, the pain becomes more than he can bear. I help him carry his bags down to a waiting SUV. Robert gives me a bear hug, climbs into the vehicle, and heads off across the desert to Amman and root canal surgery in Beirut.

Epilogue

Remember me when I am gone away,
    Gone far away into the silent land;
    When you can no more hold me by the hand,
Nor I half turn to go yet turning stay.
Remember me when no more day by day
    You tell me of our future that you plann'd:
    Only remember me; you understand
It will be late to counsel then or pray.
Yet if you should forget me for a while
    And afterwards remember, do not grieve:
    For if the darkness and corruption leave
    A vestige of the thoughts that once I had,
Better by far you should forget and smile
    Than that you should remember and be sad.

Christina Rossetti, "Remember"

I stay on for ten days in Iraq after Robert's departure. I think of him often, guessing what he would say about the stories I work on, how he would write them.

The seeds of the slaughter of the coming decade – which Robert will summarise as "suicide bombers, throat-cutters and fast-firing Americans" – are already writ large when the regime collapses. Outside Saddam Children's Hospital, I find an Iraqi civil defence worker digging up the decaying bodies of civilians killed in the battle for Baghdad. He shouts and points at the American Humvee parked beside him. "I would like to commit suicide in front of this vehicle," he tells me. The Humvee gunner is indifferent to the Iraqi's anger, but complains that the smell bothers him.

I interview the turbanned director of the main hospital in the Shia slum of Sadr City. Sheikh Tassin al-Ikabi studied theology in Najaf. Ammunition boxes and grenade launchers outnumber the microscope cases and crutches stored in his office. I write articles about the symbiotic relationship between Iraqi Shia and Iran. On Easter Sunday, Chaldean Catholics tell me they felt more secure under Saddam. Though Saddam will not be captured until December 2003, I cover the arrests of his half-brother, Barzan, and his foreign minister, Tariq Aziz, in April. Iraq's new proconsul, US General Jay Garner, explains the growing anarchy in Baghdad thus: "Iraq has been in a dark room with no light for thirty-five years, and two weeks ago we opened the door and pushed them out in the sunlight and they cannot see yet."

℘

Robert writes to me from Ireland in mid-June 2003, saying he is "tired and exhausted and I wonder why I wasted so much time last year preaching against the war in Iraq". Yet he believes his lectures had some effect. "Fight the good fight, you always told me – though sometimes I wonder to what purpose."

He seems equally ambivalent about us. We had suspended our discord for a month of collegial companionship in Baghdad, but nothing is resolved. Robert says repeatedly that he wants a new life. "I don't want to wake up one morning and find I'm living part two of the old life." He notes that our annoyance with each other "emerged, once or twice, during the war in Iraq... admittedly under pretty difficult circumstances". He is nonetheless optimistic and even alludes to a possible holiday together in Tuscany at the end of the summer. "We spent a whole month together in which we did not once let the grief of the past ten years damage us." The holiday never happens, but he writes again in August to tell me how happy he was to talk to me on the telephone. "I love you always, beloved Lara. And I don't give up hope for us."

We are back on the merry-go-round, though I suspect neither of us really believes we will light the candle in Saint-Sulpice that Robert still refers to. In 2004, when we briefly cohabit – in separate bedrooms – in our home in Ireland, Robert scolds me for telling the owner of the bookshop in Dalkey that we have separated. "But we *have* separated," I protest. "I still think we might get back together," Robert replies. I remember Carl Sandburg's poem, "If we ask you to gleam through the tears, / Kisses, can you come back like ghosts?"

Robert and I confide in each other about our private lives, though we invariably disapprove of each other's entanglements. He never mentions the young woman at the origin of our break-up. I assume she is out of the picture, at least temporarily. Or perhaps he does not want me to know. Between 2003 and 2007 he talks about Victoria, Cécile and Peyruz, all young, beautiful, intelligent women. I have forgotten others.

In October 2003, we team up for a reporting trip to Fallujah, 65 kilometres west of Baghdad, where we come upon a discreet unit of the 82nd Airborne Division, working almost under cover in the hope of staving off the flood of anti-American sentiment in the Sunni heartland.

The US and British occupation is rapidly descending into bloody chaos. The Hamra Hotel, where Robert is staying, is full of journalists, so I rent a modest suite at a family-owned "aparthotel" in the shopping district of Karrada. The threat of kidnappers and bombings have closed most of Baghdad's restaurants. Robert shares dinners prepared by the wife of my hotel receptionist.

We are both in Baghdad again on 31 March 2004, when gunmen ambush four armed American security contractors in Fallujah. A mob pulls them from burning vehicles, drags them through the streets and hangs their corpses from a bridge over the Euphrates. The video footage shown by Arab networks is so shocking that no western television station will broadcast it. We head for Fallujah, but halfway there Robert accuses the driver of ignoring orders to slow down. One does not go to such a dangerous place with an unreliable driver, Robert says. He is right, of course, but I suspect the old Robert would have risked it. I wonder if he has lost his nerve, perhaps as a result of the beating in Pakistan.

A few days later, we spend a pleasant afternoon, hiring a boatman to row us across the Tigris. We linger at a bookseller's in al-Mutannabi Street. Whole libraries were looted when Saddam fell, and there are treasures to be unearthed amid the dusty stalls. I feel ill at ease buying stolen books but tell myself we are saving them from oblivion. Robert purchases an exquisite volume of reproductions of Giotto's frescoes in the Upper Church in Assisi for me, printed by Scribner's in New York in 1954. The cover is damaged, so I have it rebound in red linen in Paris. It is one of many treasures I associate with him.

Iraq spirals into insurrection and civil war. Both of us continue to work there, though we never again happen to be there at the same time. On departing, each leaves leftover supplies for the other. Throughout the 2000s, we save newspaper clippings for each other and consult on stories, not only about Iraq.

Robert seems to be searching for some kind of stability, perhaps like that he knew with me for the first five years of our life together. In October 2006, he is asked by Kirsty Young, presenter of the BBC's Desert Island Discs programme, if he has "lived the life of an action movie hero". No, Robert replies:

> I was thinking the other day whether I actually enjoyed the life I've had, and I think I haven't. I might have been passionate about it, but I don't think I've actually enjoyed it. I was sitting on the boulevards in Paris, watching families walking down the street in sunlight, and I went back to Beirut and sat on my balcony and asked myself 'did I really want the last thirty years of war? Couldn't I have lived a more happy, serene and secure life?' I wondered whether I had perhaps wasted it.

Robert complains to me of depression. In November 2004, he writes of his frustration over the deterioration of our house. The large fissures in the walls, which I had seen as an allegory for our marriage, continue to widen. In a typical Celtic Tiger swindle, Kevin the builder blames Tony the architect who says it's the fault of Tom the engineer. Robert hears the house creaking and has hired a new solicitor to sue all three men. "It is causing me great distress," he writes.

Robert lives in Dalkey while he completes *The Great War for Civilisation: The Conquest of the Middle East.* "The book is making me very tired," he writes in the same letter. When completed, *The Great War* weighs in at 1366 pages. "While reading this massive, unruly book, I imagined Fisk emptying all his drawers on the bed," Augustus Richard Norton writes in a mainly favourable review in the progressive American newspaper *The Nation*.

Robert sends me a complimentary copy of *The Great War for Civilisation* in October 2005. When I read the dedication to his parents, Bill and Peggy, I think again how sad it is that he makes peace with The Unforgiven only when it is too late. I am touched by his inscription: "To Beloved Lara – who shared many of these adventures with love and courage supreme – as ever Robert."

The first decade of the new century is difficult for both of us. I endure a long professional crisis when the then *Irish Times* editor Geraldine Kennedy refuses to give me the promotion she promised. "You must never sue your own newspaper," Robert advises me. As usual, he is right. "Every newspaper has a personality," he says. "It changes over time." No newspaper is perfect, and just as Robert was the love of my life, *The Irish Times*, which has employed me for the last quarter century – more than three times as long as *Time* magazine – is the newspaper of my life.

Robert and I seem to be communicating vessels; when one of us is up, the other is down. At New Year's 2006, he sends a card showing willow trees on the banks of the Litani River in southern Lebanon. "If only I could find the same joy and courage that you do," he writes. "You are an example to me." He must have seen me on a good day. The following month he is up, signing a note "from the New Beloved Robert".

I have never known Robert to suffer from self-doubt, but in later years he seems haunted by a sense of futility. He has often recounted that he vowed to become a journalist after seeing Alfred Hitchcock's 1940 film *Foreign Correspondent* at the age of twelve. "Excitement, adventure, reporting scoops, beautiful women, spies. Sounds like the job for me," he says in the 2019 documentary *This Is Not a Movie*.

The title of the documentary is an avowal of Robert's own past naïveté. In his early seventies, Robert is admitting that being a war correspondent is not a game, that he is not Hitchcock's fictional reporter Huntley Haverstock. And unlike the Allies' World War II triumph over Nazi Germany, there is no happy ending in the Middle East. "I don't believe anything I wrote ever made an iota of difference," Robert says. "I feel more angry than I used to, because I don't think what we do has an effect."

Yet Robert has not lost his idealism. "As a journalist, you have got to be neutral and unbiased on the side of those who suffer," he says. There could be no better summary of his vocation. Despite the ultimate futility of our work, he says we have to keep on fighting. He wants "to leave a direct and emotional account for people not yet alive, so that no one can say 'We didn't know'."

Although Robert never joined a political party – indeed, never voted – his oeuvre constitutes one of the most convincing denunciations of war and of weapons proliferation in existence. When we described the effects of Israeli, American and NATO attacks on civilians in our articles, we were often accused of "war porn". The politicians who initiated wars and the weapons manufacturers who enabled them were the pornographers, not us, Robert argued. "If people saw what we see, they would never, ever support a war."

Robert scorned the very concept of "just war", elaborated over the centuries by the likes of Cicero, Saint Augustine, Saint Thomas Aquinas and Hugo Grotius. For him, all wars were evil, full stop. It is not surprising that he chose to write his doctoral thesis on Irish neutrality in World War II, and that he sought Irish nationality in the last years of his life. Irish governments have since the 1950s promoted all forms of disarmament. It was an Irish foreign minister, Frank Aiken, who first floated the idea of the nuclear Non-Proliferation Treaty.

Only one of the wars we covered together, the 1991 Gulf War to drive Saddam Hussein out of Kuwait, could be said to be "legal", inasmuch as it was fought under the auspices of UN Security Council Resolution 678. Robert nonetheless opposed that war vehemently, in part because of the West's double standards: no one ever proposed enforcing by military means Security Council resolutions 242 and 338, which require that Israel withdraw from the Palestinian land it occupies.

Robert was disgusted by then Archbishop of Canterbury Robert Runcie's conclusion that the 1991 war was just. "I thought I would be sick," he said while promoting *The Great War for Civilisation* in 2005. "I mean, are we still going to have religious divines telling us about just wars? Give me a break."

At the beginning of his chapter on the 1991 war in the same book, Robert quoted Tolstoy in *War and Peace*, calling war "an event ... opposed to human reason and to human nature". In a war, Tolstoy wrote, men commit more theft, arson and murder than in whole centuries, without even regarding these acts as crimes.

Robert and I endured fierce criticism from British and American colleagues for opposing the 2003 invasion of Iraq. The Bush and Blair administrations fabricated the case for war with lies about non-existent weapons of mass destruction. It was not a war of self-defence, and was not sanctioned by the UN Security Council. UN Secretary General Kofi Annan said in September 2004 that from the UN's point of view "it was illegal".

In 1991, I had wavered. Saddam Hussein clearly did not intend to withdraw his troops from Kuwait. Robert had no answer as to how he should be dislodged. I thought it would be dangerous to allow Saddam's aggression to go unpunished.

Like Robert, I knew there was no such thing as a clean or *just* war, but I thought that in some circumstances war might be *justifiable*. In those days I might have said, like Barack Obama twelve years later with regard to the invasion of Iraq, "I don't oppose all wars ... What I am opposed to is a dumb war."

Robert saw wars of resistance or liberation as a form of self-defence. He would have supported the right of Algerians to rise up against French colonial rule. When Hezbollah or Palestinians attacked Israeli forces, he reminded me that the right to fight occupation is enshrined in the UN charter.

By systematically opposing all wars, Robert was able to dodge all manner of theoretical questions regarding, for example, whether the flawed prosecution of a war invalidated its justification. When Soviet troops became the first Allied forces to enter Berlin in April 1945, they pillaged, raped and murdered on a large scale. Yet historians still recognise the essential role played by the Soviet Union in the defeat of Nazi Germany.

Faced with such questions, I am compelled to reply, as Robert did, that Saddam and Milošević were not Hitler. The shamefully sloppy prosecution of the 1991 and 1999 wars brought me closer to his point of view, though I understood the arguments for those conflicts. The bombing of the Amariya shelter and the massacre of Iraqi soldiers fleeing Kuwait threw into question the morality of the 1991 Gulf War. The Serbs had committed genocide against Bosnian Muslims and appeared determined to do the same in Kosovo. Yet NATO acted without a UN mandate. Atrocities including the bombing of the train at Grdelica and the bus at Lužane, the deaths of Milena Malobabić and of Voja Milić's family, and NATO's killing of seventy-three Kosovar refugees, seriously undermined its claim to the high moral ground.

The concept of "humanitarian intervention" – the use of military force to prevent human rights abuses – which was advocated by Obama's ambassador to the UN Samantha Power and the French foreign minister Bernard Kouchner – was discredited by the disastrous western intervention in Libya.

One hears it said that a certain number of civilian deaths are the price to pay in any war. The terrible paradox cited by the French writer and statesman André Malraux in his 1928 novel *The Conquerors* is at the heart of the argument: *Une vie ne vaut rien, mais rien ne vaut une vie.* A life is worth nothing, but nothing is worth a life.

Three-quarters of a century after the end of World War II, arguments continue about the firebombing of Dresden and the use of nuclear weapons at Hiroshima and Nagasaki. There are no easy answers, but I find the flippant way in which politicians and commentators brush off atrocities committed in the pursuit of "just" wars unbearable. Unlike Robert, I am willing to admit that the 1991 and 1999 wars may have been *necessary*, but having seen what I did, I could not have voted for or authorised either had I been in a position to do so. If that is moral cowardice, so be it.

Robert's war on war took three forms: description of the needless suffering it inflicted, ridicule of the political and military leaders who initiated conflicts, and going after the arms dealers and manufacturers whom he alluded to as "merchants of death". He shamed the American makers of the Hellfire missile which Israel fired into a Lebanese ambulance by following a missile part back to them. As I write this, there are at last questions being raised in Congress about US arms transfers to Israel. When Robert collected serial numbers of weapons casings in fields strewn with the dismembered bodies of Kosovar refugees, NATO was forced to admit that it – not the Serbian Air Force – was at fault.

Robert refused to be drawn into discussions about what he would have "done about Hitler". Had he been alive during World War II, I believe that, like the great intellectual and pacifist Bertrand Russell, he would have declared the necessity of defeating Hitler and Nazism an exceptional circumstance.

The greater Middle East underwent at least eight major upheavals during the forty-five years that Robert lived and worked there: the collapse of Arab unity, precipitated by Anwar Sadat's separate peace with Israel in 1978; the Soviet invasion of Afghanistan and the Iranian revolution in 1979; the 1980–88 war between Iran and Iraq; Israel's invasion of Lebanon in 1982; the 2003 invasion of Iraq; the advent of Sunni extremism and the rise of al-Qaeda and Isis; the failed revolutions of the so-called Arab spring.

Robert was in the forefront of coverage and commentary on all these stories. Notwithstanding his protestations of futility, few journalists have had a greater influence on public opinion about the Middle East. He reminded readers that the US and other western powers supported Iraq, the aggressor, in the Iran-Iraq war. His three interviews with Osama bin Laden are a unique and precious historical record of the mindset of the man responsible for the deaths of nearly 3,000 people on 9/11. Unlike the majority of his colleagues, Robert and his friend and colleague Patrick Cockburn, the Irish-born journalist, author and Middle East specialist, refused to cheerlead for the invasion of Iraq or the Arab spring. They knew that both would spell disaster.

Robert was one of a handful of authors and intellectuals, along with Noam Chomsky and Edward Said, who refused to allow the Palestinian question to die. Despite Israeli and US attempts to marginalise the Palestinians, the injustice done to them remains an open wound, the original sin that condemned the Middle East to instability and carnage. Robert's oeuvre gives the lie to the claim of the Israeli settler who told him, "The Palestinians are so passé, so last century".

ॐ

Much as I admired Robert, he could still hurt and exasperate me, years after we separated. Though he was often generous and thoughtful, he could also be self-centred and tone-deaf. In April 2008, he took me to Aqua restaurant on the West Pier in Howth, to celebrate my birthday. Before we left for dinner, he insisted on showing me a new documentary about himself. As we walked along Howth Harbour, I told him about a short-lived affair with a television journalist whom he disliked. "Oh Lara, how *could* you?" he said, reverting to the refrain of yesteryear. We had not gone forward.

Six weeks later, we met for dinner at La Méditerrannée, one of my favourite restaurants in Paris. He no longer hides from me the fact that he has settled with the young woman who wrote to him from her journalism school back in 1997. He talks non-stop about a project for a feature film about his life, which never comes to fruition. He describes a scene in which his father Bill will march through a village in Picardy in World War I uniform. In the screenplay, the woman whom Robert would marry the following year was to toss a rose to his father from a balcony. "She will meet Bill!" Robert exclaims. "The power of cinema!" Robert always swore he did not want revenge, but he could not find a more cruel way of telling me that I have been replaced. He does not seem to notice my tears.

I suspect that Robert's tendency to self-obsession is normal for the only child of an adoring mother. Several friends suggest he was a genius, and that geniuses notoriously crush the women who love them. One has only to read Françoise Gilot's book about her life with Picasso.

My older brother Bob never developed a rapport with Robert. In the early 2000s, not long after his own divorce, Bob spends Christmas with me in Paris, and tries to cheer me up by making light of my crumbling marriage. "Thank God we got rid of Robert!" he says every morning at breakfast. When Robert dies, Bob rings me to say he is sorry. "You told me he was egotistical," I remind him. "We just didn't have anything in common," Bob says. "Robert earned his ego," he adds. He certainly did.

Had it been left solely to me, I probably would have poisoned our relationship with anger and resentment. Robert managed to preserve something of our love for one another. He never stopped addressing me as "beloved Lara" in speech and letters. He sent cards and gifts, usually books, for my birthday and Christmas.

I recently found the inscription "Christmas 2007, To beloved Lara, with love, Robert" in the front of Irène Némirovsky's *The Dogs and the Wolves*. Robert believed in the written word, and the written record he left me often contradicts memories of our break-up. Earlier that same year, Robert decided he wanted to take full possession of the house we built, which we had continued to share. He took me house-hunting and helped me to purchase a home in Howth. Tactful as he tried to be, the experience was painful.

In the spring of 2009, when Robert asks for a divorce so he can remarry, he gives me a book entitled *We Declare: Landmark Documents in Ireland's History*. The frontispiece is a facsimile of signatures on the 1921 Treaty Between Great Britain and Ireland. "Happy Birthday, Beloved Lara," Robert writes at the top of the page. "This is the first time I've signed a document also bearing the signatures of our old mates Michael Collins and Churchill!"

I move to Washington DC for *The Irish Times* in August 2009. Robert's last letter to me arrives that autumn. I am surprised that I don't recognise his handwriting on the envelope, so infrequent have become our exchanges. The letter is dated 5 October, one week after our divorce became final. He does not mention the divorce, but congratulates me on having landed the Washington job I so wanted. The tone is friendly but detached. He signs it, "With love, Bobić," my pet name for him during the Yugoslav wars. I never reply. I do not want to disturb Robert in his new life.

ષ્ઠ૩

When I was a child, we had two trees in the garden that grew entwined. One died, and when it was taken away, the imprint of its trunk remained on the side of the other. Robert and I were like two trees that grew together.

If one of us had been kidnapped or killed in a war, sympathy and support would have poured in. But a failed marriage is shameful. Only a few close friends witness your sorrow.

I joke that the world's longest engagement – nearly ten years between the time we started living together and our marriage – overlapped with the world's longest divorce. Depending how one counts, our break-up could be said to have lasted longer than the Lebanese Civil War. I often wondered how a man who could decide in a split second which road to take in a war zone, who could compose flawless newspaper copy spontaneously in his head, could torment us both for so long with indecision.

With time, I force myself to see positive aspects in the breakdown of our relationship. Nietzsche was right: what didn't kill me made me stronger. I achieved a degree of self-reliance and self-confidence I would not have attained had we stayed together. Robert always said there was nothing as sad as someone who does not recognise their own good fortune. I must recognise mine. I write for a fine newspaper. I live in a lovely apartment in Paris. I am blessed in friendship. I believe Robert found happiness with his new wife, at least I hope so. I think she gave him a kind of admiration that he needed, and which I was no longer capable of. It was better for him to be happy without me than unhappy with me.

Sometimes I spotted my former home from the window of an aeroplane, or from the DART train on my way to visit friends in Wicklow. When I surveyed Dublin Bay and the coast to the south from Howth, I thought of Robert in Dalkey. We passed a decade thus, me flying in from Paris, Robert from Beirut, metaphorically gazing at each other from opposite sides of an expanse of water, from swerve of shore to bend of bay.

In the immediate aftermath of Robert's death, jealous competitors attack him. Now that he is no longer there to defend himself, several accuse him of faking stories, or of supporting Bashar al-Assad's regime. A shameful obituary by Christophe Ayad in *Le Monde* is particularly painful, because I worked with Ayad in Gaza and Baghdad and considered him to be a friend. I spend a weekend writing a riposte to Ayad's shabby obituary of Robert.

There is, of course, praise too, and the praise outweighs the slander. "Robert Fisk wasn't only a magnificent journalist, but a historian of the present who illuminated the world," Patrick Cockburn, who was a friend and colleague of Robert's for their entire adult life, writes in *The Independent*.

I find the words "I don't know how close you were..." which precede some expressions of sympathy annoying, as if my sorrow at Robert's passing is any less real because the marriage was long over. I am surprised and touched to receive dozens of warm messages of condolence. After all, I am not the legitimate widow.

Some of the tributes bring me to tears. "I am very proud that I worked with him during those very difficult times in the NATO bombing," Maša Matijašević, our interpreter in Belgrade, writes. "He was a really great journalist. I will also always remember his unpleasant questions asked from the first row in the NATO briefing room [in Brussels]. They were broadcast in Belgrade, and I remember being wowed every time Robert asked a question. He was really brave."

During the bombardment of Belgrade, I told Maša that she would one day look back on those terrible times with nostalgia. Sure enough. "And I will never forget how we used to drink plum brandy at sunset on the balcony of your royal suite at the 'Titanic', sorry, 'Majestic'. Those were the days, my friend," she concludes.

Imad Saidi, our dear friend and interpreter in Beirut, sends a stream of consciousness message, all in lower case, which I have abbreviated and punctuated:

> Memories of journeys around Lebanon with him, with both of you and with you, driven by Abed. [Robert] always tenaciously wanted to get to the crux of the story, never accepting hearsay and secondary sources, stopping for *manousheh* [a sort of Lebanese pizza] along the way, his impersonations of Churchill among others, asking me whether I believed in life after death, to which I would answer I'm still not sure there is life after birth. At the end of the journey he would always hand me the dollars wrapped up in a sheet of paper telling me not to spend it all on recreational drugs. His wit always shone through. I was very lucky to have known you guys then. And I still treasure the memories of a time in Beirut that no longer exists.

Perhaps the loveliest message comes from Seán Hogben in Australia, a former sub-editor for *The Times*, whom I never met. Hogben recalls the first time he read a telex message from Robert, during the 1982 Israeli invasion:

> He was far away in Beirut, yet I heard him so clearly over the clamour of the Gray's Inn Road newsroom. I was the most junior casual sub on *The Times* home desk, an Australian to boot, and for some reason the chief sub had presented me with Robert's copy for the back page colour piece. The chief sub said to me: 'Be careful with this copy, Fisk is very sensitive about how it is handled.'

'Don't rewrite it,' a colleague muttered. Rewrite it? I memorised it, so honoured did I feel to be given the tiniest trim and heading jobs on the work of a great man. Foreign did their pages and Fisk was their prince ... It was all Maggie T, the Falklands wash-up and tedious matters of Palace and record. But Fisk, he was exotic, like a sit-down with mint tea, baklava and a hubble-bubble. The Israelis were about to lay waste to south Beirut, their war machine marching up from the border with unstoppable power. Robert was taking the temperature on his street, passing pleasantries with his Druze and Christian neighbours. The story described an achingly blue sky streaked with fighter jet vapour trails. I think I had to cut about twenty words. But the intro took me right there, teleported me.

"Today, Beirut is at its most surreal..."

I was not quite twenty-eight but having been around newsrooms and newspaper folk all my life, I knew good copy.

⁊ᴀ

When things were bad between us, Robert pleaded, "Think kindly of me". He loved Christina Rossetti's poem "Remember", and told me to read it when he died. I send it to Imad in Beirut, to thank him for his message. It is, Imad emails back, "pure magic".

I was probably daunted by the sheer volume of what Robert called "Fiskery", and assumed I knew what was in the book, so I merely dipped into *The Great War for Civilisation* while he was alive. In the months after his death, I plunge into his magnum opus (though I still prefer *Pity the Nation*) and am touched to find him quoting Christina Rossetti's poem on the last page. "I think in the end we have to accept that our tragedy lies always in our past," he writes. "How to correct history, that's the thing." He means it in the context of the Middle East, but to me it reads like a personal message.

As Imad recalled in his message of condolence, Robert often asked "Is there a life after death?" He said it in jest, but the question interested him. Now he has gone, as the Czech Nobel laureate Jaroslav Seifert wrote, "to where the little flames of blown-out candles fly noiselessly". I am an agnostic bordering on atheism, but several times as I wrote this book, I had to shake off the feeling that Robert was communicating. Hadn't he promised to be the first journalist to file from beyond the grave?

When I have doubts about this project, there's a double rainbow on my daily walk to the end of the East Pier in Howth, like the one on the day of his funeral. As recounted in Chapter IX about former Yugoslavia, I open his book *The Age of the Warrior* one night and fall upon an answer to my request for his thoughts on journalists testifying before international tribunals. On the day I begin writing about the Qana massacre, I open a storage box for no particular reason and discover Pascal Beaudenon's photograph of Robert and me interviewing an Irish officer inside an armoured personnel carrier in southern Lebanon, taken hours before the slaughter at Qana. That photograph becomes the cover of this book. Surely just coincidences...

Revisiting the decades when Robert was in my life caused me to experience the same gamut of emotions. I hear his voice when I reread his books. I feel he is in the room with me when I listen to radio and television clips of interviews with him. I doubt I will ever reconcile the immense gratitude I feel for all he gave me with the sense of betrayal that comes with the break-down of a marriage. But I still love him. I still admire him. I am proud to have been his wife and I miss his presence in the world.

ঙ্গ

26 October 2019

I go to the ladies' room after disembarking from an Air France flight at Dublin airport. Should I bother combing my hair, putting on lipstick? I ask myself. Yes, I decide. One never knows whom one might meet in an airport.

Then I see him, planted in front of the baggage carousel. Only Robert, as if a spotlight shines on him. How well I know that pose. Shoulders slumped slightly, arms crossed over the chest, legs apart, chin and pelvis thrust forward. His eyes are fixed on the conveyer belt, but the look of concentration shows he is thinking about something else. I've known Robert long enough to know he is *always* thinking about something important.

I quickly survey the other passengers. She is not with him. What do I risk? Would it be awkward or upsetting, talking to him after a decade of radio silence?

I could keep walking, pretend I didn't see him. Then I realise we were on the same flight from Paris, and I have a bag to retrieve. There is no escaping this reunion. It's OK. I am having a good day, starting a week's holiday. There is no reason to avoid him. *Comme le hasard fait parfois bien les choses.* Sometimes chance does things well.

I walk up behind my ex-husband and summon my cheeriest, most melodic voice. "Hello, Dr Fisk!" Robert spins around and bursts into laughter. "Lara!" he exclaims. He pronounces my name as no one else does, drawing out the "a" and the "r" so it sounds like "Laarra". We embrace for a long moment, pull apart and stare at each other with silly, delighted grins.

"We must have been on the same flight from Paris, and I didn't see you! Where were you sitting?" I ask.

"Seat 16A. I got in early this morning from Beirut and went to the lounge."

"Ha! I was supposed to be in 16B, but I changed my seat because I like to sit near the front!" I laugh. Faint memories of missed opportunities for reconciliation flicker past me. I briefly wonder if sitting next to Robert on a plane for an hour and a half would have been a pleasure or an ordeal.

"I wish I had known you were in the airport. I would have got you into the first-class lounge," he says.

For years we lived like deluxe migrants, quaffing free champagne and scoffing food in airport lounges, devouring courtesy newspapers and raiding duty-free designer boutiques. In Cairo airport once, I spotted a magnificent Cartier silk shawl and wistfully told Robert about it. He slipped away a few minutes later, to buy it as a love offering. I wore it when we married.

Shopping bags from Hermès and Ladurée, the macaroon-maker, sit in the metal tray of his luggage trolley. Robert used to buy me Hermès scarves in airports. Now I assume he buys scarves for her.

His thinning hair has turned white. His girth has widened. I am surprised to discover that I am slightly taller than he is. Could he be shrinking?

He wears a blue cashmere jumper which I am sure is the one I purchased for him in Knightsbridge to celebrate a press award in 1999. The same Clarks we called boats, size 11, the same corduroy trousers. If not the ones I chose for him, replacements as they wore out.

His voice and facial expressions are animated. The impression of an old man dissipates. Robert still has the buoyancy I noticed in 1983, at the press conference in Damascus. We agree that neither of us has changed at all. We both know we are lying. We squeeze ten years into fifteen minutes.

"I read you in *The Irish Times*, every day when I'm home," he says, to my pleasure. "I remember the piece you wrote about becoming a French citizen. It was so … joyous."

"Which article? I wrote about it at least three times! You're right. I was very happy," I reply.

"And *I* am about to become Irish!" he announces proudly. I congratulate him.

There are momentary pauses, then a rush of words when we accidentally interrupt one another. Robert is thrilled with the way young people flock to his lectures, relieved that an American university had agreed to preserve his archives.

We talk about the war in Syria, and he mentions the final report of the Organisation for the Prohibition of Chemical Weapons, which concludes that sarin gas was not utilised at Douma. Chlorine probably was, the report says, though the OPCW would not say by which party.

Western media and politicians had believed allegations levelled by the Syrian opposition that Assad used sarin at Douma. Donald Trump seized on the reports as a pretext for a missile strike. Robert went to Douma and found no evidence to support the accusations. He was pilloried for his articles, and he considers the OPCW report a vindication.

I did not cover the Syrian civil war. The details of chemical weapons usage are still being disputed. But I remember the Bush administration's lies about Saddam Hussein's alleged weapons of mass destruction and I instinctively trust Robert.

Robert wants to know how *The Irish Times* is treating me, if I have kept the apartment in Paris, how are my girlfriends Cathy, Manijeh and Tala. We share news of mutual friends whom we have lost track of. With few exceptions, the divorce relegated them to one side or the other, not through animosity, but because we no longer frequented the same people.

"Imad is fine. Cynical as ever," Robert says. "I fought hard to get *The Independent* to pay Abed's pension, but they paid every penny."

Mustafa the landlord has taken a backseat to his niece Samira in running the building where I lived with Robert in Beirut for eight years. Robert talks to Patrick Cockburn every week or two on the phone. He asks about Spike the cat, whom we went to fetch together in Bray at Christmas 2000. "He's still alive, getting very old," I say. (Spike dies the following year, three months before Robert.)

"Like us!" Robert exclaims. We briefly summarise our respective ailments and operations. My suitcase arrives. I tell Robert I will wait for him.

"You know, it's funny, but I think I am growing superstitious. Perhaps it is age," I tell Robert. "More and more, I ask myself what my instinct is. Silly things like what I should wear today, which table to sit at, whether to accept an invitation…"

"I'm exactly the same!" Robert says.

We talk about everyone and everything except his wife. I glance at the Hermès and Ladurée bags, and assume she is waiting in the house I built with him. "Are you still married?" I ask.

"Yes!" he declares happily. "Are you?"

"No." I laugh. "I don't understand why anyone gets married any more...." I pause for a moment. "I always knew we would run into each other one day," I say. "I pictured it here, or at Pearse Street DART station."

"I did too! I thought it would happen in Paris or Dublin airport," Robert says.

He piles suitcase after suitcase onto the trolley. He spent a fortune in excess baggage over his lifetime, for the books and papers that overflowed from his library shelves.

We push our trollies out to the taxi stand, chattering gaily. Anyone watching us would assume we were just old friends, which is, I suppose, what we have become. Our brief, chance encounter has restored something precious.

Another bear hug. More smiles. Robert and I have at last found a gentle way of parting, what T. S. Eliot described as "Some way incomparably light and deft, / Some way we both should understand, / Simple and faithless as a smile and shake of the hand."

"You take the first cab," I tell him. "You have farther to go."

Acknowledgements

The idea for this book germinated in the mind of Simon Hess, the managing director and owner of Gill Hess Ltd, publishers' agents, when he read my article in *The Irish Times* a week after Robert's passing. Simon approached my agent, Jonathan Williams, who contacted me. I initially thought it would be too painful to plunge back into my years with Robert. But I could not stop thinking about the proposal and eventually rang Jonathan back. He negotiated a contract with Neil Belton, the publisher at Head of Zeus in London. This book would not have happened without the happy conjunction of these three men.

I am particularly grateful to Jonathan for his friendship, wisdom and careful proof-reading of successive drafts. Neil brought many years of experience and astute judgment to the project and devoted a great deal of time to a thorough edit of my manuscript. Matilda Singer and Georgina Blackwell shepherded the text through the editing process with patience and efficiency. Jessie Price did a great job on the cover. Elodie Olson-Coons and Janet Walker were careful, meticulous copy-editors and Christopher Phipps was equally meticulous with the index.

I thank *The Irish Times* for sending me on many of the reporting trips recounted in this book, including the 1996/97 trips to Algeria, the 1999 war in Serbia and Kosovo and the 2003 invasion of Iraq. I am grateful to *Irish Times* editor Paul O'Neill for granting me leave to write the book, and to foreign editor Chris Dooley and deputy foreign editor Dave McKechnie for being so understanding about my long absence and sporadic distraction through its completion. I thank Conor Goodman, the editor of the weekend section, for commissioning the article about Robert which caught Simon Hess's eye and eventually led to publication of this book.

My friends were especially kind after Robert's death and provided advice and encouragement while I was writing the book. Some helped with photographs, translations and the seeking of permission to quote other works.

From the bottom of my heart, I would like to thank the following people, in alphabetical order:

Hervé Algalarrondo, Iradj Amini, Anne Anderson, Mohsen Ashtiany, Fadhil Al-Azzawi, Pascal Beaudenon, Ben Benant and Cathy Bubbe, Hugh Byrne, Frank Callanan, Nicole Chardaire, Harry Clifton, Robert Cochran, Anne-Elisabeth and Jean-Paul Credeville, Stéphane Duroy, Kathy Gilfillan, Bridget Hourican, Siham Jabbar, Sammy Ketz, Jean-Pierre Lafon, Deirdre Madden, Ljiljana and Maša Matijašević, Paul McGuinness, Marie McRee, Fawzi Moutran, Hasan Mroué, Tim Mücke, David and Melissa Neckar, Patricia O'Brien, Conor and Zhanna O'Clery, Liam O'Flaherty, Olivia O'Leary, Lisa Perrine, Margo Rietbergen, Alyn Roberts, Imad Saidi, Nicole Schmid, Tala Skari, Eamonn Smyth, Ted Smyth and Mary Breasted Smyth, Birgit Svensson, Rima Tarabay, Manijeh Teymourtache, Frédéric Vitoux, Michael von Graffenried and Henk Werner.

Some of the people listed above knew and loved Robert Fisk. I hope they will find this book an accurate portrayal of him and that they will forgive any aspects they might disagree with. Most of all, I hope that this book will impart to those who did not have the privilege of knowing Robert a sense of the character of an extraordinary man and a truly great journalist.

Index